The Men Who Flew the F-4 Phantom

Martin W. Bowman

Pen & Sword
AVIATION

First Published in Great Britain in 2017 by
Pen & Sword Aviation
an imprint of
Pen & Sword Books Ltd
47 Church Street, Barnsley, South Yorkshire S70 2AS

Copyright © Pen & Sword Books 2017
ISBN 9781526705846.

The right of Martin W Bowman to be identified as author of this work
has been asserted by him in accordance with the
Copyright, Designs and Patents Act 1988.

A CIP catalogue record for this book is
available from the British Library.

Typeset in 10/12pt Palatino
by GMS Enterprises PE3 8QQ

Printed and bound in England by
TJ International Ltd, Padstow, PL28 8R

Pen & Sword Books Ltd incorporates the Imprints of Pen & Sword
Aviation, Pen & Sword Family History, Pen & Sword Maritime, Pen & Sword
Military, Pen & Sword Discovery, Wharncliffe Local History, Wharncliffe
True Crime, Wharncliffe Transport, Pen & Sword Select, Pen & Sword
Military Classics, Leo Cooper, The Praetorian Press, Remember When,
Seaforth Publishing and Frontline Publishing.

For a complete list of Pen & Sword titles please contact
PEN & SWORD BOOKS LIMITED

47 Church Street, Barnsley, South Yorkshire, S70 2AS, England
E-mail: enquiries@pen-and-sword.co.uk
Website: www.pen-and-sword.co.uk

Contents

4

Most Vietnam vets who were fortunate enough not to have left the combat base in body bags probably figure their one trip to Khê Sanh was enough to last a lifetime. I led a column of 'Dusters' (M42A1 self-propelled light tanks) and Quad 50s out of Khê Sanh at the end of a 75-day siege. When the siege began on 21 January 1968 the Marines were ill prepared for a static defence of the base and engineers hurriedly began to dig trenches and lay additional rows of concertina wire around the perimeter. Trenching machines were flown in to cut into the rock-hard surface before the attacks reached a peak in late January through mid-March 1968. During good weather, tactical aircraft flew extensive missions, dropping napalm and high explosives on enemy positions across the hills and the plateau in front of our northern perimeter. Some strikes were so close to our positions that the intense heat from the napalm was enough to singe our eyebrows. In March, under cover of fog and darkness, enemy troops dug a network of tunnels and zigzag trenches within a few metres of the perimeter wire on the east end of the runway. They went undetected until the weather broke the following morning, when F-4 Phantoms resumed tactical operations and spotted them from the air. The NVA had evidently hoped that they could tunnel under the wire and the runway to plant mines or explosives that would destroy inbound aircraft and/or the runway surface. Had penetration of the perimeter from this unlikely approach succeeded, our gun positions on the east end would have been the primary weapons responsible for repelling the enemy assault. The F-4s immediately launched heavy air strikes with napalm and high explosive ordnance to destroy the trenches. F-4s and 'Puff the Magic Dragon', a DC-3 with machine guns and a Vulcan cannon in the doorway, made multiple sorties. Poor visibility, however, often limited tactical air strikes, leaving the air support to the B-52 Stratofortresses. Under the code name 'Niagara' General William Westmoreland personally directed the activities of the Strategic Air Command, which flew numerous sorties around the clock, dropping unprecedented tonnages of explosives in defence of the base. The area around Khê Sanh would soon have the unenviable distinction of being 'the most bombed place on earth.'

2nd Lieutenant Bruce M. Geiger USMC, who celebrated his 23rd birthday in a perimeter bunker at Khê Sanh on 20 March 1968 with his platoon sergeant and a fifth of 'Johnny Walker Black'.

Preface

Norfolk understands the mentality of the navy's jet jockeys, so it would probably understand racers, too. The clean-cut, mild-mannered young Scott Campbell is a flight instructor in VF-171 (for which he says the main requirement is that 'well, you can't be a dirt bag'). 'VF,' in the infinite wisdom of the Navy, stands for 'Fighter Squadron,' and '171' designates one unit assigned to Oceana Naval Air Station, in this case, the squadron consisting of three dozen officers and 50 enlisted men training 40 or so officers and 150 enlistees for duty as replacements with the Atlantic Fleet.

The navy PR office in Washington says that by the time a pilot is fully qualified in something like an F-4 about \$1 million will have been spent on his training. Now, that's not a bad investment in light of the planes' cost, but when you consider that all fighter pilots should be regarded by all the rest of us (except maybe race drivers) as solidly entrenched in mental-defective status, the investment seems a little less sound. The job of the fighter pilots, after all and their source of greatest joy, is simply to go out and light the wick on the McDonnell Douglas F-4 Phantom. It is one of the most potent airplanes ever built and this qualifies its pilots for instant admission to the Navy Home for the Brave and Giddy.

McDonnell Douglas's description of its creation is innocuous: 'The two-seat, twin-jet, all-weather, supersonic F-4 Phantom is a versatile multiple-mission air-superiority fighter, fighter bomber, advanced interceptor, ground support, tactical strike and reconnaissance aircraft.' Sounds okay, we need some of those. Your all-purpose airborne plague. Any yo-yos get cross-eyed and we send over an F-4 to rearrange their furniture. The F-4 can deliver 16,000 lbs of destruction, after which it can turn around and beat a path back home at almost 1600 mph. Well... that boom-boom and straight-line stuff is okay, but the F-4 really is good at everything. The Encyclopaedia of World Air Power describes the Phantom II as 'the first aircraft which could detect, intercept and destroy any target which came within radar range. Other types in the same era still needed assistance from surface-based radar units.'.

Design work on the F-4 began way back in 1953 and a drastic revision to the navy's original concept required the plane to have broad capabilities. The F-4 came out so well that McDonnell Douglas built 5057 of them for sale in the United States and licensed still more construction overseas. A peak production of 72 per month was reached in 1967 and F-4s have been used by eleven countries, the final US delivery having taken place in October 1979. .

Scott Campbell, now 30, was one year old when his F-4 was designed. His boss at VF-171 is Commander C. Flack Logan (yes, that's his real middle name), a California hot rodder and racer in his youth. Logan describes the Phantom as being 'like a dragster. We didn't think in my day that anybody needed to have a wing on the back of a race car. We didn't know about aerodynamics. Look at the F-4 and it's got an itty-bitty tail and look where the weight distribution is. It's a very heavy airplane; it lands solid. We call normal carrier landings 'controlled crashes.'

'That's the design. Since then we've gotten smarter and we do things now that have some pretty jazzy lift capabilities. The manoeuvering flaps and slats, the sweeping [movable] wings, these are things that parallel aerodynamic developments in race cars.

'Low and fast,' continues Logan 'is the F-4's territory. If they're shootin' missiles at you, you're down in the weeds. Some of the MiG kills in Viêtnam were 50 to 100 feet off the ground. You're just trying to get where the F-4 does things that other people can't. If the other guy's trying to get rid of you, he's going to try to dust you off, but the MiGs had a problem above 580 knots or so when they were very low: their sticks got squirrelly, so you'd just stay with 'em until they started to lose it and then shoot 'em down. Or just let 'em lose it themselves. .

'In a war-type ACM [air combat manoeuvre - dogfight, to us], after a minute either you've shot somebody down or somebody's shot you down. We're a missile shooter, don't have any guns. We shoot AIM- 7s, Raytheon radar missiles with a range of about 27 miles at high altitude, but in our game we really have to see the guy before we can shoot at him.'

Interjects Scott Campbell, 'You can spot a medium airplane like the F-4 at fifteen miles if you've got a radar lock and your RIO [radar-intercept officer] in the back seat is tellin' you where it is. If you're just gonna spot somebody, he'd probably be no more than about five miles away. And if he's little, he could be only two or three miles away.'

'All the things that you learned the bullies did in grammar school,' Logan picks up again, 'are the same things you want to learn as a fighter pilot. Take unfair advantage every chance you get, so you get to fly back home and they don't. While we don't have to have great brains to do our business, it takes good hand-eye coordination and reactions. And we don't get too excited about the fact that you're gonna use a lot of gas by kicking in the afterburners.'

Ah, the afterburners. At a normal cruise speed of 450 knots (518 mph), the F-4 burns about 100 pounds of its kerosene-based fuel per minute. Kicking in the afterburners is like giving a big twist to the boost screw in an already overpowered race car and with the wick fully lit, the F-4 gobbles its 17,000lbs of fuel at 1,500lbs per minute!

The pilots live for the moment when they can put it right to the wall and go vaulting off our little sphere at any angle they deem appropriate, including straight up. At one time, the F-4 Phantom held every zero-to-altitude record in the world; it's been beaten since, but only by fractions. The Phantom's low-altitude speed record of 903 mph was unbroken for sixteen years, its absolute speed record stood at 1,606 mph, it held the sustained-altitude record of 66,444 feet and it was once the highest-flying airplane in the world, zooming to an edge-of-heaven 98,557 feet, later actually leaping over 100,000. To understand this kind of performance, consider another of the Phantom's figures, keeping in mind that, fully loaded, this is a 50,000lb airplane: the F-4 Phantom's maximum rate of climb is 49,800 feet per minute! So tweak it up and you get 830 feet per second, 6.36 seconds per mile, nine and a half miles per minute, straight up.

You know the pilots in the Ready Room have got to be loony. One 427 Corvette owner, a beady-eyed specimen of 37 years by the name of Sidner, admits to being a little boy inside, but says he's 171's oldest regular pilot and claims to need a cane and a Seeing-Eye dog to find the planes.

At the far end of the Ready Room, above the coffee cups and the door to the lockers, is the squadron's motto, spelled out in wooden letters: 'Fight to fly, fly to fight, fight to kill.' The word 'kill' is lettered in red.

The F-4 pilots have a running feud with the jocks who fly the newer, more sophisticated Grumman F-14 Tomcats. In some modes the F-14s perform better, but their complication means they require much larger crews (the F-4s themselves require 18 to 24 men to delve into their 199 external access doors, their 3,000-psi hydraulic control systems and their six fuselage fuel cells and two 'wet wing' cells in the wings' torque boxes). The F-14s are also less cost efficient than F-4s, partly because of their astronomical prices but also because of their tendency to electronic bugs and downtime.

'It's hard to believe,' remarks Flack Logan, 'but the F-4 is the throwaway model now. They were $6 million a copy in the Sixties. The newer F-14, F-15 and F-18, well, they've got a lot of bells and whistles and they're almost $30 million. But the F-4 will still give you a great ride.'

With these words, I am ushered into the locker room to climb into the Nomex and accoutrements of navy flight gear, each piece having been selected to fit me. When I emerge, the pilots present me with some nifty patches, my own personalized navy wings to be Velcroed to the front of my flight suit and kept as a souvenir and a cigarette lighter. I don't smoke, but I will keep this lighter. On one side it says, 'Phantoms Phorever' and on the other side it says, 'Better a sister in a whorehouse than a brother in F-14s.'

We laugh a lot, but it occurs to me that maybe they are giving me these mementos now because they figure I may not be able to enjoy them later.

I've had a day of training up at Norfolk in safety procedures, the high-altitude chamber, parachute techniques and the ejection-seat simulator, but I am not overjoyed at the thought of turning a knob beside my left knee in case I have to eject both myself and Scott Campbell. He offhandedly explains that this may be necessary while flying at high speed at low level if we suffer a bird strike. A bird strike in the canopy would, at the least, critically injure the pilot, but he would instinctively try to pull back on the stick and send us straight up, converting airspeed into altitude, giving me time to rotate the ejection selector so that he would be blown out, too.

Sweet mother.

Still, walking out to the plane in that peculiar crotch-harness swagger, I feel like Steve Canyon and the same calm that I always feel once I settle into a race car comes over me. Hey, the Wright brothers, Eddie Rickenbacker, Jimmy Doolittle, Chuck Yeager, 'Smilin Jack', me. The Right Stuff! Sheeit, this is easy.

I have clambered up on top of these two engines because that's all a Phantom is, is two engines, General Electric J79-GE-10 afterburning turbojets, weighing 3630 pounds apiece and shrieking out 35,700 afterburning pounds of thrust. The ground crew is strapping me to the Martin Baker ejection seat as I scan the bunged-up instrument panel. I hope the rest of this airplane is in better shape. The panel separates me from good old Scotty, up there in the driver's seat with about 100 doodads to keep him occupied. And me back here without even so much as a stick to grab hold of if we have a flat or the hood blows open or whatever it is that goes wrong in an F-4. Just me and my camera and all sorts of things marked in hornet-stripe, touch-under-penalty-of-death yellow and black paint. The cockpit, while smaller than that of the average car, is liveable if not cushy. My surprise that the seat offers no lateral support will soon fade, since all the loading in a jet fighter is straight down your spine. The blood tries to run out of your head at warp speed, so the trick to avoid passing out is to strain your muscles in a kind of sustained Primal Grunt, building blood pressure and thus maintaining at least a trickle of blood flow to the brain and eyes. The light pressure suits we have on today will only help offset about one g of loading. As he fires the whistling, oh-so-smooth engines, old Scotty still hasn't broadcast exactly how many gs he's planning to put my steak-and-eggs high-protein breakfast through. Then we're moving toward the broad taxiway.

The built-in earmuffs in the helmets will prove to keep the roar of the airflow around the canopy to about the sound level you'd hear in a 727. I am just settling back for the rigors ahead when Scott Campbell's voice comes into my helmet with the news that his radios are not working right, so I'm elected by default to do all the switching of channels that will keep us in touch with the ground.

I have already exercised the hydraulic pushrod that closes our dual canopies and we are rolling smoothly past a big sign that reads, 'Tomcat Alley.' I think of NBC's Tom Brokaw, who went up for a ride in an air force F-16 and found it so astounding he peed his pants. Upon landing, he climbed down, fanned out his trousers for the cameras to see and said, 'I couldn't help it.'

Lined up along the runway, the Navy F-14s look mantislike, slim and long; distinctly bent near the bulging eyes of the canopy. Our F-4 is more muscular, overripe with malevolence, a great, strapping tube of vile defiance of the laws of physics and man, an overblown blackjack of an airplane.

My mind flashes back to the quick one-day orientation aboard the carrier USS America: first the arresting-hook landing, then the tour of the huge ship and finally being allowed the special privilege of seeing flight-deck operations right there where the wing tips are slicing past your earmuffs five steps away at 130 mph, just as if you've been allowed to stroll out onto the runway at La Guardia. And there was the view down the spidery catwalks directly into the gray maw of the cold Atlantic, rising with a rumble from its watery thicket to meet the ship. Then in departing there'd been the fierce, almost orgasmic exhilaration of being flung airplane and all off the catapult in one stunning shot, zero to 150 mph in two seconds, knowing by heart the sound that was clanging through the ship as the giant steam-operated piston activated the catapult. I know it because I'd tried to sleep a few feet under the sound all through Night Ops, lying wide-eyed six feet under the afterburner blasts building up for destiny's leaps into the darkness, the pilots tied electronically to the dim control room and to the Air Boss in the ship's tower. The radar and computers there light up the panorama of screens with crisp, brilliantly coloured displays that enable the controllers to blow electronic marvels like F-14s off the catapults and out to dogfights several hundred miles away, shooting down other planes in the process and to return them to landings on the ship without ever having a pilot aboard.

I snap back to the present. My headset is talking again: 'Two-One-Five, clear to take off on the right.'

Oh boy.

Campbell: 'Okay, here we go... That's military power, now we put in the afterburners...'

Oh Jeeeezzussss!!!

I hope I didn't say that out loud. I've been for rides as insanely fast as David Hobbs'

McLaren BMW back in the days when it was a match for any Porsche 935 and fast enough to give me a whole new window of reference, but it simply has no bearing on what's happening in the F-4. There are none of the familiar points of reference you have in the car, corners and hills and guardrails and trees and bridges, stuff you can assimilate even at hyper-speed because it's familiar territory. The Phantom takes all that away and throws it down the supersonic laundry chute. Here we are sitting on the ground. zzZZSSHAP! Here we are at 5000 feet. This is not the Friendly Skies. The debauched cackle of a zealot copes over the headset. This is going to be the longest hour of my life.

'Here we are at 15,000 feet,' Campbell chortles. 'Airspeed up here is no big deal.'

'Okay. What do you reckon the highest is we'll go?' say I with the best syntax my lagging brain can muster.

'Oh, I dunno,' says good old Scotty. 'How high do you wanna go?'

'Whatever we've got time for,' I croak bravely.

I pray that the takeoff has used three-quarters of the fuel. We cruise south and put in a brief appearance over Kitty Hawk in North Carolina (and what would the Wright brothers think of us now?).

Campbell has us at about 15,000 feet and his zealot's brain is setting us up for a low-level run, one of those treetop jobs where you should apply for work with Weyerhaeuser. I realize from Campbell's patter that we are over a place called Dare County. No comment.

He rolls the airplane over and we go blasting down to meet the ocean. He is delicately easing the stick through fractions of its approximate inch of travel, his arm braced in his lap against the g-forces. He is saying, 'Okay, we'll go down here, uh, we're at 400 feet, 200 feet, now about 150, there's a little fisherman over here on the left...'

All I see is streaking blue water, then a flash of some poor jerk's face. By my reckoning, he should have been blown out of the boat. Campbell is unconcerned, so I make conversation as the forest ripples toward us: 'I see what you meant about the stability.'

'Oh, yeah, it's very stable... Fighters have to be inherently unstable so that they can be very responsive to your touch, but the F-4 is not so unstable that you can't fly it under control. Okay, here's the target-run-in line, we'll run on down. There'll be a little turbulence.'

What? Wait a minute, we're already at 150 feet and these trees are not short!

'There's about 600 knots,' his living-room voice says.

There is a ditch cut deep between the trees and we are going down into it. It is exactly like Cinerama - call it Theatre in the Rut - and instead of narrowing down to a tunnel, my vision collects the periphery and the flickering trees and when I swivel my head to look across into the forest 30 feet away on each side, I am surprised to see the details, the texture of the pattern, the floss of the undergrowth, the light and shadow on the bark... visible at 690 mph, 50 feet off the ground. We are down below tree level, surrounded by timber everywhere except directly in front and directly behind and the turbulence is doing a pitty-pat, linebacker head-slapping routine on the beak and wings of the Phantom.

Then, with the gentleness that always accompanies his first move of the controls, Scott Campbell lifts the grey malevolence, call-number Two-One-Five, up out of the funnel, rolls it over and aims the canopy back down into the ditch where the 600-gallon belly tank was a moment ago. We are hanging upside down at almost 700 mph, close enough to comb our hair with underbrush and Campbell is reciting, '. . . and there's the target, aaanndd we're outta here...'

As suddenly as death could come, Campbell has bent the airplane against the sky and I grunt and strain as violently as I ever have when retching with the flu, only now I am straining to hold everything in and to keep the blood in my head as the airplane tries to press it all into my toes, squeezing my legs as if I'm crushed in the arms of a hydraulic giant. I am aware that my noise is awful, desperate. My God, how can surface area forced against thin air produce this kind of violence? Lord help us. But I just say, 'That's amazing. What kind of g-loading do you suppose we've pulled so far?'

'About three and a half.'

What? Izzatall? That makes me mad and suddenly I want to tell him to deliver the whole works, but he does it without prodding. We make a run on a half-sunk target ship, skimming 20 or 30 feet off the water and slingshotting around the listing bridge as if possessed by an aberration of physics and hurtle up into the sky flash! and rendezvous with another F-4 to fly tandem for a while at about 500 mph with our wing tips overlapped. Then the other plane becomes the bad guy, we split off to about three miles, arrow straight at each other at a 1200-mph closing speed, close the last mile in three seconds, miss a head-on (zZHEW!!) by maybe 100 feet and then we chase him all over the sky. Now, oh yes, now I know what g-loading is. The airplane swivels and rolls and barrels after its prey, my eyes blinking sweat, trying to coordinate the whirling horizon with Down and the other F-4 with Where We're Going, praying they're not the same place.

I am groaning, grunting uncontrollably now, my body crushing the sound out under the pressure like a bellows as we plunge through a full-afterburner turn, a full circle and then another, the Phantom howling, the world as I know it ceasing to exist and there can never again be a sky like the one I grew up with that only produces rain and snow and sunshine and smog, a sky having nothing to do with torture and fading vision and the very breath squeezing out of you and there can never again be anything in me that will claim even the whisper of understanding of things I really know nothing about. My face is pulling away from my skull and pellets of sweat are escaping the skullcap under the Star Wars helmet and pelting my flaming cheeks above the oxygen mask like flecks of icy sleet, shards of dry ice. EeeEEUUNNGGHHH! Yes, but yes, we are winning! Kill the sonofabitch you Scott Campbell navy lieutenant or I'll never forgive you!!

Then we are behind the guy's wing line and we have won. I breathe in gasps and fight the rush of queasiness. This dogfight was not artificially staged; there were no planned moves. Campbell says we have pulled a sustained six and a half gs several times.

My voice sounds like a winding-down Victrola, cracking and dragging. But we are not done. There are Immelmanns and loops and barrel rolls and dives that make the ears pop like machine-gun fire and racing down across the water to beat a bread truck out to Cape Hatteras and then the old 'How high?' question comes up again, so he stands the Phantom on its tail and bangs in the afterburners and we fire up to 45,000 feet so fast I can't even read the single-digit numbers on the altimeter roller that indicate hundreds of feet. He cuts everything off. We settle to zero airspeed as he *neutralizes the controls and we fall over with a pop! pop! as the dead engines indulge in compressor stalls and then get themselves fired again with the growing rush of air through their turbine blades. And, oh yeah, I forgot to mention that somewhere out over the water a while back we went supersonic, Mach 1.2, available in the flash of an eye even with extraneous weapons-carrying claptrap hanging under the wings and the big belly tank mooning down like Junior Johnson's belly with a little wind-tunnel work.*

I've confirmed what I believed going in, that fighter planes and fighter pilots are like race cars and race drivers, tooth for nail, right down the line, fast and calm and desperate all at the same time, sweating bullets and living somewhere out front because they don't dare get behind. And fighter planes have rear-view mirrors just like cars, so you can make sure that there's nothing gaining on you.

The F-4 Phantom is rated for a maximum descent rate on landing of 25 feet per second (think about that one for a second) and Campbell dumps us back with a ka-bang! onto Oceana NAS in best carrier-landing fashion. But when he kicks in the afterburners in a classic touch-and-go and flings us back into the sky when I thought we were going to stay down, my stomach says enough!

For this, I award Lieutenant Scott Campbell and VF-171 my first-ever You-Guys-Make-Me-Sick Legion of Merit with Upchuck Clusters and Special Technicolor Yawn El Grande Award. But I also give Scott Campbell, VF-171 and the Department of the Navy special thanks for one of the greatest experiences of my life. I would kill to be able to fly one of these F-4 Phantoms and to have it waiting on my back-yard airstrip, fuelled and armed and ready to outrage the neighbours, the ones with the noisy motorboats and snowmobiles.

But the best part has been finding out that it was the admiral's oxygen mask that I emptied my steak and eggs into. Maybe if we just don't mention it . .

By Larry Griffin, *Car and Driver* July 1982

Chapter 1

The Gunfighters

Despite being designed as a specialized carrier-borne aircraft, the Phantom was to become the most widely used American supersonic fighter during the era of the Mach.2 missile-launching fighter era. No less than 1,264 F-4s were delivered to the US Navy and 2,640 Phantoms to the USAF. Only the F-86 Sabre/FJ Fury exceeded the F-4 Phantom in numbers produced, but in terms of longevity, the North American design had a shorter career span than the Phantom. The F4H-1F (F-4A) Phantom entered service with the US Navy on 30 December 1960 with VF-121 'Pacemakers' the Pacific Fleet RAG (Replacement Air Group) at NAS Miramar, California. On 30 March McDonnell received an order for one F-110A and a production contract for 310 F-4C aircraft soon followed. In April 1962 the Department of Defense (DoD) announced that versions of the Phantom were to become the standard fighter and tactical reconnaissance aircraft of TAC, United States Air Force in Europe (USAFE) and the Pacific Air Force (PACAF).

The Phantom men's greatest claim to fame was in the Việtnam War 1965-1973 where their MiG victories, ground-attack, ECM suppression missions and attacks on bridges with conventional and later 'smart' bombs formed the major part of their war. By the end of 1965, there were eighteen squadrons of 'fast movers' in South East Asia including six tactical fighter squadrons equipped with the F-4C. The Republic of South Việtnam was created in July 1954 using the 17th Parallel to separate it from the Communist North. However, Hồ Chi Minh's Việt Minh forces, led by General Võ Nguyên Giáp, planned to take over control of the South using a new Communist guerrilla force called the Việt Công (VC) or National Liberation Front (NLF). The VC campaign increased in intensity in 1957 and finally, in 1960, Premier Ngô Đình Diệm appealed to the United States for help. In 1961 'special advisers' were sent in and later President Lyndon B. Johnson began the first moves, which would lead to total American involvement in Việtnam.

In the autumn of 1965, after having flown in the back seat of an F-100 in Việtnam, Winston Spencer Churchill, a journalist before becoming a Member of Parliament, who in the 1950s had covered conflict in Yemen and Borneo, had still not got his Phantom strike and thought he would try his luck once again. Born at Chequers on 10 October 1940, days before the victorious conclusion to the Battle of Britain which his grandfather hailed as the nation's 'finest hour', he was the only child of Randolph Churchill's wartime marriage to the young Pamela Digby. She would enjoy a near-scandalous romantic career and eventually, after outliving the much older Averell Harriman, became President Clinton's ambassador in Paris. In the 1960s the Six Day War during which time young Churchill would meet numerous Israeli politicians, including Moshe Dayan;[1] and publish a book recounting the war, got his attention, just as Việtnam had. The first US aircraft on a mission against targets in North Việtnam in August 1964 had encountered only a rudimentary air defence system which did not severely impede the attack. The NVNAF possessed no jet aircraft or surface-to-air missiles and had only a crude radar system. These deficiencies were soon corrected, however, when in 1965 they introduced MiG-15 and MiG-17 jet fighters and other defences. The MiG-17 was a generation behind the Phantom in age, but some Americans feared it more than the newer MiG-21. Pushed through the sky by two 17,900lb afterburning General Electric J79-GE-10 axial-flow turbojet engines, the Phantom weighed ten times as much as the nimble MiG-17.

The Phantoms at Đà Nẵng operated almost exclusively on what was termed 'out-of-country' missions, over North Việtnam. Because of the significant numbers of surface-to-air missiles, heavy anti-aircraft fire and the very great difficulties of recovering downed pilots from the north, journalists were forbidden to go on such missions. But to Churchill's amazement, an in-country mission was set up, using an F-4C Phantom and two B-57s (the US designation for the British-built Canberra medium bomber). Having been kitted up as before with pressure suit, survival kit, parachute, dinghy, life-jacket and assorted gear, Churchill was briefed on the mission by Lieutenant Colonel Pasqualicchio - Call me 'Pancho' for short! - a dark, lean, distinguished-looking fellow with a well-trimmed moustache, who commanded the 480th Tactical Fighter Squadron.

'I climbed into the rear seat of the Phantom' he wrote, 'where, before take-off, I was given a full hour's briefing on the aircraft's controls and systems. The aircraft was equipped with four Sparrow air-to-air missiles which could only be fired from the navigator-bombardier's seat, which I was to occupy. Since we were so close to the North Việtnamese border and there was a danger that we might be engaged by MiGs, I was given a detailed briefing on how to bracket a target on the radar so as to achieve 'lock-on', as well as instructions for the arming and firing of the missiles. In addition to our defensive missiles, we carried on underwing pylons four pods, each containing sixteen rockets with high-explosive incendiary warheads, as well as an enormous cigar-shaped pod under the belly of the aircraft, known as 'the pistol' - a Gatling gun capable of firing 1,200 rounds in the space of twelve seconds. Though the Phantom could fly at Mach 2, or twice the speed of sound, the vast array of weaponry that we carried restricted our speed to Mach .82 or 600 mph. In the event that we were engaged by MiG-21s, we would instantly jettison all the 'garbage', as 'Pancho' described our external war-load, so as to recover the full speed and manoeuvrability of the aircraft for a dog-fight.

'Once our weapons had been armed, we taxied for take-off behind some Marine Crusaders and South Việtnamese F-5s, in company with the two B-57s that were to come with us. On this occasion, I had a vivid demonstration of the way the taxi-rank concept for the deployment of air power was used by the Americans in Việtnam. No sooner were we airborne and climbing on track towards our destination than we were switched to a different target. Five minutes later we were reassigned to a third, even higher priority target. This turned out to be a point on the la Drang River, just three miles from the Cambodian border, where a US Special Forces unit found themselves engaged in a 'fire-fight' with a sizable force of Việt Công' guerrillas on the far side of the river.

'The Forward Air Controller met us over the target area and pinpointed where he wanted us to drop our munitions on the east side of the river. The two B-57s made a shallow dive into the target and we followed close behind. They seemed to make little impression on the dense jungle with their 750lb bombs but, as we reached about 2,000 feet, we fired one of our rocket pods, followed moments later by a second one - making a salvo of thirty-two rockets. We pulled 6.5 times the force of gravity as we came out of the dive and, as we made a steep left-hand turn, we could see the jungle in flames for 100 yards or more along the bank of the river. We came round for a second pass with our bombs and rockets. Finally, we made four or five run-ins with our Gatling gun, which growled fiercely as we let fly two or three bursts on each pass, each time making a quick bank to left and to right, as we climbed away, so as to avoid the enemy ground fire which had been reported by the FAC. As we set course back to Đà Nẵng we could see a pall of smoke rising from the smouldering jungle we left behind us.

A couple of days later, when I visited the Special Forces base at Pleiku in the central highlands of Việtnam, I discovered that we had, in fact, killed no one in the strike but that it had had the desired effect of persuading the Việt Công to break off the action and make a tactical withdrawal. Shortly before we were due to touch down at Đà Nẵng, Colonel 'Pancho', who had let me fly the plane all the way to and from the target area, exclaimed: 'I don't think I've shown you how this bird performs!' We were at the time descending through 1,500 feet on final approach to the runway, when he thrust throttles abruptly forward and pulled back sharply on the stick, cocking the Phantom on its rear end, almost vertical to the ground. At the same instant the two after burners kicked in and, with an incredible surge of power, we shot up through the clouds into the brilliant sunshine above, making climbing barrel rolls as we went. Within seconds we were at 22,000 feet: two minutes later we were on the ground.

'My two air combat missions and a subsequent two-hour flight low over the jungle canopy at no more than 80 or 100 mph with a Forward Air Controller in his 'Bird-dog' gave me a first-hand insight into the lives and attitudes of fighter-bomber pilots in combat. Unlike troops on the ground, the pilot is, to a large degree, divorced from the realities and discomforts of war. Hurtling through the sky at hundreds of miles per hour with incredible power at his fingertips and the ability, at the touch of a button, to decide the fate of hundreds of his fellow mortals, he can easily come to feel like a god of Greek mythology, unleashing deadly thunderbolts from the sky. As one dive towards the target at nearly 600 mph, it is difficult to appreciate that the black ant-like creatures scrambling for cover below are in fact human beings - each someone's son, husband, father or brother. Unless unlucky enough to be shot down by a missile or by ground fire - as indeed all too many were, especially over the North - one is back at base within an hour or two in a totally secure environment far removed from the squalor and hardship of the battlefield, sipping an ice-cold lager. It is a form of warfare which can readily lead to insensitivity and callousness.

'As one who has on half a dozen occasions flown in fast military combat aircraft and felt totally exhilarated by the experience, I count it a salutary antidote that, three years later, while reporting the Nigerian civil war from Biafra, I found myself on the receiving end when a Russian-made Tupolev bomber of the Nigerian Air Force opened its bomb-bay almost directly over my head, dumping its weapon-load just a quarter of a mile away on what turned out to be a clinic for nursing mothers and their babies. Under such circumstances, one is liable to get a more jaundiced - possibly truer - view of air power. It becomes easy to understand how simple people, who find themselves defenceless in the face of such awesome destructive power, have before now, when a plane has been brought down, literally torn the pilot limb from limb in expiation of their pent-up rage and hatred, 'a fate that has undoubtedly befallen several Israeli pilots shot down over Arab lands'.

The political and physical restrictions on the basing of US aircraft in South Việtnam was to some extent solved by the permanent stationing of aircraft carriers in the South China Sea. In March 1965 the US 7th Fleet's Task Force 77 had developed a pattern of positioning carriers at 'Yankee Station' in the South China Sea off Đà Nẵng from which to launch attacks against North Việtnam. On 20 May TF 77 established 'Dixie Station' 100 miles southeast of Cam Ranh Bay from where close air support missions could be mounted against South Việtnam. The carriers developed a system that normally kept each ship on line duty for a period of between 25 and 35 days after which the carrier would visit a port in the Philippines, Japan or Hong Kong for rest and replenishment of supplies. Each carrier would normally complete four spells of duty on the line before returning to its homeport for refitting and re-equipping. However, the period spent on line duty could vary considerably and some ships spent well over the average number of days on duty. The establishment of 'Dixie Station' required the assignment of a fifth carrier to the Western Pacific to maintain the constant presence of at least two carriers at 'Yankee Station' and one at 'Dixie Station'. By the summer of 1966, there were enough aircraft based in South Việtnam to provide the required airpower and 'Dixie Station' was discontinued from 4 August.

When in 1964 two F-8 Crusaders were brought down during a reconnaissance mission over Laos, the USAF flew a retaliatory strike on 9 June against AAA sites. On 2 August North Việtnamese torpedo boats attacked the destroyer USS *Maddox* in international waters in the Gulf of Tonkin. At the time, thirteen of the 31 Navy deployable fighter squadrons were equipped with F-4Bs, one had a mix of F-4Bs and F-4Gs and one was converting from F-3Bs to F-4Bs. In addition, two RAG squadrons flew a mix of F-4As and F-4Bs. In Operation 'Pierce-Arrow' in the early afternoon of 5 August two F-4Bs, of VF-142 'Ghostriders' and VF-143 'Pukin Dogs'on the USS *Constellation* (CVA-64) made the first Phantom combat sortie of the Việtnam War when they provided bomber escort for ten A-1H Skyraiders and eight Skyhawks in an attack on the gunboats and shore facilities near the coal-mining town of Hon Gai northeast of Hànôi. Twelve more (five Skyhawks, four Skyraiders and three Phantoms) from the same carrier struck the Lộc Cháo base. On 10 August the US Congress passed what came to be known as the 'Gulf of Tonkin Resolution', committing America to direct, large-scale intervention in the conflict. The Navy began a campaign of limited bombing attacks against North Việtnam codenamed 'Barrel Roll' in December 1964 that continued into January 1965. Next to see action during the war in SE Asia War were F-4Bs of VF-92, VF-96 and VF-151, which flew combat air patrols during retaliatory strikes in February 1965 ('Flaming Dart') and early 'Rolling Thunder' raids in spring 1965.

Following the establishment of TF 77 aircraft carriers in the South China Sea in August 1964 it was six months before the US Navy was again in action although thirteen naval aircraft had been lost in accidents over Southeast Asian waters during this time. Air strikes against North Việtnam were part of President Lyndon B. Johnson's 2 December plan but they were not immediately instigated. However, VC attacks on US facilities at Sàigòn on 24 December and Pleiku and Camp Holloway on 7 February caused Johnson to order the first air strike against North Việtnam since 'Pierce-Arrow' in August 1964. In retaliation, the order was given for a strike code-named 'Flaming Dart I', from carriers in the Gulf of Tonkin. On 7 February 1965 49 aircraft were launched from the decks of the *Hancock* and *Coral Sea* against Việt Công installations at Đông Hới, while the *Ranger* sent 34 aircraft to bomb Vit Thù lù and other targets were to be hit by VNAF A-1s. The raid was led by Commander Warren H. Sells, Commander of *Hancock's* Air Wing 21. In the event, monsoon weather forced the 34 aircraft of *Ranger's* strike force to abort their mission against Vit Thù lù but Đông Hới's barracks and port facilities were attacked by twenty aircraft from the *Coral Sea* and 29 from the *Hancock*. The strike was carried out at low-level under a 700 feet cloud base in rain and poor visibility. The mission did not appear to have the effect on the North Việtnamese that Washington had hoped for. On 10 February the Việt Công struck at an American camp at Quy Nhon causing serious casualties. The immediate response to this was 'Flaming Dart 2', flown the following day when a total of 99 naval aircraft from the *Coral Sea, Hancock* and *Ranger* were sent against NVA barracks at Chánh Hóa near Đông Hới. The target was attacked in poor visibility with low cloud and the *Coral Sea* suffered the loss of an A-4C and an F-8D Crusader and one pilot lost on this raid. Bomb damage assessments at Chánh Hóa showed that twenty-three of the seventy-six buildings in the camp were either damaged or destroyed during the raid.

In March 1965 Operation 'Rolling Thunder' was launched and the Navy's first strike took place on the 18th when aircraft from the *Coral Sea* and *Hancock* bombed supply dumps at Phú Văn and Vĩnh Sơn. The US Navy's second 'Rolling Thunder' mission, on 26 March resulted in the loss of three aircraft out of seventy dispatched. The ability of the North Việtnamese air defence system to monitor US raids was a concern even in the early days of the war and the targets for this mission were radar sites at Bạch Long Vi, Cap Mùi Rắn, Hà Tĩnh and Vĩnh Sơn. The battle against the North Việtnamese radar system continued on 31 March with further raids on the Vĩnh Sơn and Cap Mùi Rắn radar sites by sixty aircraft from the *Hancock* and *Coral Sea*.

The decision to interdict the North Việtnamese rail system south of the 20th parallel led immediately to the 3 April strike against the giant Long Biên or Hàm Rông ('Dragon's Jaw') road and rail bridge over the Sông Mã River, three miles north of Thành Hòa in North Việtnam's bloody 'Iron Triangle' (Hảiphòng, Hànôi and Thành Hòa). The 540 feet long, 56 feet wide, Chinese-engineered cantilever bridge, which stood 50 feet above the river, would prove to be one of the single most challenging targets for American air power in Việtnam. In March the US Navy had attacked the Thành Hóa Bridge with AGM-62 Walleye television-guided glide bombs with a 250lb high-explosive warhead but failed to knock out the structure despite three direct hits. On 3 April a total of 35 A-4s, sixteen F-8s and four F-4s were launched from the *Hancock* and *Coral Sea*. The raids were the first occasion when the Việtnamese People's Air Force employed its MiG-17 fighters. Thirty-two Bullpups and ten dozen 750lb bombs were aimed at the bridge but when the smoke cleared, observer aircraft found that the bridge still spanned the river. The Navy flew 97 sorties and dropped 215 tons of bombs on the charmed bridge from April to September 1967 with little to show for its effort. Almost 700 sorties were flown against the bridge at a cost of 104 crewmen shot down over an area of 75 square miles around the 'Dragon'. On 27 April 1972 a flight of eight Air Force Phantoms, two carrying 2,000lb laser-guided bombs and two carrying Walleye IIs, attacked the Thành Hóa Bridge. Cloud cover prevented the LGBs from being used, but five of the Walleyes locked on, causing heavy damage to the bridge, even though failing to bring down a span. The spans were finally brought down three days into the 'Linebacker' campaign on 13 May 1972 by 3,000 and 2,000lb LGBs dropped by F-4Ds of the 8th TFW. Unfortunately, by then the Communists had built several other back-up routes around the bridge and the flow of supplies across the Sông Mã River was not seriously affected.

The first air combat victory was made on 9 April 1965 when two F-4Bs of VF-96 'Fighting Falcons' were launched from the USS *Ranger* (CVA-61) to relieve two other aircraft flying a BARCAP (Barrier Combat Air Patrol) racetrack pattern in the northern Gulf of Tonkin. However, the first aircraft to launch lost its starboard engine as it was being catapulted from the carrier and the aircraft ditched into the sea but both Lieutenant Commander William E. Greer and Lieutenant (jg) R. Bruning ejected just as the aircraft impacted the water and were rescued. Lieutenant (jg) Terence Meredith Murphy and his RIO, Ensign Ronald James Fegan were then launched and took over as section leader with a replacement aircraft flown by Lieutenant Howard Watkins and Lieutenant (jg) John Mueller as their wingman. As the two Phantoms flew north they were intercepted by four MiG-17 'Fresco's from China's Air Force of the People's Liberation Army. The two Phantoms that were waiting to be relieved on BARCAP heard Murphy's radio calls and flew south to engage the MiGs. An air battle took place at high altitude near the Chinese island of Hainan. One of the MiG-17s was seen to explode and was thought to have been shot down by Murphy during the dogfight but it was never officially credited due to the sensitivity of US aircraft engaging Chinese aircraft. Murphy's Phantom was not seen after the MiGs disengaged. The aircraft was thought to have been shot down by the MiGs but a Chinese newspaper claimed that Murphy had been shot down in error by an AIM-7 Sparrow III missile fired by another Phantom. Murphy's last radio call was to the effect that he was out of missiles and was returning to base. Despite an extensive two-day SAR effort, no sign of the Phantom or its crew was ever found.

On 9 June 1965, the first operational (non-combat) loss of an F-4 occurred when 64-0674 in the 45th TFS, 15th TFW ran out of fuel after a strike in South Viêtnam. On 20 June the first Phantom combat loss occurred when a 45th TFS F-4C (64-0685), one of the newly-arrived at Ubon, was brought down by a MiG-17 near Ta Chan during a strike on the NVA military training headquarters at Son La, North Viêtnam. The weather was too low, resulting in the Phantoms having to circle around the site before dropping the bombs and allowing the enemy time to react. Captain Paul Anthony Kari, 29, of Columbus, Ohio, the pilot of 64-0685, recalled: 'We got hit by .37mm radar tracking anti-aircraft fire, but I was close enough to the target so I dropped my bombs anyway.' Captain Curt H. Briggs, his back-seater [WSO (Weapons Systems Officer)] recalled, 'As we were jinking (rolls and turns) to make our plane a poor target, we could feel the plane being hit. They were locked on to us and just kept hitting us. The plane was one big ball of fire! The cockpit was full of heavy, dense smoke and we blew the canopies off so that we could breathe. Less than a minute later we lost all hydraulic pressure and the hydraulic flight controls went out and we couldn't control the airplane… and at the time we blew the canopies there was fire coming out of the left engine intake duct and we had lost intercom and radios. Sheets of flame were coming up over the cockpit area and I ejected as the Phantom started an uncontrollable roll to the left. When I pulled the handle to eject the g-force was enough that I blacked out. I came to within a few seconds when the parachute opened. It was really amazing to go from all that noise and smoke in the cockpit at once to the quietness of being in the parachute. You could hear the wind blowing through the parachute shroud lines. It was just very peaceful but the reality of where I was struck me and from then on it wasn't very pleasant. I could see the plane, a ball of fire, below. A quarter of a mile away I could see two more parachutes. One I surmised was a drag chute which had burned free from the fuselage of the Phantom. The other was Kari.'

'My back-seater hid until he was rescued' said Kari. Briggs was picked up by an Helio Courier of Air America, a privately owned airline operating in Laos, on 21 June. Kari, who flew 64 combat missions in seventy days, was captured really quickly. He had, on 4 June been part of a flight on the mission to destroy a vital thermal power plant and nearby irrigation pumping stations. Displaying tenacious combat instinct coupled with an utter disregard for his own safety, Kari courageously pressed his attack in the face of withering anti-aircraft fire to score direct hits and destroy the power plant almost single-handedly.

Viêt Công forces removed Kari within minutes of hitting the ground, a fall that caused him severe back trauma. But it was the torture that later came during his seven-year, eight-month stay in captivity among other American military personnel that would be the most taxing, as he recalls: 'Inhuman. Rats ran rampant. We had a leaky bucket in the corner... They put concrete blocks in the barred windows during the summer so it would get hot, about 130 degrees. In the winter they knocked the blocks out and it would get down to 30 degrees. One pair of pyjamas, sleeping on concrete or a piece of wood. The food was served sparse, ice cold... anything to demoralize you. Most of us had our faith in God and faith in our country that they would not let us down and they would come get us eventually. We thought, 'if we can make it through today, great. We can do it again tomorrow. Malnourishment and interrogations were a regular occurrence, a practice that led to lifelong shoulder ailments and severe vision impairment for him. During the time of imprisonment, Kari saw his weight fall from 173lbs to 103. We were interrogated four times a day sometimes... I wouldn't give them anything. Nothing other than my name, rank, serial number and date of birth... We were tortured severely. I was afraid I might spill my guts. They starved me to death.' Kari was moved from prison to prison 26 times during the nearly eight-year stretch. It was not until 12 February 1973 that Kari's hell ended. Kari, later named a Silver Star recipient, was on the first aircraft home, the twelfth man to be released.

On 17 June 1965 meanwhile, the first confirmed kills to be achieved by a US Navy fighter squadron occurred when VF-21 recorded its only aerial victories of the Việtnam War. The 'Freelancers' had converted from the F3H-2 Demon to the F-4B at Miramar during 1963, eventually making its sea-going debut on the USS *Midway* (CVA-41) between November of that year and late March 1964.This was the last peace-time deployment that the 'Freelancers' were to make for close to ten years. When VF-21 returned to sea in March 1965 they were bound for combat. On 17 June two F-4Bs of VF-21 were vectored to engage a flight of four MiG-17s near Hànôi while flying a 'barrier combat air patrol (BARCAP)', protecting a strike package attacking the Hàm Rông (Dragon's Jaw') Bridge. Commander Louis C. Page Jr. the unit's XO and his RIO, Lieutenant John C. Smith Jr., shot down the first MiG-17 with a radar-guided AIM-7 Sparrow missile. Lieutenant E. D. 'Dave' Batson Jr., aka 'Batman' flying 'Sundown 102' recalled: 'We accelerated to 500 knots for better manoeuvrability. Lou was to set up a head-on attack, having made a positive ID. J. C, Smith took the farther target, creating a slight off-set to the head-on attack. This caused the MiG to turn into the lead F-4. When they banked, their very distinctive wing plan was visible. Lou fired at close to the minimum range while shouting 'It's MiGs! I saw his missile fire, guide towards the formation and the warhead detonated. At first, I thought it had missed but then the outer half of the right wing came completely off the MiG and it started rolling out of control.'

Moments later 'Dave' Batson and his RIO (Radar Intercept Officer), 33-year old Montclair, New Jersey-born Lieutenant Commander Robert B. 'Bob' Doremus made it a double celebration by adding another MiG-17 to VF-21's tally, again employing an AIM-7. There is a possible second kill by Batson and Doremus, officially confirmed 32 years after the event. Batson had always maintained that a third MiG had been damaged by ingesting debris from its wingman after his AIM-7 Sparrow had exploded. The official documentation, and the backing of Batson's second kill theory by his then Carrier Air Group (CAG) CO, Commander Bob Moore, was enough for the third MiG to be officially classified as destroyed. Batson and Doremus were each awarded the Silver Star. Lieutenant Commander Doremus' citation for first of two Silver Star's reads: '...Engaging at least four and possibly six 'Fresco' aircraft, Commander (then Lieutenant Commander) Doremus accounted for one confirmed kill and contributed to a second confirmed kill by the other F-4B aircraft in the flight by diverting the remaining enemy planes from their threat to the US striking forces. With heavy antiaircraft fire bursting throughout the patrol area, his crew relentlessly maintained their vigil and pressed forward their attack, seeking out and destroying the enemy aircraft and thereby preventing damage to friendly strike aircraft in the area.'

VF-21 compiled a most impressive combat record by making six further visits to the war zone aboard *Coral Sea* (CVA-43) and *Ranger* (CV-61) between 1966 and 1973. Along the way, the 'Freelancers' took time out from the pressures of war to re-equip with the improved F-4J in 1968, continuing to operate this model until December 1979 and following up their wartime exploits with three rather less demanding post-ceasefire deployments to the 7th Fleet in the WestPac as part of CVW-2 aboard *Ranger*.

The Marine Corps had received its first F-4Bs in June 1962, with the 'Black Knights' of VMFA-314 at Marine Corps Air Station El Toro, California becoming the first operational squadron. The first Marine Corps Phantoms to go to Việtnam were fifteen F-4Bs of VMFA-531 'Gray Ghosts' which were assigned to Đà Nẵng airbase on South Việtnam's northeast coast on 10 April 1965, Initially, they were to provide air defence for the USMC and they soon began close air support missions (CAS). VMFA-314 'Black Knights', VMFA-323 'Death Rattlers' and VMFA-542 'Bengals' soon arrived at the primitive airfield. The F-4B was the only Marine aircraft which could carry two 2,000lb bombs and proved well suited for the ground attack role in Việtnam where on average loads of 5,000lb were carried. From 1965-1970 the eleven USMC F-4B squadrons operated on a rotational basis from Đà Nẵng and Chu Lai in support of USMC ground forces in South Việtnam and on 'Tally Ho' offensive strikes in the North Việtnamese panhandle and 'Steel Tiger'/'Tiger Hound' interdiction sorties in Laos. VMCJ-1 'Golden Hawks' flew the first RF-4B photo recon mission on 3 November 1966 from Đà Nẵng and remained there until 1970 with no RF-4B losses and one damaged by AAA.

Prior to July 1965, North Việtnam had augmented its MiG-15/MiG-17 force with modified versions of the MiG-21, which were equipped with Atoll infrared homing missiles, but they showed a marked reluctance to commit this jet fighter force to other than defensive roles. The NVNAF seemed more intent upon improving its electronic defences and at the same time began a considerable expansion of its surface-to-air (SAM) sites and Anti-aircraft Artillery/Automatic Weapons network. North Việtnamese MiGs were committed to lengthy training exercises against US aircraft and made dry firing passes (feinting an attack) under GCI radar vectoring, but broke off before US fighters could engage them. This training period extended from July 1965 to April 1966. The integration of GCI and MiG systems produced excellent training for inexperienced NVNAF pilots and ground controllers in developing their intercept capability.

The threat of MiG activity over Southeast Asia resulted in increased efforts to provide combat air patrols and airborne early warning and the F-4 Phantom and F-8 Crusader were tasked with air defence of the fleet and protection of strike forces but the US was fighting a 'limited war' in Việtnam and neither the military nor the political leadership had much experience with the concept. Strikes were conducted in an intermittent and highly selective fashion, constrained by 'rules of engagement (ROEs)' that told the pilots what they could and could not attack. One Air Force pilot, Captain Bill Jenkins, later commented: 'The rules of engagement were such that I sometimes felt I needed a lawyer in the back seat, instead of a WSO.' Another recalled, 'the rules of engagement were changed frequently to fit President Johnson's political strategies. Notwithstanding the reasoning behind them, they seemed designed to impede our success. We had them written on the bulletin board: 'Don't bomb or attack active military airfields, harbours or port facilities, coastal shipping, surface to air missile sites, MiGs - unless you are attacked first and agricultural dams or dykes'. There was one more, the one that irked everyone the most: 'Thou shall not bomb a village, even if they're shooting at you from it.'[2]

The B-52 strategic bomber was dedicated to tactical operations in South Việtnam while the F-4 Phantom and the F-105 Thunderchief or 'Thud' was tasked with strategic bombing in North Việtnam. Neither fighter had been designed for this mission, the Phantom being originally designed as a Navy fleet defence fighter and the 'Thud' as a USAF tactical nuclear bomber. They were handicapped by the limitations of their radar-guided AIM-7 Sparrow and heat-seeking AIM-9

Sidewinder missile armament, neither of which had been designed for fighter versus fighter combat. The great advantage conferred by the Sparrow, its ability to engage the enemy from any angle at up to twelve miles, was nullified by a rule of engagement which called for visual identification of the enemy before firing. The Sidewinder could be fired from up to one mile, but only from the rear, in a 30° cone that led to the engine's heat. Both missiles were limited by their reaction to g forces and both required a setup time that was difficult to effect in air combat.

Air Force pilots flying missions in the northern part of Việtnam during the early summer months of 1965 had discovered a pattern in enemy air activity. This was evident in the 'Big Eye' (airborne early warning radar aircraft) warnings, broadcasting the approach of MiG aircraft. These warnings, as noted earlier, were of two types. As the first US aircraft entered the area, the first warnings from 'Big Eye' flashed yellow, indicating that MiGs were airborne from Phúc Yên airfield. The warnings turned red as the MiGs approached within ten minutes flight time of the attacking US aircraft. Soon thereafter, however, the red warning would change again to yellow. Then, as the last flight departed the area following the attack, the red warning would reappear and the MiGs would follow the flight out of the area. The North Việtnamese timed their threats (the second red warning) so that the escorts, with a critically low fuel supply, would be forced to fly home and could not engage their MiGs. Apparently, MiG pilots could determine from their own radar equipment when the escorts had returned to base.

Pilots of the 2nd Air Division recognized this pattern and decided to take advantage of MiG tactics. Having observed the same characteristics during morning strikes on Saturday 10 July, the afternoon flight of four F-4Cs of the 45th Tactical Fighter Squadron at Ubon accompanied a strike package of F-105s in hopes of luring NVNAF pilots into thinking they were bombers and worth attacking. The F-4C escort flight codenamed 'Mink' delayed its take-off time for this particular mission by twenty minutes and arrived in the area as the tail end of the strike formation about fifteen minutes later than the North Việtnamese normally anticipated. Each aircraft was armed with four AIM-7 Sparrow and four AIM-9 Sidewinder missiles. Major Richard Hall, flight commander and 1st Lieutenant George Larson flew 'Mink 01'. Captain Harold Anderson and Captain Wilbure Anderson flew 'Mink 02'. 'Mink 03' was manned by Captain Kenneth E. Holcombe of Detroit, Michigan and Captain Arthur C. Clark of McAllen, Texas. 'Mink 04' was crewed by Captain Thomas S. Roberts of LaGrange, Georgia and Captain Ronald C. Anderson of Fairbanks, Alaska.

Two MiG-17s came up to intercept and the four Phantoms split off in pairs to meet them. A short dogfight followed. Holcombe decided to gain separation by executing a roll to the right and putting his Phantom into a 30-degree dive. The MiG pilot tried to follow, ending up behind and three-quarters of a mile away. Holcombe accelerated, gained more separation and turned left into the MiG, attacking it almost head-on. Due to an inoperable radar, he was unable to launch a Sparrow missile and the MiG passed head-on, firing as it went by. After the MiG passed, Holcombe made a slight turn to keep the MiG in sight and then made a 60-degree dive to 10,000 feet. Since he was still in afterburner he was able to reach 1.3 Mach. He then initiated a high-G barrel roll, with the MiG having turned behind him at about a mile. As he completed three-quarters of the roll Holcombe noticed the MiG firing again from the 7 o'clock position. As he completed the high-G roll the MiG pilot again overshot. This time the enemy jet started to turn but then levelled out and descended towards the cloud. Holcombe and Clark were now about 13,000 feet at Mach 0.95 with the MiG almost straight ahead and they fired all four of Sidewinders. Three missed, but the last detonated behind the MiG, which went up in a fireball a moment later. It was the first ever USAF F-4 Sidewinder kill. Short of fuel, Holcombe headed for recovery at Udorn. [3]

Tom Roberts and Ron Anderson were then trying to get on the tail of the second MiG. Roberts fired three Sidewinders. The first went by the MiG's tailpipe and detonated near the left wing tip. The second missile failed to track. Roberts followed the MiG down and fired his last Sidewinder, but had to give up the chase when he ran into intense anti-aircraft fire. The third Sidewinder exploded behind the MiG, sending it into a dive trailing white smoke. Total elapsed time for both engagements was less than four minutes. More MiGs came up to challenge the Americans, but the Phantoms were low on fuel and had to go home. In addition, although both Holcombe and Roberts still had their Sparrows, their radars had failed, rendering the missiles so much dead weight. These were the first Air Force air-to-air victories of the Viêtnam War.[4]

The North Viêtnamese were equipped with the best anti-aircraft weapons their Russian allies could provide, including light, medium and heavy anti-aircraft artillery and in particular batteries of Soviet-built SA-2 'Guideline' surface-to-air missiles (SAMs). The SA-2 had a solid fuel booster rocket that launched and accelerated it and then dropped off after about six seconds. While in boost stage, the missile, which had a 349lb high explosive warhead and a ceiling of almost 60,000 feet did not guide. During the second stage, the SA-2 guided and a liquid-fuel rocket propelled it to the target. Pilots who encountered the 35 feet long missile described them as 'telegraph poles. The success of the system depended almost entirely on the skill of its seven-man missile crew; the battalion commander, a fire control officer, three guidance officers, a plotter and a missile technical officer in their un-air-conditioned command van. Compared to the flak and SAMs, the NVNAF and its MiGs were an annoyance. Since most NVNAF pilots were not highly trained, they were guided or 'vectored' to formations of US aircraft by ground controllers; the MiGs would drop into the formations from high altitude, cannons blazing and then zoom off, rarely hanging around to fight. If they could disrupt strike packages and force them to jettison their bombs, the MiGs had done their job. The SAMs were the real threat but at first, the ROEs (Rules of Engagement) did not permit attacks on SAM sites, since Russian advisers were assumed to be working there. John T. McNaughton, assistant secretary of defence for international security affairs, ridiculed the need to strike the SAMs. *You don't think the North Viêtnamese are going to use them!* he scoffed. *Putting them in is just a political ploy by the Russians to appease Hànôi.*

McNaughton's surmise was soon discredited. On 24 July an F-4C was brought down by an SA-2. F-4C 63-7599 of the 47th TFS, 15th TFW was one of four Phantoms providing a CAP for an F-105 strike mission on a munitions factory at Chi Lăng. While at 23,000 feet about forty miles west of Hànôi the crew of Captain 'Pop' Keirn and Captain Roscoe Henry Fobair spotted a smoke trail tracking towards their aircraft and had just realised what they were seeing when their

Phantom suddenly exploded. They had become the first US airmen to be shot down by an SA-2. The crew had just heard a warning from an RB-66C that a SAM radar was on the air when three missiles were launched at the Phantoms. One missile scored a direct hit on the Phantom and the other two exploded behind the flight causing slight damage to the other three Phantoms. Keirn, who was on only his fifth mission, had flown fourteen missions as a B-17 Flying Fortress co-pilot in the 100th Bomb Group in the US Eighth Air Force. On 11 September 1944 his aircraft was shot down near Leipzig and Keirn spent the next nine months as PoW in a Stalag Luft. Following demobilization, he was recalled to active service in 1956 and flew F-86s and F-100s before converting to the F-4C.

Keirn's Phantom was the first of 110 USAF aircraft lost to SAMs in Southeast Asia. (The Air Force lost 40 percent of its total production of F-105s to combat in Việtnam. Approximately one out of every eight F-4s ever built was destroyed in Việtnam[5]). The White House approved a retaliatory air strike, but by the time it got there, the SAM batteries were long gone. Instead, dummy missiles had been placed at the site as a 'flak trap.' The attacking aircraft were lured within the range of concealed air defence guns, which shot down four of them.[6]

The effectiveness of North Việtnamese air defences would push the US to develop countermeasures as the war dragged on. RWRs were retrofitted to combat Phantoms and eventually became production fit. Electronic countermeasures (ECM) pods were carried by Phantoms, on a stores pylon or in some cases fitted to a Sparrow launch recess under the forward fuselage. F-4s were initially fitted with the AN/ALR-101 series of ECM pods introduced in the late 1960s, followed by the AN/ALQ-119, which went into service before the end of the war. In the post war period, they would carry the AN/ALQ-131.

Sporadic encounters between MiGs and US fighters occurred during the nine months following the initial aerial victories. During this period, American crews shot down five MiGs, while four US fighters were lost to the enemy's aircraft. When aerial encounters did occur, MiG pilots effectively used the superior turning capability of their aircraft to achieve a 6 o'clock position, which then endangered F-105 strike aircraft if they slowed down to follow or turn. MiG pilots relied on turn radius and cut-off tactics almost exclusively to attain a viable combat attack capability. They usually forced the 'Thuds' to jettison their ordnance in order to take evasive action and prepare for a counterattack. Against F-4s armed with radar-controlled and heat-seeking missiles, however, the MiG-17s were at a disadvantage when they employed turn radius and cut-off tactics since under these conditions the F-4s enjoyed superiority. MiGs were more of a threat at the higher altitudes, but this threat was more potential than real in 1965 and early 1966.

On 6 October 1965 Lieutenant Commander D. MacIntyre and Lieutenant (jg) Allen Johnson in VF-151's 'Switchbox 10' fired an AIM-7 at a MiG-17 which appeared to be doomed but future ranking 'Fresco' ace Nguyên Văn Bảy landed his MiG with more than eighty holes in his aircraft. MacIntyre, meanwhile, broke off and attacked another MiG-17 which was attacking his wingman, Lieutenant Commander Tom Ewall's Phantom. By that time MacIntyre was at only fifty feet, where the background ground clutter rendered his missiles redundant in any event.

On 17 October the Navy flew an Alpha Strike or major mission against the Thái Nguyên road bridge, thirty miles due north of Hànôi. The mission proved costly for the *Independence's* air wing although, curiously, the losses occurred not at the bridge itself but on the way to and from the target. The strike force of fifteen aircraft crossed the coast well to the east of Hảiphòng and approached Thái Nguyên from due east. The first aircraft to go down (F-4B 151515 of VF-84 'The Jolly Rogers') was assigned to the flak suppression force and was hit by AAA at 2,000 feet while still forty miles short of the target. An anti-aircraft shell burst in the cockpit and the 24-year old NFO, Lieutenant (jg) Porter Alexander Halyburton of Davidson, North Carolina, who was on his 76th mission, could not make contact with Lieutenant Commander Stanley Edward Olmstead his 32-year old pilot, who was either killed or knocked unconscious by the blast. With the aircraft out of control, Halyburton had no alternative but to eject. Other fliers saw no parachute and his radio failed. Back in the US his wife Marty knew the news wasn't good. The Navy had hunted her down in Atlanta where she was visiting. Porter's plane was shot down, they regretted to tell her. 'There wasn't much hope. 'At that point in the war, they had to make a pronouncement within 24 hours and they'd pronounced Porter KIA (killed in action). I felt that Porter had been blessed that he wasn't a prisoner of war. I'm an optimist and made myself think that if he had to be shot down; dying was the lesser of two evils.' A week later, the town packed into Davidson College Presbyterian Church for an Episcopal memorial service. An education fund was set up for Halyburton's infant daughter, Dabney. (Porter had gone off to war in April 1965, days after his daughter was born). Halyburton's mother commissioned a tombstone for the family cemetery plot. Marty remembers little about the memorial service. 'I was 23 with a baby and all of a sudden I'm a widow and the man I loved has been killed. Life was a blur for a couple of months.'

After the raid at Thái Nguyên, the strike force headed back towards the east to avoid the heavier flak concentrations around Hànôi and Haiphòng. Another VF-84 Phantom crewed by Ensign Ralph Ellis Gaither, 22, of Miami Florida and Lieutenant (jg) Rodney Allen Knutson, 26, of Billings, Montana, strayed too far east and was shot down within two miles of the Chinese border and 65 miles northeast of Thái Nguyên. Although US aircraft were not permitted by the Pentagon's rules of engagement to enter a fifteen-mile buffer zone west of the Chinese border, it was easy for an aircraft to stray into the zone by accident considering the confined air-space of the region to the east of Hànôi. At 450 knots it would have taken less than ten minutes for the Phantom to reach the Chinese border from Thái Nguyên. Gaither and Knutson ejected from their Phantom when it was hit by AAA causing an engine fire followed quickly by the total loss of control. Knutson was badly injured during the ejection suffering fractures to his neck and backbone As he landed he was fired upon by North Viêtnamese soldiers and Knutson drew his service revolver and killed two of his attackers before he was knocked unconscious by a shot at point blank range which fortunately only grazed his forehead and nose. He was lucky not be killed and was taken to Hànôi along with his pilot.

The last Phantom (150631) to be lost on this raid was from VF-41'Black Aces'. Lieutenant Roderick Lewis Mayer, 25, of Lewiston, Idaho and Lieutenant (jg) David Robert Wheat, 25, of Duluth, Minnesota was assigned to CAP duties to protect the strike force from MiGs. The Phantom was orbiting at low-level covering the strike aircraft as they left the target when it was hit by small arms fire. Mayer soon lost control of the aircraft and it crashed less than ten miles from where Lieutenant Commander Olmstead's Phantom had been lost earlier in the mission. Two parachutes were seen but it appears that Lieutenant Mayer was killed either during the ejection or upon landing. At the time the SAR operation was terminated, both Roderick Mayer and David Wheat were listed presumed dead. Later the status of David Wheat was changed to Prisoner of War when it was learned that he had in fact been captured. Whether Roderick Mayer survived his injuries or died of them is unknown since the communists refuse to acknowledge having any knowledge of his fate. [7]

At sea, the USS *Enterprise,* accompanied by the nuclear powered guided-missile cruiser USS *Bainbridge,* took up a position at 'Dixie' Station on 2 December to relieve *Bon Homme Richard* and fly missions over South Viêtnam before moving to 'Yankee' Station for operations over the North. On its first day of operations the *Enterprise* launched 118 sorties against Viêt Công targets in South Viêtnam; however, only 116 aircraft returned to the carrier's deck. Two F-4Bs of VF-92 'Silver Kings' were tasked to provide close air support to US troops about five miles north of Ăn Lộc, 55 miles north of Sàigòn and only ten miles from the border with Cambodia. Lieutenant T. J. Potter put his Phantom into a 30-degree dive and released six Mk.82 bombs at 5,000 feet. As soon as the bombs released the crew felt an explosion and the wingman reported that the Phantom was trailing fuel which had ignited. Within seconds most of the fuel had been lost and the aircraft was still on fire leaving no alternative for Potter and Lieutenant (jg) C. W. Schmidt to eject. They were picked up after some anxious minutes by a USAF HH-43 helicopter that was directed to the scene by a C-123 that happened to be in the area. The Mk.82 bombs were fitted with a tail fuse that had a 4.5-second arming delay but for some reason, the bombs had armed instantly upon release and then one bomb may have touched another causing a detonation.

F-4B 149468 of VF-96 'Fighting Falcons'from *Enterprise* also was lost on this day. Lieutenant (jg) Robert J. Miller and Lieutenant (jg) G. F. Martin were returning from a strike over South Viêtnam low on fuel and the weather was deteriorating. The seas were rough causing the carrier's deck to pitch violently and the Phantom made several approaches. The crew had difficulty refuelling from a Skyhawk tanker and ejected just before the fuel ran out. A Seasprite helicopter from the carrier's HC-1 detachment rescued the crew.

The *Kitty Hawk* also suffered its first combat loss on the 2nd. F-4B 152220 of VF-114 'Aardvarks' crewed by 42-year old Commander Carl Benjamin Austin, the CO and 25-year old Lieutenant (jg) Jacob Drummond Logan was following about one and a half miles behind a flight of Skyhawks with the intention of providing flak suppression if required. The formation crossed the coast ten miles south of Mu Ron Ma but the cloud was so low that it enveloped the hills near the coastline. The Skyhawks entered cloud and reversed their course back out to sea to attempt a penetration on instruments. However, when the formation broke through the cloud a few miles from the beach there was no sign of the accompanying Phantom. The next day searchers spotted a freshly burned patch of ground on a hillside in the location where Austin and Logan disappeared and it was presumed that the aircraft had flown into the hill soon after it entered cloud. [8]

On Christmas Day 1965 President Johnson suspended the 'Rolling Thunder' bombing campaign to induce the Communists to negotiate. The Việt Cộng responded with a counter-offensive campaign and 'Rolling Thunder' was re-started again on 31 January 1966.

There can be few experiences more memorable than to be aboard a large aircraft carrier engaged in combat operations and in March Winston S. Churchill counted himself fortunate to have the chance of spending twenty-four hours aboard the USS *Ranger*.

'*Ranger* was one of two carriers on 'Yankee Station' at the time, each taking it, in turn, to operate for twelve hours nonstop.[9] As I touched down on the deck of *Ranger,* our aircraft was brought to an abrupt halt by one of four arrester wires stretched across the deck. I arrived on board just in time for the start of *Ranger's* twelve-hour operational cycle, due to start at noon. At midday sharp, a flight of F-4Bs, A-1 and A-4 fighter-bombers, a Vigilante photo-reconnaissance aircraft, an E-2 Hawkeye with early-warning radar and a couple of tanker aircraft were catapulted off the deck at 22.5-second intervals. One and a half hours later, a second wave of aircraft, almost identical in composition to the first, was shot off the carrier and, fifteen minutes after that, the first wave returned to be refuelled and re-armed, before being launched once again against the enemy. This routine was to continue until midnight when the other carrier, the USS *Hancock,* took over. I spent much of the time on the flight deck with the launch crews, who provided me with a helmet equipped with goggles and ear-pads against the deafening combination of the thunder of the steam catapults at launch and the high-pitched scream of jet engines at full power.

'There is an especially generous streak in the American character which makes them eager to acknowledge their gratitude to others. I found this especially noticeable in Việtnam. On shore, the Americans spoke unhesitatingly of their Australian allies as 'the finest jungle troops in Việtnam'. Aboard *Ranger,* they made clear to me that the effectiveness and efficiency of their operation were largely due to three British inventions: the steam catapult, the angled flight deck and the mirrored light approach aid. I reflected with sadness on the decision of the British government of the day to build no more attack carriers - a decision that nearly led to disaster in the 1982 Falklands conflict, as it meant that Britain was unable to deploy either supersonic fighters or airborne early-warning aircraft to the South Atlantic.

'But in spite of the immense power deployed in Southeast Asia by the United States and epitomized by the USS *Ranger* with its 5,000-strong crew, the Americans by no means had it all their own way and the toll of human lives on both sides was relentless. During my brief time aboard *Ranger* two aircraft failed to return [on 1 March 1966]. One, an F-4 Phantom, disappeared at low altitude into a fog bank from which it never emerged; the other, an A-4, had been shot down close to the coast where the pilot had been picked up and taken prisoner [sic] by North Việtnamese in sampans before one of *Ranger's* helicopters, which came under intense fire, could reach him. Many of those captured pilots were never to return and I found myself lost for words of comfort when, later that same evening, I was introduced to the captured pilot's brother, who also happened to be serving aboard

Ranger.'[10]

With the growing nuisance caused by MiG tactics against strike forces, by March 1966 (when the 366th TFW arrived at Phan Rang AB with three squadrons of F-4Cs (moving to Đà Nẵng AB in October), the USAF F-4s began to fly 'MiG Screen' missions (i.e., protecting fighters were placed between the threat and the strike aircraft). When MiGs bypassed the MiG Screen flight, the F-4s left orbit to assist the strike force. When no MiGs engaged, the orbit was maintained until the last F-105 departed target and then the MiG Screen aircraft escorted the strike flights from the target area.

On 16 April F-4C 63-7677 flown by Major Samuel Robert Johnson, 35, of Dallas, Texas and 1st Lieutenant Larry James Chesley, 28, of Burley, Idaho in the 433rd 'Satan's Angels' TFS was hit by automatic weapons fire during a 'milk run' mission on armed reconnaissance sortie near Hà Lôi, 35 miles north of the DMZ. Both crew ejected and were captured. Johnson, who had flown 62 combat missions in the F-86 during the Korean War, was on his 25th mission and Chesley was on his 76th. During the ejection, Major Johnson suffered a broken back, broken arm and a dislocated shoulder. Taken prisoner, Major Johnson was to become one of the infamous 'Alcatraz 11' who was singled out for special harsh treatment because of their uncommon resistance. Larry Chesley had broken his back in three places in the ejection and received no medical treatment for it. Later he contracted beriberi, which debilitated him throughout his years of captivity and he lost over 60lbs in two months. 'While a prisoner of war at one time I was in a room of 48 men and there were five Larry's. So I asked them to give me another name. They started calling me 'Lucky', like one might call someone 'tiny' who was large. My wife divorced me etc, etc. The name just stuck. After I got home I remarried and we had three children adopted three more and had a Navajo boy living with us. Then my wife Annette and our six-week-old baby got killed in a train/car crash.'[11]

When the northeast monsoon season ended in April 1966, American activity increased against North Việtnam and there was a corresponding reaction in MiG activity. The NVNAF compromised American strike missions and affected the security of strike aircraft. Seven Phantoms and one Thunderchief shot down eight MiGs between late April and June, as NVNAF fighter pilots became increasingly aggressive. The first encounter came on 23 April with a flight of four F-4Cs of the 'Triple Nickel' Squadron, flying MiG Screen in support of Thunderchief strikes against the Bắc Giáng highway and railway bridge 25 miles northeast of Hànôi. Four MiG-17s were detected on radar at a distance of about fifteen miles and the two forces met in a near head-on pass. The flight lead and 'aircraft 02' each fired one Sparrow; Captain Max F. Cameron, 39, of Stanford, North Carolina and 1st Lieutenant Robert E. Evans, 27, of Haina, Hawaii in 'aircraft 03' fired a Sidewinder during this head-on contact. None of them made a hit. For the next ten minutes, the aircraft was in a left-turning engagement between 10,000 and 18,000 feet. Three of the MiGs gained position on aircraft 2, one of them firing without making a hit. Cameron and Evans in 'aircraft 03' and Captain Robert E. Blake, 28, of Presque Isle, Maine and 1st Lieutenant S. W. 'Dub' George, 25, of Canadian, *in Pittsburgh County* Oklahoma in 'aircraft 04' manoeuvred their F-4s to attack the three MiGs. Cameron, who could see little flashes of light when the lead MiG fired at the number two man with his cannon, quickly fired a Sidewinder missile at him and then went after the second MiG behind his flight leader's wingman. Evans said he thought the Sidewinder went up the MiG's tailpipe. 'As the MiG went down,' he said, 'it was falling apart and trailing thick, whitish-grey smoke.' [12]

Another MiG, meanwhile, achieved a firing position on both Cameron and Blake, but was unable to follow their climbing separation manoeuvre and rolled down to the right. Blake followed the MiG. 'I went into a diving roll and came straight down on the MiG. The pilot must have seen us on his tail. He applied full power and dived toward a valley. As I came out of the roll, I fired one Sparrow. I had a bad angle on him and missed but I realigned and fired again.' This one connected. 'The smoke looked like taffy streaming from the rear' 'It's all part of the big game And it came our way' Blake said. All of the aerial fighting took place in about twenty minutes. They were the first MiGs to be destroyed in an air to air combat since July the previous year. In another dog-fight, two MiG-21s engaged four Phantoms and an RB-66 aircraft on an ECM mission. The RB-66 sped home, leaving the Phantoms and the MiGs to exchange fire briefly with neither side scoring a hit.

On 25 April the MiG-21 was seen for the first time. The following day, Major Paul J. Gilmore of Alamogordo, New Mexico in the front seat of the lead F-4C in the 480th TFS, 35th TFW and 1st Lieutenant William T. Smith of Wayne, Pennsylvania in the back, claimed the first MiG-21 kill of the war. They were part of a flight of three F-4Cs flying escort for two RB-66s. Launching from Đà Nẵng, they rendezvoused with the RB-66s and proceeded north to the Red River, where one RB-66 and one F-4 split off for a separate mission. Gilmore and the other RB-66 proceeded northeast of Hànôi. Almost at once they spotted two or three MiG-21s coming high in the 2 o'clock position and closing rapidly. Gilmore and his wingman jettisoned their external tanks, lit their afterburners and broke into a hard left-descending turn while the RB-66 departed the area. Gilmore pulled out of his vertical reversal at 12,000 feet, with his wingman flying a tight wing position. They pulled up after the MiGs, which were in afterburner, heading northwest at 30,000 feet. The second MiG was descending very slowly, trailing white vapour toward the east. The F-4 aircrews lost sight of this aircraft as they closed rapidly on the first, which was making gentle clearing turns as he climbed away. Gilmore had several boresight lock-ons but was out of range for a good Sparrow shot. At a range of 3,000 feet, Gilmore fired one Sidewinder with a good tone. He then manoeuvred to the left to gain more separation and as a result did not see his first missile track. Gilmore had not realized that he had scored a victory but the missile had found its mark. Later, his wingman, flying cover for him, told him that the MiG pilot had ejected after Gilmore had fired the first missile and wondered why he kept after him but because of radio difficulties, his wingman could not inform Gilmore of his success (the first MiG-21 of the war to be shot down). Gilmore pulled up behind the pilotless MiG-21 again and fired another Sidewinder without effect. Quite disgusted, he started talking to himself and then rolled to the left again, pulled up and fired his third Sidewinder at a range of 3,000 feet. The missile went directly in the MiG's tailpipe and exploded its tail. (The North Viêtnamese have no record of a MiG-21 intercept at this date and the 923rd Fighter Regiment who covered this area still flew MiG-17s. The North Viêtnamese have no record of a MiG-21 intercept and the 923rd FR who covered this area still flew MiG-17s.

The two F-4C aircrews then descended to watch the debris impact. As Gilmore commenced his pull-up he spotted another MiG-21 tracking his wingman and called for a defensive split. He broke to the left and down while his wingman broke to the right and up. When Gilmore emerged from the roll, he sighted the MiG ahead, in afterburner and climbing away. He rolled in behind this aircraft and climbed in afterburner until he was directly behind. He fired his fourth Sidewinder, but the range was too short and the missile passed over the MiG's left wing. Because of low fuel reserves, both F-4Cs then left the battle area. The six-minute aerial battle was Gilmore's first encounter with an enemy plane 'after twelve years in the tactical fighter business.' As in Korea, it proved that in the hands of an accomplished pilot, a heavier machine could still beat a more manoeuvrable enemy fighter.

On 29 April the 'Triple Nickel' Squadron was flying MiGCAP for a force of F-105s attacking the Bắc Giáng bridge about 25 miles northeast of Hànôi when they met four MiG-17s north of the strike area. The F-4C crewed by Captain 'Bill' Dowell of Tampa, Florida and 1st Lieutenant Halbert E. Gossard of Oklahoma City destroyed one of them with an AIM-9 Sidewinder. The flight leader, Captain Larry R. Keith of Peoria, Illinois, flying with 1st Lieutenant Robert A. Bleakley of Cedar Rapids, Iowa accounted for a second MiG by manoeuvering him into a crash. Observing the two aircraft of the other element rolling into the MiGs, Keith broke off in the opposite direction. Seeing a MiG preparing to attack Gossard he quickly fired a Sidewinder to distract the pilot. The MiG then executed an evasive manoeuvre, but Keith followed in hot pursuit. At a distance of 6,000 feet behind the MiG, Keith's F-4 was just beginning to get Sidewinder tone. During his evasive tactics, the MiG inverted rolling to the left at an altitude of 2,500 feet. He crashed. The flight leader recalled later that the MiG pilot 'either lost control of the aircraft or attempted a Split-S with insufficient altitude.'

On the morning of 30 April, an element of two F-4Cs in the 'Triple Nickel' was alternating with another element in air refuelling while providing rescue combat air patrol (RESCAP) for two pilots shot down about 100 miles west-northwest of Hànôi. Two of the Phantoms were withdrawing from the area and the other two were returning when four MiG-17s flew out of the sun and waited until the F-4Cs were low on fuel before closing. They were headed directly for the Phantoms when sighted at a range of five miles. In the ensuing air battle 34-year old Captain Lawrence Herbert 'Shamrock' Golberg of Duluth, Minnesota and 1st Lieutenant Gerald D. Hardgrave of Jackson, Tennessee fired a Sidewinder into a MiG's tailpipe. The aircraft exploded. The two Phantoms, then low on fuel, hurriedly left the battle area. Golberg landed at Udorn with only 400lbs of fuel on board; enough for just four minutes.

Golberg had a quick wit, an infectious laugh and a smile. Although he was of the Jewish faith, he jokingly advertised himself as an Irishman, hence his call sign was 'Shamrock' and he sported a large green shamrock painted on the back of his brown leather flying jacket. Prior to his Viêtnam duty, he was a jet fighter pilot instructor at MacDill Air Force Base in Tampa. In a letter to his parents after his first kill, Captain Golberg wrote, 'By now you must have heard about the good work our squadron is doing even if they don't say who is doing it.'

Controversy erupted on 12 May when Communist China charged that US fighters had intruded into their airspace and shot down a Chinese aircraft when four MiG-17s jumped a flight of three F-4C Phantoms escorting an EB-66 on an ECM mission in the Red River Valley about 105 to 115 miles northwest of Hànôi, more than twenty miles south of China's frontier. China's report placed the air battle in Yunnan Province, 25 miles north of the border. Major Wilbur R. Dudley of Alamogordo, New Mexico and 1st Lieutenant Imants Kringelis of Lake Zurich, Illinois, were in aircraft 03. 'The enemy flier seemed to be a pretty good pilot, but he made one mistake,' Dudley later reported. 'He apparently had a case of tunnel vision when he bore in on the EB-66 and never knew we were behind him. That was his mistake. And one mistake is all you're allowed in this game.' Dudley missed with his first Sidewinder, fired just as the MiG began descending in what appeared to be a Split-S manoeuvre designed to regain an offensive position. When the MiG rolled out behind the EB-66, Dudley fired a second missile. It guided up the MiG's tailpipe and the aircraft disintegrated, spun out of control and crashed. The pilot was apparently unable to eject, for no parachute was observed. The battle continued a little longer without any further losses on either side and the two forces then disengaged. Before departing the area, Dudley fired a burst at the departing MiGs and again he apparently missed.

During July, August and September 1966 North Viêtnamese MiG activity increased and six more MiGs were shot down by Air Force F-4s and F-105s. During this period, MiG-17s concentrated almost exclusively upon the F-105 strike forces. The earlier MiG Screen flights of American F-4s evolved during this period into pure MiGCAP missions. The Phantoms kept watch for MiG aircraft and actively engaged them to prevent them from attacking strike forces. MiG pilots, however, at times out-manoeuvred American air-to-air missiles. On 13 July the crew of 'Rock River 216', a USN F-4B flying cover for the attack bombers, shot down a MiG-17 that had been chasing a pair of A-4 Skyhawks which was returning from a bridge strike over North Viêtnam. Lieutenant William M. 'Squeaky' McGuigan, 26, of Spearfish, South Dakota, who had officially finished his tour the previous day and Lieutenant (jg) Robert M. Fowler, 25, of San Francisco, of VF-161 'Chargers' from the *Constellation* in a F-4B (painted like all the others in the squadron in the colours of the NFL San Diego 'Chargers' team colours), scored the kill with an AIM-9D. 'I heard the skipper [Commander Lloyd N. Hoover, 41, of Wilbraham, Massachusetts, the flight leader who was also involved in a fight with four MiG-17s] calling MiGs' McGuigan said. 'We started looking around for them. The skipper was to my north and slightly west. I saw a MiG-17 behind an A-4 Skyhawk.' McGuigan fired one missile to chase off the MiG but it missed. 'This guy [the MiG-17] disappeared behind the clouds just as I identified him. I had him locked on radar. I rolled inside the cloud, knowing he'd come out the other side. We were not quite head-on. I was still above him. I reversed over the top of him. When he came back down, he was still diving. He was never in a position to fire at me.'

McGuigan let loose with a Sidewinder missile that caught the grey-brown jet in the tail at about 1,000 feet. His victory was the first to be made by a USN Phantom with an AIM-9B. The air-to-air tactics 'Squeaky' McGuigan had studied while a member of the US Nay's air test and development squadron, VX-4, prior to joining the 'Chargers' had paid off. After turning for home he radioed for permission to make a roll over the *Connie*. Mistakenly, he made it over the *Ranger* nearby! Jokingly, fellow officers radioed back, '*Are you sure it was really a MiG you shot down?*' Commander Hoover said McGuigan's fellow officers changed the spelling of his last name to 'Mig-Uigan'. As Hoover put it, 'it was a storybook finish' for McGuigan, who was soon due to return to the United States as an instructor at Key West. He had flown 35 to 40 combat missions on his two-month cruise on the *Constellation* and was aboard the *Oriskany* for eight months in 1962 before the air war began.

The first pair of MiG-21s to be destroyed by F-4Cs occurred on Thursday 14 July by F-4C aircrews of the 480th TFS, 35th TFW. Captain William J. 'Swede' Swendner, 31, of Alamogordo, New Mexico and 1st Lieutenant Duane A. Buttell, Jr., 25, of Chillicothe, Illinois flew the lead Phantom and 1st Lieutenants Ronald G. Martin, 26, of Lake Villa, Illinois and Richard N. Krieps, 24, of Chesterton, Indiana the number 2 aircraft. They were part of a flight of four F-4s providing MiG cover for an 'Iron Hand' flight (flight with special ordnance and avionics equipment with a mission of seeking and destroying SAM sites and radar-controlled AAA sites) of three F-105s. Following the Thunderchiefs north of Hànôi, the Phantom flight, in a right turn, sighted the first MiG-21 in a 7 o'clock position. The F-4s jettisoned their tanks and spotted a second MiG pursuing the third F-105. Even though the second MiG closed in on the F-105, the pilot continued his Shrike launch. Captain Swendner and Lieutenant Martin gave chase. Swendner's first Sidewinder passed close to the MiG's canopy without detonating and the MiG pilot lit his afterburner, initiating a 30° climb to the right. The second Sidewinder detonated behind the MiG, but seconds later a third one went up the MiG's tailpipe and blew the enemy aircraft into pieces. The MiG looked like a big red barn door,' Buttell said. 'We shot him down as he was on the tail of an F-105.'

Three minutes' later and 28 miles further north, Lieutenant Martin manoeuvred behind the second MiG, which was attacking the fourth Phantom. Just after the MiG missed that aircraft with a missile and initiated a climb with afterburner on, Martin fired a Sidewinder which impacted near the right side of the MiG's tail. The pilot ejected at once.

On 8 August 1966 24-year-old 1st Lieutenant Patrick Edward Wynne volunteered to fly one of the most hazardous missions yet assigned to the 'Triple Nickel' Squadron at Ubon. As a 'GIB' [guy in back] Wynne was eager to accumulate flight time and move to the front seat of a Phantom. For this mission, Captain 'Shamrock' Golberg's backseater was ill, so Wynne took his place in 63-7560. A superstitious person might have noticed that the flight was Golberg's final scheduled mission. On its completion, he was to receive the customary celebratory wet-down before being sent back to the United States. The intensely competitive Wynne was not the least bit superstitious, however. Wynne entered the Air Force Academy determined to graduate with a ranking higher than his father, Edward P. Wynne, had achieved at West Point in 1940. The younger Wynne did so, finishing in the top 10 percent of his class. He received his diploma from General Curtis E. LeMay, the legendary airman who was then the USAF Chief of Staff. After graduation, Wynne filled the time awaiting pilot training by earning a political science degree from Georgetown University in Washington, DC. Young Wynne excelled in flight school, driven by his determination to be a fighter pilot.

He won his wings and sought duty in Việtnam. Patrick was soon noted for his cheerful and relentless push to fly every mission he could.

Few missions in the Việtnam War were more difficult than that assigned 'Ozark' Flight on 8 August. The orders called for four Phantoms to fly a minimum-level armed reconnaissance mission in Route Pack 6, with the target area thirty miles north of Hànôi. Taking the battle to the heart of Hànôi was called 'going downtown'.[13] Each Phantom was armed with four pods of CBU-2 cluster bombs and four Sparrow and Sidewinder missiles. The eight crew members were surprised to learn that their sorties were routed to the target from the coast. This meant the fighters would have to fly over one of the most heavily defended regions in North Việtnam. The previous morning, six fighters had been shot down in exactly the same area.

'Ozark' Flight, Captain Daniel Wright leading, was launched on time and climbed to 21,000 feet for its first refuelling over the Gulf of Tonkin. Only three aircraft were able to take on fuel. 'Ozark 02', flown by 1st Lieutenant Heber 'Spike' Nasmyth, could not get his refuelling door to open. He had to return to base. The remaining 'Ozark' aircraft flew in echelon right with Wright still leading. Major John Hallgren moved into the No. 2 position, with Golberg and Wynne off his right wing. The three Phantoms dropped down to a mere 50 feet above water so as to penetrate North Việtnam's airspace beneath its radar screen. Going 'feet dry' forty miles north of Haiphòng, 'Ozark' Flight initially met no resistance. The Phantoms found few meaningful targets in the assigned area, but, returning on the reciprocal course, the fighters destroyed some trucks with their cluster bombs. The flight then dropped over a sharply defined karst limestone formation down into a lush valley. The airmen suddenly were enveloped in a barrage of 37mm and 57mm anti-aircraft fire. Hallgren took heavy flak hits in the lower rear of his F-4's fuselage; it knocked out his hydraulics and set off a number of red lights in the cockpit. Golberg radioed that he too was hit. Hallgren saw him pull up and drop back calling that he had control problems. He advised Golberg to check his stability augmentation system and then lost sight of Golberg and Wynne's aircraft. 'Ozark 01', Wright's aircraft, returned to Ubon. 'Ozark 02', streaming fuel and in obvious distress, nevertheless managed to make a brakeless landing at Đà Nẵng, saved by arresting gear. 'Ozark 03' with Golberg and Wynne disappeared into the jungle near the village of Làng Sơn, just south of China. [14]

For those who survived a shoot-down and being taken prisoner by the North Việtnamese incarceration meant enduring six ghastly, inhuman years and only courage and resilience would see them through. When 'Spike' Nasmyth climbed into his F-4 on 4 September 1966 to fly a combat mission over Việtnam, he never foresaw that he'd be blown out of the sky by a surface-to-air missile. The last words he heard before his jet was transformed into a lump of crumpled, metal wreckage were from his 'guy in back,' 1st Lieutenant Ray Salzurulo, a pilot systems operator: 'Hey, Spike - here comes another...' As the missile struck, the first thing in Nasmyth's mind was disbelief. 'As with all good fighter pilots, I thought I was invincible. I couldn't believe that they'd got me. But then, as I realized I was falling toward the ground at an appalling rate, I said to myself, 'Eject or die, Spike!' It looked like a movie. I was tumbling toward the ground and it just looked like it was spiralling toward me at a hell of a rate. That's what made me eject.'

After what seemed like an eternity, his parachute opened and brought him down to earth, somewhere north of Hànôi. Struggling to free himself from his canopy harness, Nasmyth realized he had been injured during the ejection. A shard of metal had gouged through his arm and gone in just below the elbow, out the other side and straight into his leg. 'It was just like a piece of red, raw meat was coming out of my right arm.' Once on the ground, he was immediately surrounded by the North Viêtnamese, some of whom started to beat him before hauling him away to collect their bounty. They took him to the infamous Hỏa Lô prison with all the creature comforts of the Bastille, built in Hànôi by the French in 1896 (American PoWs held there until 29 March 1973 would nickname the Hànôi 'Hilton'). This became the first of several prison camps which would become his 'home' for the next 2,355 days.

The first of three September MiG kills came on the 16th when at least four MiG-17s were sighted by a flight of three F-4Cs of the 'Triple Nickel' at Ubon, which was conducting a strike/CAP mission against the Đáp Câu rail and road bridge about seventeen miles southeast of Kép. At 1540 hours, 'Moonglow' flight was nearing their target when they were engaged in aerial combat by a flight of four MiG-17s from Giá Lam. The Phantoms jettisoned their external bombs before engaging the enemy fighters. During the air battle, the lead Phantom fired all of his Sidewinders and two of his Sparrows at several MiGs, but all escaped damage. Major John Leighton 'Robbie' Robertson, 36, of Seattle Washington and 1st Lieutenant Elliot Buchanan in 'Moonglow 03' fought with two MiGs. The #3 MiG-17 was flown by Nguyễn Văn Bảy, born in 1937, the seventh of eleven children, who 'went from the bicycle to the airplane with no stop in between' and who, by the end of the war was credited with seven kills. Văn Bảy was the first to spot the American flight far ahead of them. He asked permission to attack the Phantoms. The MiG's flight leader gave permission to give chase but expressed doubt that they could catch the much faster American aircraft. As the MiG-17s moved toward the Phantoms, Nguyễn Văn Bảy saw 'Moonglow 3' initiate a climbing left turn, which allowed the MiG pilot to cut the diameter of the circle and close the distance between the opposing aircraft to 100 to 150 metres to achieve an appropriate angle of attack. Buchanan reported to Robertson, 'This guy's pulling right in on us. He's going to shoot any time now.' Nguyễn Văn Bảy aimed and then fired his 37mm and 23mm cannons at the Phantom and a salvo of orange golf ball size rounds passed over 'Moonglow 3's canopies. Robertson pulled hard on the stick and then eased his turn. Hugh Buchanan saw the MiG close again. He said, 'This is going to be it. He's corrected the problem.'

Nguyễn Văn Bảy lined up, fired again and saw a wheel come out from beneath the F-4's wing and sail past his canopy. For Buchanan, everything went black. According to the WSO, 'It could have been from so many G forces pulling the blood away from my eyes, I'm not sure. My helmet was bouncing around - I really don't have a clear memory of ejecting; however, I do sort of have a dream - I can kind of imagine pulling the handle the F-4 had between your legs.' He went on to say, 'I ejected so I must have done it. I could hear loud booms, like the canopy blowing off. And I felt the wind. The next thing I knew, my parachute was opening. When I got down low, I could see people running around on the ground in a little village. I could see a guy off to the right. He looked like he had a uniform on and a rifle and he was running in my direction.'

Roscoe Epperson, who was flying an air cover for another mission, had recognized 'Robbie's voice over the radio and listened to the transmissions of the air battle. He heard Robertson say, 'This is 'Moonglow 3'; I see the MiGs. I am engaging MiGs!' He heard the entire battle from sighting the enemy aircraft through the dogfight. He also heard his friend report, 'I am hit and I'm heading for the water!'

Nguyễn Văn Bảy sped away from the burning Phantom and then rolled back to take a look. He watched 'Moonglow 3' pitch down in flames and saw one parachute as he turned his attention to the remaining Phantoms.

This was Major Robertson's 29th day in Southeast Asia and Buchanan's 17th mission and it had ended in disaster. During Buchanan's descent after ejection, (the back-seater ejects first) he could not see above his parachute to verify that Robertson had also ejected and it was thought that he died in the crash. Buchanan saw a large fire about one-half mile away, but could not say with certainty that it was the Phantom or jettisoned fuel that was burning. In the chaos of battle, the other 'Moonglow' crews did not see any parachutes and no emergency radio beepers were heard. Because the location was deep within enemy held territory, no search and rescue (SAR) operation was possible. Hugh Buchanan was immediately taken prisoner, transported to Hànôi and imprisoned in Camp Unity at the infamous Hànôi 'Hilton'. Later that day, the Foreign Broadcast Information Service in Okinawa translated a Radio Hànôi broadcast that announced the loss of two US aircraft in the area where 'Moonglow 3' was lost. About a month later, Radio Hànôi announced the names of three captured Americans, one of whom was Hugh Buchanan, whose status was upgraded from MIA to Prisoner of War.

First Lieutenants Jerry W. Jameson of Middletown, Indiana and Douglas B. Rose of Chicago, Illinois flying 'Moonglow 04' shot down the only MiG lost by the enemy that day. 'It seemed unreal,' Jameson later told newsmen. 'I think for the first three or four minutes I didn't realize what I was doing. I was just hanging on, trying to get away from a MiG that was chasing me. After I got away I started putting into practice what I had learned in training.' When Jameson had tried to get behind one of the MiGs in order to fire his Sidewinders, the slower but more manoeuvrable MiG went into a tight turn and ended up on his tail. When the MiG pilot began firing his 23mm gun, Jameson put his F-4 into afterburner, turned hard to the left and then hard to the right to escape. He then jettisoned his tanks and ordnance and returned to the engagement. Another MiG was sighted dead ahead, but Jameson was unable to pick it up with radar so he could launch a Sparrow. He overshot the MiG; ignited afterburner again, made a hard right turn and observed still another MiG at his 12 o'clock position. At about a mile out Jameson fired two missiles. Then he turned hard to the left and back to the right again to get away from another MiG that had begun firing on him. When he straightened out again he saw debris and a man in the air.

Four F-4Cs of the 366th TFW were providing escort for an EB-66 on 5 November when they were attacked by two or more MiG-21s in the north-eastern section of North Việtnam, near Hànôi and Haiphòng. The EB-66 was making its final orbit of the area and all of the escorting Phantoms were near the minimum fuel level for a safe return to their home station. The MiGs were first detected on radar at a range of eighteen miles. Shortly after the EB-66 executed a left turn, Major James E. 'Friar' Tuck of Virgilina, Virginia the 38-year old backseater in the lead F-4C ('Opal 01') piloted by 1st Lieutenant John J. Rabeni, Jr. of Southborough, Massachusetts saw the MiGs visually and called them out to his flight. The first MiG launched a missile at the EB-66 just as that aircraft broke into a diving spiral. The missile missed. The F-4s and MiGs also spiralled down and Tuck and his pilot jumped on the lead MiG and fired two Sparrows but they were just unguided rockets because he was inside minimum range. He was going 'pretty fast' and was soon almost flying close formation alongside the MiG. However, its pilot still would not break off from the EB-66's 'six o' clock, so Tuck practically 'shoulder-charged' it to one side. Finally, the MiG broke away and dived, so Tuck fired another AIM-7. It appeared to explode just ahead of the MiG, making its engine flame out, or maybe the pilot just lost control of it and bailed out.

Meanwhile, a second MiG got on the tail of Major Tuck's Phantom and his wingman, 'Opal 02' flown by 1st Lieutenants' Wilbur J. Latham, Jr. of Eagle Grove, Iowa and Klaus J. Klause of Franklin, Pennsylvania, manoeuvred to fire on it. 'We were at about 25,000 feet, cruising at 0.72 Mach' recalled Klause. 'I had picked up a radar contact at 18 miles and the EB-66 crew had picked up a coded indication of a MiG-21 radar, so they decided to turn back towards the north-west and leave. There was also a MiG call from an EC-121, but that was after we had engaged the enemy. The first MiG-21 came from our 'deep six' in a 30-degree climb from low altitude and this started the engagement. I called out, 'There's a MiG down there' and Tuck called 'I'm on him too'. The lead MiG of the four that were out there closed with the EB-66 and I saw it launch a missile as Tuck called to the '66 pilot to break to the right. My 'nose-gunner' (Joe Latham) jettisoned our three tanks, but Tuck didn't lose his. I got the EB-66 on my radar as a big blip followed by two smaller blips (a MiG chased by Tuck) and then at the end of this downward-spiralling daisy chain was another MiG-21 chasing 'the Friar'. I told Joe to lock on to this last MiG. We had the 'burners cooking, so we ate up the two miles distance from it. This silver MiG must have realised that we were behind him, for he entered a left-hand turn and pulled up. We were apparently at a range of 4,000 feet so I said, 'Hey shoot!' As the MiG pulled up against a clear blue sky, we hosed him with an AIM-9B. The missile came off the rail, jinked and exploded on him. The MiG looked as if it had just blown up and been punched over. We broke back left and almost ran over the pilot in his 'chute.'

The entire air battle lasted less than three minutes. That night there was a celebration in the 'Doom Club' at Đà Nẵng's officers' open mess. These MiG kills gave the 480th Tactical Fighter Squadron its fifth aerial victory.

At Ubon in the 'Triple Nickel' Squadron Lieutenant Ralph F. Wetterhahn, a native of New York City remembered 'the intensity of enemy resistance in the area around Hànôi called 'Route Package VI', which we shortened to 'Pak Six' that made us pay dearly for that goal. And we weren't even sure we were succeeding. Most of the pilots shot down over the past few months had been captains and lieutenants. We had noticed that the full colonels - the guys with experience - seldom flew to Pak Six. And some squadron commanders could find any number of reasons not to fly to Hànôi. But in late 1966 we flew to Pak Six whenever the weather allowed. In September alone, US Air Forces flew 12,000 sorties to the north.

'Those of us who were flying missions would get frags - fragmentation orders from the 7th Air Force headquarters in Sàigòn - the night before we were to go. They'd give you the target you were to hit, the time on target and the tankers you'd get fuel from. You'd head over to the intelligence office and get every photo they had. Then you'd have all night to think about it. There were a lot of mornings when I'd wake up tense and sweating, listening to mosquitoes buzzing around in the dark. I'd kill a few and wonder if they could somehow warn each other about this guy that was splatting them. Then I'd stagger into the latrine. Four bare light bulbs hung above the sinks. Gnats were diving at the lights and the sinks would be covered with thousands of dead bugs.'

Wetterhahn remembered 20 September in particular for so many reasons that have to do with living and dying: His second son was born and the sky was clear over Hànôi. 'We were already airborne and headed east when first light touched the South China Sea. After mid-air refuelling, Captain 'Bull' Fulkerson wheeled our flight of three toward the Viêtnam coast and sandwiched us between two formations of F-105 Thunderchiefs. Our F-4s were more manoeuvrable and carried four AIM-7 Sparrow and four AIM-9 Sidewinder air-to-air missiles in addition to four 750lb M-117 bombs. Our primary mission was to protect the heavily loaded 'Thuds' from any MiGs that might attack. If none came up, we would bomb a bridge near Hànôi.

'The reason we had only three aircraft in our formation was that our unit didn't have enough flyable airplanes to send up the customary four. So my backseater, an affable Texan, Lieutenant Jerry K. Sharp of Corpus Christi and I had no wingman. If we were bounced we'd be on our own, unprotected by another pilot detailed to spot surface-to-air missiles and keep enemy fighters off our tail.

'Fulkerson spread the formation out. The sun was well above the horizon now and light splashed across the green hills to the west. Fulkerson gave the command to arm our weapons - 'Set 'em up hot'- and I immediately felt a pounding in my chest. I flipped the switches that turned on the missiles' systems and set the bomb fuses and intervals. As we neared anti-aircraft artillery emplacements, Fulkerson ordered us to keep it moving. We started weaving left, then right, never flying in a straight line for more than five seconds so the gunners would have difficulty tracking us. We were doing 650 mph as we surged over the coastline north of the Red River delta.

'Minutes after we crossed the coast, clusters of black puffs began to dot the sky. The 85mm guns had opened up. One of the 'Thud' pilots called out that he had been hit. I saw the damaged plane ahead, clawing upward in a steep turn back toward the coast. Just then Sharp bellowed from the backseat, 'SAM! SAM! SAM!' Off at our 11 o'clock a surface-to-air missile left its launch pad in an eruption of flame and smoke. I shoved the throttles all the way and felt my spine press deep into the seat back as the afterburners ignited and we pushed over to gain speed. Seconds later, the first stage of the SAM dropped away and the warhead stage arced over, coming down at us and then veering toward the stricken Thud above us. Over the radio, I called to him to eject, but the SAM detonated right on top of his aircraft. Debris boiled out of the inferno.

'I rolled into a dive. It looked clear between patches of exploding flak, so I made one adjustment and concentrated on the bombsight, setting the bright red pipper below a small bridge. At that point, any bridge was fine with me. At 4,000 feet, Sharp yelled 'Pickle!' and I pressed the bomb button and felt a rumble as the four bombs kicked clear of the rack.

'Radio chatter had become an insane jumble of overlapping transmissions. I had lost sight of Fulkerson, so as I pulled the nose up through the horizon, I turned for the coast. A burst of flak rippled near my left wing. My knees were shaking so hard I took my feet off the rudder pedals and placed them flat on the floorboards. When I caught sight of Fulkerson, he was well out in front. Then I saw something closer, dead ahead - a white blur. I was doing 720 mph, but I swung left and barely missed the parachute. The F-105 pilot! He had survived flak and a SAM and then I had nearly skewered him.

'That's how it had been going, mission after mission. This one stands out because of the near-collision with a parachuting pilot, but the guns, SAMs, explosions, confusion and airplanes being shot down were standard. Supported by China and the Soviet Union, North Viêtnam had armed itself against the US air attacks and had 4,400 anti-aircraft guns and 25 SAM battalions in place.

'The mission stands out for another reason. Once we reached the safety of the sea, Fulkerson's wingman, 'Fitz' Fitzgerald, radioed that he was down to 900lbs of fuel, barely enough in an F-4 to fly a hundred miles, which was just about the distance to the demilitarized zone. Fulkerson had him jettison his auxiliary tanks and head south. We watched fuel spray from the open tank fittings as they slowly tumbled seaward. The tanks hadn't fed; the valves had never opened. We had a pretty good idea why: It was the same reason that Sharp and I had headed north without a wingman.

'Since the beginning of August, the 8th Wing had been directed by the Pentagon to 'investigate the desirability of increasing sortie rates per aircraft.' The same airplanes that flew day missions were to be reconfigured to fly missions at night and then switched back for daylight attacks the following morning. But switching aircraft back and forth entailed heavy work for maintenance crews. Daylight bombers carried a 370-gallon fuel tank on each wing, plus missiles and bombs. The night birds used a flare dispenser where a wing tank normally went and carried a centreline, 600-gallon fuel tank. Besides up - and downloading tanks at sunup and sundown, the crews had to 'refuel, rearm and repair' aircraft that flew around the clock. The test programme was called 'Rapid Roger.' According to wing records, between 6 August 1966 when 'Rapid Roger' began and 22 September the 'operationally ready' rate for aircraft dropped from 73.8 to 54.3 percent. It's not that the maintenance crews weren't trying. The wing record also shows that extra men and spare parts authorized for the test were never delivered.

'After midnight on 13 September, an F-4C (63-7694) crashed just after takeoff. During daylight that same day, another (63-7640) crashed after an in-flight fire, its cause undetermined. Of the ten aircraft lost in combat since July, two were airplanes ordered North without wingmen. A MiG got one; a SAM the other. And now Fitzgerald: 'About fifteen minutes after he dropped the useless external tanks - those same pesky tanks that were being disconnected and reconnected continually by overworked mechanics - he dead-sticked his airplane into a dirt strip at Đông Hà, just south of the DMZ. The F-4 - 63-7687 - went careening off the end, shedding missiles and landing gear. Both men climbed out unharmed.

'Two days after Fitzgerald slammed into the dirt at Đông Hà, 'Rapid Roger' was put on hold. The 7th Air Force Commander in Sàigòn, General William W. 'Spike' Momyer, had seen enough bad reports from Colonel Joseph Wilson our wing commander and he suspended it.' 'Rapid Roger' came to a halt at the end of January and the wing marked the occasion with a wake, held on Groundhog Day, complete with a black casket. A grave was dug outside the ops building and a casket was lowered into it and all took turns urinating on it. The entire 'Wolf Pack' joined in the funeral procession, led by Robin Olds and 'Chappie' James to bury the thousands of IBM punch cards created by the project. Olds drove a silver spike through the coffin as they buried it. [15]

On 11 November 1966 two F-4C aircraft of the 559th TFS, 12th TFW at Cam Ranh Bay were shot down in an attack by three Phantoms on a gun emplacement near Ba Bình, four miles north of the DMZ just as they were about to drop napalm on their target. The crew of 64-0743 consisting of 27-year old 1st Lieutenant Herbert Benjamin Ringsdorf who was from Elba, Alabama and his weapons/system operator 1st Lieutenant Richard L. Butt were shot down about five miles west of the city of Vĩnh Linh in Quảng Bình Province, North Viêtnam. Both men were apparently captured, but only Ringsdorf was released at the end of the war. On 10 April 1986 Butt's remains were 'discovered' and returned by the Viêtnamese and positively identified. For twenty years, Richard Leigh Butt was a prisoner of war - alive or dead. The crew of the second F-4C was 27-year old Captain Robert Irvin Biss from Cherry Tree, Pennsylvania and 25-year old 2nd Lieutenant Harold Deloss Monlux of Sioux City, Iowa who was on his 12th mission. Captain Biss served as an F-4 WSO with the 431st Tactical Fighter Squadron at George AFB, California from January 1965 to November 1966. He deployed to Southeast Asia in September and October 1965 and again from August 1966. Both men were captured and released at the end of the war.

During December 1966 MiG activity further increased, particularly against Thunderchief strike aircraft, although - as earlier - the MiG pilots generally broke off engagements once the American aircraft dumped their ordnance and prepared for offensive action.

On 2 December four Phantoms were among seven aircraft lost. Captain Robert Raymond Gregory and 1st Lieutenant Leroy William Stutz of the 11th TRS, 432nd TRW who had arrived at Udorn in July 1966 were on a reconnaissance mission north of Hànôi in RF-4C 65-0829 when they were hit by ground fire forcing them to eject about forty miles southwest of Yên Bái. After landing the two airmen spoke to each other on their survival radio before they were both captured. Gregory was unconscious when he and Stutz were put into the back of a truck for the ride to the Hànôi 'Hilton'. After arrival at the prison, Gregory was never seen again. He and Leroy Stutz had been together as a crew through advanced training and their first squadron assignment at Shaw AFB. They were on their 65th mission when they were shot down. [16]

Two Phantoms and an F-105D were shot down in a major strike on the airfield POL (Petrol, Oil, Lubricants) storage facility at Phúc Yên. The F-105 was first to fall after it was hit by 37mm AAA as it dived on the target from about 6,000 feet. The aircraft's rear fuselage was seen to be on fire and the pilot may have been hit as he was not seen to eject before the aircraft crashed about fifteen miles west of the airfield. Next over the target were several flights from the 366th TFW at Đà Nẵng led by a flight from the 480th TFS which was providing a CAP at 14,000 feet over the target. As the aircraft was manoeuvring about ten miles northeast of Phúc Yên to cut off a flight of MiG-21s, Captain Hubert Kelly Flesher's aircraft (F-4C 64-0753) was hit by an SA-2 and immediately disintegrated. He and his backseater, 1st Lieutenant James Robert Berger ejected but Berger suffered a spinal compression, a broken arm and concussion, the latter from an old peasant who beat him over the head.[17] The F-4C (64-0663) crewed by Major Donald Ray Burns of Mineral Wells, Texas and 24-year old 1st Lieutenant Bruce Chalmers Ducat of the 389th TFS, 366th TFW was hit by a SAM at about 19,000 feet as their flight was heading northwest to the northern edge of 'Thud Ridge', about forty miles northwest of Phúc Yên. Burns and Ducat both ejected but Bruce Ducat died in captivity. His body was returned to the USA on 18 March 1977. Donald Burns was released on 4 March 1973 and eventually retired as a Colonel.[18]

Lieutenant (jg) David Edward McRae, 27, of Decatur, Georgia and his NFO, Ensign David George Rehmann, 24, born in Bay City, Michigan were one of two F-4B crews from VF-154 on the *Coral Sea* assigned CAP duties during a raid on POL storage at near Kép airfield. As the Phantoms were making a last pass over the airfield to obtain a damage assessment, their aircraft (151014) was hit by AAA. The entire port wing was blown off and the aircraft became a mass of flames. Rehmann ejected to the east of Kép airfield but McCrae did not eject and he was killed in the crash. He remained one of the unaccounted MIA's for two weeks until the Communists used a propaganda film showing David being marched through a war crimes tribunal following his capture. Despite the photo's low quality of his burnt, dazed and swollen face and his loosely wrapped broken arm, his mother recognized the photo. Later, it was used by VIVA to depict the plight of PoWs in advertisements and on matchbooks and posters circulated internationally. As a result, tons of letters poured into North Viêtnam protesting their treatment and causing the enemy to alleviate some of the suffering PoWs were forced to endure. Milk given him after a week in captivity was the first food to stay in his stomach. 'Their green weed soup and rice were awfully hard to hack, Lieutenant Rehmann said. So weak he could hardly move, with fever and in shock from being shot down, he ranged from lucid to delirious for days. However, as he recovered and regained strength, guards demanded he be at the cell door to bow whenever they appeared. 'You learn quickly that you can't get used to taking beatings and although I was still weak, I would get there and bow rather than take that.'

The following day, 29-year old Colonel Kenneth William Cordier and 24-year old 1st Lieutenant Michael Christopher Lane of Notre Dame, Indiana in the 559th TFS of the 12th TFW Wing at Cam Ranh Bay were part of a flight providing fighter escort for a Douglas EB-66 on an electronic warfare mission over North Viêtnam. Ken Cordier, who was born in 1937 in Canton, Ohio was commissioned through the Air Force ROTC programme at the University of Akron on 16 July 1960 and was trained as a Minuteman Missile Launch Officer in 1961. He was awarded his pilot wings on 19 December 1964 and then completed F-4 Phantom Combat Crew Training. Being in the forefront of the USAF's combat pilots, Cordier's confidence at that stage was at its peak. He had flown F-4s in the 45th Tactical Fighter

Squadron in Southeast Asia in January 1965 while deployed to Ubon RTAFB, Thailand. He volunteered for another tour and in June 1966 left his wife Judy and two children Ann, 12 and Louis, 10 in Tampa for a tour at Cam Ranh Bay, South Viêtnam. As a 'seasoned veteran' of the fighting - 3 December would be his 176th combat mission - he felt he was invincible. (Lane, on the other hand, was on only his eleventh mission). Cordier was due to return to the United States in twelve days' time. But this day there had been portents of unease. Things had not gone right from the beginning. Worst of all, perhaps, was that, unbeknown to Cordier, the EB-66 they were escorting was not carrying jamming equipment designed to black out the SAM radars. 'Had I known this I would have devoted a little more time to watching what was going on below. I would then very likely have seen the SA-2 coming up at me.'

His F-4C (63-7608) took a direct hit in the tail section from a SAM ground-to-air missile while flying a wide orbit at 24,000 feet cruising at Mach .8 or around 500 mph. Cordier recalled: 'I felt an explosion behind and under the aircraft and faster than I can tell the sequence both engine firelights started flashing and the entire warning light panel lit up like a Christmas tree. The aircraft went into a wild fishtail manoeuvre, during which I was first pressed up against the straps and then pushed down into the seat. During this negative 'g'-positive 'g' sequence, I yelled out to my back-seater: 'We're hit. Eject!' I then grabbed the ejection handle between my legs. Later, I heard that my 'GIB' had made it out safely, too. The fact that my own ejection occurred at 24,000 feet meant that I would 'free fall' for approximately two miles before the automatic parachute-opening procedure came into play. After seeing my aircraft blow up, my natural reaction was to look down and see what there was below. What I saw and what happened in the subsequent few seconds, was even more exciting than the previous moments and is the single event in my life in which chance, or fate, played such a significant part.

'I looked down between my boots and saw, to my horror, a second missile (Soviet tactics at this time were to fire SAMs in salvoes of two) exploding just below and in the path of my seat! It was a red/orange and black fireball which looked like the gates of hell. It was obvious that I was going to fall into or through it. I just had time to close my eyes and hold my breath when I felt a hot flash and just as quickly I was in clear air again. I now experienced raw panic for the first time in my life. The thought flashed through my mind that the fireball must have burned off the drogue 'chute which would negate the automatic parachute-opening process and I would ride the seat into the ground if I didn't separate manually. Our training had stressed never to open the parachute at high altitude because of the strong opening shock in still air - and yet I just couldn't wait to see and feel, the silk canopy over the top of me... So my panic-driven decision to pull the manual seat release as soon as I pushed away from the seat and to grab the 'D'-ring to deploy the parachute, proved the correctness of what I had been taught. The 'chute opened with such force that it sounded like an explosion and ripped out two of the nylon panels. This allowed the air to spill out of the canopy and resulted in a faster fall which meant that I hit the ground a good deal harder than normal... It stunned me for a few moments, but the amazing thing was that throughout this traumatic experience I suffered relatively minor injuries. My back sustained a fracture as a result of the ejection, but other than this and the burning off of my eyelashes and eyebrows where flame had penetrated under my visor, plus powder burns on my arms, I was virtually unscathed. The extent of my luck can be seen when the kill mechanism of a Soviet SA-2 missile is explained. When the warhead detonates, the cylindrical metal casing breaks up into metal fragments which fly out in an expanding doughnut-shaped ring of shrapnel. If one is within its lethal radius, hits are virtually assured. However, the ring expands outwards and if one could pass through it along the longitudinal axis of the missile, given a bit of fortune, one should get through without a scratch, other than burns from the fireball. Plainly, this is what happened to me. Chance put me on exactly the correct flight path, at the correct speed and altitude, to fall through the hole of that 'doughnut' - and live to tell the tale... All this was only the curtain-raiser for the ensuing six years and three months. What happened after I hit the ground is another story... But the miraculous escape from the two SAMs convinced me that there was something else in store for me - something in the grand scheme of things which I had yet to do; otherwise, my story should have ended on 2 December 1966.' [19]

Endnotes Chapter 1

1   Chief of staff of the Israel Defence Forces (1953-58) and Defence Minister during the Six-Day War in 1967 and the 1973 Yom Kippur War.
2   Richard E. Hamilton.
3   See *The Tale of Two Bridges and the Battle For the Skies Over North Vietnam* edited by Arthur J. C. Lavelle (Office of Air Force History, 1985).
4   On 11 July Lieutenant General Joseph Moore, Commander of the 2nd Air Division, awarded Silver Stars to the men scoring the first USAF air-to-air combat victories of the Việtnam War; the two other aircrews were awarded Distinguished Flying Crosses.
5   *The Crucible of Vietnam Air Force Magazine,* February 2013 by Rebecca Grant.
6   Colonel (Ret.) John T. Correll writing in *Air Force Magazine,* July 2010.
7   Rodney Knutson's injuries had still not healed when he and Ralph Gaither were released over seven years later. He eventually retired from the Navy as a Captain. On 12 February 1973 Halyburton, Gaither, Knutson and Wheat emerged from the North Vietnam prison system. Ralph Gaither later wrote of his experience as a PoW in a 1973 book titled *With God in a POW Camp. Vietnam Air Losses* by Chris Hobson. (Midland Publishing, 2001).
8   Hobson.
9   From August 1964-August 1973 during the Việtnam War, 22 Navy squadrons (and one Marine squadron) made 84 war cruises to the Gulf of Tonkin; 51 with F-4Bs, one with F-4Gs 1965-66 and 32 with F-4Js beginning with VF-33 and VF-102 aboard USS *America* in May 1968.
10   *Winston S. Churchill Memoirs & Adventures* (Weidenfeld & Nicolson Ltd, 1989). The F-4B (150443 of VF-143 'Pukin Dogs') was crewed by 26-year old Lt William David Frawley of Brockton, Massachusetts (KIA) and 24-year old Lt (jg) William Murrey Christensen of Great Falls MT (KIA). A flight of three Phantoms was on a coastal reconnaissance mission about 40 miles south of Hảiphòng in deteriorating weather when they received a SAM warning. Flying under a 500 feet cloud base with less than one mile visibility the flight leader ordered a level 180° turn to head back out to sea. Half way through the turn the leader lost sight of Frawley who reported that he had

lost contact with the formation. It was thought that the aircraft flew into the water in the poor visibility while the pilot was trying to relocate the formation. A search revealed a small amount of wreckage but no survivors. The A-4E that was lost was piloted by 24-year old Lt(jg) Donald Joseph Woloszyk (KIA). When Kenneth Woloszyk posted names of the missing pilots that day he saw his brother's name on the list. *Vietnam Air Losses* by Chris Hobson (Midland Publishing, 2001).

11 Johnson and Chesley were among the 135 inmates released from the Hòa Lô prison on 12 February 1973. Johnson flew tours with the Air Force Fighter Weapons School and the Thunderbirds display team after his release. Highly decorated, he retired from the USAF as a Colonel in 1979 and became active in politics and was elected Congressman for Dallas, Texas in May 1991. He wrote *Captive Warriors* detailing his PoW experience in Viêtnam. Chesley wrote *Seven Years in Hanoi*, about his experiences, which was published in 1973. Hobson.

12 1st Lt S. W. George was KIA on 20 July 1966. His Phantom was hit by ground fire on a night mission near Vĩnh Linh and crashed during an emergency landing at Udorn. His pilot, Captain R. A. Walmsley, was seriously injured.

13 In April 1966, Admiral Ulysses S. Grant Sharp, C-in-C US Pacific Command, added a seventh area by dividing RP 6 into two sections, 6A and 6B. The Navy's Carrier Task Force 77 was assigned RPs 2, 3, 4, and 6B, as these bordered on the Gulf of Tonkin. The Air Force was given responsibility for air operations in RP 1, RP 5, and 6A.

14 See *Ring of Remembrance, Air Force Magazine* February 2009 by Walter J. Boyne. Golberg and Wynne were listed as MIA until 1976, when their remains were found and identified.

15 *Air & Space/Smithsonian*, August/September 1997.

17 Leroy Stutz was released from captivity on 4 March 1973. Robert Gregory's remains were eventually returned by the Viêtnamese. Hobson

17 Flesher and Berger were both released from captivity on 18 February 1973. Hobson.

18 Hobson.

19 *Out Of The Blue: The Role of Luck in Air Warfare 1917-1966* edited by 'Laddie' Lucas (Hutchinson, 1985). Cordier spent the next 2,284 days as a PoW before being released during Operation 'Homecoming' on 4 March 1973. Lane was released on 18 February.

Chapter 2

Memories Of Ubon

Richard E. Hamilton

It was February 1965. I was a member of the 47th Tactical Fighter Squadron, 15th Tactical Fighter Wing, stationed at MacDill Air Force Base, Florida. We were part of the United States Air Force Tactical Air Command, equipped with F-4C Phantom II fighters. The F-4C was the newest aircraft in the USAF inventory and we were one of two wings in the Air Force that were combat ready in the Phantom II. I was the squadron Scheduling Officer and was sitting at my desk, waiting for the Operations Officer to return from the weekly scheduling meeting at wing headquarters, hoping he would have the information I needed to complete the monthly sortie projections.

Our Wing Standardization and Evaluation Officer, Jack Britt, who was also at the meeting, returned first and looked in my door. 'Guess what, Dick? We're going to deploy to Thailand, to Ubon Royal Thai Air Base. We'll provide counter-air support for six F-105 Squadrons from Japan and Okinawa.'

'What?' I was surprised - shocked actually. I'd heard some scuttle-butt about a 12th Wing squadron deploying to Naha, Okinawa, but nothing about Thailand. 'When are we going? For how long?'

Jack shrugged. 'Not sure. Sometime this summer, I think. I don't know for how long.'

Just then the Operations Officer, Major Hodges, came in, overhearing Jack's comment. 'Knock it off Britt. You too Hamilton. This whole thing's classified.'

We answered in unison. 'Even in the squadron?'

'I'm telling you its classified - Top Secret. Don't talk to anyone about it. This is strictly need-to-know. And get the word out, no one can tell their wives.'

'Swell,' I said 'We're the only unit in the Air Force with deployable F-4s. This is really a dumb secret.' My only response from Hodges was a glare. That's how this whole thing got started.

Memories Of Ubon Thailand: A Fighter Pilot's Journal by Richard E. Hamilton.

'By the end of 1964, our forces were secretly embroiled in the war in both South Viêtnam and Laos, looking for ways to stop the flow of men and supplies coming from North Viêtnam. The Gulf of Tonkin 'incident' provided the excuse to expand our involvement. Although never proven, North Viêtnamese gunboats purportedly attacked two of our Navy destroyers cruising the North China Sea during 'Desoto' patrols, a covert operation to interdict supplies headed south. By asking Congress to support retaliatory strikes against the North Viêtnamese, President Johnson unintentionally committed our military to a prolonged war. And, little by little, Congress unwittingly supported the escalation. Shortly thereafter, in 1965, we began opening fighter bases in Thailand to support the war against North Viêtnam. Our war had truly started.

'In the weeks that followed our notification, we anticipated that we might start practicing for our upcoming air-to-air mission in 'that place.' No way, as it turned out, but we spent a lot of time concentrating on nuclear deliveries. Were we fooling the bad guys or what?

'Finally, I learned, through the Deputy Commander for Operations secretary, that our sister squadron, the 45th TFS, would go first, in April and we would relieve them sometime in July. We were only required to go for ninety days each, as the Air Force was planning to form a new wing there later in 1965. Their pilots' tour length would be for one year or for one hundred missions, whichever came first. Our deal sounded better, although we all wanted to be there long enough to get a MiG. Still, no one was to know. I guess I shouldn't have been surprised when my wife, Fran, asked me about the deployment shortly thereafter - seemed the Wing Commander's wife was on the 'need-to-know list.' She'd spilled the beans at a Wives Club coffee.

'The first big training exercise for the mission was a 'go, no-go exercise,' so we could deploy across the Pacific Ocean without going to sleep. We were given a ration of 'go' pills (Dexedrine) and 'no-go' pills (sleeping tablets - Nembutal and Seconal) along with a schedule for taking them. The test would take place over a weekend, of course. No sense screwing up the workweek.

'I started with a 'go' pill, followed by another after eight hours. After the second one kicked in, my eyes were in a permanent surprise-like stare. After another four hours, I was supposed to sleep. I gulped down my Nembutal and hit the pillow, but my eyes never closed once. After eight hours I took the second series of go pills. By this time I had no appetite and felt like digging postholes. That night I tried taking two Seconals but that was an utter failure as well. By now I'd been up for thirty-two hours and was speaking very quickly. I lied on my score-card about taking the next go pill series and finally got to close my eyes for a couple of hours. The next day I advised the flight surgeon that all had gone well and I could fly across the Pacific without going to sleep. About this, I had no doubts.

'Not much changed over the next few months. Our sister squadron, the 45th, deployed on schedule and two of their pilots had already shot down two MiG-17s. Their Phantoms were attacked by four MiGs during an escort mission [on 10 July]. Our guys quickly 'suckered them into their six,' meaning that the MiGs gained the initial tactical advantage, starting out on the F-4's tails - ready to shoot. Our guys managed to out-fly them however and shot down both of them with AIM-9 Sidewinder missiles.

'Although we were delighted with their success in the air, we'd heard that living conditions at Ubon weren't so hot and that the 45th pilots' morale was at an all-time low. Nonetheless, we were excited about our deployment, still thinking about downing our own MiG, until the 45th suffered their first combat loss. That made things dead serious. It also made us wonder about our commander's leadership abilities.

'We still hadn't concentrated on air-to-air mission training, but we got what practice we could between ourselves on the way home, after our mission objectives had been met. The whole deployment was still classified, even though the news media reported Air Force F-4s flying out of Thailand.

'Finally, the big day arrived. We were put into quarantine the evening before the launch, so we could get the right food and plenty of rest - away from the wife and kids. Yeah, right! What a mess. It was noisy, hot, we slept on cots and there was a shortage of pillows and sheets. Even our vaunted high-protein steaks had been full of fat and tougher than shoe leather.

'Anyway, the next day the majority of the pilots said good-bye to their families on the ramp amongst the newsmen and photographers. I'd elected to say my good-byes to the kids the afternoon before I went into quarantine. Somehow it seemed more normal. I didn't want my children thinking that this day was different or scary, that I was going off to war and might not come back. I'd hoped they'd think it was just another routine deployment - god knows they'd seen enough of those. Fran came, however, and I gave her a hug and a big kiss - one I wouldn't forget -making sure she didn't see the tears in my eyes when we parted.

'I looked around as I climbed the ladder to my plane, surveying the scene. One of the wives was waving a protest poster, which quickly disappeared. The journalists were snapping pictures and I wondered if they knew where we were going. What a way to start a war.

'Our deployment was scheduled to be a three-day affair. We'd fly to Hawaii from MacDill, our Central Florida home base on the first day, on to Clark AB, The Philippines, the second day and then to Ubon the following morning. Right at 12,000 nautical miles, give or take a few. Some of our maintenance personnel and extra aircrews had preceded us by two days on a C-130 transport and would meet us in Hawaii. They would provide maintenance support if required and the spare aircrews would step in for any sick pilots. After they serviced and launched our spare aircraft back to the mainland, they would proceed to Ubon.

'Takeoff was uneventful. We deployed in four formations of six aircraft - four of which were spares. Each formation would marry-up with three KC-135 tankers, modified Boeing 707 transports, for our airborne refuellings. Consequently, we were spread for a long ways, having twenty miles in between each section. Our four six-ship formations met with our first group of tankers over Dallas and the refuellings went well. However, we almost aborted over San Diego, as our mission leader couldn't make contact with light-ship 'November,' which was our rescue vessel. Someone finally got the frequency right and we pressed on to aloha land with a new set of tankers who would buddy-up with us for the ocean crossing.

'There is nothing so boring as to fly a heavyweight fighter in a big formation over a great big body of water. The only relief from the monotony was during air-to-air refuelling and that wasn't very often. Some of us had put our 'G' suits under our butts and blew them up every once in a while to prevent numbness. Others moved out of formation and did a couple of aileron rolls until one of the commanders told him to knock it off.

'Our GIBs (guys in back - preferred name for PSOs, Pilot Systems Operators) were a bit apprehensive about their first long flight and some of them were having the usual problems: staying alert and not being able to urinate. My 'GIB', Jim, just couldn't make himself go in the 'piddle-pac,' a sponge-lined plastic gizmo that held about a quart of liquid. It isn't as easy as you might think; those of you who have never tried it. Jim was all cramped up in the cockpit, wearing a flight suit and G suit (he hadn't put it under his butt). The pressurization and normal vibration of the aircraft made it difficult for him to get started. Hell, finding it through all of that gear was tough enough. Most guys were fine after getting that first dribble in the plastic tube. But not my guy.

'Jim was complaining loudly when I noticed my master warning light blinking, telling me my number two engine was losing oil pressure. Its diagnosis was accurate and I had to shut the engine down and leave the formation - since I was unable to maintain the same altitude with only one engine. The flight leader, after hearing that everything else was fine, told my wingman, Jack Gravis, to stay with me and we pressed on at a lower altitude with 800 miles left to Hickam, AFB. This was not a very serious problem in the F-4C. We had plenty of fuel and the other engine was doing fine. But it certainly didn't help with Jim's difficulty in mastering the piddle-pac.

'As we'd left the formation, I heard our mission commander tell the tanker that he was not going to enter the ADIZ (Air Defence Intercept Zone) within the ten-mile window. The F-4 was equipped with an inertial navigation system which was quite accurate and other members of the flight verified our position. The tanker leader told our flight leader he had a Master Navigator on board who had everything under control; since when does a fighter pilot tell a big airplane navigator about his speciality? About that time, we picked up a couple of bogies on our radar screens which turned out to be Hawaii ANG F-102 Interceptors. They advised the tanker leader he'd missed the ADIZ and they'd be required to escort his formation to Hickam. Quite a few raspberries were heard after a few choice fighter pilot comments were relayed to the Master Navigator. He deserved them.

'The rest of the flight beat us to Hickam by about twenty-five minutes and we were very happy to get our Phantom on the ground. I'd almost forgotten about Jim's difficulty until we parked the aircraft. He leapt from his seat and hit the ground tearing at his zipper - relief at last. We all stood there and watched while he shot spurt after spurt at least fifteen feet. The ground crews were mildly amused; he was embarrassed. After debriefing, we were given two hours to do as we wished until quarantine. Naturally, we hit the bar and sipped a couple of Mai Tai's until 'no-go' pill hour. All in all, a good day.

'We'd had four spare aircraft for the deployment. The original plan was to leave two of them on the ground in Hawaii, while the other two accompanied us to Wake Island, where the mission would be declared a 'go'. They would then return to Hickam and all four spares would return to MacDill the following day. The aircraft I flew from MacDill was getting an engine change and one of the others had developed a hydraulic leak. Looked like the plan was working thus far and my replacement bird was humming right along.

'Our route of flight was direct to Wake Island, direct to Guam and direct to Clark Air Base. Everything was a point to point over water. The trip was 4,500 nautical miles; give or take a few and the time of flight was about ten hours and thirty minutes. Another boring day. At least the weather forecast was good, so we expected no problems in that department.

'Jim was upbeat after his difficulty on the first day and proved himself capable within the first hour. His only problem now was where in the hell he was going to hang the bag for the next nine hours. He solved the problem by hanging the strap on the ejection seat handle, which he didn't plan to use.

'This was the first time I'd seen Wake Island. I immediately conjured up a scene from an old World War II movie where the hero, William Bendix, single-handedly fought off the first wave of the Japanese invasion, holding a hot machine gun in his bare hands as he riddled the enemy with bullets, saving his buddies, but, nonetheless, losing his life. The island was just a small dot in the gigantic Pacific and made me wonder about the men who lost their lives there. Such a high cost for such a little insignificant place.

'My thoughts were interrupted by a radio call. Our deep-ocean escort, a C-130 Hercules lost one of its four engines an hour or so out of Wake and advised us he had to abort. Since none of us had developed any problems and we were far enough along by now, the mission commander wished him well and declared the mission a 'go.'

'The rest of the mission was uneventful, except for our sore butts, until we learned that the tankers who had been scheduled to refuel us over the Mariana Islands had been needed for another mission. Consequently, we were advised to land at Anderson AFB, Guam. We would press on to The Philippines the next day.

'After landing, we raced to the Officers Club bar for our two hours of freedom. When we walked in the door, a voice over the intercom advised the membership that the 'combat crews' were entering the establishment. We thought it was nice of these guys to welcome us aboard, until it became apparent that the announcement was for the Strategic Air Command 'combat crews' who'd been sitting alert in their B-52s (eight-engine strategic bombers we called 'Buff's, big ugly xxxxers). After a few pointed remarks were made to the SAC pukes, we had a few beers and hit the sack. Another pretty good day.

'The next morning we departed for Clark AB, P.I., where we'd be leaving our aircraft. Ostensibly, another squadron in our wing, the 43rd, would use the aircraft in support of a SEATO initiative to provide Air Defence protection for the nearby signatories if required. Actually, they would be used to re-supply our squadron with replacement aircraft and aircrews if we lost any in combat - a sobering thought. Eventually, they'd join the 12th TFW, another group from MacDill that was scheduled to move to Cam Ranh Bay, a new base being built in South Việtnam.

'We hadn't required tankers on this leg, so we arrived in flights of four looking like the sharp squadron we were, ready for combat. Each flight broke in precision with exactly four seconds spacing between aircraft, hitting the runway with the nose held high, our orange and white drag-chutes billowing in the wind, we'd taxied to our parking area in close formation, feeling proud.

'We got to relax for most of the day at Clark, another beautiful and historic base, whose appearance emitted the flavours, traditions and memories established there before the second war. It reminded me of some film clips I'd seen in the newsreels at the movies when I was a kid. That afternoon a few of us hit the pool and generally enjoyed ourselves. Later we had dinner, en-masse, while listening to a twenty-one piece Filipino band that sounded very much like Glenn Miller. Although no one showed it, we were getting tense as we got closer to battle, even though our bravado was at its peak. But at the same time, a feeling of apprehensiveness prevailed. All-in-all, it was another good day. We left for Ubon RTAB, Thailand the next morning on a C-130 transport. Our war had begun.

'I'll never forget our welcome, or lack of it, when we arrived - July twenty-fourth. Hardly anyone spoke to us and a lot of the grubby-looking departing pilots and maintenance troops jumped on the transport aircraft as soon as we hit the ramp. Could this be an omen? Boy was it ever. The first news we received was that a member of our advance party, Dick Keirn and a 45th 'GIB', Ross Fobair, had been shot down that morning by an SA-2 surface-to-air missile, the first loss of the war to that potent Soviet weapon. [He had been at Ubon for two weeks and was on his eleventh mission]. We had sent eight 47th pilots to Ubon two weeks early to learn the ropes. Now one of them was declared missing. No one had seen any parachutes. Toward the end of October, we found out that 'Pop's' Keirn had been captured, but Ross Fobair never made it out of the airplane. 'Pop's' was one of the unlucky ones who were spit on and stoned by the crowd as they were paraded down the streets of Hànôi. Later, two more of our pilots would show up at the Hànôi 'Hilton'. [1]

'Ubon had sounded pretty good to me. Remembering the movie, I had conjured up thoughts of the King of Siam and all of the mysteries of the East. But after I arrived, the base wasn't exactly as I'd pictured - not nearly so glamorous. And the smell. Whew!

'Our base happened to be a renovated WWII British base that had been constructed in a rice paddy. There were 8,000 feet of runway with one taxiway and a small ramp and a number of small round parking revetments scattered about, which held two aircraft each. The place was jammed with only one squadron of F-4s; we had twenty-five total. There was heavy construction everywhere - graders and tractors working away, hundreds of Thai workers running around with two buckets of dirt suspended from a stick they carried across their shoulders. They were enlarging the size of the ramp and the runway was going to be lengthened by two thousand feet along with the associated taxiways.

'I noticed a couple of new maintenance hangers being built beside the new ramp along with a bunch of other buildings of unknown variety. Our Squadron operations building faced the old ramp and one of our GIBs had already mounted the 47th Squadron sign above the front door. Our logo was the 'turnip termite,' a creature from *Dog Patch*, taken from the comic strip, *Lil Abner*. Maybe a tough termite didn't seem very appropriate for battle, but it did kind of fit into the scheme of things. The place was surrounded on three sides by rice paddies covered with about one foot of smelly water, night-soil I guess. There were thunderstorms almost every afternoon and the air was super humid. The bright lights attracted the bugs and drove our guys' nuts. It was kind of hard to get any work done when you had a two-inch beetle crawling up your leg looking for something to bite. The heat from the lights also attracted snakes, kraits mostly, which were quite deadly. These required a more professional approach and scared the hell out of most of us.

'The housing at Ubon was unique. Except for the Squadron Commander and Ops Officer, who were assigned air-conditioned trailers, we lived in 'hooches', a long building constructed on three-foot stilts and screened on all sides with a tin corrugated roof. Two corrugated sections that protruded from the walls formed little roofs to keep the rain out during the monsoon storms. Each 'hooch' was divided into four rooms - about fifteen by fifteen feet. In each, there were two sets of double steel bunk beds known as racks, four steel lockers and our very own footlockers. The racks were covered with mosquito netting, the use of which was strongly encouraged, as the Ubon variety of these blood-suckers was enormous and always hungry.

'Fortunately, we were given the first day off to get settled in before our war began, although the paper-war started for me about fifteen minutes after I arrived. They needed this; they needed that. To hell with them; I needed some rest, a good meal and a beer. Request denied. Three hours of hard work later it was time for dinner. Compared to the Air Force, the Army knew how to eat. Their mess halls were a thing of beauty compared to this place. Here, we were introduced to our new Base Commander, a full Colonel we called 'Magellan' because he was a navigator. All priorities seemed to be focused on 'the important things': the runway, taxiway, ramp and revetment construction and the building progress on the new personnel and headquarters buildings, etc. There was no mention about improving the living conditions for us. There were no laundry facilities, at least not in the true sense.

'And for all of this, we got $1.90 daily per-diem. Yeah! No wonder our predecessors wanted on the plane before we could get off.

'Getting organized was no easy task. Even though we had done lots of pre-planning, it was never as easy as it looked on paper. We got our people settled by flights. Each flight 'A', 'B', 'C' and 'D', got their own 'hooch'. We had a total of fifty-four pilots, including the Commander, Operations Officer and the Maintenance Officer. Aircraft Commanders bunked with their GIBs. The restroom facilities were located in between the two rows of 'hooches' for ready access by all.

'On any base there are four major areas where fighter pilots hang out: the Operations desk where the flying schedules are posted every day on a big Plexiglas board, the personal equipment locker room where we played bridge and scrabble and kept our flying gear and survival stuff, the Intelligence area where the maps were and the bar; the latter being the most popular. The one thing in common about these places was that they were all air-conditioned, a definite advantage over our 'hooches', which were equipped with what looked like the original ceiling fans taken from the set of *Casablanca*.

'Following the first week, a bunch of the troops wanted to grow handlebar moustaches and wear 'go-to-hell' hats like we had seen on TV - like everyone else in Southeast Asia. These hats were similar to Australian bush hats, turned up on one side, except they were olive drab. 'You guys are going to look like the Pentagon expects, clean-shaven and professional,' our commander said. So that was that. But I couldn't help but wonder, though, who in the hell was going to know what we looked like if we weren't allowed to tell anyone we were here.

'The flying situation took a little getting used to as well, even though our squadron was very experienced. About half of the front-seaters had been recalled from the Air National Guard during the Berlin and Cuban crises. Most of us 'Guard bums' were Captains and had more flying time than our Flight Commanders, who were Majors. Quite a few of us had an edge on the Operations and Assistant Operations officers as well. We'd certainly dropped more bombs than they had. We also had more tactical experience as flight leaders. This situation was normally not a problem unless one of them got us shot at for no good reason. These problems were usually ironed out in debriefings or in private discussions at the bar but the undercurrent of mistrust prevailed during the rest of the deployment. This entire experience was becoming absolutely surreal. Not only did we have to live in this crazy environment, we had to put up with crazy leadership. All of us felt like we were walking on eggs. We would soon learn that our situation would get worse.

'Our missions in support of 'Rolling Thunder' were to bomb strategic targets - rail yards, factories, electrical plants, bridges, airfields, military barracks/camps and ammunition storage sites; interdict supplies being routed south; assist rescue efforts; maintain air superiority and to escort various reconnaissance missions that would take place in North Việtnam and Laos. Missions in Laos were called 'Barrel Roll' and 'Steel Tiger' and were generally armed reconnaissance missions against supply routes. We also got to play photo journalist for the Pentagon.

'After we had been flying for two weeks, it suddenly dawned on many of us that someone in Washington, not our commanding general, was controlling our missions. Some 'big shot' in the Pentagon was selecting our targets, our weapons, the time of day we were scheduled and deciding how many aircraft we would fly against each target.

'Even in wartime, there is never a bomb dropped or a shot fired without a written order from the top. There are orders for everything in the military. The orders that directed our war were called fragmentation orders; fragments of the general order that carries out the war plan. The 'frags' are sent to every involved unit; assigning them specific targets to attack. Supposedly, the frag orders came from the next highest command authority, which in our case was the 2nd Air Division at Udorn, about seventy-five miles north of Ubon on the Thai northern border close to the Mekong River, but for the most part, they seemed to pass straight through from the Pentagon. They came in every morning by secure teletype and we carried them out. No matter how dumb they might be.

'The Pentagon also played the number's game. The F-4 was a multi-purpose fighter that could perform both the air-to-air mission and the air-to-ground mission, including nuclear. Apparently, Secretary of Defense McNamara thought up the idea that you could count two-for-one with the F-4. They'd schedule us for an air-to-ground mission, cycle us back to a tanker after we dropped our bombs and then send us out for a MiGCAP mission because we always carried Sparrow missiles. I suppose McNamara thought it sounded good on the news when the anchor reported that we flew fifty sorties that day, instead of twenty-five. Learning of this, one of our guys asked our commander if we could also take credit for two combat missions and apply it toward an Air Medal, which took twenty-five missions to get in those days. His answer was, 'Hell no.'

'Most of us flew over enemy territory on at least one hundred separate occasions. Later, the Defense Department changed the qualification requirements for earning an Air Medal. They lowered the number of missions from twenty-five to ten, but that was only for missions flown over North Việtnam. Unfortunately, it was not retroactive. The weapons themselves were also a problem for us initially. For the first few weeks, we used primarily 700lb and 50lb bombs (Mk.117s) and really old WWII fuses. I guessed they wanted to use up the old stuff before giving us anything new and reliable. There had been cases of premature detonation caused by the bombs hitting together in mid-air and a lot of bombs weren't exploding when they hit. We wondered if the fuses were working at all. Our Munitions Officer figured that the propellers might be sticking and if he bent them a little more, they would work. On my next flight, as I was leaving the tanker en route to the target, my wingman said I didn't have one propeller on my bomb fuses, meaning my bombs were armed. The force of dropping them or even a bird strike might cook them off. Jim checked my wingman and saw his propellers were missing as well. The other element also had the same problem. I decided to press on to the target and take our chances dropping them there. Hell, it was just as risky to take them home, maybe more so - we'd be exposed longer. No one had a problem during their release and we didn't have one dud. However, we decided that our Munitions Officer needed to come up with a better solution. He did, by 'conning' our headquarters out of new fuses.

'This wasn't our only weaponry problem. Just because the F-4 could carry most of the weapons in the Air Force inventory, didn't mean that the munitions selected by higher headquarters were the right one for the job. One day I was targeted to attack a small wooden bridge with High Explosive anti-tank rockets. I hit the target, but the rockets just burned holes in the wood, causing minimal damage. Later, on a night mission with rockets, I thought I was shooting into a mirror after I'd fired. I watched the rocket plumes as they departed the aircraft and then watched them immediately turn around and attack me. Actually, it was flak coming from the enemy anti-aircraft gunners, who'd simply fired at the source of my rocket trails. In this case, our choice of weapons had uncomplicated their job for them.

'During our first month at Ubon, I was given the 'privilege' of shooting a Bullpup air-to-ground missile at the Thành Hòa Bridge, a target of infamy in North Việtnam. There were two kinds of Bullpup missiles: the big one weighed 1,000lbs and the smaller one weighed 250lbs. I fired the latter, which was designed to destroy trucks and tanks. Boy, did I get noticed. The follow the trail rule applied and I had a SAM after me in about ten seconds. It missed. So did I.

'Constant meddling in our tactics by the armchair quarterbacks in

Washington had a negative effect on our morale and sanity. It was difficult enough to attack the most heavily defended region in the history of aerial warfare, on a daily basis, without being interfered with by a bunch of amateurs. After all, we were the ones who were risking our lives, not them. It was also impossible to explain the situation to our wives and kids. So we were stuck with an impossible task and had to live or die by their decisions without having anyone to bitch to. My greatest fear was leaving Fran without a husband and my kids without a father and I didn't have any way to control it. Most of us didn't even talk about our fears among ourselves. These targeting and weapons problems taught me a great lesson; that the politicians in charge must trust the military to make the tactical decisions when fighting a war.

'It was rumoured that an F-105 pilot, trying to help his shot down wingman, strafed a small hamlet and was sent home for it. No one wanted to purposely bomb helpless civilians, but the North Việtnamese military located anti-aircraft weapons in many of their villages because they knew they'd be safe from attack. Personally, I never attacked a village and I think I could vouch the same for every pilot in our squadron. I'll have to admit I was tempted to attack a 23mm gun emplacement one day. The gun was shooting at me from a small cluster of huts while I was trying to provide cover for a helicopter that was trying to pick up a shot down F-105 pilot. Like most of the others, I gritted my teeth, held my temper and didn't drop my bombs. Incidentally, the helicopter had to back off and the pilot was captured - later I learned the pilot was Robbie Risner.[2] Sometimes the rules suck and following them just doesn't seem to make sense, especially when the people that make them up never have been to war - or make them for political reasons.

'North Việtnam was divided into six areas they called 'Route Packages'. Route PAC-1 was the farthest south and five and six were divided east and west at the top. Two, three and four were in between. The really bad packages were four, five and six. Places like Hànôi, Phúc Yên, Kép, Giá Lâm, 'Thud Ridge', Yên Bái, Haiphòng, Điện Biên Phú, Phú Thọ, Bắc Ninh, Sơn Tây, Thái Nguyên, Bắc Giáng, Lạng Sơn, Hòa Bình and Thành Hóa were all famous points of reference. There were also many barracks areas and truck parks in the lower route packages that would bring back some instant memories of danger for those that flew there; Vĩnh, Đông Hoi, Vĩnh Linh, as well as Tiger Island, quickly come to mind.

'Laos was another story. Apparently, the small country was involved in the war simply because of its location -caught up in the never-ending conflicts between the Thai, Cambodians and the Việtnamese - who had been fighting one another for centuries. The ancient Lao kingdom was originally the home of the Meo tribe (later called Hmong), an almost primitive group of people living in small groups throughout the highlands. They were like the American Indians and only fought when someone invaded their territory. And the country itself was different, almost entirely made up of heavy jungle forests interspersed with white limestone karsts, jutting from the ground like stone-age flint knives. There were several rivers and one central high plateau called the Plain of Jars, named after the enormous burial jars that were left on the plain by some forgotten people. There were hardly any major towns or roads, except in the lowlands near the Mekong River, just small villages located near burnt off clearings on the sides of the hills where tribal groups cleared the jungle to grow millet and opium poppies. Laos was an extremely beautiful country in a peculiar way; its valleys filled each morning with wispy fog. It reminded me of an old movie I'd seen about a secret land where dinosaurs still survived - still unconnected with the rest of the planet. Anyway, for whatever reason, not striking targets in Laos was just about as important as not flying out of Thailand. Even though everyone knew we were doing it, no one wanted to talk about it. I guess that's what our government called 'diplomacy'. None of us would ever forget being shot at in Laos, from Samneua, Ban Ban, Tehepone and Route 7, the main road through the Plain of Jars out of the northern Parrots Beak.

'Besides the 2nd Air Division, Udorn provided a jumping-off base for reconnaissance aircraft (RF-101s or RF-4Cs) stationed at Tân Sơn Nhất Air Base near Sàigòn, as well as an emergency landing base for aircraft with battle damage. It also supported the aircrew rescue effort with heavily armoured helicopters and provided forward air controller (FAC) aircraft, flying T-28s, for some Laotian missions. Air America, a CIA spook operation, was alive and well at Udorn and across the river at Vientiane, Laos.

'Almost every one of our missions into NVN required air refuelling. The SAC KC-135 crews flew out of Don Muang AB in Bangkok and were always there for us when we needed them. They flew in giant race-track orbits, fulfilling their role as airborne service stations. They stayed in three major positions, known as 'Red', 'Blue' and 'Brown' 'Anchors' - those were also their call signs. They were invaluable on rescue missions. And they would sometimes cross into North Việtnam to supply much-needed fuel to a damaged aircraft - disregarding their vulnerability to enemy fire.

'We had one GIF [guy in front] in the squadron who could see a mosquito at one mile. Andy routinely picked up the tanker visually before our GIBs [guys in back] could find it on radar. When he was in the flight, it was always a contest for our GIBs to pick up the target before Peter E. B. called a visual contact.

'Each Air Base had common call signs. Consequently, once on strike frequency, you had a pretty good idea who was there and what was going on. Sometimes when cycling through the refuelling operation, we would switch over to strike frequency to see how things were going - many times you heard things like: '*Watch out 'Oak 2', there is a SAM coming up at your five o'clock. Break hard right - now. Oh shit! Anybody see a chute?*' Sometimes it was better not to know and the individual aircrews played it by ear. Some of us just took things as they came. It was sometimes easier that way.

'The enemy order of battle for the air war in North Việtnam consisted of MiG-17 'Frescos', MiG-19 'Farmers' and MiG-21 'Fishbeds' at Phúc Yên, Giá Lâm and Kép Air Bases near Hànôi. They had 23mm or 37mm cannons and heat-seeking missiles. The North Việtnamese anti-aircraft situation was much more formidable, mainly because the MiGs didn't fly that much during our tour. They started with four-barrel 51 calibre machine guns and two-barrel 23mm cannons for low altitudes (below 3,000 feet), 37 and 57mm cannons for medium altitudes (2,000 to 15,000 feet) and 85 and 90mm artillery for high altitudes (15,000 to 25,000 feet). The big stuff, along with some 57mm had radar fire-control systems. They also had very distinguishable visual cues. The quad-14s fired tracer rounds that were yellowish-white, while the dual-23's tracers were a deep red. Flak signatures were just as recognizable. The 37mm detonations were a dirty brown, while 57mm's were almost white. The 85mm flak was very black and the 90mm was more whitish. All of these weapons were of Soviet design, very reliable and quite deadly. The SA-2 SAM was their primary point defence weapon on our watch. The Việtnamese versions were similarly laid out in a six-sided-star configuration, a missile at each point, with the guidance control radar in the middle. These were what guarded the principal targets around the Hànôi area. Our only real defence against the SAM was to see it first and evade it. We called it a 'SAM break'. The pilot that was attacked would wait until the missile had committed itself to his aircraft and then break, turning sharply down and into the missile. If he timed it right - the key word being 'if' - this usually caused the missile to overshoot and explode harmlessly. The aircrews that flew north in later years carried pods that jammed the missile's guidance system. They also had RHAW gear; cockpit instruments that would pick up the enemy's missile and gun radars to warn the aircrews that they were being tracked. Regardless, it was always best to see the missile first, rather than to rely completely on the electronics.

'After a few weeks, things kind of settled down and our schedule became routine - like the old saying – 'a few moments of stark terror and a lot of boredom'. Generally, we flew for two days in a row and pulled additional duties on the third day, mobile control, bread-truck driver and duty desk officer. Usually, we had the fourth day off. The cycle varied, depending on the daily mission requirements and the health of our pilots. The missions never got easier and the stress was enormous. Much of the time, I'd sleep fitfully, dreaming about the dangers I'd faced that day. I knew why I couldn't shake my inner fears - there was no one to share them with. Fran was the only person I had ever trusted with my emotions and no one else could take her place. I loved my profession, but it wasn't always easy. It was a macho thing, I guess. After all, we had our image to maintain - we would have been wimps if we had admitted we'd been scared. All of us needed something to take our minds off of the war, the lack of leadership and the rotten living conditions. But we never found it.

'The first month went by quickly and we got somewhat used to living with our fears and doubts. We had all rotated through the various types of missions by now and had gained the necessary experience to feel confident that we could do our job. Every pilot in the 47th wanted to fly every day, but our bosses tried to keep everybody exactly even sortie-wise - even if it meant flying with another flight or crewmember. It seemed that the 45th let those who wanted to fly, fly and those who didn't could just sit around. We heard that some of their pilots flew less than twenty missions. This policy had been criticized by our wing commander, so our bosses enforced the opposite extreme - never a happy medium. Almost every pilot in our squadron was eager to get into the air no matter how tough the mission, although we had one backseater who suffered from stress and was replaced early on.

'The F-4 could carry an even bigger load of munitions than the B-17s did during WWII. Most of our aircraft were configured with bombs and four AIM-7 Sparrow missiles, which we always carried. They were radar guided and required the GIBs to do most of the acquisition work. The GIF manoeuvred into a firing position and pulled the trigger. Our bomb loads varied, but were usually ten 750lb Mk-117 bombs. This configuration put us at our maximum takeoff weight, 58,000lbs and some of the takeoff rolls made you 'pucker' on our short runway. We later cut this heavyweight configuration to eight bombs because the lower ones, carried on our inboard racks, could contact the arresting gear cable located at the centre of the runway. Barriers were one-inch cables laid across the runway that was snagged by our tail hook when we couldn't stop. We had three of them; one at each end and the one in the centre. They were held about three inches off of the ground with rubber disks. Sometimes we engaged the cables right after touchdown, much like the Navy does on a carrier. We also used them when we had brake problems or when the runway was wet. I think that every pilot in the squadron took the barrier at least once and many had several chances to use the 'wire.'

'On my first combat mission, the target was Điện Biên Phú Air Base, where the French Legionaries had been defeated by Hô Chi Minh. Sixteen aircraft were fragged to hit the airfield: two flights of F-105s and two flights of F-4s. Our objective was to make the airfield unusable and each pilot was given a specific aim point in order to maximize the coverage of the bombs. There was very little anti-aircraft fire and most of the guys put their bombs on target, a little over fifty tons of them. The airfield wasn't utilized for the next six months. During the attack, Russ Kartrude, one of my close friends in another flight, got a hard light when he selected afterburner while pulling off his dive-bomb pass. This happens when one afterburner doesn't ignite immediately and when it does, it goes bang. At first, he thought he'd taken a hit and called out to his flight leader before he figured out what had happened. He took plenty of verbal abuse from his squadron mates when he returned, but we all knew secretly that we had been just as nervous and could easily have done the same thing. We had been 'blooded' in combat and felt pretty good about it.

'For armed reconnaissance missions, we usually carried a variety of munitions. Two aircraft might be configured with an SU-16 gun-pod (20mm Gatling-gun) and four napalm canisters, a gun-pod and four tubes of 2.75 rockets. The other two aircraft might have high drag bombs called 'Snake-eyes,' 500lb bombs equipped with umbrella-like fins that popped open after they were dropped. This allowed the pilot to drop them from very low altitudes without picking up debris from their explosion.

'We would travel a section of road, along the Hô Chi Minh Trail, looking for hidden trucks or supplies, hitting a pre-planned target if we didn't see anything on the roads. We also flew this mission at night, with flares. Shortly after we arrived, we were briefed on the situation in Laos. While the Laotian government was friendly to the United States, the country was divided and the entire eastern region of the country was controlled by the Pathet Lao, a puppet regime of the North Viêtnamese. The Pathet Lao had a sizeable army and guarded Hô Chi Minh Trail, the supply route that supported the Viêt Công and had it well defended with anti-aircraft weapons.

'The Royal Laotian army, totalling less than ten thousand men, were mainly based in the ancient capital of Luang Prabang and around Vientiane and were not heavily involved in fighting the Pathet Lao. The primary combat forces were a small faction of royalists approximately seventeen hundred men strong, led by a young general named Vang Pao who had fought with the French at Điện Biên Phú. He and his men were located at a secret base on the Plain of Jars near route seven, the road out of the northern 'Parrot's Beak'. General Vang Pao helped establish and defend what would be known as 'Lima' sites (landing sites). Our government, through the CIA, provided his forces with supplies, equipment and weapons. It was even rumoured that they had some Air Force pilots, flying FAC missions. In return, they helped us build and defend a few camps, usually located on top of a mountain, where we could cache fuel for our rescue helicopters and provide some navigational aids for our aircraft. They usually had a small dirt landing-strip and were re-supplied by STOL (short take-off and landing aircraft).

'Every now and then the communist Pathet Lao would attack one of these sites. We always kept a couple of spare F-4s at Ubon, loaded and ready-to-go. My Flight Commander, Ray Ramsey and I flew on one of the first missions. Shortly after takeoff, we contacted a forward air controller flying an unmarked T-28. His call-sign was 'Bongo' and he spoke with an American accent - supporting the rumour we'd heard about Air Force FACs flying in Laos. He directed us to a hill top that the Pathet Lao were threatening. It was early evening and getting darker by the minute. We were loaded with snake and nape, as well as rockets and a gun pod. Somehow, in spite of the darkness, we managed to put our munitions on target using only the light created by the napalm fires. Luckily the bad guys retreated. The next morning we got a message from our Laotian Ambassador, Mr. Sullivan, who lauded our efforts. Two days later he revoked the message and ordered it burned. He had apparently 'forgotten' we couldn't officially fly there. Besides, it was in support of a CIA operation. Oh well!

'For MiGCAP missions, we carried four AIM-9 heat-seeking missiles, Sidewinders, along with our four Sparrows. We would meet the strike force on their way into the target area and were assigned to engage any MiGs that might try to stop them. Sometimes we would cover two or three separate flights on different targets and followed the last one until they cleared the threat zone.

'The configuration was the same for escorting the 'Queen Bee,' a specially instrumented C-130 that flew back and forth along the North Viêtnamese coast gathering electronic intelligence information; enemy radio transmissions mainly. Two of us would fly a moving orbit around the aircraft while the other two stayed with a tanker until the first flight ran low on fuel. We exchanged places about every thirty minutes or so for most of the day. These missions were kind of crazy, but seemed to be necessary. The first week after I arrived I flew two of them back-to-back. They lasted for seven to nine hours. Talk about boring, it was as bad as an ocean crossing. Jim and I really got hungry on our first mission, so we requested a lunch from the mess hall for the next. After about three hours I had Jim fly and I chowed down. I bit into something awfully hard and broke a tooth. Turns out that the pork chop in my sandwich still had the bone in it.

'I also chased a couple of MiG-21s that day. The MiGs had made a mock attack on the 'Queen'. Unfortunately, they turned around before we could get close enough to engage and besides, we couldn't leave the 'Queen' unescorted long enough to catch them anyway. When the mission was over, I had to make an emergency trip down town to the local dentist, who was Chinese. His son turned the crank on his drill because he had no electricity. The slow grinding with nothing to deaden the pain was 'interesting.' He did a good job, however, and it didn't hurt again after he'd filled it.

'We generally carried bombs on interdiction targets and some were not the general-purpose variety. There was an interesting section of road in Laos that moved a lot of truck traffic. We just couldn't seem to slow them down, so the weapons types at headquarters decided to try something new. We were given long-delay bombs to seed the area. They worked as follows: the bombs were dropped on or near the road. Normally, the bomb went underground and then broached, returned to the surface and just laid there. The arming device was chemical, an acid vial that broke on impact. This melted a pin which armed the vibration sensing detonator. The enemy was supposed to think they were duds and when they tried to move them, or when a truck went by, the vibration would set them off. Sneaky!

'The first couple of times they worked great, but the ingenious Việtnamese learned to put chains over them before they were armed and then pulled the chains off from a safe distance to explode the bomb. Following the explosion, they simply filled in the holes and pressed on.

'We had an exciting incident involving these bombs. One of our pilots had a minor emergency after takeoff and decided to return to base. When you work with long-delay bombs, there is an unwritten rule that you never bring them home. You dump them in a safe area or you use the local jettison area, but you never land with them. The rule was made for a good reason. Anyhow, this guy just somehow forgot about the consequences and landed with his bombs. The Munitions Officer was furious. The munitions guys downloaded the bombs, put them on a munitions trailer, on mattresses and somehow got them to the jettison area safely over a very bumpy road. These bombs were designed to detonate after about thirty hours. Sure enough, a day and a half later... *Booooom!*

'One of our Squadron members, Cham Chesnutt, said of this particular guy, 'If it was raining soup, Marv would have a fork.'

'By the time September rolled around we were 'old heads.' Most of us had approximately thirty-five missions and had seen a great deal of what the enemy had to offer. We varied our tactics and formations in order to confuse the enemy gunners, or at least keep them guessing. The worst thing we could do was to become predictable.

'The North Việtnamese gunners always tried to lure our strike forces into 'flak traps'. They would build fake SAM sites, truck parks, or storage areas and place a heavy concentration of anti-aircraft guns on the easiest ingress and egress locations. If the attacking flight leader brought his flight down the valley one at a time, on the same heading and altitude, he solved many of the gunners' problems. They could just fire away and let the aircraft fly through their barrage. They also put explosive charges under large piles of gravel and blew them up when a flight of fighters went over a specific location, usually an easy place to regroup the flight after coming off a target. Therefore, our flight/element leaders had to be alert flak traps and have their wingmen attack the targets on different headings. Sometimes the second element of two fighters would attack from a reciprocal heading. Our Intelligence Officer always gave our flight leaders recommended attack headings based on the best possibility of seeing the target and for the best weapon effects; they were not based on survival. A good flight leader always wanted to destroy his target, but not at the expense of his wingmen.

'The wing weapons section at Korat AB invited a few of us over for an unofficial tactics conference. The idea of the meeting was to share our 'lessons learned' and figure out how the F-4s and F-105s might better complement each other. Their weapons officer had been working on some new tactics to attack SAM sites. We needed to know more about the SAM suppression mission in general and how we could provide them better protection from the MiGs. I had heard some scuttle-butt that there was a project at Nellis AFB, to develop a specialized group of aircraft optimized to attack surface to air missile sites. They were playing around with an F-100F equipped with special electronic equipment that would be used in conjunction with an anti-radiation missile. But that was in the future. In the meanwhile, we needed to find a way to shut down the SAMs with the equipment we had. We were anxious to talk with the other pilots that shared the skies over North Việtnam.

'We flew over to Korat in an old C-47 'goony bird' transport and were immediately impressed with the look of the base when we got off of the plane. Most of their aircraft were parked in revetments - ours were out in the open. We had some great tactics discussions at their intelligence facility and moved the meeting to the Officers' Club for the real talk. By the time we arrived, a group of 'Thud' pilots had the bar stools set up in tandem, because the F-4 had two seats and they didn't want our GIBs to feel out of place. Of course, they emphasized the fact that they just had one pilot to do the job and had only one engine to boot. We had a great time and returned the next day having made more friends.

'The F-105s were the real workhorses of the northern war. Most of them were of the single seat variety, originally designed for the nuclear delivery mission. I don't think there was another aircraft in the inventory that was as fast and stable at extremely low altitudes. The F-105 was nicknamed the 'Thunderchief,' but soon became known as the 'Thud,' because it was so heavy and went thud when it hit the ground. Its pilots were proud of the name. They were a haughty lot and were assigned to attack the toughest targets most of the time. Their losses were high and spawned the story: 'Do you know what an optimist is? A Thud pilot who quits smoking.' The Thud carried six 750lb bombs or eight 500lb bombs most of the time, but on occasion, they would carry two 3,000 pounders. They also had a built-in 20mm Gatling gun and shot down quite a few MiGs with it. The Phantom was also more suited to the tactical reconnaissance role than the RF-101C Voodoo, having a much better overall performance and unlike the Voodoo, it could fly night photo-reconnaissance missions.

'One of the pilots I met was shot down the following week and my flight flew MiG-CAP for the rescue effort. An Air America helicopter flew all of the way to the banks of the Black River and pulled him out. The chopper pilot had to refuel on the way back at a Lima site and hand pumped fuel into the aircraft while being fired upon by the enemy. I later met the helicopter pilot, who was Dutch. He certainly didn't look like my idea of a 'soldier of fortune,' just an average, skinny little guy that you might think was an accountant if you didn't know better. Guess a hero doesn't have to look or behave like John Wayne.

'About this time we learned that we'd be extended for at least two more months. Swell! The war seemed to be heating up too. I think the constant pressure we were exerting on the North Việtnamese was beginning to show. We had heavily damaged most of the major roads, railways and rail yards, military equipment and ammunition storage areas - and we constantly harassed their efforts to move the supplies south. The only target of consequence left was the port at Hảiphòng and that became a political problem. The politicians in Washington were concerned about sinking a Soviet or bloc-country re-supply ship - That we might start a war or something. Sometimes I wondered what were we doing here - Did we want to win or not?

'During this phase of the war, most of our tactical aircrews were very experienced and innovative as well. Our pilots always seemed to find a way to hit the target. One morning we were fragged to strike the Yên Bái rail yard along the Black River, just north of Bắc Ninh. There was a low overcast in the target area. Hoping the weather would clear, we pressed on. When we arrived, the clouds were still over the target but it was clear to the west. Undaunted, the lead 'GIB' called for 'Plan B.' He had given the other GIBs a nuclear timer setting for a level delivery at 3,000 feet, computed from a distinctive bend in the Black river. That became our IP. Our GIBs then used their ground map radars to help us line up with the target. We flew in two-ship formations with the second element about one mile in trail and set our weapons select switches for a level nuclear delivery. The GIBs 'pickled,' pushed down the bomb release button at the IP to start the timers. When the timers ran down, the front-seaters changed their switches to the direct mode on their bomb console and the bombs were away - Pretty neat.

'Our formations pulled off the target and started a slow rejoin as we headed south. About the time we levelled off, the sky suddenly turned black. Our friends, occupying a previously unknown 85mm battery at Samneua, decided to get themselves an F-4. Somehow we made it through the cloud of flak and got home without a hole. Bomb damage assessment (BDA) photos of the rail yard that afternoon showed major damage. Sometimes, there was a way.

'Our next three missions were just as exciting. Our flight was fragged to hit the Phú Thọ ammunition storage area just south of 'Thud Ridge'. Our target was very close to Phúc Yên AB and we didn't have any MiGCAP. That, along with the news that we'd be the number six flight on target, didn't make Jim and I feel very good about this one. Our flight leader decided to attack in separate elements, splitting the formation as we approached the ridge. He and his number two made a direct attack on the area from the west, popping up from low-altitude just before he got to the target. My wingman and I came down the east side of the ridge, heading south and made straight ahead pop-ups; hitting the target just behind the first element.

'I had never seen so much flak. Jim was yelling steadily, 'Coke bottles right, Tracers left, Jink, Jink (meaning manoeuvre out of the way).' Jink? No way; I just wanted to get the hell out of there in the fastest way possible, which was in a straight line. I was almost supersonic at one hundred feet. I could see guys shooting at me with rifles. The tracers were so heavy I couldn't tell which side they were coming from; probably both sides. After what seemed about an hour, but was in actuality no more than one minute, we joined up the flight and checked each other over for battle damage. No one had so much as a little scratch. I could hardly believe it. 'Mug-Wug,' god of flying, must have been with us all. It certainly wasn't talent that day.

'Shortly thereafter, Jim's wife sent us St. Christopher medals to wear on our dog-tag chains. I wore mine eagerly, along with the little Buddha and Episcopal-cross that already hung there. Coupled with my Greek 'worry-beads,' I figured I was well protected.

'About this time the Pentagon and the President were looking for a little good publicity; wanting to show the American people what a good job we were doing over North Việtnam in order to justify their actions. They wanted some favourable camera footage that could be shown on the nightly news.

'Someone in the Pentagon learned that our squadron had photographed the Mercury Capsule launches at Cape Canaveral and our aircraft had been wired to carry camera pods. With little warning, we were ordered to hang two camera pods on the aircraft, one under each wing and 'follow a few F-105s through a mission or two.' They also surprised us by sending a camera technician from Norton AFB, a Technical Sergeant, who would ride along in the back seat to get 'some exciting still shots.'

'Although we carried four Sparrow missiles, they were worthless unless you had someone in the back seat operating the radar. Great. We got to fly over 'downtown' (Hànôi), without being able to defend ourselves. Jim tried to give my 'technician' a crash course on firing a sparrow, but it mainly confused him.

'I took off and met two flights of 'Thuds' at 'Red Anchor'. My boy got a few still-flicks of their refuelling and then we followed the first flight to the target, which was Thái Nguyên, a real hot spot. I manoeuvred behind the first element as they dived down the chute on their dive-bombing pass and had to dodge most of the flak that was being shot at them. I whipped around and caught-up with the second element of the second flight as they made their bombing runs. By this time the North Viêtnamese gunners were really mad and the sky was full of flak puffs. My technician was duly impressed. I could tell because he never stopped screaming the whole time. Frantic, by this time, I tried to join up with the last Thud off the target, but he outran me. Thank god the MiGs weren't flying. I said good-bye to the F-105s and headed for home. I needed a drink. I found out later that some flak had hit my right camera pod on the lens - recording the hit for posterity, but destroying the pod - well worth it in my estimation.

'The next mission was at night. We were scheduled to attack the rail lines running east out of Hànôi toward China, between Bắc Giáng and Lạng Sơn and a section of track running from Thái Nguyên toward Kép AB. There were major supplies being brought into the country over these lines, including some new MiG-21 fighters. It was a bad area, defence-wise, including everything in the North Việtnamese inventory. The bad part of this plan was the use of flares. Each flight of four had its own flare ship, a fifth man, who was supposed to light up the target for us. This was 1965, before camouflage and our airplanes were painted light grey on top and white on the bottom which meant that the flares would light up our aircraft like reflectors, making it nice for the gunners. This mission was going to be fun.

'We were the number two flight on the eastern-most target and by the time we got there, the gunners were active. The first flare ship recommended that his counterparts dump their flares away from the target as a distraction, since the visibility from the moon was pretty good. They did and the air defences concentrated on the flares. In the meantime, we hit our targets. It didn't take them long to discover their mistake and they quickly returned their fire toward us. We were on our way out by then and the sky lit up with flak over our egress route. Our flight leader decided the Chinese wouldn't mind if we used a little of their airspace and deviated across their border. We got out unscathed.

'While we all had a deep respect for the 'Thud' pilots having to face these missions all by themselves, it was kind of nice to have someone to talk to when things got scary. Our GIBs had a tough job. They were also pilots and had to just sit back there and let the other guy fly and sometimes make mistakes. The GIBs always knew right where we were. They did most of the refuelling. They kept a wary eye out for SAMs and flak and helped with our bombing by calling out airspeed and altitude. Most importantly, they gave us someone to yell at or try to calm when it was us who really needed to vent our fear. Many of our GIBs had to return to the war as front-seaters within the next six months. At least, they were experienced and knew how not to treat their GIBs.

'September 4th, 1965 started the 'four weeks from hell' period of our deployment. On that day we experienced our first shoot-down since the day we'd arrived. During what should have been an easy road reconnaissance mission in Route-Pac I, our Ops Officer, who had consistently demonstrated his lack of understanding of sound combat tactics since the day we arrived, led his guys into a flak trap. His mistake was using standard gunnery range manoeuvering - having each aircraft attack on the same heading. By the time the number three aircraft made his pass, the enemy gunners had found the range and he got hosed badly while trying to silence one of them. Looking back, number two saw a flash and watched the aircraft roll inverted and explode after pulling off target. The crew was listed as missing, although most of us didn't think Jim Branch or Gene Jewell could have survived - taking a serious hit that close to the ground. [3]

'Fighter pilots are a peculiar lot,' Fran always told me. 'Academically speaking, fighter pilots could be categorized as a subculture. They're all full of confidence and verboseness and think they can accomplish anything. Somehow, it's impossible for a fighter pilot to show his feelings,' she'd say. 'What a shame. It's not normal to bottle them up.' I hadn't agreed with her until Ubon, where I witnessed the traits daily. Most of our pilots would sacrifice their lives for their families, country, or friends, without a moment's hesitation. When one of our friends was shot down or crashed, we'd silently go over the particulars of the incident in our minds, thinking how we might have reacted just a little bit differently and maybe survived. We didn't talk much about someone else's errors, we just vowed to remember the circumstances and never let the same thing happen to us. Mistakes are just not tolerated in the fighter business; they cost lives. Somehow, these 'mental exercises' made it easier for us to accept the dangers of our profession. It may be called a defensive mechanism by a shrink, but we all did it. We were very critical of each other in combat as well.

'September 24th 1965 we lost our third aircraft. Four flights were assigned to bomb an old army barracks area near Vĩnh Lihn that was suspected to be loaded with personnel and supplies. It was. When we arrived on target all hell broke loose. The flak was awfully heavy, especially for this area and they were good, 57mm mainly. One of our guys took a bad hit, but made it to the North China Sea and ejected. There were two chutes and two life-rafts spotted in the water, a good sign. An HU-16 Albatross, a Grumman seaplane, was immediately on the scene and made a landing near the shot down crewmen. About this time the North Viêtnamese shore batteries opened up on them, bracketing them with heavy artillery. The rescue bird picked up Wylie Nolen the 'GIB' and started taxiing towards Jack Gravis, the front-seater. The guns had zeroed in by now and the shelling was getting very close. When the para-rescue crewman had trouble getting Jack into the plane, the pilot [Major D. C. Hollenfield], an ex-football player, came back, reached out, grabbed our guy with one hand and literally threw him in the airplane. The Albatross got out of there in a hurry and returned our crew safely to the waiting medics at Đà Nẵng. Turns out the rescue pilot was the same guy who had cracked one of my ribs at Stead AFB, Nevada when I attended survival training. He got a little carried away in hand-to-hand combat practice and put a knee on my chest with a little too much gusto. I can vouch for the fact that he was strong.

'During the rescue operation, Bob Childers, the number three in Jack's flight decided to help the rescue effort - by himself. He instructed his wingman to join up with the totally confused number two aircraft pilot and take him home. Even though Bob didn't have any ordinance, he decided to search out the shore batteries that were shelling our down crewmen. He got a bit carried away and tried to distract the gunners aim by flying low over the emplacements. Our commander ordered him to rejoin the rest of us. Bob said he couldn't, as he was too low on fuel by now to return to Ubon and he would land at Đà Nẵng for refuelling. About a week later, Jack returned to the squadron after being declared fit following a medical check-up at Clark AB. Wylie had compressed his spine during the ejection and was sent back to the States for treatment. The Martin-Baker ejection seat, designed by the British, was known for hurting backs. Your spine was compressed when you were shot out of the cockpit and then stretched when the chute opened abruptly. We called it the 'Martin-Breaker.' [4]

'Six days later, September 30th 1965, Captain Chambless 'Cham' Chesnutt the front-seater and his 'GIB', 1st Lieutenant Mike Chwan had a minor problem just before takeoff. They aborted and returned to the ramp in time to man the spare aircraft and meet the rest of their flight at the tanker. Their flight was scheduled to be the number three group to attack an important target near the Thành Hòa Bridge and 'Cham' wanted to hit it. The Navy had damaged the bridge the day before and the supplies that were scheduled to cross that night had stacked up and were vulnerable. They were also heavily defended. By the time our flight rolled in the sky was full of flak and 'Cham' took a direct hit from a 57mm AAA battery during their dive-bomb run. There were no chutes. Another crew missing; our fourth airplane lost. 'Cham' Chesnutt was one of the best-liked guys in the squadron, who could always find a bit of humour in any situation. He would be missed, as well as his partner in crime, Mike Chwan.

'On 1 October we lost number five. No one could believe it. It was just another routine road-recce mission that didn't go as planned. The flight left 'Blue Anchor' and proceeded toward a section of road west of Vĩnh, letting down en route. They crossed over an unmarked 57mm or 85mm AAA battery located near the Parrot's Beak in Laos at medium altitude and the number four man took a direct hit. No one saw a chute - 'Chuck' Sharf and 'Marty' Massucci would never be found.'

'At 1110 hours, 'Gator' flight had departed Ubon 'Gator' flight to conduct a mid-day strike/road reconnaissance mission against Route 155, which was used to transport war supplies from China to Hànôi; and the NVA's Bàn Chân staging area which was a suspected truck park located near the Black River valley between Sơn La and Văn Yên Provinces and just 25 miles north of the Laotian border. When 'Gator 1' developed mechanical problems and was forced to abort the mission. Captain Charles Joseph Scharf, 32, from San Diego, California in 'Gator 3,' assumed command of the flight and the remaining three aircraft continued to the target area at low altitude to avoid detection by a known SAM missile site deployed in the vicinity of the truck park. The Phantom's performed a 'pop up' manoeuvre to roughly 15,000 feet to look for their target. Because the staging area could not be identified, 'Gator 3' and '4' did not drop their ordnance. According to other flight members, 'their intelligence was poor' consisting of just 'a picture of the jungle with a road running through it.' The crew of 'Gator 2' believed they saw the target and dropped bombs on their pass. All three aircraft were separated after the pop-up manoeuvre. 'Chuck' Scharf radioed 'Gator 2' and '4' that he was 'going up the road.' Captain Steele evidently misunderstood and instead of turning toward the north, he turned south and flew along Route 155 in that direction. Captain Marv Quist watched as the two aircraft headed in opposite directions and then followed the flight leader to the north. He had closed the distance between them to about a mile and a half when Scharf's Phantom (63-7712) was struck by anti-aircraft artillery fire. Quist and 1st Lieutenant Phil Ordway heard 'Chuck' Scharf transmit 'Mayday, Mayday, Mayday' and saw 'Gator 3' start to burn. According to Quist, 'The flame was small at first and gradually increased for about twenty seconds until it trailed the aircraft approximately one plane length.'

'After hearing the three Mayday calls, Quist told Scharf that his aircraft was on fire and he and 1st Lieutenant Martin John 'Marty' Massucci, 36, should bail out. Quist and Ordway observed the lead aircraft as Scharf jettisoned his external stores. The Phantom was surrounded by flashing debris as the ordnance separated from the aircraft and began to fall away from it. At the same time, Ordway saw a parachute in the midst of the debris field and he believed that Massucci knew they were on fire and bailed out thinking the Phantom was coming apart. Quist reported seeing 'people on the ground firing at us with small arms.' After completing a 360-degree turn, 'Gator 4' saw where the flight leader's aircraft had crashed into the jungle on the side of Phú Soung Mountain about five miles southeast of where it caught fire. During the extensive visual and electronic search, no emergency beeper signals were heard and no sign of either downed crewman was found in or around the area of loss. At the time the formal search effort was terminated, 'Chuck' Scharf and 'Marty' Massucci were immediately listed MIA. 'Marty's mother, Florence Massucci was home alone when a telegram arrived telling her that her oldest son was missing in action. She suffered a stroke a short time afterwards and died three years later. Both men were officially declared dead in January 1978.

'Once again, complacency and predictability were part of the scenario. One more mistake, two more pilots missing. One of our flights had been shot at by this battery the day before, but it hadn't been verified by the Intelligence 'weenies' and hadn't been posted on our official flak board. If a pilot reported being fired at to an intelligence de-briefer after a mission, the 'sighting' was reported up the chain of command to our headquarters. If it was a new sighting, they would schedule a reconnaissance mission to verify its existence. We had an unwritten rule to check daily with all of the returning flights to upgrade our own 'flak' maps. They didn't. It was always best to know where the flak might be coming from, verified or not.

'Five days later, October fifth, we lost number six. Our Ops Officer [Captain James Otis Hivner] on his first flight back from TDY was fragged to bomb an ammunition storage area at Thái Nguyên near Hànôi. His flight ingressed on a low-level run across the Red River Delta and they planned to pop up for their bombing runs. The flight leader realized he was off course and had to make a correction to find the target. He decided to follow the always heavily defended rail track south of the target until he found his pull-up point. Big mistake! When he turned down the track, all hell broke loose. The first two aircraft popped up early, dropped their bombs very short of the target and quickly departed the area. The number three aircraft saw the target but was hit during his pull-up. Even though he was burning he continued the attack and he and his wingman put their bombs on the target. Their bird had been badly damaged in the aft section, however, and they were forced to nurse the now-flaming Phantom toward the safety of the North China Sea. Unfortunately, he couldn't keep the aircraft flying and both pilots had to eject. Jim Hivner and Tom Barrett were captured and would spend the next seven years as 'guests' of the Hànôi 'Hilton' guards. The flight leader didn't even know he had lost his wingman until number four caught up and told him. Just another normal day at the ranch.

'By this time, we were all operating on adrenaline. We got four new aircrews from the 43rd Squadron at Cam Ranh Bay and continued to fly. I'll never forget meeting one of my best friends, Russ Kartrude, as he got off of the 'klong' from R&R. He was feeling great, wearing a smile a mile wide, until he saw my expression. 'What happened?'

'I told him we'd lost three more aircraft, bringing the total to six aircraft and ten crewmembers lost.

'Holy Shit!' he exclaimed. 'Unbelievable.'

'About this time our bomb loads were cut back. Instead of eight bombs, we carried only four on our centreline rack. In place of bombs, we loaded four Sidewinder missiles on our inboard pylons. The higher-ups said we had a bomb shortage, although the 'Thuds' seem to have plenty. Then the double counter missions started again. We dropped our four bombs on an interdiction target and then provided MiGCAP for the 'Thuds', sometimes rotating back to a tanker to refuel in-between strike flights. One mission for us; two for the nightly news. The aftermath of a loss was just as trying as the shoot-down. Every missing person had a Summary Court Officer appointed to go through his things, pack up his stuff and generally put things in order. It wasn't a very enjoyable experience to be going through someone's personal things right after a shoot-down.

'We usually reminisced about our missing friend at the bar for a couple of days and then put our feelings away, saving our grief for the night when we were lying in our beds. I vividly remember one of my roommates calling out to his lost friend in his sleep. I never told him I heard. It was not uncommon to hear a muffled cry during the night. I know, for my voice was one of them.

'Following one of our losses, the Summary Court Officer discovered that some of our personnel records were not up-to-date. When we went through the mobility processing line at MacDill before our deployment, we were given the option of signing up for a new life insurance option. The Air Force automatically gave each pilot a ten-thousand-dollar insurance policy in case he was killed during the performance of his duties. They had just started a programme that would allow a pilot to double this amount for about six dollars per month. All of us signed up for it when we went through the line, but we learned that the records had somehow been misplaced and couldn't be verified. Where did that leave our 'missing in action families?' Our personnel guys somehow 'found' their records and the insurance options were verified for everybody. As it turned out, the Air Force pretty much declared everyone who was shot down as missing in action (MIA). While it was terrible for the families not to know whether or not a man was actually dead or alive, the policy was a godsend for some of the immediate families who would have had to get by on a ten-thousand-dollar insurance policy if their husbands would have been declared killed in action (KIA). As it was, the families continued to get their normal pay and allowances, except flight pay, until the Air Force knew for sure. The military didn't do very much right during the Viêtnamese War, but this was one of their best decisions. At least it saved a lot of families from having to suffer even more.

'The situation back home was even worse. At least we knew what was going on. Our families were totally isolated. They couldn't say anything or ask anybody about what was going on because we weren't officially there. The military still hadn't released the fact that we were at Ubon, or that the F-105s were also flying out of Thailand. The remaining pilots at MacDill had access to the news but couldn't tell anyone about it either. It was frustrating for us, knowing what was going on at Ubon and not being able to tell our families. The mail took about seven days between Florida and Thailand and our letters always seemed to cross somewhere in the middle. This and security made it impossible to keep our wives informed with any sort of accuracy. Even though we still were not supposed to say anything about where we were or what we were doing, we all passed enough information to let them know what was going on, being careful not to get too graphic. All of us were worried about upsetting our wives, they had a tough enough time coping with the bills, the kids and keeping their own sanity.

'Fran, as well as others, was really having a hard time dealing with the situation, although she rarely complained to me in her letters. She was hesitant to write anything about her difficulties, being constantly afraid she might upset me. How unfair. I only heard about her problems from a couple of my close friends, whose wives had written to them about her.

'Every day the television news would announce that the Air Force had struck 'X' number of targets in North Việtnam and would also mention if any of the jets were shot down. The commentator would always tell if it was a Phantom or a Thunderchief. Since we were the only Phantoms flying over North Việtnam, it narrowed the odds quickly. When an F-4 was shot-down, Fran would hear about it on the morning radio news and then have to wait until late afternoon to find out who it was - because the chaplain wasn't given the official word until late in the day. Then the chaplain showed up at the family's front door with the bad tidings. My next-door neighbour, Bob Hibbard, who was also an F-4 pilot, made a special point to check with the Intelligence section each day about who had been shot down. He promised to tell Fran if it was me. This wasn't much relief for her, but she thought it was better than waiting and she didn't want Lynn and Robin to hear about it from somebody else.

'Even the wives of the men who were captured were told to keep their mouths shut about everything, not only about flying out of Thailand but about the fact that their husbands were prisoners of war. The Air Force told them that their husbands might be tortured if anybody found out. Consequently, they were scared to death and didn't receive comfort from anyone, even their ministers or priests. Then there was Jane Fonda. Her diatribe of our captured pilots was relentless and a favourite with the press. What a war. Some of the 'Thud' pilots wore patches about her - 'Commie Bitch' and the like. Our commander wouldn't let us wear one, although most of us had one in our lockers.

'The 'GIB' from our third shoot-down, Wylie Nolen, got home about the time that all of these problems were emerging. He told Fran that conditions at Ubon were really bad and that 'the guys were leading themselves,' which for the most part was true. This news, on top of everything else, was difficult to take for Fran and the other wives to take. The military wife is a special breed and she takes most separations in stride. She mows the lawn, fixes the car, handles the finances, takes care of the kids, does community volunteer work and does it all with a smile on her face. She keeps the family going. This situation, however, was just too much to ask. There were a lot of unhappy campers at both ends of these separations.

'Meanwhile, back at the ranch, we kept on flying. Most of us were pretty surly and were spending a little too much time at the bar complaining. Our commander thought we needed a diversion and insisted that we play a little volleyball after work, instead of going to the bar. Well, as the story goes, 'You can tell a fighter some things, but you cannot tell him much.' We didn't want to play games and we told him so. He ordered us to play, so play we did - With a vengeance. 'Combat rules,' we decided, 'no holds barred.'

'After the second night we boasted two sprained ankles, one broken finger, plus a lot of bruises, egos included. The commander let up and so did we. We might just as well make the most of it, we thought. The goal now was to survive the tour.

'The flying also became more routine. With the exception of the far north route-pacs, four, five and six, we pretty much owned the sky. We didn't have to worry about SAMs in the southern packages and the MiGs hadn't been flying much at all. The AAA was still in evidence around the major targets, but even the defences there seemed to have lightened up a bit. From then on, we spent a lot more time hitting supplies that were being moved down the 'trail.'

'On one mission, as the flight leader approached the target, he called for the other aircraft to 'arm-em-up,' reminding the flight to turn on the switches that allowed the bombs to drop. I guess the number-four man front-seater had his thumb on the bomb release button when he armed the switches and the bombs all came off, then and there, over the jungle. Instead of saying anything he just pressed on, as if nothing had happened and followed the rest of the flight through their bombing runs, getting shot at in the process. The flight leader noticed the smoking hole in the jungle when he egressed the target and figured out why he hadn't seen number four's bombs impact the target. Perhaps this was one of the reasons why so many of our GIBs had grey hair.

'Suddenly it was October and the fall monsoon had started. We had rain almost every day. Our Ground Control Approach (GCA) controllers hadn't practiced their skills much lately, so our Ops Officer decided that everyone would fly two or three consecutive GCAs when we returned from a mission, not just one. Again, his policy was overkill. Not only was it tiring, it used a lot of fuel and cut into the maintenance turnaround time. Sure enough, we had one of those 'pop-up' thunderstorms during GCA practice one afternoon and the whole flight was low on fuel. The GCA controllers had problems seeing the aircraft through the heavy rain and a simple low-fuel situation became a real emergency. The man with the least fuel took the barrier on the approach end. The next pilot made his landing from the other direction and took that approach end barrier. They were considering putting the third guy in the centre barrier and were hoping to get number one and two untangled in time to trap the last man. Fortunately, the rain let up and our barrier personnel were fast enough. We got three and four on the ground using normal landing techniques. Another day at the ranch.

'There was lots of construction around the base, some of which was beginning to show real progress. A Thai construction company had started renovating our 'hooches' with enclosed side walls and air conditioning. They were only doing them one at a time, however, so it would take a while before all of us could benefit. Our Officers Club though was about ready for the grand opening. In two weeks we would be able to order our dinner from a menu. Of course, heaven forbid, we'd lose our $1.90 per day and our mess hall privileges.

'Some things never seemed to make any progress, however. They'd been building a swimming pool across from the club for about three months now and it had never progressed further than making a muddy hole in the ground. It would never be opened on our tour. The ramp and maintenance areas were also starting to look like a real Air Force base. Even the roads were being paved.

'The modernization really sunk in when we received our first camouflaged Phantom. Boy, did it look different out there among our old dirty grey aircraft. All these changes emphasized one thing: the United States was here to stay - although no one wanted to admit it.

'The flying became routine for the most part. There were still plenty of scary targets up there, but everyone seemed to take them in stride. We even talked about them sometimes, admitting that we were scared. Maybe we were growing up. I remember a road-recce mission on a section of road just west of Hòa Bình in route pac four. I was flying with a borrowed 'GIB', Ben Ringsdorf; Jim was sick. The flight had been pretty uneventful. We hit a cave complex, where the North Viêtnamese occasionally stored ammunition and got a small secondary explosion. Guess somebody was there. As we proceeded on, I noticed something bright about a mile or so in front of me. It was moving and looked like a telephone pole. The duck (SAM) theory prevailed. 'If it's big and white, has a big fireball at one end and is following you, then it must be a SAM.'

'Cobra. SAM. Twelve o'clock level. Let's take it down.' We were only about 3,000 feet above the ground at the time.

'Cobra. It's tracking me. I'm pushing over straight ahead,' I said, watching my check-list hit the top of the canopy because of the negative Gs.

'I should beat it if I can get low enough,' I said to Ben, who was groaning as the missile passed approximately 500 feet on the right and kept climbing. Thank God. It was probably fired visually and never locked on.

'I decided against looking for the SAM site, as we only had two bombs left. Besides, you never attacked a SAM site with just bombs if you could help it - it wasn't good for longevity.

'Later, Ben told Fran he could see the veins in the tree leaves, we were so low.

'We still 'owned the skies' over much of North Viêtnam and were slowing down the supply of weapons to the south. The constant bombardments of their key targets were taking their toll. Don't get me wrong, there were still plenty of AAA and SAMs around our targets and we were still losing planes, but you could tell that we were making a difference.

'The technology advances were also starting to make a difference as well. The Navy stationed an 'Electronic Frigate' called 'Red Crown' up near the Red River estuary, that could follow inbound strike flights with its special radar and tell them if a SAM site was operating. They also called out a warning anytime a SAM was launched. The Air Force also had an EC-121 aircraft with similar capabilities that would orbit the area during 'big' missions. [5]

'One of our flights, 'Deer', was part of a group assigned to hit a bridge at Sơn Tây. As they approached the target 'Red Crown' advised 'Deer' flight of a SAM launch. The number four man, Bob Childers, heard the call, saw two missiles and made a SAM break, jettisoning his bombs during the manoeuvre. The flight leader, as well as the rest of the flight, hadn't heard or understood the call and the leader transmitted, 'Say again for 'Deer' flight.' They didn't realize that three missiles had been launched at the flight and elected to press on. Fortunately, the SAMs missed. By now, still not understanding the situation, the leader realized that number four had left the formation and called for him to rejoin. Four replied, 'Are you nuts, I just broke for a SAM and jettisoned my bombs.'

'He was told to rejoin again, but by now he was on his way to Ubon. The rest of the flight survived and RTB'd (returned to base) after they dropped their bombs. There was an inquiry and the Squadron Commander decided to send the GIF back to MacDill, to await further action. You guessed it; this was the same guy that helped RESCAP his shot down buddy.

'About this time we heard that the squadron would leave by the end of November. 'Will we be home for Thanksgiving?' someone asked. No one knew. But that news, along with the improved quarters, gave us all a lift.

'On November first, Ubon officially became the home of the 8th Tactical Fighter Wing. Our squadron, although a member of the 15th TFW back in Florida, became unofficial members of the 'Wolfpack,' the 8th TFW logo. We had a new Wing Commander in our newly opened headquarters building and, as an old fighter pilot, he provided some much-needed stability and leadership around the place. We wanted to show our new Wing Commander that we were professionals in spite of their actions. Suddenly everyone was trying to get as many missions as possible before we left. That part hadn't changed, however. Our Ops Officer still tried to keep everybody exactly equal, juggling formed crews against their will - following his orders to the end.

'At last, the big day, 20th November. After greeting the new guys and giving them the straight skinny on the important stuff, we jumped aboard the C-130 and headed for civilization.

'We arrived at Clark AB in the early evening, just before dark. The next morning we went to the BX, 'en masse' and cleaned them out of socks and underwear. Even my new stuff was red by now. We'd all saved one ratty set to show our wives; otherwise, they wouldn't have believed us. We spent one more day at Clark and sat by the pool for most of it. They moved us out of the condemned quarters, but our enlisted troops didn't fare so well - they had to stay in 'roachville.'

'The next afternoon, we boarded a couple of non-scheduled DC-8s and headed for home. The aircraft flew to Hawaii, on to Travis AFB California and from there straight to MacDill. Our families met us on the ramp and our reunions began. I kissed all three of my girls and gave Fran an extra-long hug; remembering the one she'd given me when I left. After the reunions, I learned that Faye, the wife of my best friend, Russ, had given birth to a baby girl on November 20th, the day we left Ubon. What's more, we had been asked to be her godparents. This was really a good day.

'Everyone tried to take thirty days leave, but I got hooked for a special assignment after the second week. A couple of us had been selected by the Wing Commander to debrief a group of 'experts' at the Pentagon and help them build a briefing for the Air Staff about our equipment, tactics, enemy defences, etc.

'We want both the positives and the negatives,' they emphasized during our in-briefing. My buddy and I joined six 'Thud' drivers and built the mother of all briefings. It had a few positives and plenty of negatives. We told them a lot of things they didn't want to hear: the F-4 needed a built-in gun; the F-4 needed more power - and a way to stop the engines from leaving a big black smoke trail. And everyone needed better bombs; the Sparrow missile needed improvements and a whole list of things. We made a special comment about letting the on-scene commanders have a say in selecting targets and the use of tactics.

'There were a standard list of gripes: Let a professional military man define the rules of engagement - Please stop assigning us the same times on target for JCS target - just so they'd coincide with the Air Staff briefing - It wasn't a good idea to show up on the same time every day - Just because McNamara wanted our mission results early in the day, didn't mean it was good policy - Besides, it wasn't good for our pilots longevity - Quit double logging sorties - Just let us do one mission at a time - with the right weapons for the mission - We weren't photographers - stop the picture taking - And for God's sake don't halt the bombing - It gave the enemy time to regroup during the pauses. All on deaf ears. The highest-ranking officer to hear the briefing was a full colonel and he about choked when he saw it. [6]

'So much for that. We returned home to find out what our new assignments would be. When we got back, the base was buzzing with the news about one of our squadron mates, Bob Childers, who was being court-martialled. Our commander had charged, Bob, who'd refused to leave the RESCAP at Vĭnh Lihn and made the SAM break at Sơn Tây with: 'Deserting his flight leader in combat.' No one could believe it. Insubordination? Maybe we'd buy that charge. Taking evasive action without being told by the flight leader? Yes, maybe, if that's against the rules. But desertion? No way!

'After the case was presented and after a couple of our pilots testified as to what really happened on the mission, the court-martial was dropped. And wouldn't you know it, all but one of the pilots that testified on behalf of the defendant were passed over for promotion. Then the record of the inquiry was classified secret and promptly disappeared.

'About this time President Johnson, in an apparent effort to bolster his ratings and appease the protesters, called for a six-week bombing halt in North Việtnam. 'In the spirit of Christmas and Tet' he'd said.

'The North Việtnamese immediately constructed three new SAM complexes in the southern route-pacs and equipped all their missiles with an optical launch capability, making them much more potent. New radar-tracking units were installed at their 57mm AAA batteries, hundreds of 23mm guns were sited along the Hồ Chi Minh Trail and every unit was re-supplied with ammunition. The runways on the northern fighter bases were repaired and new MiG-21 aircraft were added to their inventory. Their Air Defense command and control systems were also modernized, giving the MiGs a tactical advantage for the first time.

'This one 'political gesture,' in effect, had negated all of the gains and advantages we had won during our deployment. Had our ten pilots sacrificed their lives and freedom for nothing? And what about the PoWs?

'But it was over for us now; we had our wives to hold and comfort us when the bad dreams came. I was reassigned to our wing academic section where I would teach tactics to student pilots who'd be going to war. Many of the people in our squadron were reassigned. Most of our GIBs returned to units in Southeast Asia or went to Europe as GIFs. Ironically, we trained them and spent a lot of time in their back seats. I got to check out Jim, which was a real pleasure. The mood was different; the squadron was different. We got a new Commander and Operations Officer and never looked back.

'I must say that the comradeship we shared at Ubon was special. Whoever it was that said, 'Fighter pilots who fought together were bonded for life,' knew what he was talking about.

'Fran often asked me 'What does it feel like to be a fighter pilot?' I could never give her a very good answer. I couldn't take her with me in the cockpit, although I'd always wished I could. There was always something missing between us when it came to flying and it seemed impossible to share the emotional side of it. How could I explain to her that fighter pilots didn't 'feel' when they were flying. Oh yes, they felt exhilarated when they added power for takeoff or flew a low-level mission at 100 feet and 500 knots. They also felt good when they did things right. It is something every pilot is brought up with. My first flight instructor told me: 'Imagine that someone is always watching you. You should strive to make the perfect takeoff, hold the perfect position in formation, fly the perfect instrument approach and make the perfect landing - every time you fly. You must constantly aim for perfection,' he'd said. 'That's the way you stay alive in this business.' Another key to becoming a good pilot is control. First, you must learn to control your machine. You must completely understand how all of your aircraft's systems operate in order to get the most out of your machine. You must understand what the aircraft can and cannot do and how your skills fit into the process. These are the easy things to control through study and practice. Next, you must learn to control your environment. Of course, you cannot control the weather, but you can make the smart choices when you are flying in it. The tactical environment is the second most difficult situation to control. You must know your enemy, both his weapons and his mind. You need to know how enemy pilots and gunners are trained and how they'd react in specific tactical situations. You must also have a general game plan about how you should react when you meet him in combat. And you had to consider your wingmen and always base your actions on their abilities, not yours. Just because you can do something well doesn't mean that they can.

'The third and most difficult situation to control are your emotions. There is simply no place for emotions when you're flying a fighter, especially in combat - they interfere with common sense. I'm not saying that fighter pilots don't have emotions, I'm saying that they need to save their emotions for later - after the flight. Sure, we all experienced fear when we first 'came-up' on strike frequency and heard someone being shot at - Or when someone was calling from the ground on a rescue mission. But emotions come in phases. When we'd 'roll-in' on the target, the focus was to achieve the perfect bombsight picture at release altitude, nothing more. Later you could look for the flak, or check that your wingman was safe. Once the join-up was completed and the battle damage check was over, then you might discuss a few emotional things with your 'GIB'. 'Wow! That flak scared the shit out of me.' But mostly we talked about whether or not we got our bombs on target, or where the enemy guns were located so we could tell the debriefer. The things that might save lives on the next mission.

'Later, while lying on my rack, I'd remember the mission I'd flown that day. How helpless I'd felt when that 'Thud' took a hit. If the mission hadn't been up to par, I might wonder why I'd reacted the way I had or wondered why hadn't I done better? If the mission went very well I always wondered why I'd excelled that day, but couldn't do it every time? I can still remember all the 'successes' and 'failures' to this day.

'We all worried, privately, about the consequences of our bombings and whom we might have killed. But we couldn't dwell on that if we wanted to succeed and keep our sanity. We also had our own feelings about our comrades who'd been shot down, but very few of us could share those feelings with a friend. Every now and then, someone might mention: Remember old 'X,' how he used to do this or that? Then everyone would grow quiet and the subject would change.

'I always had difficulty discussing the loss of a colleague with Fran. When I did, she would sometimes cry and that made me uncomfortable for bringing up the subject - not wanting to appear weak by showing my true feelings. I also didn't want to hurt her or burden her with the reality that the next time it might be me.

'It's hard to understand emotions when you're taught not to show them your whole life - in my age group this was especially true. Regardless, I think a person needs to have a certain mind-set in order to be a successful fighter pilot. At times we're all bravado and always seem to be having fun. But many times it's a method for controlling the pressure - at least it was for me. Fighter pilots are taught to cope with the most difficult situations and cope they do. It's part of the profession.

'In the new millennium, our young fighter pilots fly the most advanced and sophisticated aircraft in the world. Yet they're not that different in spirit to us. They'd have fit in nicely at Ubon.

'I returned to Southeast Asia in 1970 for almost a year. I flew another one hundred combat missions in South Việtnam, but the feelings and motivations were never the same as they'd been at Ubon.'

Endnotes Chapter 2

1   On 12 February 1973 only Keirn was released from captivity.
2   James Robinson 'Robbie' Risner, a double recipient of the AFC, had become an ace in the Korean War and commanded a squadron of F-105s on the first missions of Operation 'Rolling Thunder' in 1965. He flew a combined 163 combat missions, was shot down twice and was credited with destroying eight MiG-15s. Risner retired as a brigadier general in 1976.
3   Captain James Alvin Branch, 31 and 1st Lieutenant Eugene Millard Jewell, 23, of Topeka, Kansas were killed.
4   In an ejection operation, once the handle is pulled, the seat is designed so that the remainder of the sequence is all automatic until the pilot hits the ground. After ejecting at high altitude, a small drogue 'chute deploys, which stabilizes the seat and pulls out the main 'chute after the seat falls to an altitude of about 14,000 feet. Then a barostatic device initiates the man-seat separator after which the personal parachute deploys automatically..
5   The 'Red Crown' early warning radar ship was officially designated 'Positive Identification Radar Advisory Zone Ship', while the airborne counterpart, the EC-121, coded 'Disco', provided MiG warnings. 'Red Crown' was more effective along coastal areas and 'Disco' in inland areas.
6   Disheartened, McNamara left office on 29 February 1968. In his memoir, *In Retrospect,* he said, 'I do not know to this day whether I quit or was fired.'

Chapter 3

'Operation Bolo'

Of the 379 USAF aircraft lost in 1966, 42 were F-4Cs in combat and fourteen operational losses. In 1967 seventeen MiG-21s were shot down by the USAF - sixteen by the F-4Cs and one by a 433rd TFS, 8th TFW F-4D - for the loss of 95 F-4Cs and 23 RF-4Cs. Remarkably, January-June 1967, USAF jets shot down 46 MiGs, including seven MiG-17s by two Phantoms and five F-105s on one day, 13 May. From April-July 1967 the USN accounted for a dozen MiGs. In May 1967 Colonel Robin Olds, CO, 8th TFW at Ubon RTAB, became the leading MiG-killer in South East Asia to add to his WWII score of thirteen enemy aircraft destroyed.

All during the Christmas holidays the lights burned late in the operations complex at Ubon Air Base in north-eastern Thailand. A bold plot was being hatched. Only a handful of men knew about it yet, but if it worked, a task force of American fighters would lure North Việtnam's new MiG-21s up from their sanctuaries and destroy them. It was December 1966, the 23rd month of the air war over North Việtnam. The war had recently entered a more aggressive phase. The North Vietnamese pilots, now flying MiG-21s as well as the older MiG-17s and -19s, had stepped up their attacks on American fighter-bomber formations. When one of the 'Wolfpack's pilots, Captain John B. Stone, the wing tactics officer, came up with a plan to allow the 8th TFW to pull a trick on the MiGs, Olds was willing to listen. Stone possessed neither the rank nor the background to become the lead planner for the largest, most complex fighter operation in the Việtnam War to date. A country boy from Coffeeville, Mississippi, he graduated from the University of Mississippi in 1959 and nearly joined the Forest Service in Montana. He loved the excitement of fighting fires, but figured that flying fighters with the Air Force was probably even more exciting. After an assignment flying the F-102 at Soesterberg RNAFB in Holland, 'eating lots of Indonesian food and drinking Indonesian beer,' Stone returned to the United States with four other 102 drivers to train in the F-4 and head to Southeast Asia. Of this original group only Stone would escape being shot down or killed.[1] Stone's suggestion was simple: fly formations of Phantoms fitted for air combat just as if they were a strike package of F-105s and then take on the MiGs when they came up to attack. Olds gave the OK for Stone and other pilots to begin planning the mission. Late in December, Seventh Air Force ordered the first fighter sweep of the war against the MiGs in the Red River Valley north of Hànôi. It was to be called 'Operation Bolo' named after a Filipino traditional knife and there had been little debate about who should plan and lead it. 'We gave the job to the man most likely to succeed,' an Air-Force general would later tell the *New York Times*. 'We gave it to Olds, of course.'

The phrase is a good description of Colonel Robin Olds,' the *Times* commented: 'All-America tackle and Captain of the football team at West Point; husband of Ella Raines, the actress; quadruple ace in World War II; full colonel at 30 years of age; and now at 44, everybody's choice as the hottest pilot of the Việtnam War.'

Born on 14 July 1922 in Honolulu, Robin Olds was the son of Robert Olds, a fighter pilot in World War I and later an aide to Billy Mitchell. Eloise, Olds' mother, died when he was four and he was brought up by his father, who gave him his first flight at the age of eight, in an open-cockpit biplane. In his later years, Robin Olds would speak with admiration of the great leaders - Ira C. Eaker, Carl A. Spaatz and others - who met often at his home, as his father eventually rose to the rank of Major General. Robin began to gain prominence while a cadet at West Point, where he played tackle on both offence and defence and was named an All American. He graduated from West Point in 1943 - the year of his father's early death - and months later graduated from pilot training, with his wings being pinned on by General Henry H. 'Hap' Arnold himself. Young Lieutenant Olds was well-trained, with more than 650 hours in aircraft, including the Lockheed P-38 Lightning, when he entered World War II combat. He flew with the abandon of a man who knows he is invulnerable and for whom the enemy is only a target. Olds began his sensational rise as a fighter pilot in Europe. He flew with the 479th Fighter Group and was given command of a squadron at the age of 22. He flew 107 missions, scored twelve aerial victories and destroyed another 11½ enemy aircraft on the ground. His knowledge of air combat grew with his victories and so did his willingness to speak out about his beliefs - no matter how contrary they were to current doctrine. It was a trait that would work more often against him than for him.[2]

Ralph F. Wetterhahn was a 24-year-old first lieutenant when he first met Robin Olds, who had arrived at Ubon on 30 September. 'We had heard about Olds. He had flown P-51 Mustangs and P-38 Lightnings over Europe in World War II. We'd also heard that he had been on the general's list some years before, but had been redlined from promotion. We were curious to meet this resurrected bad boy and soon after his arrival, everybody got the opportunity. He ordered all pilots to come to the main briefing room - the first time we'd all been brought together. I wouldn't have wanted to address that crowd. We had no respect for leaders because they weren't flying and couldn't talk to us about flying. And we had all the discipline (and about half the maturity) of the Los Angeles 'Dodgers' in a dugout brawl. But the room was quiet. And Olds gave the first version of what J. B. Stone, a captain with the outfit and its savviest tactician, came to call the colonel's 'I'm-the-new-guy speech.'

Stone recalled. 'He got everybody together and just laid down the rules. After he told us how it was going to be, he'd say, 'I'm the new guy. You know a lot that I don't know and I'm here to learn from you. But in two or three weeks, I'm gonna be better than all of you. And when I know more about your job than you do, you're in trouble.'

'Over the next few weeks', continues Wetterhahn 'Olds began flying combat missions with the 433rd. He had flown on the first Air Force jet aerobatic team and was a hell of a pilot. He continued giving the speech every now and then, always ending it with the challenge 'I'm gonna be better than you.' He also visited the other squadrons and all the maintenance areas. He talked to us in the officers' club. Almost overnight, it seemed, he knew all our names. During the three months prior to Olds' arrival, the wing had lost an entire squadron's worth of airplanes. Twenty-two pilots were dead or missing. Getting to the magic number to finish a combat tour -100 missions over North Viêtnam - seemed impossible. Olds had turned things around and not a single member of that wing ever wanted to fail in his eyes. By November the wing's operationally ready rate had increased nine percent and losses had dropped dramatically.

'Some pilots seem born for combat. They thrive on a steady dose of danger. Robin Olds was one of those. I remember him as a disciplined, professional officer, but he was also a fierce fighter who bristled at and frequently outmanoeuvred, the political constraints that kept his wing from doing damage to the enemy. Olds began sporting a handlebar moustache and he and his vice commander 'Chappie' James, the first black officer to rise to four-star rank, got new nicknames: 'Black Man and Robin.' [James, 47, had flown 101 combat missions in P-51 Mustang and F-80 aircraft in Korea. He would fly 78 combat missions into North Viêtnam, many in the Hànôi/Hảiphòng area.] We also referred to Olds, who was all of 44, as 'Old Man.' We were still wise-asses, but we weren't screw-ups anymore.

'On a typical evening at the officers' club bar, *Snoopy Versus the Red Baron* would be playing on the jukebox for the sixth time and half the place would be singing along. Olds would be knocking back scotch the way you empty a water glass. He might catch you out of the corner of his eye and his eyes would lock onto yours so hard somebody'd get hurt if they walked between the two of you. After he had a few drinks, conversation with him was like toying with a cobra. He could turn on the most innocent of comments. Olds made it clear to us that he didn't care much for statistics. He was after results. He stalked onto the stage of the briefing room one morning with a fistful of papers - decoration requests that flight leaders had filled out for his signature. He said there was a lot of interesting reading in the forms about flak, SAMs and MiGs, but not very much about targets being destroyed. 'Some of you want medals for just showing up' he said and dropped the stack of papers in a trash can.'[3]

Advance word on 'Operation Bolo' was on a strict need-to-know basis. Every pilot in the wing was put into intensive training for the role he would play in the MiG Sweep, but great care was taken to make this seem part of a more general training programme. Air crews who would fly 'Operation Bolo' were not told about it until Sunday morning. Ground crews knew only that something big was coming as they laboured to get the airplanes into peak condition. 'They didn't know what was afoot, but every man felt the sense of urgency,' Colonel Olds would write later in *Air Force Magazine*. 'I found one crew chief hobbling about his bird on crutches, his broken leg dangling in a cast. He told me he didn't know what was going to happen, but he was making blankety-blank sure his bird was ready for it.' As for Colonel Olds, he divided his time between preparations at Ubon and shuttling back and forth to brief other Southeast Asia wings selected to participate in 'Operation Bolo.'

So far in the Viêtnam War, American pilots had shot down 27 MiGs and fourteen of these were by the 'Wolfpack' at Ubon. Their success in 'Operation Bolo' would hang on a classic deception: could they mislead the enemy into thinking that their F-4C Phantoms were bomb-laden F-105s and thereby get Hànôi Air Defence Command to commit its MiGs against what appeared to be an irresistible target? MiGs could differentiate F-105s from Phantoms from the electronic signature emitted by their QRC-160 pod which jammed the 'Fan Song' range-finding radar of the SA-2 surface-to-air missile battery. 'Fan Song' got its name from its horizontal and vertical fan scanning antennas and its distinctive sounding emissions, which could be picked up by warning equipment. 'Fan Song' performed two functions: target acquisition and missile guidance. It acquired as many as four targets before firing. After launch, it guided up to three SA-2s against one target. According to John Stone, the QRC-160 transformed a blip on a SAM operator's radar to a solid line. When a flight of four or more aircraft flew with their pods turned on in a tight formation, these solid lines blurred together and rendered Fan Song useless. Stone believed that if the jamming pod was installed on the 28 F-4s and using F-105 tanker anchors, refuelling altitudes, approach routes, approach altitudes, airspeeds and radio call signs and communications to simulate a normal Thunderchief strike force, the MiGs could be tricked into thinking that they were the more vulnerable F-105s and attack. The Phantoms would fly every leg of their mission just as the F-105s would. Normally, fighter pilots did not talk much to each other in transit, but they would put out a few radio calls to simulate Thuds making checks and so forth. Instead of bombs, the F-4Cs would be armed with heat-seeking Sidewinders and radar-guided Sparrows.

'Operation Bolo' was laid on for Monday, 2nd January. Weather conditions over the target area were poor and considerable cloudiness and overcast was forecast. A one-hour delay was instituted to await more favourable weather over Hànôi. Annoyed at having stayed sober for New Year's Eve, many of the Eighth's pilots (including Olds, briefly) went directly to the bar and began to party. At 'Oh dark thirty' on the night of the first, Stone and Olds decided that the mission was a 'go'. Stone ate his dinner of liver and onions outside the briefing room that evening. [4]

On 2 January all other flying was cancelled for the day and all designated units went into high gear to carry out the operation. The 'Bolo' task force consisted of 56 F-4Cs organized in two groups with seven flights of four aircraft each, one group from the 8th TFW and the other from the 366th TFW; six flights of 24 F-105 regular 'Iron Hand' Thunderchiefs in the 355th and 388th Wings for defence suppression; four flights of F-104s; four EB-66 jamming aircraft and supporting flights of EC-121 'Warning Star' and KC-135 aircraft. The 'Warning Star' was known to pilots in theatre as 'College Eye' and later 'Disco' for its call sign. The fighter forces were drawn from the 355th, 388th, 8th and 366th Tactical Fighter Wings. Another hundred aircraft were to perform diversionary strikes. The F-4Cs of the 8th TFW became the West Force and were to bring the MiGs up and cover suspected orbit areas as well as Phúc Yên airfield and Giá Lâm Airport on the outskirts of Hànôi. The F-4Cs of the 366th TFW, designated the East Force, were assigned to cover Kép and Cát Bi airfields and to block approach routes to and from the north.

Monday at Ubon was tense and the tension grew when, during aircrew briefings, the order for an hour's weather hold on the mission came through from Seventh Air Force. Then, finally, the word flashed from Sàigòn to execute 'Operation Bolo.'

'OK, you Wolf pack, let's get 'em,' Colonel Olds shouted.

The pilots and backseaters suited quickly and climbed into their waiting fighter planes. Almost every flyable F-4 in the wing was going. Phantoms strung out in seemingly endless file waited their turn to wheel onto the runway. Then they were off two by two, into the afternoon sky. Even the spares, those aircraft standing by to fill in for last-minute aborts, went. It was an awesome air armada. There were fourteen flights of Phantoms: seven from the 'Wolfpack' and seven from elsewhere. In addition, six flights of F-105s would accompany them in and strike at SAM sites in Route Pack Six.

The 28 Phantoms of the 8th TFW departed first, with twelve Phantoms in a first wave that took off at about 1225 local time, followed by fourteen aircraft about a half-hour later. Pilots and backseaters had tired of the jumbled code words issued in the daily frags from the 7th Air Force, nonsense like 'Rolleye' and 'Junetime,' which might be friendly aircraft call signs one day and SAM warning codes the next. They were too difficult to use in the heat of battle. So they named their flights after cars: 'Olds', 'Ford' and 'Rambler'. Colonel Olds' call sign, chosen with a sense of humour by someone on the operations staff at Seventh Air Force, was 'Olds Lead.' The first wave was divided into three flights, with Robin Olds commanding the 'Olds' flight, Colonel Daniel 'Chappie' James, Jr., commanding the 'Ford' flight and John Stone commanding the 'Rambler' flight with 1st Lieutenant Clifton P. Dunnegan of Winston-Salem, North Carolina, three minutes behind 'Ford'.

Across the Black River, they swept, on the typical F-105 ingress route. Below them was an unbroken floor of clouds. Their centre-line auxiliary fuel tanks ran dry and were dropped. 'Olds Flight' increased speed and crossed the Red River. Phúc Yên airfield at the southern end of 'Thud Ridge' was six minutes, 23 seconds ahead. The cloud deck below hid the peaks of 'Thud Ridge'. Everything the North Viêtnamese knew about how the Americans operated indicated that this was a large strike force of F-105s. The American flyers had hoped for better weather. With clouds stretching all the way to the horizon, the Hànôi air defence commander tracking the inbound formation of aircraft might not commit his MiGs, even if he fell for the deception. He might figure that the undercast would so limit the effectiveness of visual bombing by the Thuds that it was not worth the risk to try stopping them. Furthermore, if the MiGs did come up, the clouds would offer them a place to hide from the F-4s.

Olds, knowing he might only get one shot at executing this plan, pressed on. He led the flight to a point twenty miles from Hànôi and called 'Green Up!'(F-105 jargon for 'Arm bombs') Much to his surprise, no MiGs showed up to meet the decoy flight. About two minutes from Phúc Yên, Colonel Olds' back-seater, 1st Lieutenant Charles C. Clifton of Fort Wayne, Indiana, momentarily picked up a radar blip, possibly a low-flying MiG, but lost it. 'Olds' Flight passed Phúc Yên and circled back. Still no MiGs. 'Ford Flight' arrived and hurtled by, a thousand feet away.

'Olds 3' then picked up a fast radar return about seventeen miles from his 12 o'clock. The MiG was closing at a very high rate, indicating a head-on situation. The MiG zoomed under the flight and ducked into a cloud layer. Olds, continuing to lead the flight toward 'Thud Ridge', spotted several MiG-21s coming up through the cloud layer. He immediately initiated a hard-left turn to gain a firing position. For Olds, this would be his first engagement with an enemy jet. In his excitement, he almost shot all his missiles trying to get his first MiG. First, he salvoed two radar-homing AIM-7Es at minimum range. The missiles failed to guide. Next, he launched two heat-seeking AIM-9 Sidewinders at the MiG-21, now a mile and a half away, but these missiles guided on the clouds instead of the MiG. Meanwhile, another MiG-21 started closing on the flight from the rear quarter and started firing its cannon at 'Olds 3'. Ralph Wetterhahn flying aircraft 2 as Olds' wingman remembered that moment distinctly. 'I'm watching this MiG about to kill us and my backseater's [First Lieutenant Jerry Sharp] getting a little bananas.'

After Olds' Sidewinders failed to guide Wetterhahn immediately salvoed two AIM-7Es at the MiG in front. The first missile simply fell off the rail, but the second missile did guide and exploded just behind the MiG. 'I saw this fireball behind his tail,' Wetterhahn explained 'and I thought, 'God damn, I missed him!' The MiG continued flying for a few more seconds and then went end over end 'shedding large portions of the aft section. The aircraft, now emitting black smoke, went into a flat spin, falling through the clouds like a leaf.' The Sparrow's warhead, which consisted of expanding rods, had unfolded like a carpenter's ruler and, in the words of Wetterhahn, 'basically cut the ass end off this MiG-21.' [5]

In the 13 January 1967, issue of *Time* magazine, Olds would describe the ensuing dogfight as 'a swirling battle that covered a huge part of the sky.' Crews pulled and positioned and launched missiles for what seemed like hours, but the fight really lasted only nine minutes.

'Olds 4', flown by Captain Walter S. Raedeker III of Asheville, North Carolina and 1st Lieutenant James E. Murray III of McKeesport, Pennsylvania later reported: 'We continued the right turn when 'Olds 03' called contact below the cloud layer. The flight then turned left and down, but the contact passed under the flight, exceeding radar tracking capabilities. As the flight began climbing again, 'Ford' flight, which had just entered the target area, called MiGs at 'Olds' 6 o'clock.

'Olds!' called out Captain Everett T. 'Razz' Raspberry in 'Ford two'. 'You have MiGs at your six o'clock!' Raspberry, 34 was a 'good ol' boy originally from Macon, Georgia, latterly Fort Walton Beach, Florida. His first jet assignment was with the 309th Strategic Fighter Squadron flying the F-84F Thunderstreak and later he flew the F-100 Super Sabre. Eventually, he flew nuclear alert with them while station in Korea and afterwards was sent to USAF Fighter Weapons School at Nellis AFB, Nevada where he 'really learned to fly and fight'. He graduated the 'Top Gun' of his class. He was selected as an instructor for the inaugural F-4C Fighter Weapons School at Nellis - 'one of the first group of guys to fly the Phantom'. When he first laid eyes on the F-4 he thought 'Boy oh boy, this is a big mother!' 'The more you saw of it, the bigger it got. It seemed bigger because the fuselage was so much wider and it seemed you could have a basketball game inside the thing.' He arrived in SE Asia on Thanksgiving Day 1966. He began his combat tour by flying regular missions anticipating that 'Wild Weasel' Phantoms would be arriving shortly but they never came. By Christmastime, he had almost half of his 100 missions in. [6]

Olds saw MiGs pop through the clouds off his wing and looking over his shoulder, saw the one Raspberry had seen, coming at him from behind. Olds broke his flight to the left.

'Olds babe, you've got one right on your ass!' 'Olds two' sang out.

Olds tightened his turn. Now the MiG could not bring its guns to bear and Olds shifted his attention to another MiG, this one in front of him. Clifton obtained a radar lock-on, which would guide the Sparrow missiles toward the MiG's fuselage. The missile leapt forward, guiding true, but the radar broke lock. Olds quickly fired a heat-seeking Sidewinder, but that missed, too and the MiG disappeared into the clouds.

'Rambler' Flight, coming in along the east side of 'Thud Ridge', heard over their headsets the crackling exchanges between 'Olds' and 'Ford' Flights in the battle area.

'Olds, where are you?' queried Captain John Stone in 'Rambler' Lead.

'Find your own' came the answer from someone. By now, MiGs were not that difficult to find. As Major Phil Combies of Norwich, Connecticut would later recall, 'There were MiGs all over the sky.'

Radeker and Murray reported: 'Olds 01' and '02' concentrated on two MiGs, one at 8 o'clock and one at 10 o'clock. We then performed a high-speed yo-yo which afforded us an excellent advantage on one MiG-21, who passed under us apparently tracking 'Olds 03'. The second MiG-21 was no longer visible behind us so we dropped down behind this MiG. Initially, we had a very poor Sidewinder tone. We then added some power and climbed slightly and the Sidewinder tone became excellent. The missile was fired after the radar-heat switch had been transferred to the heat position and guided right into the MiG. It struck slightly forward of the tail, immediately resulting in a burst of black smoke and a violent tuck-under. The MiG was observed to be uncontrollable and violently falling, still trailing smoke.'

As Radeker's and Murray's MiG entered the overcast, 'Olds lead' and 02 had just completed successful attacks on their MiGs. Olds and Clifton had headed southwest and saw another MiG come up through the clouds, going east at Olds' 10 o'clock position. Olds broke sharply in pursuit, slammed full afterburner, pulled in hard to gain position and prepared to attack with Sidewinders. 'Olds explained, 'I pulled the nose up high, about 45 degrees, inside his circle. Mind you, he was turning around to the left so I pulled the nose up high and rolled to the right. This is known as a vector roll. I got up on top of him and half upside down, hung there and waited for him to complete more of his turn and timed it so that as I continued to roll down behind him, I'd be about 20 degrees angle off and about 4,500 to 5,000 feet behind him. Frankly, I am not sure he ever saw me.'

Olds pulled up low and behind the shiny MiG-21, got a good growl from his Sidewinders and squeezed the trigger twice. The first Sidewinder hit the MiG, tearing the right wing away in a bright red flash. What was once an aircraft outlined by the sun against a brilliant blue January sky became a twisting, corkscrewing, tumbling hunk of metal and it fell end over end into the clouds. No one could see if the pilot had ejected. Looking for other MiGs, Colonel Olds checked his fuel level and gave the order to head for home when Radeker reported 'Bingo' fuel. (Reaching a minimum predetermined fuel state that would allow a particular sequence of events or RTB (return to base).

Colonel James commanding 'Ford' Flight had entered the target area just as the MiGs began to engage and had seen 'Olds lead' blast the wing off the MiG from a few miles away. James noted the NVNAF tactic of double attacks from MiGs located at different positions of the clock: 'My flight was attacked by three MiG-21s, two from 10 o'clock high and one, simultaneously, from 6 o'clock low. I did not see the MiG at 6 o'clock at first, as I had already started to counter the attack of the two closing from the front quarter. My rear seat pilot called me (very urgently), stating a MiG was closing from 6 o'clock and was in missile firing range on my number three and four aircraft. I was a bit hesitant to break off the attack I already had started on the other two MiGs, as I had just seen Olds flight pass underneath us a few seconds before and I had a fleeting thought that this was who my rear-seater was seeing. However, I quickly max rolled from a left bank to a steep right and observed the low MiG as called. I called a hard right break for 03 and 04. As they executed, the MiG broke left for some strange reason and for a split second was canopy-to-canopy with me. I could clearly see the pilot and the bright red star markings.'

A lone MiG decided to jump 'Ford' Flight's right flank. If he could bring either his 30mm gun or his Atoll missiles to bear, he was in excellent position to make a kill. 'Chappie' James had seen the MiGs attack develop and had something more than escape in mind. As the MiG drew nearer, James ordered 'Ford Three' and 'Four' to break hard right. 'As they did so,' recalled James 'the MiG broke left for some mysterious reason and for a split second we were side by side. We were so close that, besides the red stars in his wings, I could clearly see the pilot's face. I began a horizontal barrel roll to get away from him and into an attack position. Once in position, I launched a Sidewinder. The missile missed because the evading MiG broke left at full throttle. But when he did it, he put himself in the line of fire of my number 2, Captain Raspberry. I told him to press the attack as the two aircraft that I had initially engaged had now swung around into range, head-on. I had a good missile growl and fired two AIM-9s in rapid succession at them. I immediately rolled over to reposition in fighting wing position on Captain Raspberry. We continued down and remember thinking he was getting a little inside optimum missile parameters.

Captain 'Razz' Raspberry and 1st Lieutenant Robert W. Western of Carrolton, Alabama in 'Ford 02' executed a rolling manoeuvre, placing them in perfect position to fire the AIM-9B at the MiG's 6 o'clock at a range of about 3,500, Raspberry assuming that the MiG pilot was not aware of the F-4C's position. Raspberry recalled: 'As a wingman, my job was to protect my leader and that's what I was going to do. I headed for the MiG and he broke into a right turn as I went into a hard left. At one point we were 50 feet away from one another, canopy to canopy, as I rolled over the top of him. As I chased him I knew I had one shot because only one AIM-9 was working. I also knew through all my training that I had to fore that sucker between minus 1g and 2g and be a certain distance behind him. As we manoeuvred around I realized that I was in too close and was concerned my missile wouldn't track properly. I was becoming even more disappointed when I saw him make a run for the clouds and knew an infrared missile would not have a good chance tracking him. I thought he was going to get away. Suddenly, just before he got to the cloud deck, the MiG-21 reversed his turn and I knew this was my one chance. I went to zero-g and had my pipper right on him and squeezed the missile off. That AIM-9 shot out like a bullet and impacted between the cockpit and tailpipe. The MiG swapped ends and stalled out and went into a slow spiral and fell into the undercast.' [7]

Colonel James followed it down and observed the MiG disappear into the clouds and bursting into flames. He called Raspberry and directed him to rejoin in wing position. James headed for the 'Olds flight' but they were already rejoining to proceed out of the area. James covered their egress from 6 o'clock high and departed the area with them.

The third West Force flight fought in two separate engagements. Captain John Stone had monitored the radio chatter of Olds and James and had asked if his flight could assist, but he received no intelligible reply. Nearing Phúc Yên, 'Rambler 02' in Stone's flight observed MiG-21s at 3 o'clock and at a distance of six nautical miles, coming up out of an overcast in an easy left turn. Because of his radio failure, however, he could not alert Stone and the other members of the flight and himself take the lead, a practice which was a pre-briefed procedure for a flight member making MiG contact. Major Philip Combies and 1st Lieutenant Lee R. Dutton of Wyoming, Illinois at 16,000 feet in 'Rambler 04' also observed the flight of four MiG-21s and an additional two in trail at a distance of two or three miles. Stone sighted two of the MiGs crossing over Phúc Yên in a 3 o'clock position about 4,000 feet below at a range of two nautical miles. As Captain Stone's flight began closing, the MiG flight leader broke left and Stone steepened his turn to follow. This placed 'Rambler 04' on the outside of the echelon, in a position where he had to go high to clear the other members of the F-4 flight, who were turning into them.

Combies later described the chase and the victory: 'Shortly after completing the turn to the northwest we spotted a flight of four MiG-21s in loose formation, 2 o'clock low at six to eight miles. At one to two miles behind were two more MiG-21s. Due to their position 'ahead of the beam' I wondered if they were being vectored against us or possibly against 'Olds' or 'Ford' flights, who were initiating their egress from the area. As the MiGs crossed in front of Stone, he started in on them, breaking left and down. This caused the flight to slide to the right and I wound up high and right from the remainder of the flight. I went 'burner' and held minimum 'burner' throughout the initial engagement. The MiGs broke left and our flight commenced the engagement. Dutton secured, by boresight, a full system lock-on one of the MiGs. I had selected radar and interlocks out and had no difficulty in tracking the MiG. I don't think I pulled over four g's at any time during the whole battle. Using the Navy tactic of disregarding the steering dot, I pulled lead on the MiG using the reticule. When I felt I was where I wanted to be, I pulled the trigger, released, pulled again and held. I did not see the first Sparrow at all. However, I saw the second from launch to impact. 'We were about a mile behind the MiG, in a left turn, at approximately 12,000 feet at the time of launch. The second Sparrow impacted in the tailpipe area followed by a large orange ball of fire and a chute sighting.'

'I was startled to see his chute hanging there,' Combies said later. 'How could he get out of the airplane before the explosion? I suppose he saw the missile coming and ejected. He could have seen the rocket fire coming out of the Sparrow's tail.'

Meanwhile, two MiGs (probably the fifth and sixth aircraft) manoeuvred to gain an advantage on Stone and his wingman who were attacking MiGs 1 and 2 from the flight of four. One of the pursuing MiGs passed low between the two F-4s and the other fired cannon at angle off, with no effect. Captain Stone and 1st Lieutenant Clifton Dunnegan in the lead aircraft broke right in an evasive manoeuvre and reversed back to the left to continue attacks on the first and second MiGs. Stone in the meantime lost his wingman, who ended up in a left barrel roll, high, where he mistakenly joined 'Rambler 04', thinking he had rejoined Stone. Stone again closed behind the same two MiGs and fired three Sparrow missiles. He recalls: 'I called for boresight and continued to turn to position for the kill. Due to the excessive chatter and not knowing for sure whether we were locked on, I fired three AIM-7Es. I maintained illumination of the target by tracking with the pipper. I planned to fire in salvoes of two. The first Sparrow was not observed, so I fired two more. The second missile detonated just at the wing root. The MiG caught fire and the pilot ejected.'

'Rambler 03' piloted by 37-year old Major Herman Ludwig Knapp in the 433rd 'Satan's Angels' had also attacked a MiG, probably the fourth plane in the four-ship flight, which had been in pursuit of Stone. Knapp, who was from Roselle, New Jersey, had locked on at 2½ miles and launched two AIM-7s at a 1½ mile range as the MiG dived into a left spiral. The first Sparrow did not guide and the second followed the MiG into the clouds. No impact was observed and this MiG could not be claimed. [8]

Minutes later, Stone's flight had its second encounter. Stone picked up three radar contacts to his right and at a distance of twelve miles. He turned right to identify these contacts, but then he visually acquired two more MiGs at 10 or 11 o'clock, three miles away in a left turn. He turned left for position on these MiGs, intending to launch a Sidewinder, but he was unable to do so because at that moment 'Rambler 03' called a MiG on the tail of an F-4.

'I turned toward my 7 o'clock,' said Stone 'and saw a MiG at 700 feet, firing. I initiated a hard break up into the MiG. When I reversed I could not see the MiG nor did I have my wingman. I then unloaded to make separation.'

'Rambler 02' and 'Rambler 04' had tailed in behind other MiGs, which split, with one or more going left and down and one going right and up. 'Rambler 02', flown by 1st Lieutenants Lawrence J. Glynn of Arlington, Massachusetts and Lawrence E. Cary of Pawnee City, Nebraska followed one of the MiGs. 'Rambler 04' followed another. Glynn fired two Sparrows at his MiG; the second one hit and the MiG exploded. He flew through the debris, which caused some damage to the underside of his aircraft. The MiG pilot bailed out, thus raising the day's score to seven victories for the 'Wolf pack'. Glynn then fired a Sparrow at still another MiG, but it passed about 2,000 feet in front of the enemy aircraft.

Combies and Dutton in 'Rambler 04' lined up on the MiG they had been pursuing. The North Viêtnamese pilot, who had been after Combies but lost him, rolled out, rocking his wings and looking for the Phantom as he climbed. Combies fired two Sparrows at the MiG but neither missile made contact with the target and he launched his four Sidewinders. Two detonated near the aircraft and as the last two Sidewinders were about halfway to the MiG and looking good, Combies suddenly heard one of the F-4 pilots on the radio yelling 'F-4C, I don't know your call sign but there's a MiG on your tail. Break hard right!'

'Cripes, every F-4 up there broke right' Combies said.

When Combies broke hard right, he failed to see what happened to his missiles. 'Later, we learned he was warning John Stone, who had a MiG-21 firing at him, but who evaded and knocked one down. I cleared myself and rolled back, to the right where my MiG was. No MiG, just a guy hanging in a chute. His airplane and mine were the only two in that particular piece of the sky that I knew about. The MiG probably blew up or fell through the clouds. I put him down as a probable.'

Glynn spotted two more MiGs, but could not attack because his radio was out and he did not desire to break formation with Combies. Before the flight departed Phúc Yên, one other MiG attacked 'Rambler 02' with cannons and eight to ten rockets, but Glynn pulled hard left and escaped the barrage.

'Olds', 'Ford' and 'Rambler' Flights, running low on ordnance and fuel, headed out. Colonel Olds passed command to Major Fred Crow in 'Lincoln Lead'. But the battle was over for the MiGs, too. They had retreated into the clouds and would not rise again. The shooting part of the MiG Sweep had involved only the first three flights of Phantoms.

A crowd was gathered on the ramp at Ubon and the first flight of birds made traditional victory passes. The first F-4 touched down and taxied in. As it passed the wing command centre, Olds raised his hands and clasped them together, indicating that the mission was a success. When the last Phantom touched down, there was a silence as figures were being compared, then a yell of 'all safe,' a gasp of air and the thoughts and sounds of victory were all around.

Colonel Olds herded his pilots off to de-briefing. As yet, no one had an accurate count on how many MiGs had been shot down.

'Okay,' said Olds. 'Let's have one at a time, starting with lead flight.' Gradually, they pieced the story together.

They had shot down seven MiG-21s - of which North Viêtnam had but 15.

When Colonel Olds met with reporters, somebody asked him what he thought of MiG-21 pilots. 'I think,' said the master of the MiG Sweep, 'they are very aggressive. I think seven of them made mistakes. We out flew, outshot and outfought them.'

Without the loss of a single American aircraft, Operation 'Bolo' had accounted for the destruction of seven enemy MiG-21s - nearly half of the North Viêtnamese operational inventory at that time. Had the weather been more favourable, Olds' 'Wolf pack' would probably have destroyed several more enemy aircraft. Although these losses hurt the enemy, the NVNAF had more MiG-21s stored in crates at Phúc Yên. Operation 'Bolo', however, did without question establish the air-to-air superiority of the F-4C over the MiG-21.

'It was quite a day,' said Phil Combies, 'but you should have seen the night. My head hurts thinking about it.'

Crews were decorated with Distinguished Flying Crosses and Olds received his third Silver Star. He threw a huge party for the maintenance crews. After that, the parties seemed to go on continuously.

Colonel Olds missed the evening's celebration. He was in Sàigòn, making a personal report that brought a broad smile to the face of General William W. 'Spike' Momyer, the nail-hard fighter tactician who commanded Seventh Air Force. The 'MiG Sweep' created quite a clamour in the press. It had, said *Time Magazine*, 'chopped Hô Chi Minh's air arm off at the elbow.'

An opportunity to perpetuate another ruse presented itself a few days later when RF-4C weather reconnaissance aircraft was forced to abort their planned weather reconnaissance missions in North Viêtnam because of MiG attacks on 3 and 4 January 1967. To lure the MiGs into the air, two F-4Cs on the following day flew, in close formation, a route similar to that normally flown by weather reconnaissance aircraft. The intent of the F-4Cs was to deceive the enemy radar operators into believing that only one aircraft was flying a weather reconnaissance mission. The F-4Cs flew above cloud formations topping out at 7,000 to 7,500 feet, but they made no radar contacts nor encountered any enemy aircraft.

Scheduled MiGCAP for an F-105 strike mission was cancelled due to weather conditions on the 6th and the 'Wolfpack' decided to try the ruse one more time. Two Californians, Captain Richard M. Pascoe of Lakeside and 1st Lieutenant Norman E. Wells of Redwood City crewed 'Crab 01' the lead F-4C; Major Thomas M. Hirsch of Rockford, Illinois and 1st Lieutenant Roger J. Strasswimmer who was from the Bronx manned 'Crab 02'. They flew in a 'missiles-free' environment, i.e., any sighting or radar con-tact could only be an enemy. When they encountered radar-controlled AAA near Phúc Yên, Pascoe turned on the ECM pod to deflect the radar lock and caused the flak to become inaccurate, falling either short or wide of the flight. Pre-planned tactics called for an attempt to establish radar contact with MiGs, manoeuvre the F-4s to Sparrow parameters, (i.e., within the linear range of the missile) and then proceed from there. The ruse worked.

The flight made radar contact with four MiGs about 25 miles northwest of Hànôi and immediately Pascoe pounced on them. Pascoe reports: 'I manoeuvred the flight by use of airborne radar to effect a visual identification of four MiG-21C aircraft and fired two AIM-7 radar missiles at the enemy flight leader. The second missile struck the MiG aircraft in the fuselage midsection and detonated. The MiG-21 was seen to burst into flame and [fell] in uncontrollable flight through the clouds.'

Hirsch had launched an AIM-7 at this same aircraft, but his missile apparently did not guide and there was no detonation. Pascoe continued the attack, on the second MiG, which dived into the clouds. Seeing the third and fourth MiGs at Hirsch's 6 o'clock position, he barrel-rolled into them at their 6 o'clock, but they also disappeared into the clouds. Pascoe continued turning hard right, assuming the MiGs would continue their turns in the clouds.

When the third and fourth MiGs came out of the clouds in wing formation, level, Pascoe barrel-rolled left to decrease lateral separation and to drop to the rear of the enemy aircraft. But they spotted him during the roll and turned into him. As soon as he completed his roll, Pascoe put his gunsight pipper on the fourth MiG's tailpipe, switched to heat, heard a Sidewinder tone and fired an AIM-9 to 'keep their attention,' even though he realized that his angle was too high. The missile passed about 300 to 400 feet behind the MiG. He fired another Sidewinder, which passed close to the MiGs tail but did not detonate.

The two MiGs reversed and the fight degenerated into a slow-speed scissors during which Pascoe fired a third Sidewinder. It missed. The third MiG pilot seemed to realize he was getting into a disadvantageous position and left the area, but the fourth MiG continued the scissors manoeuvres.

Hirsch wrote in his report about locking on to the fourth MiG: 'In rolling to watch one of the enemy aircraft dive away I lost sight of the flight leader. Approximately one minute later I picked him up and saw two MiG-21s reappear from the undercast in a climb. The lead F-4 engaged the MiGs as I turned to close on them. As I approached I obtained a radar lock-on to a MiG-21 which was in a right climbing turn. As I slid in from his 4 o'clock position to his 5 o'clock, I fired an AIM-7 with full radar computing system. The MiG steepened his climb to near vertical and appeared to lose airspeed. When next observed the MiG was in a nose-down attitude and rolling slowly. Just prior to entering the undercast in this attitude, both crewmembers in the #2 F-4 observed the MiG pilot eject and separate from the seat.'

Because he was in a turning manoeuvre, Hirsch could not follow the missile's track. The AIM-7 did not seem to detonate, thus the MiG either flamed out, or the pilot lost control.

The two MiG-21 kills of 6 January and the seven enemy losses earlier in the month dealt a serious blow to the North Viêtnamese. For the next two months, NVNAF fighters showed an understandable lack of aggressiveness. The NVNAF was obviously stunned by its losses and entered another intensive training phase. Although American strike forces occasionally sighted MiGs in their normal operating areas, none of the MiG pilots challenged them to combat. During the latter part of January and through February and March, the northeast monsoon was in full swing. MiG activity was therefore curtailed as much by weather as by the need for additional training. The lull in the air-to-air war was only temporary. The MiGs began to venture forth once again during March as American air strikes intensified. Although no longer rising in force, only in four-aircraft flights, the North Viêtnamese patrolled only their own bases. A few MiG-21s did attempt single aircraft attacks against American strike forces, while MiG-17s conducted their attacks on a more or less random basis, following the well-established tactic of attacking just as the strike aircraft entered into or recovered from a bombing run.

Endnotes Chapter 3

1 *Fast Movers: Jet Pilots and the Vietnam Experience* by John Darrell Sherwood. (2000).
2 *The Robin Olds Factor* By Walter J. Boyne *Air Force Magazine,* June 2008.
3 Originally published in *Air & Space/Smithsonian,* August/September 1997.
4 *Wolfpack Assassin,* by Lieutenant Colonel Everett T. Raspberry as told to and written by James P. Busha, *Flight Journal,* 2 April 2014
5 Colonel Wetterhahn would fly F-4C Phantoms on 180 missions over North Viêtnam in three combat tours. Later he flew Navy A-7E Corsairs.
6 *Wolfpack Assassin,* by Lieutenant Colonel Everett T. Raspberry as told to and written by James P. Busha, *Flight Journal,* 2 April 2014.
7 See *Wolfpack Assassin* by Lieutenant Colonel Everett T. Raspberry as told to and written by James P. Busha, Flight Journal, 2 April 2014.
8 On 24 April 1967 Major Knapp and 25-year old 1st Lieutenant Charles David Austin of new Canaan, Connecticut were killed after their flight of four Phantoms had just bombed their target, a five span bridge four miles north of the centre of Hànôi.

Chapter 4
Tailhookers and MiGCAP

'We have driven the MiGs out of the sky for all practical purposes.'
Lieutenant General William W. Momyer, commander of the Seventh Air Force in a report on 16 August 1967 to a Senate subcommittee While General Momyer's statement was momentarily true, the picture soon changed and in late August the North Viêtnamese pilots introduced new tactics. These called for the MiGs to approach American forces at low level, climb quickly to altitude, make a single firing pass and then run for their home bases (including some in China).

For the men of the 'Tonkin Gulf Yacht Club' 1967 was, for the most part, a repeat of the previous year although tragedy was to strike both the *Forrestal* and *Oriskany* and both carriers were taken out of the line. For the other carriers operating in the Gulf of Tonkin, operational highlights during the year included strikes against North Viêtnamese airfields beginning on 24 April from the *Kitty Hawk* and the continuing rivalry between Crusader and Phantom crews. By the summer of 1968, F-8 pilots would lead the Phantom crews by seventeen to twelve but no victories were scored by either aircraft between September 1968 and March 1970 and from spring 1972 onwards F-4s went on to score all the victories. The Crusader was known as the 'MiG master' but it was the Phantom which scored the most Navy MiG kills; 36 - double that of the F-8. Altogether, seventeen attack carriers made a total of 73 combat cruises and spent 8,248 days on-the-line during the nine years between the Gulf of Tonkin Incident and 1972. Attack carrier fighters scored 56 confirmed and four probable victories. The most victories were by squadrons embarked aboard the *Constellation* with fifteen kills. Navy operational losses during the war totalled 299 fixed-wing aircraft and 35 helicopters. Marine Phantoms from VMFA-531 'Gray Ghosts' were assigned to Đà Nẵng airbase on South Viêtnam's northeast coast on 10 May 1965 and were initially assigned to provide air defence for the USMC. They soon began close air support missions (CAS) when VMFA-314 'Black Knights', VMFA-323 'Death Rattlers' and VMFA-542 'Bengals' arrived at the primitive airfield. Marine F-4 pilots claimed three MiGs (two while on exchange duty with the USAF) at the cost of 75 aircraft lost in combat, mostly to ground fire and four in accidents.

By 1967 VF-151 'Vigilantes' and VF-161 'Chargers' on the *Coral Sea* attributed three of their seven combat losses to SA-2 missiles, On 4 January Air Wing 2 from the *Coral Sea* mounted a major strike against a road bridge at Thúy Diễm on the coast twenty miles south of Haiphòng. One of VA-22's Skyhawks that bombed the target it was hit by ground fire causing a fuel leak and had to be abandoned soon after crossing the coast when the aircraft started to burn furiously. The pilot was picked up safely by a Navy SAR helicopter. About ninety minutes after the first strike another wave of aircraft from the *Coral Sea* attacked the Thủ Thiêm Bridge. This wave included Phantoms of VF-

154 'Black Knights' dropping Mk.82 bombs. Just as Lieutenant Alan M. Vanpelt had dropped six bombs in a shallow dive, his cockpit lit up with fire warning lights and his port engine was seen to be on fire. The fire spread rapidly and a wingman reported pieces of the aircraft falling off. A few miles out to sea he and his backseater Ensign R. A. Morris ejected and they were picked up by a Navy helicopter. As no AAA had been observed during the attack on the bridge it was assumed that these two aircraft were the victims of chance hits by small arms fire or automatic weapons.

In the late afternoon of 20 February 1967 an F-4B flown by Major Russell Clemensen Goodman, 33, of Salt Lake City, Utah, a USAF pilot serving on an exchange posting with the Navy and Ensign Gary Lynn Thornton, 25, of Porterville, California took off from the *Enterprise,* part of a section of two Phantoms of VF-96 assigned to attack a railway siding at Thiên Lin Đông eight miles southwest of Thành Hóa. As Russ Goodman's aircraft (150413) approached the target at about 1727 hours he popped up to 11,000 feet and commenced a dive to drop Mk.82 bombs on the railway trucks that were sitting in the siding. As Major Goodman started to pull out of his dive his aircraft was hit either by AAA or a surface-to-air missile (SAM) in the left front section. Ensign Thornton could not establish contact with Major Goodman. Before he ejected from the badly damaged jet at just 250 feet altitude, Thornton noted that Goodman was either dead or unconscious because his head was down and wobbling back and forth. Thornton ejected but there was no sign of Goodman. [1]

During March and early April 1967 F-105s destroyed seven MiGs and then on 23 April three F-4Cs of the 366th TFW encountered two flights of two MiG-21s each. In 'Chicago 03' Major Robert D. Anderson of Tulsa, Oklahoma and Captain Fred D. Kjer of Allen, Nebraska made the only MiG kill during this encounter. They saw two MiG-21s in a staggered trail formation entering a left climbing turn into the strike force and jettisoned bombs and left outboard external wing tanks to engage. Anderson was unable to turn tight enough to decrease angle-off and reversed to the right to rejoin the strike force. The flight immediately sighted two more MiG-21s in staggered trail passing off the right wing. They entered a right climbing turn at maximum power. 'Chicago 01' began a right turn, attempting to set up an attack on the lead MiG. The other MiG was in the contrail level in a left turn. The missile fired from 'Chicago' lead was tracking the MiG when both went into a cirrus cloud.

'Chicago 03' continued accelerating to attack the other MiG. With the pipper on the MiG, a boresight radar lock-on was obtained and then a full system lock-on. The range was marginally close for a successful Sparrow shot. A climbing turn to the outside was initiated and the pipper placed again on the target. The radar was still locked on. One missile was fired that left the aircraft going slightly right of the MiG-21, but guided back to the target, striking the MiG in the right aft fuselage. A large explosion was observed and fire and fuel began streaming from the MiG. It continued the left turn and bank increased until inverted and went straight into the ground. The MiG was hit around 32,000 feet and impacted at about sixteen miles northeast of Thái Nguyên. No chute was observed.

'The one thing I learned,' Anderson later commented, 'is that you can't afford to be complacent up there. You have to keep looking around. The MiG pilot thought he was out of the fight, home free. He made no evasive manoeuvres. I don't think he ever saw me or knew what hit him.'

After two years of political indecision, the first major strike on the MiG bases took place when Kép and Hòa Lac airfields were attacked on the 24th resulting in the loss of two naval aircraft at Kép. The strike force was protected by a TARCAP flight of six F-4Bs of VF-114 'Aardvarks' from the USS *Kitty Hawk.* They were led by 35-year old Lieutenant Commander Charles Everett Southwick, who was born in Fairbanks, Alaska, with Ensign W. Laing as his backseater. Southwick had attacked North Viêtnamese patrol boats during the original Gulf of Tonkin incident in August 1964. As the Phantoms and the strike force approached Kép they came under heavy and accurate anti-aircraft fire. Southwick's aircraft (153000) was hit by AAA as he escorted the first wave of bombers out of the target area. The aircraft appeared to be little damaged but in any case the crew were faced with a more pressing problem when they were attacked by eight MiGs of the 923rd Fighter Regiment. The Phantoms reversed course and headed towards the MiG-17s, four low down and four at the same altitude as the Phantoms. One of the MiGs passed over the Phantoms and Southwick reversed his course again, caught up with the MiG and shot it down. However, there was little time for celebration as Southwick's wingman warned him of another MiG-17 that was on his tail. Another Phantom flown by Lieutenant H. Dennis 'Denny' Wisely, who had shot down an An-2 Colt biplane on 20 December 1966[2] and Lieutenant (jg) Gareth Laverne Anderson, 25, of Falmouth, Massachusetts, destroyed the MiG before it could do any damage for the first of their two victories in North Viêtnam.[3]

As the Phantoms retired towards the coast Southwick discovered that he could not transfer fuel from the wing tank. Unable to reach a tanker in time, Southwick and Laing ejected over the sea about twenty miles south of Hon Gai and were rescued by a Navy helicopter. On 14 May Lieutenant Commander Southwick and Lieutenant David John Rollins his backseater were shot down on a strike on the Thành Hóa Bridge was accompanied by a flight of F-4s that attacked the densely packed anti-aircraft defences around the target. Southwick rolled in from 9,000 feet and at 500 knots in a 30-degree dive he fired his Zuni rockets. As the aircraft (F-4B 153001) pulled out of its dive both engines suddenly flamed out. Probably as a result of ingesting debris from the Zuni's. The crew ejected as they could not restart the engines and both were quickly captured. [4]

On 26 April the 366th TFW destroyed another MiG-21. This one was hit by Major Rolland W. Moore Jr. of Barberton, Ohio and his pilot, 1st Lieutenant James F. Sears of Milan, Missouri, flying 'Cactus 01', the lead aircraft in a MiGCAP flight dispatched to cover a large F-105 strike force attacking the Hànôi transformer site. The flight met about ten MiG-21s with Moore engaging three of them in turn. Moore looked up at 9-10 o'clock and picked out one of the several MiG-21s orbiting to the left over Phúc Yên. Sears turned hard, nose high, to get at the MiGs at a 7 o'clock position. He got one in his sight reticule and selected radar, while Sears went boresight until he obtained a full system lock-on.

'We've got him,' called out Sears. 'Fire!'

Moore depressed the trigger. The AIM-7 tracked smoothly toward the MiG's 6 o'clock position. The deadly missile gained on the MiG - 2,000 feet, 1,000 feet, trailing steady. The MiG rolled out of the turn and disappeared from Moore's sight into the cumulus clouds at the southern end of 'Thud Ridge', but this manoeuvre was not sufficient to escape the explosion.

This air battle had taken place near Phúc Yên airfield, where the F-4s came under AAA fire in spite of the proximity of the MiGs. All flight members felt that the MiGs could have landed at the airfield at any time, but chose instead to lure the flight over the field, where the enemy appeared to be coordinating the attack between SAMs, MiGs and AAA.

Since the beginning of the year, F-4s had been employed more for strike missions than for MiGCAP, but if the bombing campaign was to be continued without unacceptable losses of strike aircraft, it would be necessary to divert a portion of them back to MiGCAP role. Accordingly, the USAF began to sandwich a flight of F-4s behind a lead flight of F-105s and to place another Phantom flight in trail behind strike forces. As a result, during May, 26 MiGs were destroyed with a loss of only two Phantoms in 72 USAF and USN MiG encounters. Most of the MiG victories were credited to USAF fighters. While fifteen of them were the victims of the MiGCAP Phantom crews, six were shot down by aggressive F-105D Thunderchief pilots. The first victory in which F-4Cs were providing MiGCAP barrier for F-105 flights came on 1 May, while the F-105s were on a RESCAP mission.

In the 390th TFS, 366th TFW, North Dakota born Major Robert G. Dilger was flight leader in 'Stinger 01'. 1st Lieutenant Mack Thies from Houston, Texas was his back-seater. Dilger detected two or three enemy aircraft approaching from his 12 o'clock position at 8,000 feet and descending, at which time he warned his flight of the MiGs, which then pulled up vertical and rolled to the right, enabling the F-4s to end up in a 6 o'clock position to the first two MiGs. Dilger and his wingman engaged the enemy and one of them fell. Dilger wrote: 'I acquired a boresight lock-on and fired an AIM-7. The MiG-17 dived for the deck and made a hard turn into the attack. The missile missed. I yo-yoed and again was at the MiG's 6 o'clock. I fired a Sidewinder which could not turn with the MiG-17, as he broke into the attack and went even lower. In exactly the same manner I yo-yoed and fired two more missiles from his 6 o'clock. On each attack, he would violently break into the missile. On the fourth pass he broke hard right and struck the ground while trying to avoid the missile, which was tracking toward his 6 o'clock. He spread in flames across a large area.' [5]

On 4 May the 'Wolfpack' at Ubon provided two flights of Phantoms for MiGCAP for five F-105 flights of the 355th TFW which was on a strike mission. Colonel Robin Olds, the 8th Wing commander, led the rear flight, flying as 'Flamingo 01' with 1st Lieutenant William D. Lafever of Losantville, Indiana. The other F-4 flight was sandwiched midway in the strike force. MiG warnings crackled on Olds' radio just before his wingman sighted two MiG-21s at 11 o'clock, attacking the last of the Thunderchief flights. Colonel Olds' account picks up the encounter at this point: 'The MiGs were at my 10 o'clock position and closing on 'Drill' [the F-105 flight] from their 7:30 position. I broke the rear flight into the MiGs, called the F-105s to break and manoeuvred to obtain a missile firing position on one of the MiG-21s. I obtained a boresight lock-on, interlocks in, went full system, kept the pipper on the MiG and fired two AIM-7s in a ripple. One AIM-7 went ballistic. The other guided but passed behind the MiG and did not detonate. Knowing that I was then too close for further AIM-7 firing, I manoeuvred to obtain AIM-9 firing parameters. The MiG-21 was manoeuvering violently and firing position was difficult to achieve. I snapped two AIM-9s at the MiG and did not observe either missile. The MiG then reversed and presented the best parameter yet. I achieved a loud growl, tracked and fired one AIM-9. From the moment of launch, it was obvious that the missile was locked on. It guided straight for the MiG and exploded about 5-10 feet beneath his tailpipe.

'The MiG then went into a series of frantic turns, some of them so violent that the aircraft snap-rolled in the opposite direction. Fire was coming from the tailpipe, but I was not sure whether it was normal afterburner or damage-induced. I fired the remaining AIM-9 at one point, but the shot was down toward the ground and the missile did not discriminate. I followed the MiG as he turned southeast and headed for Phúc Yên. The aircraft ceased manoeuvering and went in a straight slant for the airfield. I stayed 2,500 feet behind him and observed a brilliant white fire streaming from the left side of his fuselage. It looked like magnesium burning with particles flaking off. I had to break off to the right as I neared Phúc Yên runway at about 2,000 feet, due to heavy, accurate, 85mm barrage. I lost sight of the MiG at that point. Our number 3 saw the MiG continue in a straight gentle dive and impact approximately 100 yards south of the runway.'

Colonel Olds then took his flight to the target area and covered the last of the 355th TFW strike aircraft as they came off the target. Leading his flight to Hòa Lac airfield and dodging two SAMs on the way, he found five MiG-17s over that airfield. 'We went around with them at altitudes ranging from 1,500 to 6,000 feet, right over the airdrome,' Olds reported. The F-4s ran low on fuel before any real engagements occurred, however, and were forced to break off this encounter.

Another raid on the NVA barracks at Hải Dương took place on the 12th. Forty-four year old Colonel Norm Carl Gaddis of the 390th TFS, 366th TFW at Đà Nẵng was flying wing for Colonel Frederick Corbin 'Boots' Blesse in a CAP flight of F-4Cs. Blesse graduated from the United States Military Academy in 1945. He flew two combat tours during the Korean War, completing 67 missions in F-51s, 35 missions in F-80s and 121 missions in F-86s. During the second tour in F-86s, he was officially credited with shooting down nine MiG-15s and one La-9. At the time of his return to the United States in October 1952, he was America's leading jet ace. General Blesse remained with fighter aircraft for practically his entire military career. During the 1955 Air Force Worldwide Gunnery Championship he won all six trophies offered for individual performance; a feat never equalled. He served two tours in Southeast Asia;

while on his first tour in 1967-1968 he flew 156 combat missions. General Blesse again volunteered for combat duty and in April 1967 was assigned as director of operations for the 366th Tactical Fighter Wing at Đà Nẵng. During this one-year tour of duty, he flew 108 combat missions over North Viêtnam and another 46 in Laos and South Viêtnam. He was decorated for valour for helping unload the bombs from a burning F-4 Phantom during a rocket attack.

At the age of eighteen, armed with a dream of flying and the desire to serve his country, Norman Gaddis enlisted in the Army Air Corps in the months following the bombing of Pearl Harbor. He was commissioned in 1944 and flew P-40s and P-51s in the USA before being demobilised in 1945. He was recalled to active duty in 1949 and flew F-84Gs on ground attack missions during the Korean War. After many appointments including tours with the 81st TFW at Bentwaters in England and the Fighter Weapons School at Nellis AFB, Nevada he was posted to Cam Ranh Bay in November 1966. By 1967 he was the director of operations of the 12th TFW but was flying with the 366th during an exchange programme where the DOs of F-4 and F-100 fighter wings flew with other wings for a short period to exchange views on tactics. As the strike force was retiring from the target a couple of SAMs were fired at it then several MiG-17s appeared on the scene. Gaddis's aircraft (63-7614) was damaged by AAA over the target and was lagging behind the others when it was hit by cannon fire from one of the MiGs near Hòa Lạc airfield.

His WSO was 26-year old 1st Lieutenant James Milton Jefferson, who left Florida to attend the United States Air Force Academy, where his brother had graduated in 1959, graduated in 1964 and had embarked on what seemed to be a promising career with the Air Force. He ejected first followed by Colonel Gaddis who was quickly captured. During interrogation in prison, the Colonel was shown items of flight clothing belonging to Jefferson but it seems that the young WSO had been killed in the incident. Gaddis was on his 73rd mission when he was shot down. He spent the next 2,124 days as a prisoner of war in the infamous Hànôi 'Hilton' before being was released on 4 March 1973 but there is still no confirmation as to what happened to his WSO although the Viêtnamese claim to have buried him close to the aircraft crash site. He was the first full Colonel to be captured by the North Viêtnamese.

On 13 May two Phantoms and five Thunderchiefs shot down seven MiG-17s in aerial combat. One of two F-4 flights providing MiGCAP for the Yên Viên air strike was leaving the area when crews observed the air battle between F-105s and MiG-17s. Major (later General) William L. Kirk, 35, of Rayville, Louisiana and his pilot, 1st Lieutenant Stephen A. Wayne in 'Harpoon 01' and their wingman immediately broke off to go after the MiGs, while 'Harpoon 03' and '04' remained high to provide air cover. Kirk saw two MiG-17s firing at an F-105 which was in a hard left turn. 'The F-105 reversed underneath and dived for the deck. The MiGs started to reverse and then pulled up and started a left turn again. In this reversal, I switched to heat-mode for Sidewinder missiles, obtained a good tone and fired two Sidewinders. The first missile tracked well and exploded approximately thirty feet behind the MiG. The MiG started a very tight left diving spiral turn. It was on fire from the trailing edge of his left wing to the tail section. I lost sight of the MiG in this spiral, as he went underneath my aircraft.'

Kirk saw two more MiG-17s and fired a Sidewinder at them, but the missile did not have a tone and missed. He then attacked a third MiG with a Sparrow missile, but both the aircraft and the missile disappeared into a cloud with unknown results. Kirk, however, would destroy a total of two MiGs during his tour of 130 Phantom missions he would fly with the Wolf Pack before his return to the United States in January 1968.

Lieutenant Colonel Fred A. Haeffner of Fargo, North Dakota and 1st Lieutenant Michael R. Bever of Kansas City, Missouri in 'Harpoon 03' had observed Kirk's successful AIM-9 attack on the MiG just before Haeffner dived after two MiGs chasing Thunderchiefs. Haeffner attempted to fire two AIM-7 missiles from an overhead position but inadvertently fired three. Dropping below the nose and out of sight, the first missile failed to guide and missed the MiG by about 100 feet. The second fired from a slightly lower altitude, dropped out of sight, but reappeared. Haeffner and Bever saw it hit the MiG on the fuselage just behind the canopy. The MiG disintegrated. The third missile was last seen guiding to the vicinity of the destroyed MiG-17. Major Ronald E. Catton, flying in 'Harpoon 04' said 'the MiG seemed to blow up on the spot. The second missile powdered the MiG; it broke up into many disorganized pieces.'

Over the months of air-to-air combat, many MiGs escaped destruction by the F-4s simply because there was a deficiency in the Phantom's short-range kill capability. At medium range, they could use the infrared heat-seeking AIM-9 Sidewinder; at long range, they had the radar beam-riding, AIM-7 Sparrow. But aircrews were unable to manoeuvre their F-4s to fire these missiles at short range and many of the MiGs escaped. The fighters were handicapped by the limitations of their radar-guided AIM-7 Sparrow and heat-seeking AIM-9 Sidewinder missile armament, neither of which had been designed for fighter versus fighter combat. The great advantage conferred by the Sparrow, its ability to engage the enemy from any angle at up to twelve miles, was nullified by a rule of engagement which called for visual identification of the enemy before firing. The Sidewinder could be fired from up to one mile, but only from the rear, in a 30-degree cone that led to the engine's heat. Both missiles were limited by their reaction to g forces and both required a set up time that was difficult to effect in air combat. The cannon pods were not as accurate as the internal gun of the F-105 and some felt that it was a net disadvantage, as it induced drag and displaced other stores. Some also thought it might induce the Phantom pilot to attempt to dogfight with the more manoeuvrable MiGs - not good practice. In May 1967 however, the F-4s began carrying the SUU-16 gun pods to complement the missiles and immediately the short-range deficiency was corrected (and later, the F-4E arrived, modified to carry an M-61A1 rotary 20 mm cannon internally).

The first MiGs fell to the SUU-16 on 14 May when the 366th TFW destroyed three MiG-17s when the F-4s provided MiGCAP during an F-105 strike on the Đông army barracks and supply depot. The first flight encountered sixteen MiG-17s, destroying two of them; the other flight encountered ten MiG-17s and destroyed one. Major James A. Hargrove Jr. of Garden City Beach, South

Carolina and 1st Lieutenant Stephen H. DeMuth of Medina, Ohio in 'Speedo 01' fired Sidewinders and Sparrows against three MiG-17s and missed all three. On the fourth engagement, DeMuth elected to use the SUU-16 gun pod and opened fire at approximately 2,000 feet and continued firing until at about 300 feet flame erupted from the top of the MiG fuselage and it exploded. Two Texans, Captain James T. Craig, Jr of Abilene and his back-seater, 1st Lieutenant James T. Talley of Nixon in 'Speedo 03' then shot down a MiG with a 20mm gun after missing two other MiG-17s with Sparrow missiles. Major Samuel O. Bakke of Fort Morgan, Colorado and Captain Robert W. Lambert of Virginia Beach, flying in 'Elgin 01', the lead aircraft in the second flight, got their victory at the same time that Craig and Talley made their kill. Unlike Hargrove's aircraft, Bakke's Phantom was not equipped with SUU-16 gun pods. Bakke fired two Sparrow missiles while pursuing the target in a left turn. One missile did not guide and the other 'homed in' on the target, causing an explosion and fire in the right aft wing root of the MiG-17. 'The kills with the gun mode could not have been made with a missile,' Craig later commented.

Remarkably, January-June 1967 USAF jets shot down 46 MiGs and from April-July 1967 the USN accounted for a dozen MiGs. By the end of August 1967 four aircraft carriers, the *Bon Homme Richard, Constellation, Kearsarge* and *Ticonderoga* and their protecting forces had arrived in position in the Gulf and started a pattern of line duty that continued until August 1973. The threat of MiG activity over Southeast Asia resulted in increased efforts to provide combat air patrols and airborne early warning. The versatile F-4 Phantom, along with the F-8 Crusader, was tasked with air defence of the fleet and protection of strike forces. Phantoms and MiGs met each other in the sky over Viêtnam on many occasions throughout the first half of 1967 and American crews also continued to run the gauntlet of SAM missiles and ground fire. The 19th of May - Hô Chi Minh's 77th birthday - proved to be one of the worst days of the war when the first Navy raids on targets in Hànôi itself resulted in the loss of six aircraft and ten aircrew over North Viêtnam.[6] The three participating carriers, the *Enterprise, Bon Homme Richard* and the *Kitty Hawk* each lost two aircraft.

The first of three 'Alpha' strikes that day was on the Văn Điển military vehicle and SAM support depot near Hànôi, an area of town American pilots commonly referred to as 'Little Detroit,' which had been bombed on 14 December 1966 when two aircraft were shot down. Weather conditions included rain showers earlier in the morning, scattered clouds and visibility of ten miles. The strike aircraft, call sign 'Raygun,' were A-6A Intruders from the *Enterprise*. When the various elements of the strike package arrived in the target area, each element's flight leader established radio contact with the Airborne Battlefield Command and Control centre (ABCCC) responsible for controlling all operations in the region. After being given clearance into their individual targets, each element commenced its briefed attack on their targets. At the same time the attacks began, the NVA gunners opened fire on the American aircraft from their well-entrenched AAA batteries and SAM sites that were dispersed throughout Hànôi and the surrounding countryside. At 1112 hours, an A-6A Intruder flown by Lieutenant Commander Eugene B.

'Red' McDaniel and Lieutenant James K. 'Kelly' Patterson, radar intercept officer; was struck by a SAM forcing them to immediately eject from their crippled aircraft. Both men landed roughly a mile from the wreckage of their aircraft and a mile apart.

A minute later and within seconds of hearing another pilot call 'two good chutes' for 'Red' McDaniel and 'Kelly' Patterson, the North Viêtnamese obtained a SAM lock on 'Showtime 01', leading the CAP flight of F-4Bs of VF-96 and flown by Commander Richard Rich, 42, of Stamford, Connecticut, the Squadron executive officer. His backseater was Commander William Robert 'Bill' Stark, 37, of Michigan City, Indiana. At this time the Phantom was about twelve miles south of Hànôi at 18,000 feet and heading toward the southwest. Rich's wingman reported that enemy defences, both anti-aircraft fire and SAMs were extremely heavy. Volleys of SAMs were fired at the formation forcing the aircraft down to a lower altitude, which was dangerous due to the intense AAA and small arms fire. Commander Rich and 'Bill' Stark obtained a visual sighting of a SAM and successfully performed a 'Split S' manoeuvre, which brought the Phantom down to an altitude of 12,000 feet. The SAM exploded to the rear and left of the aircraft. Even though Commander Rich's cockpit instruments were all green, his wingman quickly examined 'Showtime 01' for any sign of battle damage and then gave Rich a thumbs up confirming there was none. Then the wingman heard another transmission from Rich that indicated that his aircraft had been damaged and was responding sluggishly. Two minutes later, with 'Showtime 01' even lower, a second SAM launch was detected coming from the same general direction of the first. Rich again obtained a visual sighting of it and commenced performing another 'Split S' manoeuvre. The second missile also exploded to the rear of the lead aircraft shaking it violently. Stark later reported he remembered hearing a garbled voice transmission from. Rich stating, 'I can't .... (do something).' After the second SAM detonation, the wingman lost visual and electronic contact with his flight leader in the chaos of battle as he dodged other missiles and intense AAA fire that was being directed at the other American aircraft. In the cockpit of 'Showtime 01', a command ejection sequence was initiated by the NFO. Bill Stark was knocked unconscious by the ejection and suffered compound fractures of the lower vertebrae, a broken arm and a broken knee. He landed just east of the Song Côn River and the Hà Đức village located along both sides of the river about eighteen miles south-southwest of Hànôi. There was no sign of Commander Rich, who is presumed to have been killed in the crash. Visual contact was completely lost and repeated radio calls to Commander Rich produced negative results. The wingman found no trace of Rich's aircraft, there were no emergency radio signals and the wingman saw no parachutes. Search and rescue efforts were impossible due to the high threat in the Hànôi area. Electronic surveillance of the area produced negative results.

The *Kitty Hawk's* CAP flight fared no better when it took over about one hour later and it also lost one its F-4s. The SAMs were still being fired in great numbers and despite violent evasive manoeuvres; F-4B (153004) in VF-114 'Aardvarks' was hit in the belly by an SA-2. The Phantom was piloted by Lieutenant (jg) Joseph Charles Plumb, 25, who was raised in a three-room

Left: Lieutenant Scott Campbell of VF-171. 'Aces'.

Below: 35th Tactical Fighter Squadron, 12th Tactical Fighter Wing group photo at Đà Nẵng AB, South Việtnam in May 1972.

Top left: Captain Charles Barbin 'Chuck' DeBellevue, one of only five Americans to achieve flying ace status in the war in SE Asia and the first Air Force weapon systems officer (WSO) to earn ace status. He was credited with a total of six MiG kills - four with Captain Richard S. Ritchie and two with Captain John A. Madden, Jr.- the most earned by any US aviator during the war, He is a recipient of the Air Force Cross.

Top right: Lieutenant Curtis Dosé of VF-92 'Silver Kings' aboard the *Constellation* on 10 May 1972 explains how he manoeuvred his Phantom behind a MiG before shooting it down, for which he received the Silver Star.

Below: MiG killers head for a pre-mission briefing at Udorn. Captains 'Chuck' DeBellevue and Richard S. Ritchie (front row) and Lieutenant Colonel Carl G. 'Griff' Baily and Captain Jeffrey S.Feinstein (back row). In 1972, while flying as a WSO for four different pilots, Feinstein downed five enemy aircraft, thereby becoming a flying ace, the last of five US aviators to become aces during the war in SE Asia.

Top left: Major John Leighton 'Robbie' Robertson (pictured) and 1st Lieutenant Elliot Buchanan (PoW) who were shot down by a MiG-17 flown by Nguyễn Văn Bảy on 16 September 1966.

Middle: Captain Paul Anthony Kari pilot of the first Phantom lost in combat on 20 June 1965. His backseater, Captain Curt H. Briggs was rescued and Kari was taken into captivity.

Top right: 1st Lieutenant William 'Buddy' Stone Hargrove of the 555th 'Triple Nickel' Squadron in the 432nd TRW. He and his backseater, Captain Calvin Bryan Tibbett (25) of Waynesville, MO (right) scored two MiG-21 victories, on the 9th and 16th September 1972 but were killed on 21 November 1972 when their Phantom crashed following a control failure during a training sortie over Thailand.

Below, right: 1st Lieutenant Charles Lane, a backseater in the 'Triple Nickel' Squadron, who was KIA on 23 August 1967.

Below, left: Lieutenant (jg) Henry Adams 'Black Bart' Bartholomay of VF-161 'Chargers'.

Above: F-4J BuNo155508 of VMFA-235 'Death Angels' during aerial refuelling from A-4E BuNo 150056 of Fleet Composite Squadron 1 (VC-1) in the Caribbean on 1 March 1977. While with VMFA-333'Shamrocks' this Phantom was written off in a runway accident at MCAS Iwakuni, Japan on 4 November 1983.

Below: Lieutenant Colonel Robert F. 'Earthquake' Titus and his backseater, 1st Lieutenant Milan Zimer celebrating their 2nd and 3rd MiG kills on 22 May 1967.

Left: F-4E 67-0374 of the 4th TFW attached to the 8th TFW was the last US aircraft lost to enemy action when it was shot down by ground fire on a strike mission in Cambodia on 16 June 1972 Captain Samuel Blackmar Cornelius, 30, and 27-year old Captain John Jackie 'JJ' Smallwood (pictured) were killed. Sam Cornelius was on his third tour having flown over 360 combat missions.

Right: 1st Lieutenant Wayne Ogden Smith, 25, of Clearwater, Florida, who with his F-4D pilot, Major Kenneth Adrian Simonet, 44, of Chicago, Illinois both of the 435th TFS in the 'Wolfpack' destroyed a MiG-17 on 18 January 1968 with an AIM-4.

Left: Captain James Alvin Branch, 31 (pictured) and 1st Lieutenant Eugene Millard Jewell, 23, of Topeka, Kansas were killed on 4 September 1965. In 1994 the remains of Captain Branch were returned and identified and his status changed from MIA to KIA.

In 1975 35-year old Colonel James Daniel 'Chappie' James Jr. became the first African American to reach the rank of four-star general. James went to Ubon Royal Thai Air Force Base, Thailand in December 1966, as deputy commander for operations, 8th TFW. In June 1967, under Colonel Robin Olds, he was named wing vice commander. Both in their mid-40s, they formed a legendary team nicknamed 'Blackman and Robin'. James flew 78 combat missions into North Việtnam, many in the Hanoi/Haiphong area, and led a flight in the 'Operation Bolo' MiG sweep in which seven MiG-21s were destroyed, the highest total kill of any mission during the Việtnam War.

Above: Colonel Robin Olds (back row far left) with pilots of 555th 'Triple Nickel' TFS, 8th Tactical Fighter Wing 'Wolfpack' at Ubon RTAFB on 4 May 1967. The squadron scored its first two aerial victories 23 April 1966. One week later, the 'Nickel' gained the distinction of being the first Ace squadron in SE Asia with six kills. While stationed at Ubon the 'Triple Nickel' downed an additional 13 MiGs including four MiG-21s on 2 January 1967. The Nickel was now the only 'Quad ace' fighter squadron in this operational theatre, with twenty MiGs confirmed destroyed.

Right: Colonel (later Major General) Robert Maloy (left) and Captain William S. Paul (right) of the 366th TFW after being rescued by an H-3E Jolly Green Giant from the 37th Aerospace Rescue and Recovery Squadron on 15 October 1967. Enemy fire hit their F-4 over North Viêtnam, but they reached open water before ejecting. Maloy fractured his back and Pararescueman (PJ) Airman 1st Class Roger Klenovich (centre, wearing red PJ beret) went into the water to help him.

F-4B 151450 of VF-31 'Tomcatters' on the *Saratoga* in 1967. On Sunday 18 May 1969, now with VMFA-314 'Black Knights' , MAG-13 at Chu Lai, 151450 was lost near Phú Bái, just south of Huê during a routine operational tanker mission with a KC-130F tanker (149814) of VMGR-152 'Sumo's' piloted by Major Jimmy D. Sells, which had departed Đà Nẵng AB at 12:05. 151450 crewed by Major J. D. Moody and 1st Lieutenant Griffiths and 152270 crewed by Major A. Gillespie and 1st Lieutenant V. Maddox and the KC-130F were descending in a 'tobogganing' maneouvre while heading southbound in the vicinity of the South Việtnam coastline. At the same time a separate F-4B (151001) of VMFA-542 'Bengals', MAG-11 crewed by Captain John Laurence Nalls, Washington DC and his RIO, Captain Charles William Pigott, East Providence, RI, was heading in a generally westbound direction toward the Huê Phú Bái military area. As 151001 and the KC-130F approached each other nearly head on with a closing rate of approximately 700 knots true air speed, 151001 hit the tanker head-on in the vicinity of the No.4 engine and the starboard refuelling pod on the KC-130F. The radome on the F-4B cleared the propeller on the No.4 engine as the cockpit initially impacted with it. 151001 crashed and Nalls and Pigott died instantly. The KC-130F crashed into the sea with the loss of all six crew. 151450, which was plugged into the starboard drogue, was sprayed with fuel and apparently ingested an undetermined amount of debris into both engines. The F-4B flipped uncontrollably to an inverted position while the drogue and a portion of the hose remained attached to the aircraft. Its engines could not sustain power and the fighter crashed at sea. Major Moody and 1st Lieutenant Griffiths ejected safely and were recovered. The second refuelling F-4B, 152270, was plugged into the port refuelling drogue and sustained limited damage in the form of two small holes in the port aileron and a half inch hole in the starboard wingtip. Major Gillespie observed the spinning tanker and when it was apparent he could render no further assistance returned to Chu Lái AB without further incident.

Above: F-4J of VF-33 'Tarsiers' assigned to Carrier Air Wing 6 (CVW-6) being catapulted from the USS *Independence* (CV-62) during a deployment to the Mediterranean from 28 June to 14 December 1979.

Below: F-4N 152318 of VMFA 323 'Death Rattlers' at full afterburner on the catapult of the USS *Coral Sea* (CV-43) in 1979. This Phantom went to MASDC on 19 October 1983 and was salvaged in November 2004.

Left: Commander Harley Hubert Hall USN.

Below, right: Eight victory ace Nguyễn Hông Nhị.

Left: Commander Harry Lee Blackburn the 37-year old Executive Officer of VF-92 'Silver Kings' on the USS *Constellation* who was shot down and killed on 10 May 1972 . His 26-year old RIO, Lieutenant Anthony Rudloff was released on 28 March 1973 and later became an F-14 Tomcat instructor pilot. Commander Blackburn is presumed to have been killed either during or soon after capture. His remains were returned to the USA on 10 April 1986.

Left: Lieutenant (later Commander) John C. 'Inchworm' Ensch of VF-161 the 'Chargers'. In July 1966 'Jack' joined VF-21 'Freelancers' and made two deployments to SE Asia, one aboard the USS *Coral Sea* and one aboard the USS *Ranger*. In January 1971 he joined VF-161 'Chargers' and in April 1971 deployed to SE Asia aboard the USS *Midway*. On 10 April 1972 he made his second deployment to SE Asia with VF-161 on Midway. On 23 May 1972 he and his pilot, Lieutenant Commander. Ron McKeown were credited with two MiG kills over North Việtnam. On 25 May 1972 'Jack' and his pilot, Lieutenant Commander Mike Doyle (KIA) were shot down by a SAM. Jack Ensch was captured immediately after ejection and spent seven months in captivity, being released with the last group of PoWs on 29 March 1973.

Right: VF-84 'The Jolly Rogers' carrier pilots in 1965. VF-84 made several Mediterranean cruises on board the *Independence* (CVA-62) flying the F-8C Crusader for several years prior to being introduced to the F-4B during 1964 and flew the F-4J and the F-4N until they transitioned to the F-14 Tomcat in early 1976. In 1965 the squadron deployed for seven months on board *Independence* assigned to Attack Carrier Air Wing Seven (CVW-7) in the Gulf of Tonkin and flew 1,507 combat sorties, logging 2200 flight hours over both North Việtnam and South Việtnam.

Above: F-4B-26-MC BuNo153018 NH-205 of VF-114 'Aardvarks' ready for takeoff on the steam catapult for a CAP mission over Việtnam. VF-114 was assigned to Carrier Air Wing 11 (CVW-11) aboard the USS *Kitty Hawk* (CVA-63) for a deployment to Việtnam from 18 November 1967 to 28 June 1968. On 13 March 1969 the port engine on this Phantom flamed out due to stuck throttle and crashed into the Gulf of Tonkin. Lieutenant (jg) E. L. Brazil and Lieutenant (jg) K. J. Oden ejected

Left: Lieutenant Commander Stanley Edward Olmstead of VF-84, the 'Jolly Rogers' USN, born 12 November 1933 at Gage, Oklahoma, who was one of two aircraft captains with their RIOs in VF-84 'The Jolly Rogers' from the USS *Independence* that were shot down on 17 October 1965. Olmstead and his RIO, Lieutenant (jg) Porter A. Halyburton and Lieutenant (jg)'s Ralph E.Gaither and Rodney A. Knutson were taken prisoner.

Marine KC-130F Hercules tankers in 1972. Nearest to the camera is F-4J BuNo 155811 which was shot down by a North Vietnamese MiG-21 with an 'Atoll' missile on 26 August 1972 on the border of Laos and Vietnam in Houaphanh Province near the city of Sop Hoa, the only Marine jet ever to be lost to enemy aircraft during the Vietnam War. The crew ejected, the pilot 1st Lieutenant Sam Gary Cordova was captured and died in captivity, the RIO 1st Lieutenant Darrell L. Borders was rescued. The NVAF pilot who shot the Phantom down was Nguyễn Đức Soát of the 3rd Company, 927th Fighter Regiment; his fifth of six aerial kills.

'Wolfpack' pilots of the 8th Tactical Fighter Wing carry their Commanding Officer, Colonel Robin Olds (14 July 1922 - 14 June 2007), following his return from his last combat mission over North Việtnam, on 23 September 1967. This mission was his hundredth 'official' combat mission, but his actual combat mission total for his tour was 152! His philosophy regarding fighter pilots is quoted as: 'There are pilots and there are pilots; with the good ones, it is inborn. You can't teach it. If you are a fighter pilot, you have to be willing to take risks.' Colonel Olds boldly led the 8th TFW 'Wolfpack' from September 1966 to September 1967, as it racked up 24 MiG victories, the greatest aerial combat record of an F-4 Wing in the Việtnam War. Olds was a 'triple ace' with a combined total of sixteen victories in World War II and the Việtnam War. By the end of his combat service in WW2 he was officially credited with twelve German planes shot down and 11.5 others destroyed on the ground. Olds is regarded among aviation historians and his peers as the best wing commander of the Việtnam War, for both his air-fighting skills and his reputation as a combat leader. Colonel Olds assumed the position of Commandant of Cadets at the US Air Force Academy on 1 December 1967. His inability to rise higher as a general officer is attributed to both his maverick views and his penchant for drinking. He retired in 1973 as a brigadier general.

Above, left: Lieutenant Ralph F.Wetterhahn.

Above, right: The capture of 1st Lieutenant (later Captain) Michael Thomas Burns, 23, a back-seater in the 433rd 'Satan's Angels' Tactical Fighter Squadron at Ubon. He and Colonel Carl Crumpler his front seater were shot down on 5 July 1968 attacking a gun site in the panhandle of North Việtnam and were imprisoned in the Hànôi Hilton' after enduring a journey time of 35 days in the back of a truck.

Below: Major John R. Pardo and 1st Lieutenant Stephen A. Wayne of the 433rd TFS, 8th TFW who destroyed a MiG-17 on 20 May 1967. This was Lieutenant Wayne's second aerial victory; a week earlier he had flown with Major William L. Kirk, when the pair had shot down a MiG-17.

Above: Lieutenant Colonel 'Pancho' Pasqualicchio (far right) who flew Winston Churchill in a Phantom in Việtnam later on in his career.

Left: Winston Churchill was aboard the *Ranger* on 1 March 1966 when F-4B 150443 of VF-143 'Pukin Dogs' crewed by 26-year old Lt William David Frawley (pictured with sunglasses) of Brockton, Mass and 24-year old Lt (jg) William Murrey Christensen (below, right) of Great Falls MT were KIA by a SAM during a coastal reconnaissance mission about 40 miles south of Hảiphòng in deteriorating weather. A-4E 152057 VA-55 'Warhorses' that was lost the same day was piloted by 24-year old Lt (jg) Donald Joseph Woloszyk (left, who was KIA). When Kenneth Woloszyk posted names of the missing pilots that day he saw his brother's name on the list.

home in Mission in rural Kansas who was on his 75th mission, with five days before he was to return home. His back-seater was Lieutenant (jg) Gary L. Anderson (who it will be remembered was Denny Wisley's RIO on 24 April 1967 when they were credited with destroying a MiG-17 over North Viêtnam). The aircraft became a mass of flames and the engines wound down rapidly. As the tail section began to disintegrate Plumb and his back-seater decided that it was time to leave and ejected near Xan La, twelve miles southwest of Hànôi. Charlie Plumb recalls. 'Our F-4B lay crumpled in smouldering wreckage near a small village. The peasants stripped me of all my flight gear, blindfolded me and put me into a pen with a buffalo bull where I got the opportunity for the first and hopefully the last time in my life, to play matador. But having no red cape, I was unable to attract a great deal of attention from the fairly docile bull. So it was necessary for the Vietnamese to run around to the aft side of this animal and harass him into making sweeps upon my innocent body with his horns. I received no permanent injury. And I look back upon it with more humour than terror. being captured by peasants and thrown into a pen where a bull buffalo was goaded by the villages into charging the pilot. Fortunately, the bull was less than enthusiastic about the whole affair.' The two fliers were incarcerated in the 'Hànôi Hilton'. [7]

North Viêtnam lost no MiG aircraft to USAF aircrews for the next four days, although air-to-air engagements continued daily. On the 20th, however, two MiG-21s were destroyed by aircrews of the 366th TFW and four MiG-17s were destroyed by the 'Wolfpack' aircrews. Both of the MiG-21s were defeated by a Phantom flight providing MiGCAP for a strike force attacking the Kính Nô motor vehicle repair yards. They approached the target area, two MiG-21s were attacking the departing strike force. The F-4s immediately broke off to attack the enemy. Major Robert D. Janca, (who had flown left wing in the Thunderbirds 1959-1961) the flight leader, of Hampton, Virginia with 1st Lieutenant William E. Roberts Jr. of Quitman, Oklahoma as his back-seater, reported: 'I spotted a MiG-21 at my 9-10 o'clock high position. The MiG started turning left into us. I lowered the nose and began a left turn into the MiG, at which time the MiG reversed to the right and started to climb. I continued in the left descending turn to close and then commenced a climbing turn. As the MiG continued to climb I put the pipper on him, received a good tone and fired an AIM-9 missile with the MiG about 4,000 feet ahead, zero angle-off and framed against the blue sky. The missile guided straight with very little flutter and detonated about fifteen feet to the right of the MiG's tail. A large piece of the tail came off along with other small pieces. The MiG pitched up and began a roll off to the right from about 8,000 feet and then appeared to enter a spin. I continued my turn, watching the MiG as he disappeared from my line of sight at approximately 1,000 feet AGL (actual ground level). My pilot, Lieutenant Roberts and 'Elgin 02' [Captain Daniel S. Burr and 1st Lieutenant William A. Norton] saw the MiG strike the ground.'

Meanwhile, Lieutenant Colonel Robert F. 'Earthquake' Titus, 39, of Hampton, Virginia and 1st Lieutenant Milan Zimer, 29, of Canton, Ohio (flying 'Elgin 03'), who had initiated the attack, accompanied by aircraft 4, pursued the two MiG-21s they had seen as they entered the area. (Robert F. Titus was born on 6 December 1926 in Orange, New Jersey. On 15 April 1955 Captain Titus, fresh out of Test Pilot School, working with the Joint Parachute Test Group, strapped himself into a F-51D Mustang at Naval Air Station El Centro and took off on the very last official USAF Mustang sortie. Titus was no stranger to the Mustang, having flown over 100 combat missions on the type during the Korean War. His second tour was in the F-86 Sabre as flight commander. Titus was also shot down in an F-86, parachuting down over enemy lines and having to fight his way out to safety. In May 1966 he assumed command of the 'Skoshi Tigers,' the only F-5 squadron in the USAF at Biên Hòa Air Base. In January 1967 he became commander of the 389th Tactical Fighter Squadron at Đà Nẵng. He would fly 400 combat missions in North and South Viêtnam and destroy three Mig-21s in aerial combat.).

Before they could fire, someone called 'break' and the flight broke off. The MiGs turned away, so the flight started to rejoin the strike force when Titus spotted yet a third MiG. He attacked. Zimer reported the engagement quite tersely: 'While en route to target and at the north end of 'Thud Ridge', the strike flight was attacked by several MiGs. Colonel Titus and I engaged three MiGs, of which we shot down a MiG-21C with a Sparrow missile. We were moving in for the kill on the first MiG we engaged with a full system lock-on when 'Elgin 04' called 'MiGs at 6 o'clock'. Colonel Titus immediately broke off the attack. We then rejoined the strike flight. We observed another MiG-21C and engaged him; with a full system lock-on, we fired three missiles. The first two did not guide, but the third missile destroyed the MiG-21 C. [The] kill was observed by all members of the flight. We were returning to strike flight when we engaged a third MiG. This engagement we broke off because aircraft 4 was [at] minimum fuel. Major Robert Janca confirmed the Titus victory, observing how Titus fired 'an AIM-7 missile which impacted on the right side of the MiG-21. The MiG exploded in flame and a short time later I observed the pilot, who had ejected, floating down in his chute.'

The other four MiGs destroyed during the afternoon of 20 May fell victims to two flights of the 'Wolfpack' at Ubon, which were flying MiGCAP for an F-105 strike force attacking the Bắc Le rail yards. The first flight of Phantoms flew line abreast with the second Thunderchief flight. The other F-4 flight was high and to the right of the last F-105 flight. An EB-66 support and an 'Iron Hand' SAM suppression flight were included in the strike force.

The force came in from the Gulf of Tonkin. As the aircraft crossed the coastal islands, the Phantoms jettisoned their centreline tanks. Shortly thereafter, about twenty miles east of Kép airfield, two SAMs streaked from the ground at the American aircraft and the 'Iron Hand' flight attacked the site with Shrike missiles. The SAMs immediately stopped guiding. But with the appearance of the SAMs, there simultaneously came a MiG warning. The mission called for the F-105 force to divide and strike two targets at the rail yards, with one Phantom flight accompanying the first division and the second remaining with the other division, so that each part of the strike force would receive protection. Fifteen miles short of the target, however, the first flight of F-4s sighted MiGs. The other flight sighted more MiGs several miles away. In the next twelve to fourteen minutes there was a massive and aggressive dogfight with eight F-4s battling 12-14 MiG-17s. Elements of each flight acted separately to provide support to other elements. While the F-4s engaged the MiGs, the F-105s proceeded to assigned targets.

Four MiGs were destroyed in a span of five to six minutes. The first fell to a Sidewinder of Major John R. Pardo, the aircraft commander and 1st Lieutenant Stephen A. Wayne, the back seat pilot in 'Tampa 03'. Pardo reports: 'As our flight approached the area of the sighting, I observed four MiG-17s turning in behind the F-105s. Colonel Olds fired one missile and told me to 'go get him.' I launched one Sparrow, which did not guide. I then launched one Sidewinder which guided and struck the number four MiG-17. I broke left to negate other MiGs at my 8 o'clock. I continued a 360° turn while positioning on another MiG-17 and observed an aircraft burning on the ground near where I observed my Sidewinder hit a MiG-17. The remainder of the missiles I fired did not guide or were not observed due to evasive action necessitated by the tactical situation.'

This was Lieutenant Wayne's second aerial victory; a week earlier he had flown with Major William L. Kirk when the pair had shot down a MiG-17.

Two other MiG-17s became the victims of Colonel Robin Olds and his pilot, 1st Lieutenant Stephen B. Croker of Middletown, Delaware. These were aerial victories three and four for Olds, making him the leading MiG-killer at that time in Southeast Asia. Olds termed the events of 20 May 'quite a remarkable air battle.'

'F-105s were bombing along the northeast railway; we were in our escort position, coming in from the Gulf of Tonkin. We just cleared the last of the low hills lying north of Haiphòng, in an east-west direction, when about ten or twelve MiG-17s came in low from the left and, I believe, from the right. They tried to attack the F-105s before they got to the target. We engaged MiG-17s approximately fifteen miles short of the target. The ensuing battle was an exact replica of the dogfights in World War II.

'Our flights of F-4s piled into the MiGs like a sledge hammer and for about a minute and a half or two minutes that was the most confused, vicious dogfight I have ever been in. There were eight F-4Cs, twelve MiG-17s and one odd flight of F-105s on their way out from the target, who flashed through the battle area.

'Quite frankly, there was not only danger from the guns of the MiGs, but the ever-present danger of a collision to contend with. We went round and round that day with the battles lasting twelve to fourteen minutes, which is a long time. This particular day we found that the MiGs went into a defensive battle down low, about 500 to 1,000 feet. In the middle of this circle, there were two or three MiGs circling about a hundred feet - sort of in figure-eight patterns. The MiGs were in small groups of two, three and sometimes four in a very wide circle. Each time we went in to engage one of these groups, a group on the opposite side of the circle would go full power, pull across the circle and be in firing position on our tails almost before we could get into firing position with our missiles. This is very distressing, to say the least.

'The first MiG I lined up was in a gentle left turn, range about 7,000 feet. My pilot achieved a boresight lock-on, went full system, narrow gate, interlocks in. One of the two Sparrows fired in ripple guided true and exploded near the MiG. My pilot saw the MiG erupt in flame and go down to the left.

'We attacked again and again, trying to break up that defensive wheel. Finally, once again, fuel considerations necessitated departure. As I left the area by myself, I saw that lone MiG still circling and so I ran out about ten miles and said that even if I ran out of fuel, he is going to know he was in a fight. I got down on the deck, about fifty feet and headed right for him. I don't think he saw me for quite a while. But when he did, he went mad, twisting, turning, dodging and trying to get away. I kept my speed down so I wouldn't overrun him and I stayed behind him. He headed up a narrow little valley to a low ridge of hills. I knew he was either going to hit that ridge up ahead or pop over the ridge to save himself. The minute he popped over I was going to get him with a Sidewinder.

'I fired one AIM-9 which did not track and the MiG pulled up over a ridge, turned left and gave me a dead astern shot. I obtained a good growl. I fired from about 25 to 50 feet off the grass and he was clear of the ridge by only another 50 to 100 feet when the Sidewinder caught him.

'The missile tracked and exploded 5 to 10 feet to the right side of the aft fuselage. The MiG spewed pieces and broke hard left and down from about 200 feet. I overshot and lost sight of him.

'I was quite out of fuel and all out of missiles and pretty deep in enemy territory all by myself, so it was high time to leave. We learned quite a bit from this fight. We learned you don't pile into these fellows with eight airplanes all at once. You are only a detriment to yourself.'

The final MiG destroyed that day fell to the leader of the first flight, Major Philip P. Combies, with 1st Lieutenant Daniel L. Lafferty of Eddyville, Illinois flying rear seat, in 'Ballot 01' for Combie's second MiG victory. Having engaged several MiG-17s without results, Combies climbed to re-engage when he saw a MiG-17 in hot pursuit of Olds, about 1½-miles away. When Olds broke hard left, the MiG overshot and headed directly toward Kép airfield, about 8 miles distant. Combies got behind and fired an AIM-9 with good tone: 'The missile impacted in the tailpipe area of the MiG and the MiG caught on fire. The MiG was at approximately 1,500 feet at the time of missile launch. The MiG went 'belly up' and into an uncontrollable dive and eventually impacted into the ground.'

Two days following this air battle, on 22 May, Lieutenant Colonel Titus and his backseater, 1st Lieutenant Milan Zimer, while leading a flight of four F-Cs in 'Wander 01', repeated their earlier success. Titus' flight was one of two that was providing Phantom MiGCAP for a strike force directed against the Hà Đông army barracks and supply depot. Titus later related the afternoon's events: 'I was carrying a SUU-16 two days later [May 22] when I got two more MiGs, the second with a SUU-16. In that particular case we were escorting the Thuds [F-105s] inbound to the target, headed for the heart of Hànôi and I had a feeling that we would get some kind of reaction. The MiGs had been flying that month and, of course, with the strike force headed for Hànôi, it did seem to be a fruitful mission to get on, although I had just happened to chum up on the mission that day.

'I was leading the first flight that time and we were south of formation, line abreast of the first two flights at about 16,000 feet, headed west to east, when suddenly out in front eleven miles I spotted a couple of MiGs. I happened to see the sun reflecting off them. I called my backseater and told him to go boresight and immediately called that I was 'Padlocked' [a code word meaning, essentially, 'I'm attacking the MiGs'] and accelerating. I went into afterburner and started pushing forward. Because of numerous MiG calls in the area, I had already cleaned off my external tanks, so we were in a good fighting configuration.

'The MiG that we locked on to started a left turn and I lost sight of him and followed him on the radar. He made a turn around to the right, a hard climbing turn. I was unable to get lead on him. I could merely keep him on the right hand of the scope. He stopped his climb and we levelled off. He was in a descent; he climbed again. Finally, I told my back-seater that I thought there was something wrong with the radar. He agreed and we joined the 'Thud' formation.

'We were still in burner, came alongside the formation and came out of burner. I looked over my left shoulder and a MiG was making a pass on the formation. He fired a missile. I called him and turned into him just about the time he fired the missile. Having fired the missile, he started to climb - possibly after he saw me coming at him. In that particular area, there was a scattered overcast condition, cirrus deck. It must have been around 20,000 feet. As I closed he went through the cirrus at a very high climb angle. I was in close pursuit, had a very strong Sidewinder tone and I fired the missile. The missile was tracking as he disappeared into the cloud. The missile went through the same hole. I deviated slightly to the right, came out on top of the cloud deck and noted some debris in the air and smoke off to the left. I don't know what it was, but there was some foreign matter in the air - very discernible. I mentioned it to my back-seater.

'Then, almost instantaneously, I saw from my 1 o'clock position another MiG-21 about a mile away. I turned toward him and put the pipper on him and got another Sidewinder tone and fired another missile. Almost immediately the MiG started a hard descending left turn and we went from, I would guess, 25,000 feet down to about 2,000 feet while he was doing all sorts of twisting, turning reversals, rolling all sorts of hard manoeuvres. It was very impressive to see the rapid roll response and directional change ability of that airplane. I proceeded into the dive with him. We could not obtain a radar lock-on, presumably because of the ground return. We were right in the vicinity of the Hòa Lạc airport. There was quite a bit of flak; SAMs were going off.

'The MiG made a very high-g pull-out and levelled at approximately 1,500 to 2,000 feet above the ground. In his pull-out, he was at wing level so I got the pipper on him and fired a long burst of the SUU-16 at him. I did not observe any impacts and thought I had missed him. However, he did slow down quite rapidly. I overshot, pulled up to the left, did a reversal, came back around and called for my number two to take him. About this time number two had overshot and came up to my right. I turned off watching the MiG and called for number three and as I did so I observed the MiG was in a shallow, wing-rocking manoeuvre and continued on down in the shallow dive and impacted with the ground.

'Where he was hit I don't know, but apparently, he was out of it after the first hits were taken.'

After these two MiG-21 kills, USAF crews flying into North Viêtnam encountered a lull of several days during which no enemy aircraft were shot down. The air-to-air posture was improved somewhat on 28 May when the 'Triple Nickle' Squadron received F-4D aircraft. This improved Phantom model soon entered combat.

On 21 May another strike on the Văn Điển SAM and vehicle support depot resulted in the loss of a single aircraft and the rescue of its crew. The TARCAP flight was once more provided by the F-4Bs of VF-114 on the *Kitty Hawk*. One of the Squadron's Phantoms was flown by Lieutenant Dennis 'Denny' Wisely who had shot down a MiG-17 on 24 April. His back-seater was Ensign James 'Jim' H. Laing. Their F-4B was hit as it was retiring from the target at low level. The TARCAP flight had evaded three SAMs but came down low and ran into intense flak. The aircraft was peppered with automatic weapons fire and suffered failures of the hydraulic and pneumatic systems. The pilot decided to make for Thailand rather than risk the gauntlet of the intense air defences between Hànôi and the coast. The decision was a wise one as the aircraft crossed the Laotian border before becoming uncontrollable forcing the crew to eject near Sai Koun, 85 miles southwest of Hànôi. Jim Laing's parachute started to open the instant his ejection seat fired with the result that he broke an arm and sprained his other limbs. Both men were picked up safely by a USAF HH-3 after a Navy SH-3A had to be abandoned in Laos after running out of fuel during the first rescue attempt. This was the second ejection and rescue for Ensign Laing who had been shot down with Lieutenant Commander Southwick on 24 April. [8]

On 2 June Colonel Olds flew an F-4D in a flight otherwise composed of F-4Cs. Providing MiGCAP for an F-105 strike force the flight engaged eight to ten MiGs. Three 'probable' MiG kills resulted, one of them claimed by Olds. Had his kill been confirmed, he would have become the first 'ace' of the Southeast Asia war.

USAF Phantom pilots scored three more victories on 5 June. One flight of four F-4Ds of the 'Triple Nickel' Squadron shot down the first of the enemy trio while flying MiGCAP for an 'Iron Hand' flight in the vicinity of 'Thud Ridge' during the mid-afternoon. Several MiG-17s jumped aircraft 3 and 4. During the ensuing engagement, the F-4s became separated and departed the area. Major 'Razz' Raspberry, leading a flight of four F-4Ds on a MiGCAP for some F-105 'Wild Weasels' on an 'Iron Hand' flight near 'Thud Ridge', was flying as call sign was 'Drill 01' and his 'GIB' was Captain Francis M. Gullick. 'Drill 01' and Captain Douglas B. Cairns his wingman attacked seven or eight other MiGs in a 'Wagon Wheel' formation. 'Upon sighting the MiG-17s,' recalled Raspberry, 'I immediately engaged them to prevent the MiGs from attacking an 'Iron Hand' flight patrolling the area. Although the MiG-17 wasn't as fast as the MiG-21 it was still a nasty little bugger because it could turn on a dime and carried a great big old 37mm cannon in the nose that could ruin your day in a hurry.' After making several turns with the MiGs, I disengaged and flew southeast 3-4 miles and then turned back into the MiGs.' Approaching them for the second time, he spotted one at 12 o'clock high and attempted to hit him with an AIM-4 Falcon missile. However, the missile did not guide.'

Again he left the fight to gain separation and once again came back - at low altitude. With a radar lock-on, he fired an AIM-7 at a MiG in his 11 o'clock position and missed.

'On my third approach to the MiGs, I was between 500 and 1,000 feet actual ground level on a north-westerly heading. I could see three MiG-17s; one in my 12 o'clock, slightly high and two more in my 11 o'clock position, slightly low. My 'GIB' locked on to a target which was obviously one of the MiGs I had seen in my 11 o'clock position as I turned slightly left and down to centre the steering dot. I observed the rate of closure to be 900 knots. When the ASE circle was maximum diameter, I fired an AIM-7. The missile appeared to be headed straight for the oncoming MiG. I was unable to watch the impact because Colonel Olds, [flying lead aircraft in the adjacent flight] called me to break right as a MiG was in my 4 o'clock and firing. My wingman was able to see the AIM-7 as it approached the MiG and observed the MiG as it struck the ground. I would estimate the MiG's altitude at the time of [missile] impact at 100-300 feet.'[9]

About five minutes later Major Durwood K. Priester, 36 of Hampton, South Carolina and his rear-seater, Captain John E. Pankhurst, 27, of Midland, Michigan, were leading a flight of four F-4Cs on MiG combat air patrol in 'Oakland 01' when inbound to the target area Priester observed three MiG-17s at his 3 o'clock low position. Priester's flight dived from 17,000 to the MiGs altitude of about 8,000 feet. The number three MiG pulled up vertically as Priester started his dive. 'I pulled up and in trail with the number three MiG, as it executed a hard right turn. I fired a short burst but saw no evidence of the 20mm hitting the MiG. I did not have a gun sight and relaxed stick pressure while assuming I had overled the MiG due to the close proximity while firing. The MiG-17 started to reverse his turn and I fired another burst of 20mm. Two large balls of flame exited the MiG's tailpipe, but the aircraft failed to burn. I rolled over and observed the shallow dive, wings level and straight course of the damaged MiG as it impacted the ground and exploded. The pilot did not eject and crashed with his aircraft.'

A few minutes later Captain Richard M. Pascoe and his back-seater Captain Norman E. Wells[10] flying 'Chicago 02' as wingman for Colonel Olds destroyed a MiG-17 - the second aerial victory for both officers. Olds' flight was on MiGCAP for a strike force and was covering the departure of F-105s. Monitoring the radio chatter of Priester's engagement with the MiGs, Olds' flight immediately reversed course to join in the fight. Proceeding south along 'Thud Ridge', Pascoe saw four MiG-17s battling Priester's flight and single MiG-17s high at 9 o'clock and 3 o'clock. Olds and Pascoe pursued the MiG at 9 o'clock and 'Chicago 03' and '04' of his flight attacked the one at 3 o'clock. Olds expended all AIM-4 and AIM-7 missiles without effect and then passed the lead to Pascoe. 'We picked up a single MiG-17 at approximately five nautical miles in front of us,' reported Pascoe and then: 'I fired two AIM-9s as the MiG started a slight climb and observed the first to impact at the extreme tail end and the second about three feet up the fuselage from the tail. The MiG continued in his left descending turn and struck the ground as the canopy was seen to leave the aircraft. The aircraft was totally destroyed.'

Olds and his back-seater, 1st Lieutenant James L. Thibodeaux saw the two AIM-9s of their wingman hit the MiG. The pilot ejected just before the MiG crashed 'with a large fireball.'

The heavy losses sustained by the NVNAF between April and June 1967 seriously undermined the effectiveness of the North Viêtnamese fighter force. After 5 June the NVNAF seldom ventured out during the remainder of June and July, but they did continue to train and to practice intercepts whenever US forces were not in the north-eastern corner of North Viêtnam. In this period, American aircraft losses to MiGs were minimal, but beginning on 8 June, SAMs and AAA began to take a heavy toll on them. As dusk turned day into night over the southern part of North Viêtnam on 8 June two F-4C Phantoms in the 389 TFS, 366 TFW at Đà Nẵng began an armed reconnaissance mission. As the aircraft were following a broad river valley near Khê Phát, 25 miles northwest of Đông Hoi, they encountered heavy ground fire. Captain Victor 'Joe' Apodaca, who was of mixed Spanish-American and Navajo Indian parentage, piloting F-4C 63-7425 radioed his leader that his Phantom had been hit and was told to climb and head for the sea. A later radio message told of control and hydraulics problems and this was followed soon after by an emergency signal from a SAR beeper, which indicated that at least one of the crew had ejected. The leader had to return to base to refuel but an electronic search was conducted with no success. Nothing more was heard until the spring of 1988 when remains identified as being those of 1st Lieutenant Jon Thomas Busch, Apodaca's backseater were handed over, along with a charred map and a battered nameplate bearing Victor Apodaca's name.

The 366th TFW lost a second Phantom on the same day during an armed reconnaissance mission around Chap Le near the coast and only ten miles north of the DMZ. F-4C 64-0667 in the 480th TFS was hit by 37mm anti-aircraft fire as it was strafing a storage area. Major C. A. Colton pointed the Phantom out to sea and he and 1st Lieutenant R. D. Franks ejected about twenty miles off the coast where they were picked up by a USAF helicopter.

Two days' later F-4D 66-0236 in the 555th 'Triple Nickel' Squadron in the 'Wolfpack' at Ubon was lost when it ran out of fuel during a CAP mission. Both crew were rescued. On the 11th two F-4Cs in the 366th TFW at Đà Nẵng were lost in a mid-air collision at 14,000 feet about ten miles northeast of Kép during a MiGCAP mission. F-4C 64-0786 in the 390th TFS was crewed by Lieutenant Colonel Hervey Studdie Stockman and Captain Ronald John Webb who ejected and they were taken, prisoner. Major Donald Martin Klemm and 1st Lieutenant Robert Harvey Pearson flying F-4C 63-7706 in the 389th TFS were killed. During the Second World War Stockman had flown P-51 Mustangs from England with the Eighth Air Force while Webb had been a navigator on KB-50 tankers in the early 1960s. Both men were released from captivity on 4 March 1973.

On 12 June Major V. D. Fulgram and Captain William 'Bill' K. Harding in the 'Triple Nickel' Squadron flying F-4C 63-7673 were lost on an armed reconnaissance mission over the southern provinces of North Viêtnam. Fulgram's aircraft was flying at 4.500 feet near Ấn Lộc, twelve miles northwest of Đông Hoi when it was hit by AAA in the starboard wing. Uncertain that he could reach Ubon safely, Fulgram decided to make for Đà Nẵng and almost made it but just a few miles short of the runway the aircraft became uncontrollable and the crew ejected at sea. They were rescued by a Marine Corps helicopter. A second 'Triple Nickel' F-4C was lost when 63-7710 developed problems with its hydraulic system after takeoff forcing Major Martin G. 'Marty' Slapikas and Lieutenant Theodore R. Bongartz of Catonsville, Maryland to eject. The third Phantom lost was F-4C 64-0662 in the 558th TFS, 12th TFW, part of a flight of Phantoms from Cam Ranh Bay crewed by Captain Edward Arthur Lapierre and 1st Lieutenant Lawrence Jay Silver, which was shot down by ground fire while attacking a VC storage complex near Trực Giáng in the Mekong Delta. Having expended most of his ordnance Captain Lapierre was making his sixth pass over the target using his 20mm cannon. The aircraft was seen to dive into the ground close to the target without either crewmember ejecting. On 14 June the 366th TFW lost its fourth Phantom in six days when 1st Lieutenant Edward John Mechenbier and 1st Lieutenant Kevin Joseph McManus' F-4C (64-0778) in the 390th TFS was hit by an 85mm round at 6,000 feet as it dived on the Vu Chùa railway yard near Kép. The aircraft burst into flames and the crew ejected a few miles away and were captured. Mechenbier had flown a total of 113 missions, 79 of them over North Viêtnam, while 1st Lieutenant McManus had flown over 140 missions in two tours of duty.

On the 19th F-4B 150439 of VF-142 'Ghostriders' on the USS *Constellation* crewed by Lieutenant Commander F. L. Raines and Ensign C. L. Lownes was lost while flying as escort to an RA-5C to obtain photographic coverage of Route 1A between Hànôi and Nam Định, a city in the Red River Delta about 45 miles southeast of Hànôi. The Phantom was hit by anti-aircraft fire just as the Vigilante was finishing the photo run less than two miles south of Hànôi. Everything seemed normal so the pair headed out to sea and rendezvoused with the carrier. However, as Lieutenant Commander Raines extended the undercarriage and the flaps on the downwind leg of the approach, the Phantom's hydraulics failed completely and both crew ejected. They were picked up by one of the *Connies* Kaman SH-2 Seasprites.

Three days' later, on 22 June, RF-4C 65-0861 in the 12th TRS, 460th TRW at Tân Sơn Nhứt collided with Lockheed Constellation N6936C of Airlift International four miles north of Sàigòn. The Constellation was operating a mail contract flight from Manila to Sàigòn and collided with the Phantom as it commenced its approach to Tân Sơn Nhứt. Captain A. T. Dardeau and 1st Lieutenant A. J. Lundell ejected safely but the seven crew on board the *Constellation* were killed when it crashed out of control. On 26 June the 366th TFW lost yet another F-4C (63-7577). Major J. C. Blandford and 1st Lieutenant J. M. Jarvis in the 390th TFS were ferrying an F-4C either to or from Clark AFB in the Philippines when they were intercepted by Chinese Air Force Shenyang

J-5s (MiG-17) about 25 miles off the southern tip of Hainan island. Badly damaged by cannon fire from the MiGs, Blandford and Jarvis reportedly ejected at an altitude of about 25,000 feet but they were both killed.[11]

On 28 June Commander William 'Bill' Porter Lawrence, 37, of Nashville, Tennessee, executive officer of VF-143 'Pukin' Dogs' on the *Constellation* led a flak suppression section during a raid on an important trans-shipment point ten miles northwest of Nam Định. A noted pilot who became the first Naval Aviator to fly twice the speed of sound in a naval aircraft, (1,300 miles per hour in the Navy's F8U 'Cruiser III' on 15 September 1958), he was also one of the final candidates for the Mercury space programme. He was released from the programme only because of a small heart murmur discovered during flight training. His backseater in F-4B 152242 was Lieutenant (jg) James William Bailey, born in 1943 in Kosciusko, Mississippi, a veteran of 183 combat missions over Southeast Asia, having flown with VF-143 on board the *Ranger* in 1966.The Phantoms were at 12,000 feet and were preparing to roll in on the target when Commander Lawrence's aircraft was hit by 85mm flak. With the aircraft's hydraulics failing. Lawrence released his CBUs on the target and had difficulty in pulling out of his dive before part of the tail section separated from the Phantom. The crew ejected and were captured and suffered the usual torture and beatings. Along with fellow prisoner, Commander (later Vice Admiral) James Stockdale, Lawrence became noted for resistance to his captors. Additionally, he memorized every PoW by name and rank while in captivity. He developed a code by tapping on the prison walls to communicate with other prisoners. [12]

On 29 July one of the greatest tragedies of the war in Southeast Asia occurred as the result of a simple electrical malfunction. The Atlantic Fleet carrier *Forrestal* (which in 1955 had been the first carrier built to handle jet aircraft) had left Norfolk, Virginia on 6 June after a major refit and was assigned to TF 77 on 8 July. After working up in the South China Sea, the Forrestal took up her position at 'Yankee Station' on 25 July for her combat debut off Việtnam. Four days later, after flying just 150 combat sorties; she was limping away from Việtnam towards Subic Bay in the Philippines for temporary repairs before returning to Norfolk, Virginia on 14 September for a major refurbishment. On the morning of 29 July, as a launch was under way, a stray voltage ignited a Zuni rocket pod suspended under F-4B 153061. One of the rockets fired and zoomed across the deck to hit a Skyhawk's fuel tank, causing a chain reaction of explosions and fire on the flight deck. The Skyhawk pilot, Lieutenant (jg) D. Dollarbide, was incredibly fortunate to escape and be rescued by his plane captain. The aircraft on the deck were soon well ablaze, the fire fed by over 40,000 gallons of aviation fuel together with bombs and other ordnance. Bombs detonated blowing holes in the armoured deck through which fell burning fuel and ordnance that set fire to six lower decks. After the inferno was eventually brought under control the next day a total 134 men were dead, 62 more injured and 21 aircraft destroyed with another 34 damaged.

Captain Tom Wimberly, XO of VF-74 'Be-Devilers' on 29 July recalls: 'A photo of the folded port wing is that of the F-4B Phantom I was manning at the start of the fire. I was amidships, port side, chained down with the engines running, no ground crew in sight. I looked back when the fire first started and said to my RIO, Lieutenant (jg) Jim Martin 'this is really going to screw up this launch.' It looked like just one aircraft on fire. Little did I know. When the fire spread across the after end of the flight deck, I was anxious to get unchained and taxi forward. I told Jim that if no one came to unchain us, I would go into burner to try to break the tie-downs. At that moment, a plane captain named Dale Goldinger came running aft, toward the fire and unchained me and also wingman John Orsburn's F-4 and we scooted up the deck. It was obvious we needed as much separation as possible from that fire. At about one minute twenty seconds after the fire started, the first bomb exploded. It was like it went high order like it was properly fused. The difference between the bombs exploding and the fuel tanks previously exploding was infinite. The bomb explosions severely jarred the whole ship. Until the first bomb went, I was calm. When the first bomb went, I switched to the extremely scared mode. My knees were knocking and doing a dance on the cockpit floor. Having taxied forward, there were no tie-down chains. Goldinger showed up again and gave me the signal to do what plane captains did to avoid having to sit holding the brakes in the process of being towed. They would loosen the seat belt and put it around the emergency pneumatic brake handle, then tighten the seat belt. I did that and was satisfied the plane would be OK, so I got out. I headed for the ready room, thinking my RIO would follow. Reaching the ready room and not finding Jim behind me, I retraced my steps to the catwalk. There was Jim, taking photos. (RIOs were required to carry cameras to record battle damage if possible.) I am sure he got some of the most spectacular photos of the fire.'

With *Forrestal* heavily damaged and out of action, aircraft from the *Constellation, Oriskany* and *Intrepid* continued to strike at bridges, depots, SAM sites and airfields before the monsoon set in.

During April-July 1967 the Navy accounted for another dozen enemy aircraft. On 10 August Lieutenant Guy H. Freeborn and Lieutenant Bob Elliott his RIO and Lieutenant Commander Robert C. Davis and his RIO Lieutenant Commander Gayle O. 'Swede' Elie of VF-142 'Ghostriders' from the *Constellation* each shot down a MiG-21 with Sidewinders.

A contributing factor that aided MiG tactics after the June-July 1967 stand-down was the diversion of F-4s from MiGCAP to strike missions, leaving strike forces without adequate protection. Heavily-laden strike aircraft were unable to outrun the supersonic MiG-21s and strike pilots were briefed to avoid confrontation whenever possible; and if MiGs were sighted, the former were to continue to the target at increased speed. When they could not outrun the MiGs and if the situation so dictated, the last strike flight could jettison its ordnance and attempt to short-stop the attack by engaging the enemy. Such a situation persisted in August and part of September. In the first half of 1967, the North Viêtnamese had realized they could not directly confront US fighters in air-to-air combat, so they changed their procedures for the deployment of their numerically inferior MiG units. To take advantage of the MiG-21's speed and small size, pilots flying the type were instructed to intercept targets only at high-speed behind or above US strike formations. Then, as they approached their target, the MiG-21 pilots would make a supersonic diving pass against trailing or isolated flights, so they could position themselves for a missile kill. The action of 23 August demonstrated that the VPAF (Viêtnamese Peoples Air Force) had successfully executed their new procedure, which was helped by more skilful ground controllers who directed the MiG fighter towards their targets. Indeed, the new procedure gave MiG pilots the ingredient they needed to achieve a kill over their US opponents; between August 1967 and February 1968, the VPAF achieved a kill ratio of 1.1:1 against the USAF, with the loss of twenty aircraft for twenty-two victories

The 23rd of August was the worst day for the USAF in North Viêtnam since 2 December 1966, when they had lost five aircraft in a single day. Consequently, the actions of 23 August became known as 'Black Wednesday' amongst US pilots who participated in air operations over Hànôi on that particular day. The USAF officially confirmed the loss of three F-4Ds during the raid against the Yên Viên rail yard. The action gave the VPAF their first major victory since Operation 'Bolo'. The US Navy lost an F-4B (149498) of VF-142 from the USS *Constellation*. Lieutenant Commander Thomas Walter Sitek, 32 and Ensign Patrick Lawrence Ness, 25 of Minnesota. Minneapolis was killed on a flak suppression mission during a Navy strike on railway sidings at Lạc Đạo to the east of Hànôi. Sitek was a veteran pilot. Ness, however, was on his first tour of Viêtnam. Married shortly before he shipped out, Ness had joined the Navy in July 1965 and learned to fly. Before he was shot down on 23 August he had been shot down twice and rescued. The third time, he was not so lucky. Over the target, Sitek's aircraft encountered intense flak and SAMs in profusion and was seen to successfully evade two missiles but was hit by a third as the F-4 levelled out momentarily at 8,000 feet. The aircraft quickly became a mass of flames from wingtip to wingtip and the fire spread to the fuselage as the fuel cells exploded. No ejections or parachutes were seen. Search and rescue efforts were not feasible since the location was deep inside enemy territory. The two men were presumed to have died in the crash of the aircraft, probably having been wounded by the explosion of the SA-2.

Late in the day the USAF lost an F-105 and an O-1E and four F-4D Phantoms in the 'Triple Nickel' at Ubon, which were taking part in a strike against the Yên Viên rail yards by five flights of F-105s and four flights of F-4Ds, one of which was designated as the MiGCAP flight which flew to the left rear of the F-105 box. The five F-105s rendezvoused with the four F-4 flights in the refuelling area and then they crossed the Red River six miles southeast of Yên Bái, proceeding from there down 'Thud Ridge'. The F-105 'Iron Hand' flight (two F-105Ds and two F-105Fs) led the force to the target area. The force then split into two 'cells,' the F-105 strike aircraft in a box formation and the F-4 strike aircraft following in a triangular formation.

As 'Ford' flight turned down 'Thud Ridge' at 15,000 feet about fifty miles northwest of Hànôi, someone warned on the radio, *Bandits, northwest at sixty miles, heading 360°.* Two MiG-21s then descended out of a 25,000 feet overcast and attacked from 6 o'clock. The number two F-4D aircrew saw the enemy missile which passed their left wing and impacted with the lead F-4D. Major Charles Robert Tyler ejected and was knocked unconscious and taken prisoner but his WSO, Captain Ronald Nichalis Sittner was killed. From this point on, the air battle turned into a confused dogfight. The sky over North Viêtnam was filled with numerous engagements: F-4Cs, F-4Ds and F-105Ds battling many MiG-21s and MiG-17s. In the confusion, one F-4C aircrew fired two AIM-7 missiles at what they thought was a MiG but was actually an F-4D. Luckily, the aircraft commander identified the friendly aircraft in time. 'I told the guy in the backseat to break lock. It was no problem,' he later commented. The missiles, one of which had been tracking well, went ballistic as soon as the radar lock-on was broken and they did no damage. The aircrew fired upon was unaware of the incident, but continued down 'Thud Ridge'.

A second enemy missile hit 'Ford 04's tailpipe and the Phantom exploded in a ball of flame. Captain Larry Edward Carrigan of Arizona survived and was captured three days later. His backseater, 1st Lieutenant Charles Lane, 24, from Yankton, South Dakota was killed, flying on his 92nd mission. Once Charles told his mother, Bea, that flying was like baseball. He wrote that it gave a good feeling, like 'if you sat on the bench one minute and were playing in the World Series the next.' Another F-4 was also destroyed in the attack. Of the four men in the two Phantoms, three parachutes were seen 'descending to the ground.' It is believed that Charles was killed instantly. Carrigan said he flew quite a distance before he crashed and Charles, had he ejected, should have fallen down sooner. The USAF's confirmation of the loss of 'Ford 4' to a MiG gave Nguyễn Văn Cốc his second air-to-air victory. On 2 January 1967 he was among a group of pilots who fell into the trap set by the 8th Tactical Fighter Wing and he and four other Viêtnamese pilots were shot down. All ejected safely. Nguyễn Văn Cốc eventually became the leading VPAF ace pilot of the war with nine kills.

Soon after the loss of 'Ford 04' 1st Lieutenant David B. Waldrop III, an F-105D pilot shot down a MiG-17. 'It was beautiful,' reported Colonel Olds, flying the lead MiGCAP F-4D. 'The MiG-17 was diving toward the ground with flames coming out of his tailpipe. It wasn't the afterburner; he was on fire. There was that great, great, huge Thud right behind him with fire coming out of his nose. It looked like a shark chasing a minnow.' Olds saw no parachute.

Following close behind 'Ford' flight was 'Falcon' flight. Major Robert Ralston Sawhill avoided the MiGs but ran into an intense barrage of AAA as he dived on the target. His aircraft was hit and he and 1st Lieutenant Gerald Lee Gerndt ejected close to Giá Lâm Airport. Both men were quickly captured and spent the rest of the war as prisoners until released on 14 March 1973. A fourth Phantom in the 555th was hit by the intense AAA over the target but managed to escape from the area and head towards home. Major C. B. Demarque crossed North Viêtnam and Laos into Thailand but he and 1st Lieutenant J. M. Piet his WSO were forced to eject near Wanon Niwat, about sixty miles northwest of Nakhon Phanom when they ran out of fuel before reaching a tanker. They were both picked up by a rescue helicopter, having suffered only minor injuries.

The loss of four aircraft on a single raid was a severe blow to the 'Triple Nickel' and the threat of the MiG-21 was becoming very apparent. The VPAF had revised its tactics by approaching the strike force at low level and zooming up to attack with a single pass before heading for base or China. The tally might have been worse as an F-4C crew launched two Sparrow missiles at what they thought was a MiG but was then identified as another Phantom. The crew broke radar lock and the missiles went ballistic and fell into the jungle.

The MiG tactics employed during the 23 August engagements came 'as a complete surprise' to Olds. Had he been informed, the commander felt, he could have avoided the mass confusion. He found out later that higher headquarters knew that the MiG-21s had changed their tactics prior to this engagement, 'but the word hadn't filtered down to our wing. That made me pretty mad because I lost two aircraft because of this new tactic. If I had known about the new MiG tactic, I would have split my MiGCAP elements up; 3 and 4 would have accelerated below the strike force and ingressed 10-15 miles ahead of them. My wingman and I would have turned easterly toward the Ridge prior to the strike force... accelerated... gained 15-20 miles separation ... and swooped over the force as they turned south-easterly down the Ridge. The GCI controller would already have picked us up on radar; he would have observed our turn. I'll bet you one hundred dollars that he'd called off the MiGs. He probably would have said, 'Break, break, they're on to you.' Then we would have turned in behind the strike force and continued ingress.'

F-4 crews mostly flew air-to-ground missions in South East Asia armed with conventional and retarded bombs with standard or extended fuses, rocket launchers, CBUs (cluster bomb units), or BLU firebombs. At the end of May 1967 the 'Triple Nickel' at Ubon re-equipped with the F-4D and on 24 August the AGM-62A Walleye TV-guided bomb was used in a successful attack on a bridge. On 25 May 1968 F-4Ds of the 'Wolfpack' launched GBU-10 laser-guided bombs for the first time. F-4Ds of the 25th TFS seeded ADSID-1 acoustical sensors along the Hô Chi Minh Trail and Mk.84 EOGBs (Electro-Optical Guided Bombs) were first dropped by Phantoms of the 8th TFW on 6 April 1972.

From 24 August to 17 October 1967, there were no further MiG kills by USAF fighters. During this period the Air Force assigned a larger number F-4s to a purely MiGCAP role, but apparently, the North Viêtnamese elected to avoid confrontations. Strike forces, meanwhile, continued to pound enemy support and war-making installations. On 18 October, MiG pilots once again initiated a campaign of dogged opposition against US air forces. A strike force composed of four F-105 strike flights, one F-105F 'Iron Hand' flight and one F-4D MiGCAP flight struck the Dai Loi rail bypass bridge on that afternoon. Three of the four strike flights encountered MiG-17s in the target area and one MiG was shot down by an F-105D. The F-4D MiGCAP flight trailed the Thunderchiefs into the target area and also encountered MiG-17s, but destroyed none.

Renewed MiG opposition prompted Pentagon officials to authorize for the first time in the war a strike against Phúc Yên airfield, the largest of North Viêtnam's air bases. Accordingly, six days after the Dai Loi strike, four strike forces of F-105s and F-4s, working with US Navy aircraft, struck the airfield.

Pilots of the 8th, 355th and 388th Tactical Fighter Wings reported all bombs on target; the mission was highly successful in rendering the sprawling base unserviceable. Post-strike reconnaissance photos showed four MiG-21s, four MiG-17s and one MiG-15 destroyed or badly damaged.

Seventh Air Force planners had anticipated a loss of 3 percent of the strike force to MiGs, flak and SAMs during the Phúc Yên raid, but not one US aircraft was lost. One MiG-21 was destroyed in air-to-air combat during the initial attack. It was shot down by Major William L. Kirk (who had destroyed a MiG-17 on 13 May) and his backseater, 1st Lieutenant Theodore R. Bongartz who were leading a MiGCAP flight protecting a strike package of F-105s in 'Harpoon 01'. 'Disco', an EC-121 'Warning Star' and a Navy cruiser ('Red Crown') were watching the airspace over North Việtnam on radar and warned Kirk that bogeys were approaching. The Phantoms turned to meet the attackers, Kirk recalling: 'As I rolled out of this turn, I met a MiG-21 head-on. It was highly polished - a beautiful little airplane - and as we passed within twenty yards of each other I thought: What a shame to have to shoot at him.'

'This kill wasn't quite the same one as my first one last May 13,' Kirk, nearing the end of his Việtnam tour, commented. 'That one was a MiG-17 and there was only one pass. I got him with my air-to-air missile. This time it was a good old-fashioned dogfight and we fought him for a long time.' He had to protect the F-105s, however, and so climbed up to reverse his course and get on the MiG's tail. To his surprise, he found that the MiG was doing the same thing. The PAVNAF rarely liked to dogfight and the MiG pilot would have been better off to have gone on to disrupt the formation of Thunderchiefs. The Thuds were his priority target and the MiG-21 was fast enough to make pursuit difficult. The two aircraft wheeled through two vertical loops, the Phantom held back by its external fuel tanks. Kirk finally managed to discard his tanks, which confused the MiG pilot and allowed Kirk to get on his tail. Bongartz fired a Sparrow, but it exploded short. Kirk fumbled for the switches to arm his cannon pod: 'It couldn't have taken more than a couple of seconds, but when I looked up I had a windscreen full of MiG-21! He was in a hard left turn and the gunsight pipper was right in the middle of his back. I squeezed the trigger and the 20mm Gatling sawed a hole right through him between the wing roots. He bailed out immediately.

'We took position as fragged and I positioned my flight line abreast, high and to the left of the trailing F-105 flight. MiG calls were heard as we entered NVN. They proved to be extremely accurate. When the MiG calls indicated that the MiGs were 6 o'clock at eight miles I turned our flight back into the attack. As I rolled out of the 180° turn Lieutenant Bongartz acquired a radar lock-on to a target 306 right at 4 miles. I immediately looked to that position and visually identified a MiG-21.

'At initial contact, the MiG was slightly right and head-on. He appeared to go into a steep climb, initially, but as I started up with him he then rolled into me and put his nose back down. He appeared to be aggressive for the first 360° turn and then it appeared he was trying to disengage.

'After several hard manoeuvering turns and reversals, in which the MiG would run through a cloud at every opportunity, I acquired AIM-7 missile firing parameters and launched two missiles. The first guided well and exploded very close to the MiG. I did not observe the second missile. The first AIM-7 could possibly have damaged the MiG, even though I could see no visible damage, in fact, I had the impression that the MiG started to decelerate immediately after missile detonation. I then switched to guns, closed to about 500-700 feet and started firing. The HEI impacted on top of his fuselage between the wing roots ... I could see large pieces coming off the fuselage and the entire fuselage section was engulfed in flames. The pilot bailed out; the MiG-21 rolled to the right and crashed. I then turned and flew by the MiG pilot, hanging in his chute. I was not able to get a look at his face in that when he saw me approaching he turned his back.'

MiGs continued their aggressive assaults and on Thursday, 26 October six MiG-17s jumped a flight of four 'Triple Nickel' F-4Ds flying MiGCAP for a photographic mission three miles northwest of Phúc Yên airfield. As soon as the MiGs appeared the reconnaissance aircraft departed. In the ensuing battle, three of the MiGs were shot down by air-to-air missiles. The first victory went to the 'Ford' flight leader, Captain John D. Logeman, Jr. who was from Fond Du Lac, Wisconsin and 1st Lieutenant Frederick E. McCoy II of Sheboygen, Wisconsin his backseater.

'Approximately six nautical miles before reaching Phúc Yên,' recalled Logeman 'I observed four MiG-17s climbing up through a cloud layer at our 2 o'clock position. I called the flight to turn into the MiGs, who were in a right climbing turn approaching our 4 o'clock position at approximately five miles range. I also called the reconnaissance flight to egress the area. As I completed my right turn, heading approximately 090° at 17,000 feet, I placed the pipper on the lead MiG-17 and fired two AIM-7E missiles in boresight mode. Range to the MiG was 2.5 to three miles. The first missile did not guide. The second missile came up into the reticule and appeared to be on a collision course with the MiG. We were head-on and his cannons were firing. I pulled up to avoid the cannon fire and did not observe missile detonation. I immediately turned hard left to re-engage the MiGs on a west heading. During this left turn, I observed a parachute in the area of intended missile impact and a MiG-17 was descending inverted, trailing sparks from the fuselage. 'Ford 02' [Major John A. Hall and 1st Lieutenant Albert T. Hamilton] observed this parachute at the same time. Another MiG-17 was attacking from my 10 o'clock position. He turned away at a range of about two miles. My rear seat pilot obtained a boresight, full system lock-on and I attempted to fire two AIM-7E missiles. One did not leave the aircraft, but the second missile fired and appeared to be guiding. I broke off the attack at this point to manoeuvre away from a MiG-17's cannon attack from my 7 o'clock position. At this point, I called the flight to egress for 'Bingo' fuel.

The second victory went to 'Ford 03's Captain William S. Gordon III of Wethersfield, Connecticut and 1st Lieutenant James H. Monsees of Santa Clara, California minutes after Logeman's. Watching the attack come in from 3 o'clock, Gordon turned his element to attack the eight MiGs, but he was too close to fire a missile. 'I disengaged,' he reported, 'then gained lateral separation and re attacked.' He observed: 'Two MiG-17s were in the pipper head-on. My pilot obtained boresight, full system lock-on and I attempted to fire two AIM-7E Sparrow missiles... Only one fired. I was unable to see the missile detonate due to evasive manoeuvering necessary to avoid the attacking MiGs. I disengaged again and reversed back into the fight. A MiG pilot was hanging in a white parachute in the same location that I had fired the missile. The MiG had been at approximately 16,000 feet in a slight climb. I disengaged and reengaged two more times without obtaining a good position to fire. On the next attempt, I had a MiG-17 in my pipper for a tail shot. By the time I selected AIM-4Ds, cooled the missile, listened for a tone and fired the missile with self-track selected the MiG had turned to a head-on firing attack. I fired the AIM-4 with a full system radar lock-on at a range of approximately 6,000 feet. Again I was unable to observe the missile impact due to evasive action necessary to avoid the attacking MiG; however, it appeared to guide straight for the MiG. My pilot observed another chute at lower altitude, approximately 8,000 feet. At the same time, he could still see the high parachute that we had observed first. After I had shot my second missile, my wingman observed two MiG-17s egressing the battle and pursued them, finally destroying one. Then Captain Logeman called the flight to egress due to low fuel.'

The third victory went to Captain Larry D. Cobb of Lambert, Missouri and Captain Alan A. LaVoy, 27, of Norwalk, Connecticut flying 'Ford 04'. LaVoy, who had been on duty in Vietnam since May, was home recently on R&R after logging 65 missions over enemy territory. Cobb recalled: 'Gordon turned us into the MiG-17s and started to accelerate. On the first turn, we were unable to fire, so he left the fight for separation. We then turned right and re-entered the fight. We were both able to fire a missile on this pass and we continued through the MiGs and out the other side of the fight. Gordon carried us out and up to the left. Again we turned to re-enter the fight. I observed an enemy chute in the middle of the battle. We again went through the battle but were unable to fire. We continued using these tactics during the attack. On our last pass a MiG-17 obtained a 6 o'clock position on Gordon, but when I told him to break left, the MiG-17 broke off the attack. I observed two MiG-17s at my 10 o'clock position. I cooled an AIM-4D Falcon infrared-guided missile, obtained a self-track lock-on and fired the missile with 10-15° lead angle. The AIM-4D impacted on the tail of the MiG-17 and he exploded and started to roll right. The pilot ejected and his plane spiralled earthward in flames.' (Disappointing results with the Falcon - it accounted for a total of five victories in the war - led to the 8th TFW modifying its F-4Ds to once again carry USN-developed Sidewinders).

Heavy North Viêtnamese MiG losses during October, both in the air and on the ground, were sufficient reason for another stand-down and more training, but the NVNAF did not resort to this action. Rather, in the next two months, they gained a slight edge in the air-to-air war. As American aircraft losses mounted, USAF air strikes were conducted against every jet-capable airfield north of the 20th parallel except Giá Lâm Airport on the outskirts of Hànôi. Many NVNAF aircraft dispersed on a temporary basis to bases in China. Repairs in the meantime were made to North Viêtnamese airfields and their MiG losses were replaced. By the end of 1967, the MiG inventory was thus still reasonably high. Yet, significantly during this 2-month period, USAF fighter crews succeeded in downing five MiGs in aerial combat.

On 24 October 1967 seven hours after Kép airfield was bombed, the Navy and Air Force made a coordinated attack on Phúc Yên, the first time this major air base had been attacked. The raid was accompanied by several flights of Phantoms that flew CAPs over various points in North Việtnam. Radio Hànôi announced that in the afternoon that eight US warplanes had been shot down during a strike on the Hànôi, Hảiphòng and Vĩnh Phú region of North Việtnam and that a number of pilots had been captured. Two F-4B Phantoms of VF-151 from the *Coral Sea*, one piloted by Commander Charles R. Gillespie, 38, of Meridian Mississippi, the CO of VF-151 'Vigilantes' and his NFO (Naval Flight Officer or navigator), Lieutenant (jg) Richard Champ Clark of Tacoma, Washington and the other flown by Lieutenant (jg's) Robert F. Frishmann and Earl G. Lewis, were brought down by SAM missiles. As the raid was flying down 'Thud Ridge', still thirteen miles north of the target, it was engaged by a SAM battery. Commander Gillespie saw one of the SA-2s and dived to 14,000 feet to avoid it but moments later the aircraft was hit by another missile that the crew had not spotted. The aircraft burst into flames and the hydraulics failed leading to loss of control. The cockpit filled with smoke, the intercom system failed and Gillespie gave an emergency hand signal to order abandonment. He ejected safely but was not able to tell if his NFO escaped from the aircraft. Earl Lewis saw Gillespie eject. He also maintained constant visual contact with the disabled Phantom and saw Clark slumped over in the back seat. Other members of the flight observed two good parachutes, heard one electronic beacon signal and observed one unidentified crew member on the ground. They remained overhead near 'Thud Ridge' to provide cover for the rescue attempt. An electronic and visual search was immediately put into action but when no voice contact could be established with any of the four downed crewmen and the single beeper stopped transmitting, the search effort was terminated. Gillespie was captured but he did not see Dick Clark again. It seems that his NFO did not appear in any of the PoW camps.

About fifteen minutes' later another Phantom was hit by a SAM. Lieutenant Frishmann was flying straight and level at 10,000 feet when it was damaged by a missile that exploded behind the Phantom. One of the engines failed and caught fire but before the crew could take any action another SA-2 exploded just in front of the aircraft. The Phantom immediately rolled out of control and both crew ejected. Frishmann relates; 'I wasn't even diving when they hit me. I was flying. Bad luck!' Frishmann thought his NFO had been killed but the pair met up after more than four hours on the ground but both men were found and captured by the Việtnamese. Frishmann's arm was badly injured by missile fragments when the SAM exploded. A North Việtnamese doctor removed the elbow joint, shortening the arm by eight inches.

On 26 October an F-4B of the VF-143 'Pukin' Dogs' on the USS *Constellation* flown by Lieutenant (jg) Robert P. 'Burner Bob' Hickey Jr. and Lieutenant (jg) Jeremy G. 'Jerry' Morris destroyed a MiG-21. Lieutenant Commander James 'Jaybee' Burton Souder, 32, born in Elizabethton, Carter County, Tennessee where he spent his boyhood, was a RIO in another Phantom in the flight.

Slightly less than perfect eyesight prevented him from becoming a pilot but he won his Naval Flight Officer wings of gold and served as an F-4 RIO. He had detected the inbound bogey that turned out to be a MiG-21 on his radar at 17 miles. But 'Jaybee' was unable to pick up the threat on his instruments so he directed both Phantoms in a 'wild, full-burner, clawing-climbing intercept' to up around 30,000 feet, finally putting the F-4s at the MiG's 6 o'clock. When 'Jerry' Morris finally got radar lock-on, problems in 'Jaybee's Phantom prevented a missile launch so he told Hickey to shoot the MiG. He did and his AIM-7E Sparrow destroyed the enemy jet, whose pilot ejected successfully to fight another day. Nguyễn Hồng Nhị went on to score a record eight US aircraft destroyed. 'Burner Bob' Hickey and 'Jerry Morris each received Silver Stars. 'Jaybee' Souder was awarded the DFC. On 27 April 1972 he and his pilot, Al Molinare, became unwelcome guests in the most infamous 'Hilton' in the world. 'Jaybee' Souder recalled: 'The greatest inspiration I experienced in Hànôi came to me my first day there. I was extremely tired, hungry, thirsty and aching all over from that long truck trip north. The interrogators had begun their work. I looked to myself for strength but found I had little to offer. I wondered how I would sustain myself during the long months and possibly years ahead. Then the thought came to me. 'You are in the presence of the greatest men in the world.' I thought of Captain Bill Lawrence, under whom I'd served in 1967 and Captain Jim Stockdale and Jerry Denton and Colonel Robbie Risner and the many others who had endured the pain and hardships of PoW life for so long. Then my job became a very easy one compared to theirs.

The *Constellation's* last kill of her deployment came on 30 October during a raid on the Thành Hóa Bridge when the Northern Phantom MiGCAP flight of VF-142 'Ghostriders' was vectored onto a flight of four MiG-17s near Haiphòng. Lieutenant Commander Eugene P. Lund and Lieutenant (jg) James R. Borst shot down one of the MiGs with a Sparrow and then positioned his Phantom behind the MiG's wingman and fired another Sparrow. The missile accelerated away from the aircraft but suddenly exploded about 100 feet in front of the Phantom and badly damaged the engine and the undercarriage. Lund managed to reach the *Constellation* but without a serviceable undercarriage was unable to land the aircraft and so he flew alongside the carrier at 5,000 feet and he and his backseater ejected. They were picked up by one of the carrier's helicopters.[13]

On the afternoon of 6 November, 1967 two forces were sent out to strike Kép's airfield and rail yard. The 'Wolfpack' provided the MiGCAP F-4Ds. Captain Darrell D. Simmonds of Vernon, Texas was the flight leader in 'Sapphire 01' with 1st Lieutenant George H. McKinney Jr. of Bessemer, Alabama as his rear seat pilot. Since this flight was the only MiGCAP, it split into two elements to protect each side of the strike force should MiGs be sighted. Approach to the target was uneventful; no SAM and no MiG warnings were issued but as the 'Iron Hand' flight recovered from its Shrike release on Kép airfield, the first MiG warning came. The first F-105 strike flight was recovering from its bomb run when it was attacked by four MiG-17s. The F-4s at once turned south to engage the MiGs but made no visual contact. The

MiGCAP then turned back to the northeast to rejoin the departing strike force and now made MiG contact. In the next few minutes, the two pilots in the lead aircraft destroyed two MiG-17s in short order. Captain Simmonds recalled: 'My initial contact with the MiGs came when my flight was on a 90° beam heading to the egressing force. A flight of four MiG-17s (not the same flight that we turned into) was closing in on the last egressing flight and started firing. I closed on the firing MiG and caused him to stop firing and take evasive action. After several manoeuvering tactics, I closed to within 1,500 feet of the MiG and fired my gun. At that time, the aft section of the MiG-17 burst into flames. We then pulled up and to the right and observed the canopy blow off, but no ejection occurred until just before impact with the ground. The chute of the MiG pilot streamed and disappeared into the trees just as the MiG impacted in a large orange fireball.

'I turned the flight back toward the egress heading when my back seat pilot spotted a lone MiG-17 at our 4 o'clock position, low and heading away from us. I called to the flight that we were going back in and turned to close on the MiG-17. He saw us coming and dropped to about 200 feet off the ground and started up a small valley. I dropped just below him and closed. When he saw me moving into lethal range, he broke hard left and climbed, giving me a tracking position. I moved to within 1,000 feet and opened fire. The MiG-17 disappeared in a large fireball and plummeted to the earth in many pieces. Again I turned my flight toward the egress heading. MiG calls indicated that there were MiGs following us at six miles and closing. We did not have the fuel to engage and elected to accelerate and depart the area.'

On the night of 9 November 1967, for his 52nd combat mission, 40-year old Lieutenant Colonel John Armstrong and 25-year old 1st Lieutenant Lance Peter Sijan of the 480th TFS, 366th TFW at Đà Nẵng were tasked with a bombing mission to Ban Laboy Ford on Highway 912 in Laos. As they rolled in on their target to release their ordnance, their F-4C (64-0751) was engulfed in a ball of fire, due to the bomb fuses malfunctioning and causing a premature detonation on their release. Sijan managed to eject from the aircraft and although likely rendered unconscious in the ejection, his parachute landed him on a rocky limestone karst ridge adjacent to the target. No electronic or radio signals was heard from either Sijan or Armstrong until early on the morning of 11 November, Sijan came up on the radio and made contact with a 'Misty' FAC F-100F that was flying over his crash site. The USAF launched a massive effort to locate his position and 'soften up' the numerous enemy air defences in his area. At dusk, the SAR forces were finally able to position a 'Jolly Green Giant' helicopter near Sijan's position. (During this overall rescue operation, over twenty aircraft were damaged by anti-aircraft fire and many had to return to base. One A-1H aircraft was shot down, though its pilot was soon rescued by a SAR helicopter on station). Sijan, refusing to put other airmen in danger, insisted on trying to crawl to a jungle penetrator lowered by the helicopter and he directly opposed the helicopter's Para-Jumper coming down to find and rescue him. After the 'Jolly Green' hovered for an agonizing 33 minutes and upon hearing no further radio transmissions from Sijan, the on-scene SAR commander flying a A-1H Skyraider suspected a trap and thus ordered the

'Jolly Green' and the entire SAR effort to withdraw. Search efforts continued the very next morning but to no avail.

During his violent ejection and very rough parachute landing on the karst ridge, Sijan had suffered a fractured skull, a mangled right hand and a compound fracture of the left leg. He was without food, with very little water and no survival kit; nevertheless, he evaded enemy forces for 46 days. During this entire evasion and escape period, Sijan was only able to move by sliding on his buttocks and back along the rocky limestone karst ridge and later along the jungle floor. After managing to move an astonishing several thousand feet, Sijan crawled onto a truck road along the Hô Chi Minh Trail, where he was finally captured on Christmas Day 1967. Terrifically emaciated and in poor health, Sijan was placed in custody in an NVA camp. Soon thereafter, in his emaciated and crippled condition, he overpowered one of his guards and crawled into the jungle, only to be recaptured after several hours. He was then transferred to another prison camp where he was kept in solitary confinement and interrogated at length. During interrogation, he was severely tortured; however, he did not divulge any information to his captors. He was soon transported to the Hànôi 'Hilton', where, in his weakened state, he contracted pneumonia and died on 22 January 1968. His remains were repatriated on 13 March 1974 and were positively identified on 22 April 1974. He was buried with military honours in Arlington Park Cemetery in Milwaukee. Sijan received the Medal of Honor posthumously in 1976 for his invincible courage and extraordinary devotion to duty.

On 19 November two VF-151 'Vigilantes' F-4Bs from the USS *Coral Sea* were on a MiGCAP patrol escorting A-4s from the USS *Intrepid* into the Red River Valley to strike airfields and bridges near Haiphòng. The North Viêtnamese sent up two MiG 17s in front of the F-4s to bait the F-4s into jumping them. Behind the F-4s were four MiG 21s waiting for the Phantoms to take the bait. 'Switchbox' flight was providing TARCAP coverage in the vicinity of Hàiphòng and the two Phantoms were stalking a flight of MiGs when they were themselves engaged by other MiGs just south of Hàiphòng. The MiGs were from Giá Lâm but were operating undetected from a forward airfield at Kiên Ân.

Lieutenant Commander Claude Douglas Clower, 37, of Beaumont, Texas and Lieutenant (jg) Walter O. Estes, 28 of Williamston, Michigan, were in the lead aircraft. Their wingman was Lieutenant Commander James Erlan Teague, 24 of Harrisburg, Arizona and his RIO was Lieutenant (jg) Theodore Gerhard Stier, 27, of Pasadena California, a veteran of 155 missions. Ted Stier recalled: 'We were flying in a combat wing formation and MiGs were known to be operating in the target area as we were receiving transmissions from 'Red Crown'. Jack Teague and I were on Doug Clower's left at about the 9 o'clock position about 500 feet out when Walt Estes called 'MiGs 3 o'clock high'. I rogered and looked up and saw two MiG-17s sweeping into firing position. I called their clock positions - three, four, five o'clock - to Jack but he stayed in position as Clower continued on the same course and took no evasive action. Next, I saw a Sidewinder leave Clower's aircraft. About the same time the two MiG-17s were settling in on a firing position and I yelled to Jack 'let's get the hell outta here'.

Teague's aircraft was hit. He began an immediate course change towards the coast. His aircraft was intact except for small fires burning around the radome and air conditioning.

Clower saw the first MiG-17 at about 170° nose-on closing fast. He knew the MiG could not manoeuvre into a position to do anything right then and let him pass behind him. He immediately picked up the second MiG-17 with a tone from his sidewinder. The MiG-17 was in front of him in a shallow left turn. He commenced a 1-2g left turn to get inside the MiG-17 for a better tone and track for the sidewinder. As the tone got better he fired an AIM-9B. It just missed and detonated close by due to the proximity fuse. He swung his F-4 in tighter on the MiG and got a good tone with an AIM-9D. He was right on top of the MIG-17 and fired the sidewinder. At that same moment, he got a frantic call from his wingman to 'Break left', so he was unable to see the missile hit, but there is no way it could have missed. As he was breaking left a missile came up under his right wing and detonated just in front of the wing of his Phantom; the right wing was gone. He called 'get out' to his RIO and ejected.

'As far as the 'Break' call' recalls Ted Stier 'perhaps Walt called it or maybe I transmitted in the open when I told Jack 'let's get the hell outta here' and Doug took that to mean 'break'. The missile Doug fired exploded but I didn't see it hit an aircraft. There was an explosion in front of his aircraft about a mile, plus or minus but I didn't see any aircraft in front of him. Maybe I was too busy watching the two MiGs closing in on us. I then saw Clower's aircraft explode in a ball of flames and saw one chute. Jack and I then came under fire as tracers enveloped our aircraft. The MiG firing and tracking us broke off the engagement for whatever reason and went his merry way. I could tell that our aircraft wasn't responding properly and asked Jack 'what was wrong.' He replied 'we've had it, stay with me'. I gave him a heading to the coast and as he slowly turned the aircraft, we lost flying speed and the aircraft went into a flat spin like a leaf falling to the ground. I told Jack I was ejecting.'

Stier thought that his aircraft was hit by cannon fire from a MiG but it is also possible that the aircraft was damaged by debris from Clower's aircraft, which had just exploded close by. Stier ejected but his pilot was not seen to escape from the aircraft.

As Clower's parachute deployed he descended through 4,000 feet. That was when he noticed a mustard coloured parachute in front of him at about his 11 o'clock. He then turned and noticed another chute behind him at his 5 o'clock. The Navy used all-white chutes at that time so this had to be his RIO, Walt Estes. There was only one explanation for the yellow/mustard parachute in front of him; it had to be from the MiG-17 he had just fired his Sidewinder at.'

The downed aircrews landed close together on the open, flat coastal plain covered in rice fields on the south side of a northwest to southeast running primary road that paralleled a small river located just to its north. The area was laced with rivers and roads of all sizes running through the densely populated and heavily defended site approximately four miles east-southeast of Đội Cứu Hộ Trên Không, eleven miles southwest of Hảiphòng and 52 miles east-southeast of Hànôi. The region in which the aircrews landed was also seven miles due south of Kiến An airfield and ten miles southwest of Cát Bi airfield.

Within days of the loss, Radio Hànôi and Radio Havana boasted that MiG-17s had shot down two American aircraft and captured the four crewmen. Subsequent to his capture, Clower was visited in the PoW camp by a North Viêtnamese pilot claiming to be the one that shot him down. Doug Clower was told of the tactics of using two MIG-17s to sucker and four MiG-21s to jump the American fighters. The North Viêtnamese pilot communicated the tactics they used by drawing the engagement in the dirt. The NVAF pilot would not confirm or deny the MiG kill. Some documentation suggests that Clower's Phantom was brought by down by 37/23mm gunfire from the MiG 17s. The MiG 17 did not carry air-to-air missiles. Clearly, from the accounts of Clower, Stier and the NVAF pilot, he was brought down by a missile. So where did the missile come from that blew off his wing? It had to be from a MiG 21. Doug Clower remained positive that he had a MIG kill, although it was not officially confirmed by the Navy.[14]

On 17 December 1967, a US Marine Corps aircraft commander flying with the 432nd TRW teamed up with a USAF pilot for the next aerial victory when eight F-105 and two F-4D flights were scheduled three targets in Route Package 6A. In support of the effort were two flights of F-105 'Iron Hand' aircraft, four flights of F-4D MiGCAP aircraft and two flights of EB-66 ECM aircraft. The entire effort was divided into two forces, one striking the Làng Lau rail bridge and the other hitting Phúc Yên airfield. Captain Doyle D. Baker, a Marine Corps exchange pilot, commanded 'Gambit 03'. His 'guy-in-back' was 27-year old 1st Lieutenant John D. Ryan, Jr., eldest son of General John Dale Ryan. According to their pre-flight briefing, if their flight leader could obtain an immediate visual contact on any MiG which another flight member called out, he would give that aircraft permission to attack. As the strike force crossed the Red River and headed toward 'Thud Ridge', the F-4 flight trailed south of the main force by about eight miles. Suddenly came the warning: 'Red bandit airborne out of Giá Lâm.' Shortly thereafter, 'Gambit 03' and '04' established a visual contact and Baker requested and received permission to attack.

Baker turned right, made a high-speed diving pass at the MiG-17 and fired his SUU-23. The MiG turned into him and attempted to evade the attack. Passing beneath the hostile aircraft, Baker performed a high-speed yo-yo, followed by a scissors manoeuvre as the MiG reversed his turn. Keeping the MiG-17 in sight, Baker waited for separation, then performed a Split-S and made a second high-speed pass and fired his SUU-23. The MiG continued to turn into the attack, so Baker returned to 10,000 feet to allow separation. He made another high-speed pass, trying to fire the SUU-23, but discovered it was empty. The MiG turned into the attack. Baker overshot and made a high-speed yo-yo to 10,000 feet to try to get more separation. The MiG then levelled his wings at 2,000 feet and headed 120° at approximately 0.6 Mach. Baker manoeuvred his Phantom into a two-nautical mile stem attack and launched one AIM-4D while in a 10° dive, passing through 3,000 feet. The Falcon's lack of a proximity fuse would limit kills with this missile to just five in total but on this occasion the missile hit the tailpipe of the MiG and Baker observed persistent fire and black smoke trailing from the hostile aircraft. The left wing of the MiG dropped sharply and it began an uncontrollable downward roll from 2,000 feet. Baker executed a climbing right turn and lost sight of the kill. Under the rules at the time Baker and Ryan each received a half credit for the kill.[15]

MiG opposition proved extremely heavy and an F-105D and F-4D 66-7774 in the 497th TFS in the 'Wolfpack' crewed by Major Kenneth Raymond Fleenor, 37, of Bowling Green, Kentucky who had flown 87 missions and 1st Lieutenant Terry Lee Boyer, 29, of Visalia, California who had flown forty missions, were shot down on the raid on the Làng Lau railway bridge. The MiGCAP Phantom fell to the cannon of a MiG-17 during a dogfight near Yên Bái. The crew ejected and came down near the town of Più Thơ on the Red River and were both captured. Fleenor was on his 87th mission when he was shot down, while Boyer was on his 40th.[16]

F-4C 64-0782 in the 559 TFS, 12th TFW at Cam Ranh Bay crewed by Colonel C. Brett and 1st Lieutenant Myron F. Smith was shot down near Vĩnh Linh, five miles north of the DMZ, during an armed reconnaissance mission. The aircraft was making its second pass over an automatic weapons site when it was hit by 57mm AAA. The aircraft crashed close to the target but only Colonel Brett survived the ejection and was rescued by an HH-3E of the 37th ARRS. As night fell a third Phantom was shot down over North Viêtnam. F-4D 66-7757 in the 497th TFS, 8th TFW crewed by Major Laird Guttersen and 1st Lieutenant S. P. Sox was taking part in a strike on a ferry at Hun Hung, four miles south of Đông Hới when it was hit by ground fire. Guttersen coaxed the damaged aircraft out over the sea and he and his WSO ejected about eight miles off the coast and were rescued by a Navy helicopter. Guttersen's good fortune ran out on 23 February 1968 when he was shot down over North Viêtnam by Nguyễn Văn Cốc and captured.

By mid-December 1967 MiG-21s were coordinating their attacks with those of MiG-17s each from different quadrants, in multiple passes. These tactics were observed on the 19th when two large strike forces were sent into North Viêtnam to hit Viêt Trì and Tiến Cường rail yards. The first force, which never reached its target, consisted of four F-105 and two F-4D MiGCAP flights. It was attacked by six MiG-21s and four to eight MiG-17s. The USAF aircraft jettisoned their ordnance and jumped into the numerous engagements. None of the aircraft was damaged and one of the MiGCAP aircraft - 'Nash 01 - crewed by Major (later Major General) Joseph D. Moore of Spartanburg, South Carolina and 1st Lieutenant George H. McKinney Jr., poured enough gunfire from their underwing pod gun into a MiG-17 to receive credit for a half share in a MiG kill; the other half was awarded to Majors William M. Dalton of Stephens City, Virginia and James L. Graham of Lancaster, Pennsylvania in 'Otter 02', an F-105F 'Iron Hand' aircraft in the second force. Major Joe Moore, son of Lieutenant General Joseph H. Moore, tried to find where the MiG-17 had impacted but he could not tell an aircraft crash from all the bomb detonations. Whatever they blew up, it was not part of the rail yards targeted. Despite the loss of the two MiGs of forty strike aircraft, 24 jettisoned their bombs.[17] Moore flew 135 combat missions in F-4s including 100 missions over North Vietnam, 53 of them around Hànôi. Following his tour of duty at Ubon, Moore was selected to be commander-leader of the 'Thunderbirds' US Air Force Air Demonstration Squadron at Nellis Air Force Base. He planned and guided the team's successful conversion from F-100s to F-4s in 1969.

Early in 1968, President Johnson forbade all strikes further than the 19th Parallel and on 1 November he ordered a halt to all bombing of North Việtnam. 'Linebacker I' as it was called began with raids against road and rail systems, to prevent supplies reaching the Communists operating in South Việtnam. On 8 May A-6 Intruders sowed minefields in Haiphòng, Hon Gai and Cẩm Phả in the North and in five ports in the South. At this time the North Việtnamese had one of the best air defence systems in the world, with excellent radar integration of SA-2 SAMs, MiGs and AAA. Losses, though, were kept to within acceptable limits.

Beginning in January 1968, MiG pilots were less prone to flee toward China. Instead, they became more aggressive and frequently returned for a second pass against American strike aircraft. The number of their kills increased and the MiG threat became more significant. US forces therefore scheduled more MiGCAP missions and, at the same time, reduced the size of strike forces to provide better force protection. The first confrontation of the New Year took place on the morning of 3 January. The strike force was involved in a major effort and consisted of two separate forces. 'Alpha Force', which aimed at the Đông Dau rail bridge in the Hànôi area, was made up of four F-105 strike flights and two F-105 'Iron Hand' flights. 'Bravo Force', consisting of three F-4D strike flights, one F-4D flak suppression flight and two F-4D MiGCAP flights was directed against the Trung Quảng rail yard. The two forces approached from different directions and at different times, thus effectively splitting the MiG forces. 'Alpha Force' was attacked by MiG-21s on its approach to the target. 'Bravo' Force' was attacked by MiG-17s during withdrawal. 'Bravo' force engagements resulted in the destruction of two MiG-17s, one by a strike F-4D and the other by a MiGCAP aircrew. 'Olds 01' the strike aircraft was crewed by Lieutenant Colonel Clayton K. Squier of Oakland, California and 1st Lieutenant Michael D. Muldoon of Perry, New York in the 435th TFS, 8th TFW. Squier reported: 'I engaged four MiG-17 aircraft in a head-on pass during egress from the strike target about six miles south of Bắc Giáng. The MiGs passed within 200-300 feet of my aircraft, going the opposite direction. I channelled in, afterburner to the left, cooling an AIM-4 missile for the re-engagement. After approximately 360° of turn, I visually acquired two MiG-17s three miles ahead, in trail and in a gentle left turn. I selected the trailing aircraft, tracked, closed to positively identify the type aircraft and launched the AIM-4. The missile tracked directly to the aft section of the MiG-17, impacted in a ball of fire and smoke. The MiG immediately started a solid trail of grey/white smoke and continued in a gentle left turn with no manoeuvering observed. As I passed to the right rear of the MiG-17 and slid to the outside of the turn, other aircraft in the immediate area diverted my attention and I lost sight of the smoking aircraft. I gathered my flight together and continued the egress.'

While Squier was firing his AIM-4, he was attacked by another MiG-17 which aimed cannon fire at him from a range of 1,000 feet but missed. His wingman in 'Olds 02' was also fired upon by a flight of two MiG-17s, but again with no damage resulting.

Meanwhile, the F-4 MiGCAP flight observed the engagements and descended to get a closer look. Major Bernard J. Bogoslofski of Granby, Connecticut and Captain Richard L. Huskey of Cleveland, Tennessee, flying 'Tampa 01' the lead aircraft, observed a MiG-17 firing on Squier's wingman and decided to get it. Bogoslofski reported: 'The MiG-17 was tracking one F-4 in a tight left turn and gunfire was observed coming from the MiG-17. I was high and 5 o'clock to the MiG-17 and rolled in on him from 11,000 feet. I tracked the MiG-17 and began firing 20mm. The MiG-17 tightened his left turn and I performed a vertical pirouette left in order to continue tracking him, using high-G and at least 80° of dive angle. A burst of fire appeared to fragment the MiG's left wing as I initiated a recovery.'

Major Albert S. Borchik, Jr., in 'Olds 04 and Major Ronald L. Markey, commanding 'Olds 03', saw the pilot eject and the MiG hit the ground.

On 18 January three large strike forces hit targets in North Việtnam. 'Alpha Force', scheduled against the Bắc Giáng thermal power plant, comprised one F-105 'Iron Hand' flight, one F-4D flak-suppression flight, one F-4D strike flight and one element of an F-4D MiGCAP flight; the other element aborting before entering North Việtnam due to ECM malfunctions. 'Bravo Force' consisting of four F-105 strike flights, one F-105 'Iron Hand' flight and one F-4D MiGCAP flight meanwhile, headed for the Hà Giá railroad siding, but strong resistance from two MiG-17s and two MiG-21s, in coordinated attacks, forced the Thunderchiefs to jettison ordnance two minutes short of the target. 'Charlie Force', composed of one F-105 'Iron Hand' flight, four F-105 strike flights and two F-4D MiGCAP flights which was assigned the Đáp Câu rail by pass returned unscathed.

As 'Alpha force' approached the target it encountered co-ordinated attacks from SAMs, AAA and MiG-17s. Captain Robert L. Rutherford, flying an F-4D in the fourth slot, observed two MiG-17s at 1 and 2 o'clock, in a climbing left turn. 'Otter' flight, which was led by Major Kenneth Adrian Simonet, 44, of Chicago, Illinois and 1st Lieutenant Wayne Ogden Smith, 25, of Clearwater, Florida was then at 12,000 feet altitude, above the MiGs and beginning a descent to the target. In addition to dropping normal weapons, 'Otter' flight was tasked to drop AGM-62 Walleye television-guided glide bombs with their 250lb high-explosive warhead, which involved going 'down the chute' at 30 or so degrees while trying to acquire the target on an often fuzzy TV image to automatically track light or dark spots.

'Otter' flight picked up the Bắc Giáng thermal power plant and rolled in. 1st Lieutenant Robert Campbell Jones of Madison New Jersey, the 24 year old 'backseater in 'Otter 02' piloted by Captain Robert Bruce Hinkley of Springfield, Massachusetts, recalled: 'Normally we'd go one plane after another but because once each Walleye went off the smoke would obscure the target so we all had to hit pretty much at the same time. And you had to get pretty close with the Walleye to get a steady lock before releasing the weapon.

It was so accurate that in a flight of four one guy would get the front door, another guy the chimney and another, a window which the Walleye could go through without touching the sides. When everyone was locked on, the lead said, 'Okay, ready, ready, pickle' and we punched the weapons off. Then we pulled off in a hard right climbing turn into two-ship formations for mutual support.'

In an air-to-air engagement the F-4D strike flight lost the first of two 'Wolfpack' Phantoms when 'Otter 01' was shot down but not before Major Simonet and 1st Lieutenant Wayne Smith had destroyed one of the MiGs. Simonet, who was serving on his second tour in Southeast Asia, had enlisted in the US Marine Corps on 2 December 1942 and served with the 1st Marine Raider Battalion and the 4th Marine Regiment in the Pacific during World War II. Lieutenant Smith was on his 70th combat mission. Simonet maneuvered left, cooled an AIM-4D and fired the missile. It went up the tailpipe of the MiG-17, which caught fire, went out of control and crashed. No parachute was observed. During this encounter a fourth MiG-17 pulled in behind Simonet, firing his cannon. 'Otter 01' took hits and began trailing smoke. The MiG broke off the attack and Simonet turned east, attempting to withdraw but he and his back-seater had to eject. Their parachutes were observed descending to the ground.

Captain Bob Rutherford then heard 'Otter 02' call out: 'They're shooting' and seconds later their Phantom was on fire. Bob Jones recalled: 'Coming off the target we were kind of slow and low, so we punched off all external fuel tanks and missiles we were carrying to get light and immediately started going into defensive turns. Tracers were going by our plane. I looked back and there were two MiG-17s 'parked' about 500 feet behind. What had happened to the rest of the guys in my flight? They were all gone. This whole thing happened probably in ten seconds. All of a sudden we were hit. The plane jostles and kind of goes out of control and the radome comes right off and then the airplane pitches over and we're hanging. The controls are worthless. The airplane's burning and the flames are coming right out of the intakes and into the cockpit. We both said 'Let's get out of here.' Yeah, absolutely; it's time to exit the airplane. The whole thing takes maybe a quarter of a second. Like they said, 'If you ever have to do this, you're gonna think that's a long time.' Thoughts went through my head. If the ejection seat doesn't work you have to unstrap and climb out like in World War Two and jump over the side. I'm thinking 'I'm gonna have to do that' but then all of a sudden the rocket seat works and 'boom' there you go. The canopy blows away and my helmet goes flying off. And so you go from a chaotic situation in that cockpit where you're in mortal trouble to hanging out in a parachute and its quiet.'

Bruce Hinkley who was flying his 76th mission and Bob Jones, who was flying his 33rd, had ejected about fifteen miles southeast of Kép. Other members of the flight had seen their Phantom crash about two miles from the target

'I looked down' continues Jones 'and my airplane's burning on the ground. I could see Hinkley off to the side maybe 100 yards away. As far as being rescued, we knew that once you're above the Red River they're not coming. If you could land in the mountainous area it was a little less populated. Off to the right was 'Thud Ridge' and 'MiG Ridge', but they were forty miles away. You're supposed to check your parachute right away and I looked up. I had got two or three panels blown out of this 24-foot canopy so I was coming down pretty fast. On the horizon, I see a MiG. I don't know if it was the guy that shot us down or one of the others, but he's coming right at me. I said to myself 'this guy's gonna shoot me right out of this parachute. I had a little .38 pistol and I'm thinking 'if this SOB is gonna shoot me, I'm gonna get some shots off.' This little peashooter would go out about fifty feet and this guy's got a 20 millimetre cannon, so not much of a challenge there. But we had put tracers in the pistol so that if we were shot down we could fire through the trees to signal other aircraft. I thought if I shoot first, he's gonna see this so maybe he's not gonna shoot me. He goes right over the top of me, thumbing his nose at me or whatever and flew away. Then I heard shooting from the ground.

'I landed like a ton of bricks. I weighed 185lbs but with all the gear I was carrying I weighed 240. Bruce comes running over. 'We gotta get out of here' and I said to him, 'Where are we going? There is nowhere to go.' Immediately this giant ring of people started closing in. It seemed that there were 1,000 people. There were probably 100 at least. Some of them had a military shirt. Some had a hat. Some had pants. Everyone - old ladies, kids - had a weapon: bamboo rifles, M-15s, M-16s, AK-47s, pistols, sharpened rocks, anything they could pick up. I looked at Bruce and said, 'Well this it.' The initial capture was probably the most dangerous time when guys were killed or never showed up. So we emptied our guns, tossed them in. We broke our radios because you don't want them to make bogus calls and call in a helicopter and then shoot it down. Right then the mass of humanity descended on us. They took our flight suits, cut our boots off and left us sitting against an earthen embankment on the side of a rice paddy bare-foot and shivering in our underwear. Then about five or six younger guys with rifles lined up. Bruce says, 'They're going to shoot us.' I remember saying 'Nah, they wouldn't do that' And I'm thinking ''the hell they won't.'

'All of a sudden this old guy with a long Hô Chi Minh beard comes out of the crowd and he's arguing with these people. They're pushing him away and he's coming back. It's one of those deals where my whole life passed in front of my face like I was out of my body and God was looking down at me. And this voice said, 'You're pretty young but you still had it better than most'.

'The old guy was telling them, 'hey, look, these guys are worth a lot more alive than if you just kill them right here.' Obviously, he won the argument. We were paraded blindfolded through a couple of villages where 'hate rallies' worked up with bull horns and they were told that we were 'bad guys'. They pulled our hair back and yanked our blindfolds off. Later that night two tiny militia girls dressed up like Pancho Villa with bandoleers of ammo, rifles, knives and stuff and a film crew arrived to film us for propaganda. They each held us by a rope as the film crewed filmed us. We made it through that and we were taken to the Hànôi 'Hilton' in the back of a jeep hogtied. And that's the last time I saw Bruce Hinkley for five years'. He went one way, I went the other.'

Hinkley and Jones and Simonet and Smith would spend 1,883 days in captivity. They were released during Operation 'Homecoming' on 14 March 1973. Major Simonet and Lieutenant Smith's commanding officer had submitted on their behalf a claim for the destruction of enemy aircraft.

The next victory came on 5 February 1968 when a small strike force attacked a target in the Thái Nguyên area. The US Air Force lost a Thunderchief and shot down a MiG-21. The force consisted of one F-105 'Iron Hand' flight, one F-105 strike flight and two F-4D MiGCAP flights. A MiG-21 shot down one of the F-105s while the MiG pilot's wingman was destroyed by 'Gambit 03', a MiGCAP Phantom crewed by Captain Robert G. Hill of Tucson, Arizona and 1st Lieutenant Bruce V. Huneke of Hanford, California. Inbound to the target, the strike force had received MiG warnings: 'Two blue bandits airborne, Phúc Yên.' The warnings continued, indicating two MiG-21s headed northwest out of Phúc Yên, apparently intent upon intercepting the approaching strike aircraft. Hill was the first to see a MiG. His flight leader instructed him to take the lead and go after it. While the flight turned left to attack, the flight members lost sight of the MiG-21 and an F-105 was destroyed by his air-to-air missile. The American pilot safely ejected moments before his aircraft rolled over and disappeared into the undercast. Hill and his wingman were rolling out of their 360° turn at 23,000 feet when the F-105 was hit. Suddenly Hill saw a second MiG-21 at his 10 o'clock position, low, as he was breaking off from an attack on an F-105 climbing toward them. 'I immediately attacked and positioned myself in his 6 o'clock. The initial engagement was with the SUU-23 and 100 rounds were expended with no visible effects. I then cooled an AIM-4D Falcon. It never got a high tone but I fired it, thinking 'it may track.' The missile did not appear to guide. The second AIM-4D worked exactly as advertised and detonated on the MiG-21's aft section. I then selected radar and fired two AIM-7Es and attempted to fire a third. The first missile was launched with a boresight lock-on and did not appear to guide. The second AIM-7E was fired with a full system lock-on and appeared to guide. The third missile did not fire. 'Gambit 04'called a break as we were passing through 40,000 feet with a second MiG-21 on our tail, firing a missile.'

Hill's second Falcon had hit the MiG in the tailpipe, resulting in a 40-foot diameter, grey-white explosion. The MiG then exploded in a large red fireball of flame, blowing off the tail section. It fell straight down and impacted. No parachute was observed.

American forces were often successful against such multiple MiG passes because of improved MiG warnings and vectoring by the warning platforms. At times, too, MiG pilots became careless and screamed down on US aircraft without benefit of their ground control. One such attack occurred on 6 February. 'Buick' flight of four F-4Ds providing MiGCAP for a strike mission were egressing the target area when a MiG-21 suddenly appeared, making a pass from the rear quarter, high. The flight broke up and went after the MiG. Three F-4D aircrews missed with their missiles, but 'Buick 04' crewed by Captain Robert H. Boles of Lexington, South Carolina and 1st Lieutenant Robert B. Battista of Montgomery, Alabama found the MiG-21 directly in front of their aircraft. 'After several MiG calls' recalled Boles, 'we turned into the threat and engaged two MiG-21s. I visually acquired the MiGs at approximately three miles. One MiG made a climbing turn away from the flight, while the lead MiG turned left and down. The flight leader and his wingman went down after the MiG while Captain Joel S. Aronoff in 'Buick 03' and I stayed high, initially. During the ensuing engagement 'Buick 1, 2 and 3 each fired several missiles at the MiG. Although I had a radar lock-on and was within delivery parameters, I did not fire because Captain Aronoff did not immediately answer my radio transmissions when I asked if I were cleared to fire.

'During the engagement, the MiG tried evasive manoeuvres which consisted mainly of climbing and descending turns. When Captain Aronoff cleared me to fire, I was line abreast, 1,500-2,000 feet out from his plane. I attempted to fire two AIM-7s. The first missile did not come off. The second missile fired as advertised and guided toward the MiG. At firing, I held the MiG at 12 o'clock... The interlocks were in and we had a full system lock. The aim dot was centred. We were in a slight climb at the time. I watched the missile guide and just prior to impact the MiG either initiated a left turn or rocked his wings to the left in order to look back at our flight. The missile detonated at the left aft wing root section and the MiG exploded. I then exclaimed over the radio that I got the MiG and Captain Aronoff confirmed the MiG's destruction. At that time the flight leader called for the egress.'

Kép airfield was the target for a mission on 12 February, but en route the primary mission was aborted because of adverse weather. The strike aircraft, accompanied by two MiGCAP flights from Ubon's 'Wolfpack', proceeded then to the alternate target: Cao Nùng rail yard. The two MiGCAP flights escorted the withdrawing strike flight to the coast and returned to sweep the target area. While withdrawing for the second time, each flight tracked two MiG-21s. Only one flight met with any success; the lead aircraft, 'Buick 01' crewed by Lieutenant Colonel Alfred E. Lang, Jr. of East Orange, New Jersey and 1st Lieutenant Randy P. Moss of Great Falls, South Carolina, shot down a MiG-21. 'I sighted two bogies at my 9 o'clock position approximately 4,000 feet high in a shallow left turn about 75 miles east of Hànôi,' said Lang. 'As I closed on the bogey, Moss continually advised me of the bogey's azimuth, altitude, range and our overtake speed. He also had me recheck my armament switches and fuel status. At eight miles he reaffirmed that the aim dot was centred, that we were in range and then called out ranges at one mile intervals until I fired. At six miles I identified the second bogey as a MiG-21 and fired two AIM-7Es at 4½-miles, approximately 60° off his tail, with a full system lock-on, 600 knots overtake and the steering dot centred. Altitude was approximately 34,000 feet and airspeed 1.3 Mach. I also cleared Colonel Spencer to fire.

'Lieutenant Moss and I both tracked our missiles visually and observed the first missile to explode in the MiG's 7-8 o'clock position and the second missile exploded in the 10 o'clock position. As the MiG flew through the explosion he rolled inverted, yawed 30-40 degrees right to the direction of the flight and then entered a tumbling spin. The pilot did not eject and the aircraft continued in an uncontrollable spin. I then sighted the other MiG, which had been approximately 3 miles in front of the destroyed MiG. We acquired lock-on from dead astern and closed to 9-10 miles, but had to break off the attack because aircraft 4 was minimum fuel. We recovered at our home base.

Colonel (later Brigadier General) Robert V. Spencer flying in 'Buick 03' with 1st Lieutenant Richard W. Cahill as the rear-seater had in the meantime fired two AIM-7 missiles at the lead MiG. The first guided and tracked toward the target, detonating short of the enemy aircraft and the second missile guided, tracked and exploded very near the MiG's 6 to 9 o'clock position. The MiG then pitched violently upward and fell into an uncontrolled, tumbling spin. Seventh Air Force later confirmed the kill by Lang and Moss but denied the claim submitted by Spencer and Cahill.

The next aerial victories for the US Air Force were the last before a four-year hiatus set in. Two MiG-17s were destroyed during a strike against Phúc Yên airfield on 14 February. In the strike force were two flights of 'Iron Hand' F-105s, one F-4D strike flight and two F-4D MiGCAP flights (one fragged as 'fast' CAP and the other charged with 'slow' CAP). All of the MiGCAP aircrews were briefed to expect the standard coordinated MiG-17/MiG-21 effort, with the MiG-17s flying a low 'Wagon-Wheel' orbit and the MiG-21s flying high altitudes and both under GCI control. One F-4 flight was armed with AIM-7 and AIM-9 air-to-air missiles; the other with AIM-4 and AIM-7 missiles and SUU-23 gun pods. MiG warnings proved to be excellent and the second F-4 flight turned to approach two MiG-21s as the strike force was inbound to the target. The F-4s obtained a radar lock-on, but the MiGs withdrew without contact and the flight rejoined the strike force near 'Thud Ridge'. These two MiG-21s avoided the F-4s, but then attacked one of the trailing F-105 'Iron Hand' flights. After a brief engagement, one element of the F-105s returned to Korat while the other continued on to the target area. As the strike force continued, the F-4 flight sighted four MiG-17s at 11 o'clock, range three miles and headed toward it. The MiG-17s were performing a left-hand 'Wagon Wheel' manoeuvre at 8,000 feet over the flats northeast of Phúc Yên as the F-4 flight commenced a climbing spiral to the right to gain separation and to set up for a pass. The flight leader, Lieutenant Colonel Wesley D. Kimball in 'Nash 01' and his wingman, Major Ray M. Burgess went through the 'wheel' with Kimball attempting to get a MiG with an AIM-4 Falcon. The missile did not get a high tone, so he did not fire. Kimball and Burgess dived through the MiG orbit pattern, pulled up at 7,000 feet and started to climb.

It was at this moment that Major Rex D. Howerton of Oklahoma City and 1st Lieutenant Ted L. Voigt II of Nelsonville, Ohio in 'Nash 03' (F-4D 66-7554) in the 'Triple Nickel' appeared. One of the MiGs attempted to fall in behind the number one element. Howerton saw this and began his attack. 'I rolled in approximately 2,500 feet behind the MiG and fired an AIM-4D missile, which appeared to guide, but thinking that I might be inside minimum parameters I selected guns and began firing the externally mounted SUU-23 cannon. Hits were noted on the MiG and shortly thereafter it exploded and began to break up. The missile was not seen to impact or destruct. The MiG went down in flames with one wing and the tail section separated.' The MiG-17 tumbled in a nose-down snapping spin and with what appeared to be pieces of the tail fluttering downward before impacting in rice paddy terrain northeast of a large river, close to the foot of 'Thud Ridge', exploding in an orange fireball.[18]

Kimball and Burgess then made another pass at another MiG. Kimball fired 350 rounds of 20mm from a range of 2,000 feet but saw no hits. Very low on fuel at this point, his flight left the area.

Within a few minutes after this engagement began, the other MiGCAP flight attacked these same MiG-17s. The lead aircraft, 'Killer 01' crewed by Colonel David O. Williams Jr. of Rockport, Texas and 1st Lieutenant James P. Feighny Jr. of Laramie, Wyoming soon destroyed one of them. Williams reported: 'We sighted four MiG-17s in a left-hand orbit pattern approximately ten miles northwest of Phúc Yên, at about 15,000 feet. Lieutenant Colonel Kimball's flight executed an attack on the MiGs and then rolled in behind his 3 and 4 on a trailing MiG, which started a right-hand turn and dived down from approximately 24,000 feet to his 5:30 to 6 o'clock position at about 1.2 Mach. I asked my rear seat pilot if he was locked on. He said he was, but wasn't sure it was the right target, so he asked me to put the pipper on him and he selected gyro out and relocked. We were now locked on to the MiG. I fired one AIM-7E Sparrow missile at approximately ½ mile. The missile tracked perfectly and detonated near the left side of the fuselage. The MiG immediately shed its empennage and burst into a bright orange fire in a flat spin. I yo-yo-ed high and then rolled over to clear my tail. As I looked back the MiG was burning profusely. At about the same time I saw a bright orange parachute with a man hanging from it.'

USAF F-4D Phantom crews destroyed eight MiGs in aerial combat during January and February 1968. The percentage of losses to MiGs was a mere 1 percent during 1965, 3 percent in 1966 and 8 percent during 1967. But this figure leapt to 22 percent during the first three months of 1968. With this increasing threat and the end of bad weather, it seemed an opportune time for another major American effort against the MiG force but on 31 March President Lyndon B. Johnson announced that effective 1 April, all bombing north of 20° North latitude would cease and North Việtnam were invited to begin peace negotiations. Two days later, the bomb line was further moved southward to 19°, permitting air strikes only in Route Packages 1, 2 and the southern third of 3. As a result, almost all of North Việtnam became a MiG sanctuary; the only jet-capable airfields within the limited operating area of American forces were not being used by the NVNAF for MiG operations. Following two USAF victories on 14 February 1968, there was an interruption in shoot downs that would last more than four years. After 3 April MiGs ventured south of the 19th parallel, for the most part, under radio and radar silence. They continued their high-speed, hit-and-run tactics but usually retreated north of the 19th parallel after making single firing passes.

On the afternoon of 7 May 1968, three flights of MiG-21s from the VPAF 921st Regiment were flying towards Thọ Xuân Air Base, as part of redeployment in response to the US bombing halt above the 19th Parallel. The flights were led by Đăng-Ngọc Ngự, Nguyễn Văn Minh and Nguyễn Văn Cốc. Due to the lack of coordination between the different sections of the VPAF 921st Fighter Regiment and the ground-based air-defence forces, the MiG-21 flights were mistakenly identified as US fighter-bombers and were fired upon by North Viêtnamese anti-aircraft artillery. Moments later, Ngự also mistook an escorting flight of MiG-21 fighters flown by Nguyễn Đăng Kính and Nguyễn Văn Lung for US fighters. He dropped his fuel tanks to prepare for an attack which was promptly aborted when he realized they were North Vietnamese.

Later, Ngự and Cốc arrived over the skies of Do Luong, north-east of Vĩnh and they made three circuits over the area when they were told that enemy aircraft were detected coming from the sea; these were real US fighters. The US flight detected were a formation of five F-4B Phantoms of VF-92, USS *Enterprise*, led by Lieutenant Commander Ejnar S. Christensen; call sign 'Silver Kite 210'. Over North Viêtnamese airspace, a US Navy EKA-3A electronic warfare aircraft tried to jam North Viêtnamese communications but failed and Ngự's flight of MiG-21 fighters was guided towards their target by ground controllers. While trying to engage the VPAF MiGs, the F-4B formation became separated due to confusion in radar control. In the ensuing dogfight, two AIM-7 missiles were fired by the US Navy fighters but missed. Ngự then noticed two F-4B Phantoms about three miles to starboard, but could not get into a suitable firing position. Cốc was right behind Ngự at the time, but he wanted to disengage from the fight as his aircraft was running low on fuel. However, Cốc quickly changed his mind after he spotted an F-4B ahead of him at an altitude of 8,200 feet. It was 'Silver Kite 210' crewed by Lieutenant Commander Christensen and his Radar Intercept Officer, Lieutenant (jg) Worth A. Kramer which was flying out to sea. Cốc immediately gave chase and successfully scored a hit after he fired two R-3S 'Atoll' missiles from an altitude of 4,900 feet. The Phantom burst into flames and crashed into the sea at 1844 hours. Christenson and Kramer ejected safely from their aircraft before impact and were recovered a short time later. The action gave the VPAF their first aerial victory over the airspace above the Military Zone IV of North Viêtnam and Nguyễn Văn Cốc, his seventh aerial victory.

Only on 23 May did any sizeable force of MiGs venture south of the bomb line. One MiG-21 was shot down by a US Navy Talos missile. Some MiGs were lost to the Navy later in that year, but the US Air Force scored no additional aerial victories and losses occurred.

On 29 May 1st Lieutenant (later Captain) Michael Thomas Burns, 23, a back-seater arrived at the 433rd 'Satan's Angels' Tactical Fighter Squadron at Ubon. He found the Thais 'real friendly' but the weather was 'hotter than blazes'. 'It was very humid and the primitive air base was scraped out of the jungle.'

'Out of pilot school in 1968, some guy named Robert McNamara, or someone like him, had this bright idea about two pilots in a fighter was better than one, but two fighter pilots in the same airplane never works. They kept that concept up for about two years and then abandoned it so my job was to assist the 'guy in front'. I ran the radar and sometimes landed it from the back seat and flew formation. You were a pair of eyes to look out for other airplanes, missiles or targets. Some of the missions were the kind where they drove you up to about 20,000 feet and they vectored you around and told you when to drop your bombs through the clouds. But most of the flights were flying around at about 5,000 feet driving up and down roads looking for anything moving. I watched F-4s come back from missions with huge holes in the wings that you could almost squirm up through. It was a rugged airplane and if you didn't hit the hydraulics underneath the belly it would take a lot of hits. I flew a few night missions where we were driving around in absolute dark and you couldn't tell up from down except from instruments and you could see twinkles of light; soldiers shooting at you with their guns, but it didn't get heavy. There were one or two times where we were bombing something in a valley, blowing up a bridge and we were flying with a 'Thunderbird' pilot. He went down in this valley, just under the mach and dropped the bombs and pulled out about 7g pull out. We got below the hills and I could look out the side and see white tracers of a fifty calibre. He was right even with us, but he wasn't leading us. And I could see the bullets coming out but going behind us. But this guy just hauled ass through that valley. I had a couple of other missions like that until the last one; my eighteenth mission, on 5 July when I was shot down.

'We were on an armed reconnaissance with one other F-4. We were two, lead was out about one mile ahead of us and we would look at the maps before we would go out and decide exactly where we'd fly up and down what rivers. We were driving up and down this road at about 1,500. Forty-one year old Major Carl Boyette Crumpler, my front-seater said he saw some guns at the base of this hill, probably about a thousand feet high, down to our right, so we jacked up the airspeed and we rolled in at about 5,000 feet.'

'As we went down lining up on the guns, we got pretty low. We released the bombs and all the traces came up. They were red and they say the red ones are 35mm. I could feel this thumping on the bottom of the airplane. We pulled out well over 500 knots, right over the trees, right over that hill and as we pulled out and banked, I looked back to see where a bomb hit. The last two-thirds of the airplane was a ball of fire. I couldn't see the tail and I don't think Crumpler noticed that we were burning. He was getting ready to make another bomb run. So I told him that we were hit and head for the South China Sea and out there to the right, to the east. We headed for the South China Sea and started driving that airplane. When we got to about 8,000 feet one of the engines died; it was just zero. The other engine was on afterburner and we got real slow - about 200 knots - and then the airplane jerked up and down real hard, threw us around in the canopy and then it just fell out of the sky. I could see the earth go by, then the canopies, then the blue sky, then the earth. We ejected and I came down through the clouds and landed in a wide open field. It was a perfect parachute-landing roll. I rolled my chute up and hid it. I could hear 'rat-tat-tat-tat' coming from all around. It was gunfire way out in the distance and they were shooting in my direction, so I couldn't see anybody.

'Once I hid the chute, I got my radio out and I pulled out the antennae. I called the other airplanes. I said, 'this is Burns. I am on the ground and I am OK.' A voice said they didn't see our chute. 'Give us a reading from that smoke in the hills'. I looked over at the hills that we were bombing at one time and there was a black column of smoke and that was our F-4 burning. I took my compass out and dropped it on the ground and it said 045 so I said '045 about two miles'. The voice said 'head west we will try a pick-up in the morning'.

So I started running to the west. I soon got real tired. I still had my G-suit on (the 'fast pants' we called them) so I had to unbuckle that, throw it in the weeds and keep running. I could still hear gunfire from different directions and so I crawled into a huge stand of bushes, pulled all the weeds up behind me like I was taught in survival school and I sat there. It got quiet. I could see the sun slowly going down. Time was passing. I took my .38 out. I figured if there was someone between me and that helicopter I'd use it. But I didn't need it. So I put it in the dirt next to me and I just waited. Then I heard a crackling noise behind me. I turned around and there was this little Viêtnamese, about 60, with a black T-shirt and black shorts. He took two cautious steps into the weeds, bent down and looked but he didn't see me at first but finally, his eyes met mine. He was about ten feet away and his eyes got real big. He kind of fell backwards and started screaming. As I turned around about five Viêtnamese piled through the bush and I was looking up the barrel of four or five AK 47s with great big barrels like a nickel or a quarter.

'Crumpler also got captured. We were trucked up to Hànôi and we arrived at the 'Hànôi Hilton' thirty-five days after I was shot down. That prison camp all was grey; like purgatory almost. It felt like life had ended. Well, it doesn't. You either quit or adapt to it. That first year I was full of rage. You are cut off from everybody. You can't talk above a whisper. There's no distractions, just you. You're stuck there. And you can tap on the walls to the cell mate next to you. And you'd better be careful. It is not that you are in jail and you can go out in the courtyard and you can talk with one hundred guys. You are in a 9 x12 cell with one person for a year and a half, or maybe a year with two people. There was a loud speaker in every cell. Our bathroom was a black bucket, about a foot and a half high and we called it the 'black stallion'. In one cell an American PoW read out loud about how the 'glorious' war was going in the south and how we lost 10,000 men today and had eighteen planes shot down. I thought to myself, 'God, what did they do to that guy?' It sounded awful. I got used to it. Well, at some point I decided I was going to keep my head, take care of my friends and stay in close touch with my comrades.'

On 10 July Lieutenant Roy Cash, Jr. and Lieutenant Joseph E. Kain, Jr. of VF-33 'Tarsiers' in an F-4J destroyed a MiG-21 with an AIM-9 about twenty miles northwest of Vĭnh for the USS *America's* first kill of the war. (The next Navy Phantom kill came on 28 March 1970 when Lieutenant Jerome E. Beaulier and Lieutenant Steven J. Barkley of VF-142 'Ghostriders' from the *Constellation* in an F-4J shot down a MiG-21 with an AIM-9). After 28 September 1968 MiG activity virtually ceased and on 1 November all bombing in North Viêtnam was halted by Presidential proclamation. The next incoming President, Richard M. Nixon, confirmed this policy in January 1969 and the ban on bombing of the North remained in force until May 1972 when the North Viêtnamese offensive prompted Nixon to authorize a resumption.

In the meanwhile, American PoWs had to sit out the war in appalling conditions. In Orange Park, Florida Major Carl Crumpler's wife, Jane, sons Mike (16), Todd (13), daughters, Beth (11) and Leigh (10) awaited his return.

Endnotes Chapter 4

1   Gary Thornton was released on 4 March 1973 (the last airman to serve a full six years as a PoW). He retired from the United States Navy as a Commander. In January 2010 the Department of Defense PoW/Missing Personnel Office announced that the remains of a US pilot, missing in action had been identified as Major Goodman's and would be returned to his family for burial.

2   His RIO on that occasion was Lt (jg) David L. Jordan. Also, Lieutenant David A. McRae and Ensign David N. Nichols of VF-213 from the USS *Kitty Hawk* in an F-4B shot down an An-2 with an ASIM-7E on that date.

3   On 19 October 1966 Wisley and Anderson had a narrow escape when their Phantom was hit by an A-4 following KA-3 refuelling and the port wing was sliced off the A-4 whose pilot ejected.

4   Both men were eventually released on 4 March 1973. The wreckage of F-4B 15.3001 is currently on display in Hànôi.

5   On 11 August 1967 F-4C 63-7593 crewed by Major Robert G. Dilger and his backseater 1st Lt G. L. Rawlings was damaged by 57mm AAA during an attack on a truck convoy near Thành Lãng Xã. The aircraft limped back towards Đà Nẵng but the crew were forced to eject and came down in the sea just south of Marble Mountain off the coast and were immediately picked up by a rescue helicopter. Another 366th TFW Phantom (F-4C 63-7634) crashed as it was landing at Đà Nẵng. Major Kenneth Richard Hughes was killed. 1st Lt H. B. Cox survived. Hobson.

6   Though a Navy aircraft from the USS *Bon Homme Richard* scored a direct hit against the Hànôi power plant with a Walleye. The Navy hit the plant again with the bomb two days later, knocking out Hànôi's major source of power.

7   On 11 November 1976, the Department of the Navy declared Richard Rich dead. William Stark was released on 4 March 1973 and resumed his career until retirement as a Commander. Plumb was released on 18 February and Anderson on 4 March 1973. Joseph Plumb acted as the PoW's chaplain when conditions in the camps allowed such social activity. *Vietnam Air Losses*, Chris Hobson (Midland Publishing, 2001). Gary Anderson died during a military training flight on 21 June 1976.

8   Horner. RADM 'Denny' Wisely flew 350 missions on F-4s of VF-114 on three tours of SE Asia. He was Commanding Officer of the 'Blue Angels' in 1980 and 1981.

9   Lieutenant Colonel Raspberry completed 130 combat missions with 100 as flight leader and mission commander in North Vietnam. He returned to the USAF Fighter Weapons School as an F-100/F-4 project pilot and programme manager, He returned to SE Asia and flew an additional 55 combat missions. He retired from the USAF in 1977 with over 5,000 hours of fighter time.

10 Pascoe and Wells were promoted following their aerial victory of 6 January 1967 - Wells to Captain and Pascoe to Major. Pascoe however, had not yet donned his gold leaves.

11 This Phantom was flown by Major Robert G. Dilger and 1st Lieutenant M. Thies when they shot down a MiG-17 on 1 May 1967.

12 James Bailey was released on 18 February and Commander Lawrence was released on 4 March 1973 *Vietnam Air Losses*, Chris Hobson (Midland Publishing, 2001).

13 James Borst later got his pilot's wings but was killed in an A-7 in the USA during an air combat training mission. Hobson.

14 On 14 March 1973 Ted Stier and Doug Clower were among 591 Americans released in Operation 'Homecoming' from prisons in and around Hànôi. The remains of Lieutenant Estes and Lieutenant Teague were repatriated on 30 September 1977. Clower's aircraft was one of the 27 Navy F-4Bs that had been loaned to the USAF for use by the 4453rd CCTW in 1963. *Vietnam Air Losses*, Chris Hobson (Midland Publishing, 2001).

15 In 1971 General John Dale Ryan, Chief of Staff of the US Air Force changed the rules governing a victory so that a pilot and his backseater each received full credit for a victory; the revised rule being made retroactive to 1965. Captain John Ryan Jr., 29, was killed on 12 January 1970 when his Phantom crashed into San Pablo Bay, San Francisco on a flight from Hamilton AFB to its home base at Holloman. His backseater, Captain J. Travis Nelson, also 29, died with him.

16 Kenneth Fleenor was one of the first USAF pilots to convert to the Phantom and commanded the 12th FTW after his release and attained the rank of Brigadier General before retiring from the Air Force on 1 August 1980. Horner.

17 by Wayne Thompson

18 A red star victory symbol was painted on the Phantom's left hand splitter plate and a second was later added for another kill but confirmation was subsequently withdrawn.

Chapter 5
'Barrel Roll' Backseater

Rayford 'RK' Brown

The Tiger FAC Hunter-Killer missions were always flown in flights of two F-4Es; one low aircraft acting as the FAC and one escort flying above to provide cover and to strike targets identified by the lead. Tigers were configured with two CBU-52 canisters and two LAU-68 rocket pods, while the escorts were configured with twelve MK-82 (500lb general purpose) or seven Mk.83 (1,000lb GP bombs). The Tiger missions averaged about 4.5 hours for each sortie, just as before, with two in-flight refuelling per mission. Tiger missions generally started at Stoeng Treng or Kratié, Cambodia and continued along the roads and rivers searching for lucrative targets. In May strikes caused the enemy to change his tactics revealing that NVN land and water routes into the Republic of Viêtnam were being used, bypassing routes previously used. The termination of USAF activity in RVN after the ceasefire accounted for the change. Truck and water traffic remained at a low level in June, but air strikes against the traffic were increased to discourage any future increases in the use of the Cambodian logistic supply lines.

These missions were not a favourite for the heavily loaded 'escorts' or the 'killers'. For one thing when the Tiger leads no longer carried CBUs, the trailing F-4Es had a very high fuel flow rates and used much more fuel, due to their significantly greater weight and drag. While the Tiger lead was far much streamlined with only two LAU-59 rocket pods and 7 rockets loaded in each and two external fuel tanks. The wingman carried typically twelve MK-82 500lb bombs and the same wing tanks making them heavy and fugly - fat and ugly.

This caused the wingmen to constantly try to save fuel by cutting across any angles but seemingly always either on the verge of a stall or worse. Wingmen heavily loaded with bombs always had to terminate that portion of the mission in order to head for a refuelling tanker.

And to make matters worse, the dedicated tanker for Tiger was at 28,000 feet; far too high for bomb laden wingmen to reach without using four times as much fuel in afterburners as the Tiger FAC leader. Where the Tiger FACs loved it, the wingmen hated it and left the wingmen to ponder, 'Whatever happened to wingman consideration, a time honoured responsibility and tradition of flight leadership?'

The Tiger FAC lead wanted wingmen to save their bombs for the second and third sessions in case of lucrative targets. The wingmen wanted to dump their loads as soon as possible. Mutually opposing objectives set up by poor planning and weak leadership, or a lack thereof.

Then there was the matter of call-signs. The Tiger FACs each had their own Call sign. Tiger 01, the most senior and generally the most experienced…leader. Tiger 02 was next based upon longevity as a Tiger, or I suppose since this group was chosen all at the same time, I guess the next highest rank or date of rank or they drew straws?

Individual Tiger call signs was traditional for Tiger FACs since 1971 and was good since fast-FACing was a single-ship mission. But with two aircraft it was a mess. The wingman became 'Tiger 02 Bravo'. For a decade or more the terms Alpha and Bravo traditionally had been used to identify the front pilot (Alpha) and rear seat occupant (Bravo) for SAR missions and in general. But now, Tiger 02 had two descriptions; Tiger 02 - his personal call-sign and Tiger 02 'Alpha'. While Tiger 02 Bravo, the wingman, also had multiple different identifiers; Tiger 02 Bravo 'Alpha' - wingman pilot and Tiger 02 Bravo - Bravo - wingman backseater. Confusing and showed a further lack of mature leadership and competent decision making.

In December 1970 Kathleen Brown, 1st Lieutenant Rayford 'RK' Brown's wife of almost two and a half years had arrived in Thailand on a charter DC-8 with 250 other wives to be with her husband for the last three months of his tour at Korat. Her husband was a F-4E backseater in the 469th TFS, 388th TFW at Korat RTAFB which had converted from the F-105D in November 1968. He and Kathy had a 'hootch' in a compound in Nakhon Ratchasima just outside Korat. Next door lived Captain Stevens the 34th TFS flight surgeon, his wife Karen and baby daughter. Stevens had a new pair of Leica roof prism binoculars that had the most fantastic clarity and weighed a fraction of what the beat up old artillery spotter glasses the backseaters carried weighed. The previous afternoon Rayford Brown had declined his generous offer to let him use them on the flight on Saturday, 2nd January 1971. The night before Kathleen had trimmed his horns back into the quick. On Saturday morning she fixed a big breakfast of fried pork and scrambled eggs. Life was as perfect as Brown could ask for. He had no regrets. His mind was at ease.

F-4E 67-0359 'Tiger 02' mission, crewed by Captain Harvey Weir and 1st Lieutenant Rayford 'RK' Brown was controlling a strike on the northern edge of the Plain of Jars. The northern part of Laos, 'Barrel Roll', was overcast with stratus and the tops were low. The solid overcast didn't seem to be more than 1,000 to 1,500 feet thick. Rayford Brown did not remember anything remarkable about the period leading up to the first refuelling.

'We had flown directly from Korat to the Barrel and were just cruising around looking for a workable area anywhere in 'Barrel Roll'. For F-4s to drop their bombs we needed no more than scattered clouds up to about 10,000 feet. All the Air Force fighters had to be able to visually acquire the target before dropping their bombs.

'7th Air Force would issue a fragmentary order each day. This order was referred to as the 'Frag'. It had sections for each unit's taskings. Each task or flight had a line or two that would give ordnance loading, number and type of aircraft; refuelling time and off-load for the flight from a specific tanker track; and a time on target or rendezvous with a particular Forward Air Controller - FAC. This process was referred to by the crews as being 'fragged'. The term 'hits or hitting' came from when aircrews shared a bottle at a social event and if you wanted a bit more scotch in your glass you asked for a 'hit'. When a fighter would intercept and join into formation with a tanker and then take on fuel we referred to it as 'hitting' a tanker, a KC-135. In our case, it was the 'Orange Anchor' refuelling track north of Udorn RTAFB in north central Thailand and south of Ch 108, a TACAN located on top of a mountain in central northern Laos. We were configured with two rocket launchers, each with seven Willy Petes -White Phosphorus 2.75 inch folding fin aerial rockets, 620 rounds of 20mm High Explosive Incendiary (HEI) in the nose gun and two 370 gallon external wing tanks. F-4s burned 17 gallons/minute at .85 mach cruise and more than ten times that amount in afterburners. These external fuel tanks would usually go dry twenty minutes after takeoff because of the fuel consumed by start, taxi and take off.

'On our first refuelling, we filled-up to 'no flow'. The F-4 could signal the tanker through the boom that it was full and that turned off the refuelling pumps on the KC-135 resulting in 'no flow' and then the pilot punched the Air to Air Refuelling disconnect button to release the boom from the refuelling receptacle. If you were not fragged for enough JP-4 - Air Force grade jet fuel, to go to 'no flow' the boom operator could read the pounds of fuel that he had transferred.

'After tanking we proceeded northeast to the 'PDJ' (Plain de Jars), which was a relatively flat area that years of war had left a no-man's-land covered with bomb craters and pock marked with CBU, cluster bomb unit, scars. We found a hole in the thinning overcast and got underneath. I estimated the cloud bases were still 1,500 to 2,000 AGL - above ground level, maximum. We passed 'Roadrunner Lake'. Yeah, it looked like a roadrunner's profile on the map and headed for the gap in the mountains that indicated where Route 7, a major line of communication (LOC) left the PDJ and entered the mountains.

'From there Route 7 wound east to North Việtnam. Our intent was to determine if interdiction point SC900 was passable again after previous bombings. The mountain tops were not obscured by clouds. Our speed was somewhere on the north side of 480 knots, all we could get in military power - maximum power without using afterburner. The gunners would not hear us coming for very long. About 1445 local time we noticed that the cold weather of the night before had caused all the leaves to fall off all the potted plant camouflage on the truck- hiding revetments - bunkered stalls, along Route 7. The limbs were barren and there were miles of revetments.

'I suggested to Harvey Weir, aka 'Tiger 02 Alpha', that we have 'Bullwhip', the RF-4C out of Udorn, run a strip photo. He concurred so I got out my big 1:50,000 map book from beside the seat and opened it. It filled the entire front of the cockpit. I started reading a set of start and stop UTMs, metric meter grids used by the Army and Frag to designate targets down to the nearest ten metres, to Bullwhip over the radio.

'While doing this I called Harvey off a rocket pass for a 'known 37mm gun site' that we were going to fly over if we continued the pattern. He tapped the afterburners - moved the throttles outboard and forward to engage the afterburners and started a repositioning turn under clouds. I struggled to get the coordinates transmitted intelligibly to Bullwhip against the constant G forces. To keep our position close enough to maintain sight of the target area we had to make a level turn with 60-70 degrees of bank pulling 2-3 times our body weight. I didn't understand why he wanted to shoot a 'Willy Pete' just to make a puff of white smoke. We had no fighters and it would be dissipated long before Bullwhip would be on scene. However, I failed to object to the pass. This was a Lieutenant mistake distinguishing between brave and stupid.

'About this time Harvey asked 'Which one?' meaning which revetment to shoot at. I switched from looking out the side to out the front. I answered, 'We're too low.' He had managed to position our jet into a 20 degree rocket pass under a 2,000 feet cloud layer and as I looked past the side of the top of his ejection seat and out the front I could see that the trees had leaves. Harvey began an immediate pull to just slow on the angle of attack (AOA) indexers. The F-4 had AOA indexer lights to obtain the optimum/maximum lift AOA. There were four of the lights, two on either side of both cockpits and each consisted of an up and a down chevron and a circle. Too high an AOA gave a down chevron, slightly high gave you a down chevron and a circle, etc. Too high of an AOA meant you were too slow on landing. I can still see the bright red segmented circle with the inverted chevron over it as the indexer light glowed brightly under the dimness of the overcast. This indexer light was located directly in my line of sight when peering through the hole between the canopy bow and the front ejection seat. Harvey immediately eased up to the 'on speed' donut and I felt the aircraft mush with a 15+ degree nose up angle of attack. We had 300-320 knots and were very heavy, perhaps still feeding the external fuel tanks. Jettisoning the tanks and rocket pods would have been a good idea at this point but it did not occur to either of us. There was a vertical karst - jagged nearly vertical limestone mountain, ahead now and there was no way we could clear it. We had been on a south to north pass perpendicular to Route 7 and aimed at a revetment on the north side of Route 7 and on the west side of a small pork chop shaped valley. 'Harv' had rolled right and moved over into the valley.

'Time was slowing down. I thought about an F-4, call sign 'Falcon' that had just landed the week before with the backseater having ejected for unknown reasons. We were still mushing but now level and just above the trees. There was still no way to make the turn to get over the karst growing larger rapidly in front of us. The thought went through my mind, 'Will the radar come to me or will I go to the radar?' I started pulling the lower handle out of its bracket. Suddenly I was tumbling and disoriented. The chute opened smoothly and I automatically looked up to check the canopy per my jump training at Fort Benning five years earlier.

'I was surprised there were several blown panels in a white and orange parachute. Whattt? I thought it was supposed to be olive drab. I felt the survival kit deploy and suddenly to my left, there was a large and greasy black-orange fireball. I thought to myself that at least the jet was not going home without me and I had made the right decision. I did not know if Harvey had gotten out or not.

'Before I could look back from the fireball rising from two-thirds of the way up the karst I was hung up just under jungle canopy. No feet together toes on top of each other, chin tucked in and arms crossed over my chest like they taught me at jump school. My parachute canopy and survival kit were snagged across the top of the jungle canopy. I was hanging in the clear about three feet from the 8-9 inch tree trunk. My sunglasses and oxygen mask were still on. It was just like the Jungle Survival movie I had watched at Clark.

'I immediately heard yelling and firing around me but I didn't see anyone or hear any rounds hitting in my tree. I pulled on one riser a couple of times to swing to the tree trunk. The shooting and yelling continued from the south based upon my orientation to the eastern ridgeline behind me.

'My weight was still in the harness with my legs wrapped around the trunk of the tree. The lack of hearing and vision from the helmet were making me claustrophobic. I decided to drop my helmet while I shinnied down the tree.

'In survival school, they had cautioned us to be sure to keep our helmet for the recovery. It would provide needed protection during the ride up to the chopper.

'I carefully determined the uphill side of the tree, reached my helmet out as far as I could and released the chin strap. The helmet fell and grew smaller. It was still falling. 'Damn, this tree is much taller than I thought.' I heard the helmet hit the ground and roll down hill but I could not see it.

'I disconnected my parachute by holding the tree with one arm and my legs and releasing the Koch - (pronounced Cook) quick release, fittings with my free hand. I was still restrained by the survival kit. I pushed the left side release and it swung clear. I was still caught by my tree lowering device. One hundred and fifty feet of nylon strap was stored in my lumbar pad and fed under my arm to the hardware on the front of my parachute harness. It had snagged as I came through the tree canopy and started to play out. I considered again the tree lowering device but decided it would take too long to untangle. I had climbed many trees as a kid on a rural Oklahoma farm and this would be a lot easier with my G-suit and gloves on.

'I easily slipped out of my harness and evaluated the mini survival kit in a small pocket in the back of my harness and decided it would not be needed. Granddad Martin had told me that the fish wouldn't bite if I talked, so I knew the fishing was not going to be any good with all the shooting and yelling going on.

'I shinnied down the trunk with G-Suit and gloves. This was fun. Not even a raspberry. I stopped at the foot of the tree and took off my four leg restraint garters from the Martin Baker ejection seat. I decided to keep my G-suit because of the time it would take to move all the water bottles and stuff from the pockets to my flight suit. I replayed in my mind the Jungle School movie of the pilot wandering off leaving a trail of equipment. That was a good flick.

'Once cleaned off, I pulled my camo golf hat out of my G-Suit pocket, since there was no trace of my helmet. I still had my corrective sunglasses on. You see I was a product of the Air Force policy to hire the visually handicapped as navigators.

'I got out my radio and established contact with 'Bullwhip on Guard' - the 243.0 MHz frequency dedicated for emergency use. 'Tiger 02 Bravo is down in a ravine two or three valleys west of SC900E and he is uninjured.' I heard a momentary emergency beeper from Harvey.

'I stowed my radio, got my .38 revolver out and climbed NE away from Route 7 and toward the military crest -1/3 of the height of the hill below the crest, of the east side of the valley. I tried to put some immediate distance between me and my orange and white parachute strung out across the top of the jungle canopy.

'After moving about twenty yards along the contour of the very steep hill I came to the edge of what I thought was a partially overgrown slash and burn clearing. It would not provide adequate cover for moving so I turned right and climbed uphill toward the military crest. I was moving carefully to be quiet and not to leave a trail of broken foliage. Ahead I saw a limestone out-cropping about three and a half feet tall with vines hanging over the front. It was undercut enough that you could not look over the top and see into it. The slash and burn area made for a great field of fire.

'I had my .38 calibre revolver with five rounds loaded. Those guys with fully automatic AK-47s were not going to have a chance. I figured I had two rounds each for two Pathet Lao soldiers and one for me. I'd heard that 'Raven 23's body had been found skinned and his gonads sewn up in his mouth. 'Raven' FACs flew O-1 Bird Dogs, small single reciprocating engine powered aircraft. They were assigned to a unit at Ubon but left their AF ID cards there and flew in civilian clothes carrying US Embassy ID Cards because 'there were no American troops in Laos'. They lived and flew out of small strips in their areas of responsibility but mainly at the secret base, Long Tiene, or also known as 'Alternate' or '20A'.

'I was not going to be captured alive if I could help it. I had an additional ten rounds of .38-ammunition on my survival vest if I had time to reload. My new home was only about sixty yards from my parachute, 100 yards above the valley floor and well below the crests of the surrounding hills. The valley in front of me was approximately 1 kilometre across - a little more than half a mile. I was about a kilometre north of Route 7.

'I crawled under the vines and backed up against a rock with my .38 out. The shooting and yelling had continued to my left, which I thought was south.

'We had been bombing the caves on the northeast side of the karst to my back and NE of where the aircraft impacted for the previous week or two so I was sure I would be welcomed by the locals.

'Concealed behind the vines and radio out of my survival vest, my next call was on 282.8 for any Air America helicopter. However, due to my location down near the bottom of the ridge my radio range sucked. I switched to Guard. 'Raven 26' immediately answered my call. I could hear his aircraft so I vectored him toward my position and he immediately gained a tally (visual) on my orange and white parachute.

'After 'Raven 26' had my parachute in sight I gave him my estimated 60-70 metre distance; NE and slightly uphill from the chute. He told me that he was going to mark my chute with a 'Willy Pete' to confirm my position.

'Did you know that 'Willy Pete' comes in with a crack - a combination of supersonic travel and a super quick fuse to scatter the white phosphorus above the ground? This was an educational experience since I had not been on this end of a 'Willy Pete' before.

'I started sharing the direction and estimated distance to the ground fire from my position. I had bailed out at almost exactly 1500 local time. This was the time on target - TOT, or station time, for the Sandys - the generic call sign for fixed wing dedicated SAR aircraft. These same aircraft and pilots sometimes flew under different call signs when not on dedicated SAR missions. 'Raven 26' was controlling the 'Sandys', call sign 'Hobo', on a different frequency keeping Guard radio channel clear. For this reason and my location, I did not hear many radio transmissions except for 'Raven 26'. The 'Sandys' arrived about ten minutes after 'Raven 26'. They began strafing and attacking enemy ground fire sites under his control. I continued to call out the ground fire to 'Raven 26'. The ground fire was now timed to the arrival of the 'Hobos' so I assumed that my importance had decreased a great deal. I was not jealous of the attention being lavished on the 'Hobos'.

'After several minutes of this I heard a single soldier, as in one and not his/her marital status, hunting through the jungle coming from my east to south and I estimated about ten yards away. Why do I say hunting? The timing of the steps was crunch - peer, crunch - peer, rather than a normal 100 beat per minute walk. I was sitting in the back of my cover facing west and could not see anything moving. I whispered into my radio to 'Raven 26' and requested a strafe pass from my parachute up the hill. The crunching of the brush was getting much too loud.

'The Hobos (A-1s) were configured with 7.62 mini-guns on one stub pylon just for such a situation. Suddenly I was spitting dirt out of my mouth as I heard the crack of supersonic rounds followed in a couple of seconds by the *Whrrrrrrrrrmth* of the mini-gun. Another teachable moment, I hadn't considered that the bullets get there way before the sound of the gun. Inside my vines, I could see three holes in the ground about a foot apart starting just short of my left foot and leading uphill to my right. My 'up the hill' and the 'Hobo's 'up the hill' had been about 45 degrees apart.

'I told 'Raven' what happened. He saved that 'Hobo' up, meaning he had him secure his ordnance and not drop or shoot anymore. I didn't hear the bad guy again. I was and remain grateful for that strafe pass even though it was very close. I continued to hear voices to the south, down the valley and they were joined by more voices coming from the NW up the valley toward where I had seen the fireball. They sounded like they were moving toward my position. 'Raven 26' obliged my request by having someone lay napalm up the valley just beyond my position. It turned out that this was also the approximate position of Harvey. Some of the napalm got really close to him. After about an hour and a half things began to slow down. I asked 'Raven 26' how much gas he had because three would make a crowd. He allowed that he had plenty of fuel left. At about 1700 'Raven 26' turned the On Scene Commander - OSC, job over to 'Raven 22', Grant Uhls. Grant was killed two months later.

'There had now been almost two hours of continuous airstrikes by a variety of fast and slow movers. Air cover had begun within approximately fifteen minutes of ejection/crash and this I think prevented an organized search for Harvey and me. Those attacks had also largely suppressed the ground fire except for some random small arms bursts. The sun was low on the western rim of the valley and I had an 'ear worm' running in my head. 'My bags are packed, I'm ready to go. Taxi's waitin', outside my dooo…' 'Raven 22' called that they had started the last chance pickup attempt from the SW over Route 7.

'Just as I saw the first helicopter in the SAR force coming over the western valley rim he turned back and the sound receded into silence. 'Raven 22' said both Jolly's took fire and a Parachute Rescue Jumper -PJ, was hit.

'By 1800L it was dark and the A-1s left. 'King', the Airborne Command Control and Communication (ABCCC) C-130, bedded us down for the night and promised a first light effort in the morning. The chill factor went down with the sun. I had been sitting on the damp almost muddy ground, plus I had been hot and sweaty in the backseat of our jet and I was wet when I jumped. Miserably cold already, I was off to a good start for a long night. It was hungry out, too.

'I felt strangely calm after the 'King' kissed me goodnight. I had been the whole afternoon. I had accepted the fact that I was already dead and worrying would not change that. No previous aircrew had been recovered alive after spending the night in Laos. In the twilight silence, I began reviewing the events preceding going to work that morning. My thoughts turned to God at this point. I considered a big prayer; however, I decided I hadn't talked with Him much before and as a stranger,

I didn't want to piss him off by bothering him now. I decided on just simple thanks for still being there, as I had already wasted several lives that day. Earlier in the quiet after 'King' had bedded us down I tried to make a deal with the Devil for hot biscuits and sausage gravy. If he showed up with a plate of 1½ tall golden brown biscuits drowned in real sausage gravy, my soul was his. *'Mai mi, Kah,'* No *have, sir,* as they said in the Officers Club when you asked for iceberg lettuce. The devil couldn't hack it any better than the 'O' Club at Korat.

'It was pitch black now and I still had my sunglasses on despite having a clear set in my G-suit pocket. My rationale was I didn't want them to see the whites of my bright blue eyes. I knew they must be open wide.

'Almost concurrently with darkness, I heard a large number of trucks start up. They were all muffled, sounded new. It completely destroyed my visions of a bunch of beat up old trucks struggling down Route 7. There was a log-floored bridge somewhere nearby and it sounded like a xylophone as each truck crossed it. All the trucks shifted at the same points, as though they knew the route very well. From my position, I could not see any lights moving on Route 7 and I guessed the trucks were on the new 'Robin Hood' road a couple of km further south. The truck sounds continued steadily for several hours.

'About 1900 the sounds of a multi-engine recip - slang for piston reciprocating engine powered aircraft, passed high over me and then died away. I stowed my radios to save the batteries for first light. I didn't want to run out of energy when it counted. Occasionally during the night, I heard high altitude multi-engine recips pass overhead, but they sounded so high I didn't think anything of it. It seems to me everyone but me got the word I was supposed to check in with them every hour during the night. The lack of radio contact during the night resulted in me being listed as MIA - missing in action and having a working radio.

'The long, long night was beginning. I was lying on my left side to keep my shooting arm free and to keep from making noise I didn't try to move. The valley was over four thousand feet elevation and the sky had cleared. I estimated the temperature in the forties with no wind. I was still damp and getting colder.

'The cold kept my thirst down and I just nursed my two pint flasks of water from my G-suit pockets. At 2330, determined from my radio-active, glow-in-the-dark, radium filled Navigator's watch, I heard dogs barking. I referred to my survival school training and came to the conclusion that the blood hounds had arrived. My heart dropped. I moved to a sitting position with my back against the wall, my knees drawn up and my arms on my knees holding the .38 with both hands. I quietly cocked my .38 by holding the trigger down as I pulled the hammer all the way back then releasing the trigger. I was ready for one dog, one Gomer - slang for communist guerrillas and me as necessary. No more barking. Later I heard voices from my back right, NE of me, on the ridge but they seemed to go off to the south toward Route 7. I still had my .38 out but returned to lying on my left side with my back to the rock wall. After midnight the truck traffic stopped.

'I kept the .38 out and my plan was to use cover until I was sure I could take out two of them should discovery be imminent or I was discovered. I planned to reload if possible. I fingered the rounds in elastic loops on the front of my survival vest, noting the direction to slide them out. I mentally rehearsed flipping the cylinder out, dumping the old rounds and reloading the new rounds one at a time so I wouldn't drop one in the dark.

'I also mentally rehearsed where to shoot myself before I could be wounded and or captured. I decided on under the chin with a 30 to 45 degree upward tilt to cut the brain stem. I figured my worst case would be if they came in with sweeping blind firing because I had no protection from the front but vines. Hide and wait. Did I tell you that it was cold and miserable?

'I may have nodded off during the night but no real sleep. Mother Nature visited during the night and I fished it out from under my G-suit and took a whiz once. I was sure it sounded like Niagara Falls despite being on my side.

'At 0600 on Sunday 3rd January with first light, I heard a fast mover - slang for jet fighter as opposed to a slow mover piston engine, fly over but was unable to make contact whispering into my radio. Then I heard a slow mover cross over and head to the SW. I could hear him holding way to the southwest, maybe over PDJ. I could just barely hear him. The weather was hazy clear and 40-ish Fahrenheit.

'It would turn out this was 'Raven 26' ('Chuck' Engle). He said he came over and confirmed the parachute was still there. The fast mover had been 'Tiger 01' (Bob Jones and Jerry Sullivan) but they had been given a survivor location nearly five nautical miles (nm) east of our actual location.

'As the first sunlight started to hit the far west hilltops I heard jets and ordnance far to the east. Scud clouds started to form as the sunlight hit the air. My bags were still packed and my radio was on.

'I heard male Laotian voices coming up the valley from Route 7. The voices were accompanied by thrashing of the bushes. This was not the 'first light pickup' effort that I wanted. I whispered into my radio and 'Raven 26' immediately answered. Minutes or hours passed and I could not tell the difference.

'The scud clouds had now formed a thin, solid layer at about 1,000 feet above ground level (AGL). I called again and made contact with 'Tiger 01' at about 0630. I expressed my concern to him with the bad guys in the valley about twenty to thirty yards away hacking my chute and survival kit down out of the tree, saying I might need some assistance. I lost contact as 'Tiger' turned away from my position and headed east again above the overcast.

'From the debrief I learned that there was a Nail FAC who flew an OV-10 out of NKP and 'King' in the area but they were both new to the SAR and also had the incorrect coordinates passed out by intelligence.

'By 0730 the bad guys had my chute down out of the tree and not knowing their intentions, I tried to raise someone on Guard. I again made contact with 'Raven 26' who had been there the previous afternoon and knew just where I was. Since my first contact he had been working in the background asking 'King' to make him OSC, but 'King' was trying to make the Nail FAC the OSC.

'This was the situation. When 'King' and the 'Hobo's' (A-1Es) bedded us down for the night they promised a first light effort. I expected a FAC to be orbiting overhead at sunlight with 'Sandys' on his wing. I got nothing but a Gomer first light effort. I could not talk to the fast-FAC long enough to vector him back to my position because he was so far away. The afternoon before when 'King' returned to base, the debriefing resulted in our position being mis-plotted by more than five nautical miles. This had resulted in the jet noise and ordnance I had barely been able to hear over to the east. The next morning 'King' could not hear me on the radio nor see my parachute, but he would not let 'Raven 26' be the OSC. Finally, 'Raven 26' got tired of listening to me whine and came up on Guard and said that if anybody wanted to play he was going to start another SAR. At this point 'King' capitulated and made 'Raven 26' the OSC.

'Two Korat F-4s, call sign 'Miller' flight, with pilots Doug Henneman with Ron Akaka in back and my roomy George Koch with Stan Hancock, from my Navigator School class, had been holding over the western PDJ. King weather aborted other flights from Korat and elsewhere, but Miller flight told 'Raven 26' they were ready to play, despite the weather and 'King.'

'Raven' told the fighters to let down over the PDJ, an area of known terrain height and head for Roadrunner Lake. Then they were to follow Route 7 until they saw smoke, turn left and then drop on the next smoke. 'Miller 1's Weapon Systems Officer (Ron Akaka) saw a thinning of the clouds where they could penetrate. George later told me they were able to hear my whining clearly while they were holding over the western PDJ and they really wanted to help. 'Raven 26' told me to take cover, as he was going to mark the opening of the valley and the location the flight was to drop their ordnance. I was still lying on my left side peering out of my vines at the voices in the valley because with my chute cut down out of the tree I could no longer see any enemy activity. My left leg was completely numb from loss of blood circulation during the night and with the Gomers twenty yards away I was afraid of the noise I would make if I tried to sit up and pull it out from under me. CRACK! CRACK! 'Raven 26' fired two 'Willy Petes' on one pass marking the play. Suddenly I was looking DOWN on the back of an F-4 with gleaming white Tiger teeth, doing the speed of heat as it passed into a little patch of orange sunlight. That image is still burned into my mind. I was only a couple of hundred feet above the floor of the valley. The F-4E was on the tree tops, banana tree tops. It rubbed off some cans of napalm and stood on its tail and disappeared into the clouds. The second F-4E laid his nape right beside lead's and disappeared vertically with at least a five-or-six-G pull-up.

'There were no more voices coming from the valley. Instead, the morning breeze brought the delightful aroma of napalm cooked bananas to me. It had now been 24 hours since I had eaten and bananas 'a la nape' smelled really good.

'Under the cover of 'Miller flight's noise, I got my fingers into the left knee hole of my G-suit and dragged my floppy paralyzed leg out in front of me and leaned back against the rocks to watch the air show and take my mind off of it. Soon I started feeling a welcome tingling sensation. After two more napalm runs 'Miller flight' switched to Snakeyes (Mk 82 500lb general purpose bombs with eight foot span metal petals to create high drag to slow the bomb and give the fighter safe fragmentation clearance). I got a little more into the air show and raised up and peered out through my vines. Did you know 'Snakes' go off *whoooomp* and not 'boom' like in the movies? Neither did I. About fifteen seconds after the first explosions I heard this tinkle - tinkle coming down through the trees. Oh shit! That was pieces of the metal petals coming back down. Now I remembered that the casings of the Mk.82s are propelled outward and upward as fragments travelling up to 6.000 feet per second, twice as fast as a rifle bullet. I got my ass back in my cave and as low as I could get.

'The SAR had now started. There were continuous air strikes. After about an hour I heard a burst of small arms fire from the west side of the valley that coincided with the arrival of a Sandy and I relayed it to 'Raven 26'. The Sandys covered the area with ordnance. I listened to chatter on the radio about ground fire along Route 7 to the southwest. In my humble unbiased opinion, the ground fire was pretty well suppressed by 0830. However, while suppressing the ground fire on Route 7 they discovered the revetments that got me into this mess in the first place and started beating them up with CBUs and high explosive - HE, rockets. Lots of missions went on beating up the area to suppress the enemy ground fire and they talked about using CS tear gas, along the LOC using code words of course. The after-action report claimed six trucks damaged or destroyed.

'About 0930 I overheard the 'Jollys' talking about going 'Bingo' in about thirty minutes, and then having to take a couple of hours to go out to the PDJ to aerial refuel off of 'King'. TWO hours!? Everyone said that it was still too hot for the helos to come in across Route 7 for the pickup.

'We had been working the area for weeks as Tiger FACs. In fact, we had been beating up the caves on the backside of the hill northeast of where I was hiding. I was sure the enemy loved us over there. I also knew that there was nothing out to the northwest of our position. Route 7 ran off to the southwest. I came up on the radio to 'Raven 26' and suggested a pickup from the northwest, ignoring Route 7.

'My bags are packed, I'm ready to go...' Two hours? I was going to miss lunch and that had started to sound important to me. 'Taxi's waiting outside your door ...' Also, Mother Nature was back violently waving the number 2 card. It turned out that January 2nd had been the first full day of operational capability for air-to-air refuelable HH-53, Super Jollys at Đà Nẵng in South Việtnam. They had launched and hit a C-130 tanker, 'King' on the way to the SAR area on Friday afternoon. The local CH-3 'Jollys' from NKP RTAFB in the NE corner of Thailand would have had to land at a 'Lima Site', a small fortified landing site held by the Royal Laotian forces and refuel in order to get deep enough to reach me and RTB. We were too far north of the border into Laos for a round trip with any hover time to pick us up. As a matter of fact, on 3 January 'Raven 22' and two CH-3 'Jollys' were deployed to 'Lima Site 32' only five miles north of the SAR, standing by if needed. The Super Jolly HH-53s were almost three times the size of the mere Jolly Green Giant CH-3s.

'Slowly things began to get organized. 'Sandys' 4 and 7 dragged down the run-in trolling for enemy ground fire. For the non-fisherpersons, trolling is driving the boat at minnow swimming speed pulling bait or lures. It was clear from enemy fire. By my count, I had not heard any ground fire for more than an hour. Two 'Jollys' started in following one of the 'Sandys' and another one S-turning above the formation and the fast movers started bombing Route 7 again as a diversion.

'All of this had been taking place under a 1,500 to 2,000 feet overcast. 'Raven 26' had been down at 1,000 feet AGL for two hours or more before being relieved by 'Raven 22' just before the pickup attempt.

'Just as the A-1 leading the 'Jollys' crossed the western ridgeline he told the 'Jollys' to start slowing down. Then he told Harvey, who was closer to them, to pop his smoke. At about the same time the 'Raven' put a smoke rocket where my chute used to be. I could hear the roar of the three mini-guns on the 'Jolly' over the rotor noise. Orange smoke began to drift up from behind the low ridge to my northwest and the nose of the 'Jolly' pitched up to what seemed like a 45 degree angle and it pivoted around the axis of the rotor and put its tail rotor into the vegetation on the steep terrain east of Harvey. He hovered and hovered, the mini-gun on the left side was hosing out toward, but below, my position since I could see the top of the rotor. It turned out that another PJ called the guy and told him to be careful for the survivor. I came out of my cover and was standing there watching the show again when I heard something in the grass in front of me. Fool.

'I got back into my hole and peered out through the vines. Finally, they dragged Harvey out of the jungle canopy trailing a vine. As the 'Jolly' turned toward me 'Raven 22' told me to pop my smoke.

'While they were picking up Harvey I prepared my smoke like they taught us at sea survival. I already had the seal broken and ripped the striker wire out of the flare. A tiny wisp of orange smoke about two inches long emitted from the flare… *Shake It, Shake It'* they had said. I shook the hell out of it and it began to spew a volcano of orange smoke.

'The 'Jolly' came to a hover about fifty yards in front of me in the slash and burn clearing with mini-guns still blazing. I waited for it to come to me. In jungle survival at Clark, they had said to not try to move to the penetrator. At the debrief I learned that the trees beside my slash and burn area had been so tall, remember the falling helmet, they didn't think the cable would reach me. I had stowed my radio, gun and camo hat under my survival vest. At this point I threw the 'Bullshit Flag' on survival school and came out of my hole, vaulting over large trees felled across the slash and burn area, racing and sliding for the 'Jolly' that was hovering at about the elevation of my hiding place with the penetrator downhill from me. At the SAR Debrief, the left side PJ gunner told me that I had startled him when I came flying out of the bushes jumping over logs and racing toward him. He had started to swing his gun my way when he realized I was wearing a flight suit.

'The terrain was quite steep and the penetrator slid further downhill from me. I grabbed the cable and started pulling it to me. They had left a couple of the petal seats down from the first pickup and they caught on some vegetation. NOT a problem.

'I was still wearing my sunglasses but knocked them off putting the penetrator strap over my head instead of unhooking it. I picked them up with one hand while holding the penetrator against my butt with the other. Now I grabbed the cable above the penetrator and pulled up and give the PJ a thumbs-up.

'They had cautioned us at survival school about getting the swivel at the top of the penetrator straight…I pulled up on the cable but failed. As the cable tightened I hugged the penetrator and put my bare head next to the swivel. I know you have this one figured out already. About half way up to the helo the swivel snapped up and bashed me in my left temple. I immediately knew what had happened as I dropped down an inch. I was still hugging the penetrator for dear life and didn't notice how much I was swinging back and forth. The technical term is oscillating, but just the same I was slammed into the bottom of the 'Jolly' so hard that I was dazed a little. No way was I coming off this thing. I held on even tighter. I'm not sure but I think I had reached around and interlocked my fingers behind my back.

'I was now beside the door and felt the PJ pulling the cable into the door way. He started letting out slack in the cable so my toes came back down to the floor as he pushed me over onto the cool anti-slip grit-coated aluminium floor of the helo. Boy did that feel good?

'I looked across the helo and saw Harvey wrapped up in a blanket. After evaluating the odds of hitting something critical on the chopper if I shot him with my .38, I just reached over and shook hands. The helo was now climbing and moving forward toward the western ridgeline. I became aware of the roar of the three mini-guns hosing out the sides and back of the 'Jolly' and the horrendous whine of all the gear boxes. There was an extra M-16 lying on the floor and I considered picking it up but decided that an additional twenty rounds from me wouldn't be much compared to the 12,000 rounds per minute combined rate of fire from the three minis. The PJs were hand signalling me to see if I was alright. I gave another thumbs-up. Too bad they didn't have faces at that time.

'We climbed to 7 or 8,000 feet MSL- above Mean Sea Level, over the PDJ. Battle damage check showed we had taken one small arms round with no leaks in the fuel or hydraulics or shorts from damaged wires.

'We joined up with 'King' for refuelling. The 'Jolly' crew let me ride in the jump seat so I could see out the front. I had not realized how far the refuelling probe extended out in front of the 'Jolly' to poke the basket towed by the 'King'. I was used to the boom being stuck into the back of the F-4 right behind my head. This was more like trying to stick the tip of a cane fishing pole into a tin can in a wind storm. Again for those deprived of pleasant fishing training, a cane pole is an inexpensive bamboo pole about 15 feet long and one and a half inches in diameter at the big end and one quarter inch at the small end. It is very floppy and flexible.

'I thanked the crew over the intercom. Compared with the F-4 it was a long shaky ride back to Udorn. The 'Jolly' crew was just visiting the area so as a local navigator I was able to assist when there was a temporary spatial disorientation discussion between the pilots.

'There had been two Super Jolly HH-53s in the area for the pickup and we were joined on the way home by two CH-3s, 'Jollys' that had been waiting at 'Lima Site 32' as backup. Now there was a four ship of 'Jollys' headed for Udorn. We lined up down the runway and the PJs popped smoke to trail behind us. At the runway departure end, we slowed and turned back down the taxiway…we couldn't do that with the F-4. We 'hover-taxied' back to the ramp and turned into the 'Valley.' The crew checked in with their Command Post whose call sign was 'Ho-Ho-Ho' of course and gave their maintenance status. It began to really settle in with that radio call and maintenance status, that things were getting back to normal…I was safe. Then I noticed the group of about fifty people with a fire hose. This would be nice, guys, but I needed to take a dump in the worst way and I was still chilled, but they had earned the privilege of hosing us down. Maybe I could borrow the fire hose if I couldn't hold it any longer.

'After we were hosed down they gave us hollowed-out pineapples filled with champagne and fragrant leis made of Plumeria blossoms for our necks. Then it was off to the hospital for medical clearance. We were checked for dislocations or broken bones and a series of back X Rays because of the ejections. My only visible damage was a couple of lumps on my head.

'Now we did run into some trouble at the hospital. They insisted against our great protest that we could not take our pineapples with us into the hospital. We and several others explained to them that their rules sucked and would just have to be changed. Didn't work and they took our pineapples. After the medical checks, we were taken to the cafeteria for some food. When I started to eat for the first time in 24 hours I was pleased to find that my iced-tea was champagne over ice. Good corpsmen.

'I was given an autovon - automatic voice network telephone system, patch from Udorn to Tinker AFB to my parents in Oklahoma. Since it had taken the Air Force about twenty hours to notify them I was MIA it was now only a couple of hours after that notification that I called home.

'Shortly we had a 'Gooney bird' ride back to Korat. After landing we were met on the ramp by the Wing CC and Wing DO for debriefing and a beautiful young lady patiently waiting in the background. My story was that we had pulled to on-speed but didn't have the G-available to turn the required corner. Harv's was a little different. The DO liked Harvey's version better and told the Lieutenant he was dismissed and get the pretty young lady off the ramp. I did.

'About two weeks later there was a SAR debrief-party at NKP. Very drunk out. Good food and friends. We had a 'Meanest Mother in the Valley' contest which consisted of seeing what one could tolerate eating or drinking. One young NKP 'Nail' FAC burped up his raw egg and was about to be disqualified when he sucked it up out of his cupped hands where he had caught it…we let him stay. There was about a three way tie at this point and I was still in the game. One of the three said he had something and came back with a can of Japanese seaweed. He opened it and the smell was the worst thing I had ever smelled. He was the only one that would touch it. He was declared the winner and summarily thrown outside the party 'hootch' along with his horrible smelling seaweed.

'There were other people involved in my SAR that need a chance to talk…my family. War is not fought in isolation. First, my wife 'Kathy.' While I was down she did not cry or break down in public. She conducted herself like the brave soldier she is. I owe her big time for what she has been through over the years. Night range missions after three of our friends were killed in two accidents. Numerous TDY - temporary duty, assignments some up to 179 days, remote tours and PCS's - permanent change of stations, where I went back to familiar work and she was left alone in many new homes with no friends.'

Chapter 6

Blue Bandits

Commander John R. Cheshire USN Retd

In World War II the US Navy's kill ratio was 14:1 (fourteen enemy planes destroyed for each Navy aircraft lost). In the Korean War American jets had a 12:1 kill ratio over enemy fighters. During the first few years of aerial combat in Viêtnam, from the Navy's first MiG kills in 1965 until the bombing halt of 1968, the Navy's kill ratio was around 2.5:1. The Navy ordered a comprehensive study of tactical aircraft, radars and missiles, as well as the training and tactics of Navy aircrews. The report found that poor missile performance was a major factor in the low kill ratio. Almost 600 air-to-air missiles were fired by the Navy and Air Force in about 360 engagements between June 1965 and September 1968 and the probability of a kill worked out to be about one kill for every ten missiles fired. On 3 March 1969 the United States Navy established an elite school for the top one percent of its pilots. Its purpose was to teach the lost art of aerial combat and to insure that the handful of men who graduated were the best fighter pilots in the world.'

'They succeeded.'

'Today, the Navy calls it Fighter Weapons School. The flyers call it...'
'TOPGUN'

In the spring of 1971, John R. Cheshire had to leave and trade his rented ocean-front house on Mission Beach that spans nearly two miles of ocean front between the Pacific Ocean and Mission Bay at San Diego, California for the USS *Midway's* junior officers' bunkroom #14. (But it was still 'ocean front' property, now wasn't it?). It was to be the first of his two combat cruises to Southeast Asia. For a former landlocked Iowa farm boy who as a child had watched in awe and respect, every original episode of the black and white TV series *Victory At Sea*, the long passage across the Pacific was a wonderfully fulfilling experience. 'From the USS *Midway's* passage south-westward beneath and beyond San Francisco's Golden Gate bridge, a week's port call in Pearl Harbor, passing by the Mariana Islands with their historic WWII battles and exotic names, through the important San Bernardino Straits of the Philippine Islands with echoes of Leyte Gulf, the ghosts of the great war in the Pacific 25 years earlier, were everywhere. It was indeed a thrill to now be in the same Navy and in the same waters that I had watched on TV. It was also inspiring to be in the same Pacific theatre as my father's good friend and the individual who initially stirred my interest in military aviation at a very young age - a WWII B-24 nose gunner and role model named Hartwig. Thus it was a great source of pride to now be a part of that same great legacy. For this and subsequent cruises - especially in heavy seas, sometimes with water over the bow - I found I was not the only one to be humming or whistling Richard Rogers' fabulous *Victory at Sea*. Unlike the one to follow a year later, this cruise would prove to be only 'mild' combat. The 1968 bombing halt over North Viêtnam was still in effect in 1971. That meant that except for a very occasional 'protective reaction strike' north of the DMZ, our missions were confined to South Việtnam, Cambodia and Laos. Since the North Việtnamese MiGs never ventured into the South, we as fighter pilots were denied our primary mission - one we had trained for and actively sought - air-to-air combat with enemy MiGs.

'As a newly minted Naval Aviator, I attended a few weeks of Maintenance Management School in Memphis. Completing that short course, I then spent a few weeks on leave at home with my family in Iowa, before finally embarking on my journey to NAS Miramar in San Diego and my post graduate F-4 training. It was a very long drive (1,900 miles) from my Anamosa Iowa farm home to San Diego, California. I made it an even longer drive (2,600 miles) by driving by way of Houston (while visiting a friend there, my car was burgled and I lost all my personal belongings) and through San Antonio (to reclaim some property loaned to another friend) before finally setting course for San Diego. The highlight of this 2,600+ mile drive was topping a long grade through a rock-cut along Interstate-8 in Arizona and having two F-4 Phantoms blow by suddenly - no more than a hundred feet above me - and at amazing, blazing speed in the opposite direction! They might have been Navy or Air Force F-4s... it made little difference. I knew I was getting ever closer to being one of 'them' with each passing mile.

'As I finally descended from the last mountain range into the glowing lights of San Diego, I began to realize how incredibly fortunate I was and how unlikely my life's journey to date had been.

'Once again, as had happened in each of my four previous duty stations, there was another tragic incident the week of my check-in to VF-121'Pacemakers', the F-4 training squadron known as the 'RAG'. An F-8 had lost its engine on approach to NAS Miramar. Although the pilot ejected safely, the stricken craft slammed into a hangar, killing and injuring quite a number of navy maintenance personnel who had been working in the hangar.

'Once established at my new duty station, I learned there was a large backlog of students going through F-4 training. Training that normally would take six months, now stretched out to over a year. So after a week of difficult and unpleasant SERE training at the Warner Springs simulated PoW Camp and a few weeks of refresher instrument training with VF-126 in the TA-4J, I ended up in a six-month pool, awaiting F-4 training. Although I was eager to commence F-4 training, I can think of no better place to be than San Diego in the spring and living once again in an oceanfront beach house, to thoroughly enjoy my sabbatical.

'Eventually, my F-4 training would begin in earnest. Those were heady times at VF-121. Naval Air was then in a major process of totally revamping F-4 fighter tactics, after some earlier, disappointing experiences in Việtnam.

'The Ault Report had suddenly and thankfully changed everything. As a result, the superb, veteran fighter pilots/ROs who were then establishing the Navy Fighter Weapons School ('Top Gun') from scratch were my instructors. Veteran Israeli and British fighter pilots joined us in sharing their expertise and in learning the new and developing tactics. For a fighter pilot, these were indeed exciting and dynamic times.

'Of my year at VF-121, two more things stand out: EW training and Night Carrier qualification flights. Throughout my training, the thought of actual combat was always remote - well 'beyond the horizon.' Yes, we did practice air-to-air and air-to-ground 'combat' tactics, daily. But we did so for the enjoyment, the learning and for the grade given for that training flight. It was never a life-threatening, exigent situation. Moreover, our simulated combat training was mostly 'offensive' and rarely 'defensive' training. It was all, great fun. But our attitudes all changed, late in our training, when the EW (Electronic Warfare) Officer came into class to give his 'secret' lecture.

'Our colourful EW Officer walked into class with his infamous, 'suitcase' EW trainer. It was a large, unfolding box that held all the classified electronic instruments that were too secret to be in our 'training' F-4s. We had never seen them. These instruments could tell a pilot if the enemy had him on radar, had him locked-up; were going to fire at him and with what weapon and from which direction and if they did indeed fire... The EW's Officer's suitcase trainer showed us the many simulated, yet scary red warning lights and directional strobes of people shooting at us. It also included the loud aural warning tones of enemy missiles racing toward you. It received everyone's attention. Our perspectives all suddenly changed. We knew, from that time forward of the immensely serious business and challenges that lie ahead.

'I have often thought that knowing what I know today, I might never have night-qualified in the F-4 aboard an aircraft carrier. I did, of course, and am eternally thankful for that! But had I truly known what I was doing at the time - the enormous difficulty and the great risks involved - I might not have.

'Though always challenging, landing an F-4 - or any Navy aircraft for that matter - during the day and in good weather, can and should be fun. However, landing an F-4 at night on a darkened carrier - especially in those earlier days of very few ship's lights, no HUD (Head Up Display), no precision guidance 'needles' and little guidance other than a spastic RMI needle, an LSO and the visual 'ball' - can sometimes (often? always?) be terrifying, be it your first or even your 300th night trap. The prospect of this CQ (carrier qualification) would become extremely challenging for me for several reasons. First, it would not be conveniently close-by off the coast of my California home. Rather it would be off the distant East Coast, in the Atlantic and aboard the USS *Forrestal*.

'But what was especially difficult was that my 'field-carrier-landing-practice' (FCLP) training had to be unexpectedly cut short. During our FCLP detachment at Yuma MCAS, the Officer in Charge (great guy and later a VF-96 Commanding Officer of some note and more) called me aside from the officer's swimming pool. He privately but kindly informed me of my father's death in Iowa. Thus instead of finishing FCLP Training, I immediately flew home to Iowa for my father's funeral.

'Subsequently, I had to attend to a number of family matters in Iowa. But following only a few days and although very short on CQ training and without ever returning home to San Diego and NAS Miramar following Dad's funeral, by my own choice (and as my father would have wanted it), I went straight to NAS Oceana, Virginia for the challenging initial F-4 CQ on the *Forrestal*.

'Despite the difficult circumstances and to my surprise, I did quite well. Nevertheless, my friend just beat me out for the top overall carrier landing grades. But once again, I was fortunate. His top landing grade sent him immediately to the Gulf of Tonkin where he joined at sea, a returning squadron, VF-154. My grade sent me to a great squadron getting ready to deploy - VF-151.

'In surfing terms, that meant I was in the perfect spot to catch the perfect wave - to join a squadron early in their cyclic wave of shore duty, work-ups and deployment to Southeast Asia, at the most opportune time. And indeed, it would become quite a long and thrilling ride!

'After encountering aircraft accidents in each of my five previous change-of-duty stations, it was not only a great pleasure to finally become a true fighter pilot - in a real, front line fighter squadron - but also to not have some unfortunate aircraft accident accompany my arrival. With VF-151, that tragic chain of events for me had fortunately been broken...forever.

'Arrival to a fighter squadron was an entirely different experience than anything of my prior 2.5 years of flight training. Nothing compared. Although I was obviously the new squadron 'FNG' and 'Nugget' and thus given all the unwanted junior jobs, it was also very apparent from day one, that I had just become a most welcome member of one of the most exclusive, elite and tight knit units of aviators imaginable. It was an immediate thrill... without yet even flying in the squadron colours.

'My initial flight with 'Fitron 151' was a radar intercept training flight launched from NAS Miramar and flown over the desert and Salton Sea. My squadron CO and his senior RO were in the other, lead aircraft. Toward the end of our training flight and as we joined up into close formation for the return to base, I noticed a lot of smoke in the CO's cockpit - I really thought he was on fire! My old-hand back-seater Dave laughed and said, 'not to worry.' 'That's just the CO's back-seater RO Denny, smoking his usual cigar. He lights up at the end of every mission.' [Smoking without securing our 100% oxygen flow was potential suicide. Smoking with it secured was still risky and obviously against regulations. Nevertheless, some months later I found myself joining our squadron's airborne smoking club... especially after combat missions.]

'Immediately I knew, after nearly three years of structured and tightly controlled training, this was going to be a whole different world ... a fighter pilot's world. It is a world that few can truly understand and far fewer ever are allowed to even see or experience... and indeed for me, it all was all coming true and about to be.

'Not long after my arrival to VF-151 and just prior to my first deployment to Southeast Asia, I was involved with 'Carrier Qualifying' aboard the USS *Midway*. This involved the completion of a prescribed number of both day and night carrier landings ('traps'). On this late winter night, the USS *Midway* was operating approximately 100 miles off the coast from San Francisco.

'During these training flight operations, there must always be an alternate airfield designated, just in case there are any problems landing aboard the aircraft carrier. On this occasion, NAS Moffett at the southern end of San Francisco Bay was our alternate airfield (what we called a 'Bingo' field).

'As the ship continues steaming, flight crews are routinely updated with the constantly changing bearing and distance to the 'Bingo' field. Each crew then calculates their absolute minimum fuel required to reach the emergency 'Bingo' field if ever needed, for their particular aircraft.

'On this dark night - for reasons still unknown to me - a serious mistake was made. The actual distance to the 'Bingo' field was far greater than what was being broadcast to those six of us who were flying in the ship's night landing pattern.

'Then suddenly, the USS *Midway* steamed into a thick fog bank, precluding any more landings. We were told to 'Bingo'!

'We (my RO, 'TA' and I) immediately initiated a climbing turn toward our 'Bingo' field... a landing field we would soon learn was now much further away than we had been led to believe. We would now need much more fuel than we had planned for us to ever make it to NAS Moffett. And there was nothing any closer, other than the very cold and pitching, black Pacific winter water.

'Flying a 'Bingo' profile is an emergency situation with a small margin for error. Checking our charts during climb-out and given the large distance error, we soon realized making it to NAS Moffett without running out of gas was very questionable. It would be close. Certainly, neither of us relished a midnight ejection into the icy cold waters of the northern Pacific and a Search & Rescue (SAR) operation. But we began to seriously prepare for that real possibility.

'To gain the greatest distance with the least amount of fuel, the charted 'Bingo' profile must be flown precisely. This involves climbing to the specific altitude mandated for the given range, then later beginning a long slow glide at idle power at a predetermined distance from the 'Bingo' field. Naturally, the bulk of the precious remaining fuel is burned in the initial climb. Very little fuel is needed for the long, slow glide to touchdown.

'Still in our fuel-burning climb, but having nearly reached our prescribed altitude, we switched radio frequencies to a different *Midway* air traffic controller. At check-in, he asked for our fuel state. We responded with, 'one-point-six' (1,600lbs).

'There was a long pause. Then, the controller finally responded with the chilling words that ring as clear to me today, as they did 35 years ago:

'Sir, you're never going to make it!'

'Luckily we did make it, but barely. It was extremely close.

'A precisely flown, long idle descent straight to landing (and with a propitious bit of a tailwind) saved us. Our fuel gauges registered virtually empty as we taxied in after landing... with my knees slightly shaking on the rudder pedals. In fact, another *Midway* F-4 just ahead of us actually did flame out for lack of fuel while taxiing inbound.

'Then once we were refuelled - just like immediately climbing back onto a bucking horse after being thrown - we launched once again into the late dark night, for our return to the ship.

'The *Midway* had by then escaped the fog bank and was now steaming in the clear, yet thick black Pacific night. Thankfully, she now had updated and accurate 'Bingo' field information. Totally drained, physically and emotionally, we finally landed aboard her at 2 am, went to our bunkroom, called it a night and collapsed!

'But in my dreams that night - as well as today, so many years later - I can still vividly hear that young air-controller hauntingly say... 'Sir, you're never going to make it!'

'I would fly fifty-six missions during this cruise until it ended abruptly for me by a non-combat, yet serious injury. This resulted in an early MedEvac and a long and arduous journey back home on a stretcher. We, evacuees, were stacked 4 high on a packed C-141 shared with a lot of other shot up guys in much worse shape than I, to the Balboa Naval Hospital in San Diego for surgery. It was both a physical and emotionally painful flight. A majority were close air support missions for US and ARVN troops on the ground. Except for missions near Tchepone or the Mụ Giạ Pass (a mountain pass in the Annamite Range between northern Việtnam and Laos, 90 kilometres northwest of Đông Hới on the Hô Chi Minh Trail) and a few other areas where heavier anti-aircraft guns and AAA were common, we otherwise rarely saw any Cross of Gallantry really heavy enemy fire. Nevertheless, a multitude of unseen small arms fire directed at us was assumed to be always present.

'On one early mission, I did once mistake some multiple and rapid flashes of sunlight that were reflecting off of water-filled bomb craters, as heavy enemy fire. The burst of veteran laughter emanating from my back seat at my naiveté quickly highlighted my mistaken rookie observation!) As a fast moving F-4, our risks paled in comparison to our engaged troops on the ground, or the low and slow and easily targeted flying FACs who courageously directed us in for our close air support. Indeed, the war sometimes seemed very distant. We flew off the carrier on 'Dixie Station' in the Gulf of Tonkin, laid our bombs relative to where the FAC (Forward Air Controller) had laid his targeting 'smoke' and then returned to the ship for a hot meal, some paperwork and if lucky, a short combat nap. It was often very routine and relatively low risk. Most of what we knew of the intense and high risk, ground war that was being waged, we learned from the daily newspaper, *Stars & Stripes*. Of course there were always the occasional, sudden and unexpected reminders of the true danger of our missions. But our 'close-calls' during this cruise were, fortunately, few and far between. Little did we know then, how different - and tragic - our next cruise to the war's end would be!

'On rare occasions during a bombing mission, we would have a problem with our bomb release mechanism. One or more of our 500lb bombs would accidentally hang up on the F-4 and couldn't be released. With this unwanted condition of 'unexpended ordnance', for safety reasons, we usually flew to Đà Nẵng to offload the bombs rather than land aboard the ship with them. Most flight crews welcomed this. It meant spending a little time on dry land and was an interesting change of venue. More inviting, it offered the opportunity of having a 'legal' cold beer, which of course, was 'prohibited' aboard ship.

'Unlike the Air Force and Marines, the Navy had only a small detachment in Đà Nẵng and its facilities were very Spartan. What substituted for an officer's club was a small annex to the officers' quarters. It only contained a refrigerator, a small bar and maybe four or five old wooden tables with chairs. We called the little place the 'Red Dog Saloon'... after 'Red', the Navy officer in charge of the Đà Nẵng detachment.

'One day we had to divert with hung bombs to Đà Nẵng. Since we were in the day's last flight-operations cycle of the *Midway*, we, therefore, had to spend the night in Đà Nẵng before returning. After dinner, my RO and I went to the 'Red Dog'. There were only a handful of people there, including a young Việtnamese girl as barmaid.

'Starting on our second beer and immersed in our own conversation of our day's events, looking up, we suddenly noticed we were now all alone in the bar. Suddenly we recalled hearing stories of whenever the Việtnamese barmaid abruptly and inexplicably disappeared, a Việt Công (VC) rocket attack was imminent.

'As the only two now left in the bar, we decided perhaps we had better go to the protection of the sandbagged bunker, just outside. As we casually made our way outside to the safety of the bunker, we heard three loud explosions on the base... but thankfully some distance away. Joining the other 'Red Dog Saloon' patrons already huddled in the bunker we realized we had just 'survived' our first Đà Nẵng VC rocket attack. And my RO and I vowed that next time we would definitely always keep an eye on the young barmaid. Next time we would be the first rather than the last to make it to the safety of the bunker... whenever she unexpectedly disappeared. [And indeed, a few weeks later when she again abruptly disappeared for a bit, (thanks to our survival-driven, steep learning curve of war), we were now the first, rather than the last to rush into the relative safety of the outside sand-bagged bunker! (Good thing too; this time, the VC rockets hit a lot closer!)]

'Following that relatively 'moderate' first seven-month cruise of mine with VF-151 and CVW-5 in 1971, the *Midway* and our air wing were scheduled to have six months at home before we deployed once again to combat in Southeast Asia. But it was not to be.

'In response to the large US troop pullout in South Việtnam, the growing strength of the American anti-war movement and the vulnerability of the South Việtnamese army, General Võ Nguyên Giáp launched an all-out Eastertide offensive on 30 March 1972 with 200,000 North Việtnamese soldiers against the South. President Nixon countered by cancelling the 1968 bombing halt in the North.

'On 6 April 1972, the *Midway* was conducting routine carrier qualification training operations, 100 miles off the coast of California when they got the word: 'Proceed immediately to the Việtnam War Zone!'

'This was nearly two months earlier than planned and without any warning!' recalled John Cheshire. 'Fortunately, the high command reconsidered, allowing at least a very quick, weekend port call in Alameda, California to prepare for what would eventually become, the longest carrier deployment of the Việtnam War. The ship rapidly steamed back into Alameda on Friday. That night I flew a commercial airline (PSA) to San Diego. The next day, Saturday, I put my Volvo 1800E in storage, loaned my red MGA to a friend, closed out the rent, said my goodbyes and packed all my belongings, putting most in storage. Then late that night I flew the last remaining VF-151 F-4B (BuNo153056) from its hangar at NAS Miramar to NAS Alameda. Since our maintenance personnel were still in Alameda or onboard *Midway*, maintenance personnel from another squadron had been working feverishly all day to repair it. But it still had some 'problems.' Nevertheless, we desperately needed it for deployment. After a tentative (and very rare if not against normal 'regs') night test flight, we had to fly it to Alameda with its landing gear locked down (there was some serious concern this 'hangar queen' aircraft could not lower its landing gear again, if they were raised - so we just left them down). The navigational instruments 'didn't work too well' either, so we just visually followed the car lights on the Grapevine and the I-5 freeway north beyond Los Angeles to the Bay area. We thankfully made it OK. In the morning, this last squadron aircraft was loaded aboard the *Midway*.

'I spent the next day - a beautiful Spring Sunday - with my girlfriend of the time. She had happened to be in Lake Tahoe for the weekend and drove to Alameda immediately when I told her the news. The next day, Monday, the *Midway* sailed underneath the Golden Gate Bridge - with its groups of both supporters and war protesters - for what would be a most arduous, record setting and intensely climatic experience of the long Việtnam War.

'Unlike the previous cruise, we all knew this one would be far different and far more difficult. This time we seriously studied maps and enemy defenses religiously, rather than potential tourist sites and port visits. We would have no navigational aids over the 'North' so we had to memorize the lay of the land. Then, 19 days and 7,800 miles later, we found ourselves back in the thick of a much angrier air war than ever before. And it would last nearly ten months more.

'Since we had deployed early and suddenly, without the normal 'work-ups', we were not fully trained, nor quite as battle-ready as we would normally have been with a longer turnaround period. So upon our arrival in the Gulf of Tonkin, instead of jumping into the hot air war over North Việtnam, we initially conducted close air support operations in the relative safety, south of the DMZ.

'One of my first missions of this cruise was in support of ARVN and the few remaining US troops in the Battle of Ân Lộc. This battle was notable to me because it was the first time I could actually see from the air, some distinct battle lines between the good guys and bad guys. For the first time, after nearly sixty combat missions, I was able to tell there was indeed a hot war going on below me. Because of the lack of trees and triple canopy jungle in the area, I could observe unobstructed, real troop and enemy positions.

'Fighter pilots of the day were just that - air-to-air fighter pilots, still taught and believing in the classic Von Richthofen, Red Baron tradition (honourable and chivalric combat, against a worthy opponent). While they relished the air-to-air missions against possible MiGs, they believed air-to-ground missions to be somewhat below them (no pun intended). Nevertheless, I must confess to one early and satisfying, 'air-to-mud' as we disdainfully called them, close air support mission.

'One day during the siege of An Lộc, a FAC (forward air controller) vectored me to an enemy target - a suspected, captured 105mm howitzer thought to be hidden in a certain clump of trees. Apparently, it had been decimating both our US and ARVN troops for some time. I dropped six Mk.82 500lb bombs on what I believed was the FAC's designated target, relative to his 'smoke'. Unfortunately, I had apparently dropped on a different clump of trees than he wanted, but only a very short distance away. The FAC began screaming about my errant miss... and then quite suddenly he was quiet... Had he been shot down? No... he was temporarily in awe.

'To our mutual surprise, there were huge multiple, secondary explosions coming from that close-by, but 'wrong' clump of trees and they continued for some time. 'Secondaries' (multiple, subsequent explosions) meant success. It meant that I had hit not only that pesky 105 howitzer and maybe others, but more importantly, I had also hit a large - and heretofore unknown - NVA stockpile of weapons and ordnance. I really believe my successful strike saved a large number US and ARVN lives by eliminating all that ordnance. (Even true fighter pilots will admit to that type of 'air-to-ground' mission once in a while.) It was a good day of many.

'Here is how we planned our 'Alpha Strikes' in Air Wing 5 aboard Midway, as depicted by multi-talented Fighter RIO Ben 'Yossarian' Thompson in his private autobiography.

'I was at the peak of my profession at age 25. I was a superior fighter pilot, fresh from Top Gun and razor-sharp. My primary mission was to shoot down MiGs and protect our guys. I was confident that I could do that without hesitation, under all conditions - even if against the world's very best fighter pilots - and that I would prevail. I was more than ready and eager to engage the enemy in aerial combat. Unfortunately, the MiGs would not cooperate. The North Viêtnamese Air Force (VPAF) had sustained some significant losses in early 1972; primarily from my fellow Navy fighter pilots. By the time we finally had worked our way north from 'Dixie Station' to 'Yankee Station' and to the air war over North Viêtnam the MiGs were starting to become very reluctant to engage Navy fighters. The Navy and Air Force would alternate their three-daily 'Alpha Strikes' over North Viêtnam. When not flying, I used to watch on ship's radar, the air strikes over the north. It rapidly became apparent in the summer of 1972 that the North Viêtnamese MiGs would routinely engage Air Force strikes, but would usually scamper and disappear during US Navy strikes. Obviously, the Navy's new 'Top Gun' school of new fighter tactics, combined with the extraordinary, recent success of Navy fighter pilots had made a real and immediate impact on the air war. Try as I might - including 'bait' and deception - I could never entice nor engage any MiGs in aerial combat. I did, however, have four close encounters with enemy MiGs. Here is one other close encounter:

'As MiGCAP for an 'Alpha Strike', the Skipper, both our ROs and I were on-station at 3,500 feet, 420 knots, manoeuvering above the North Viêtnam delta area that we called, the 'Hour-Glass' [because of the hourglass shape of the delta rivers]. 'Red Crown' (Call-sign for the Navy ship in the Gulf who observed and controlled the air war) reported two 'Blue Bandits' (MiG-21s) venturing way far south. Since their southern airfields had all been bombed, we knew these MiGs would soon have to be turning back northbound to return to Kép, their airbase. We decided to 'cut them off at the pass', with a 90-degree intercept.

'Red Crown' reported the MiGs very 'fast and very low,' so we also went lower and faster - from our usual 3,500 feet down to about 500 feet above the rice paddies and well in excess of 600 knots. We were about 1,500 feet below a solid overcast cloud layer. With us heading due East and the MiGs heading nearly due north, we became without visual or radar contact, what was known as the dreaded 'merged plot'. This meant we all were on top of each other, all in the same piece of sky, but we still hadn't spotted our enemy - a very dangerous situation.

'Had the MiGs spotted us? We didn't know. The tension was incredible. We then immediately and deliberately committed a fighter pilot's cardinal sin - we turned on a merged plot.

'Turning on a 'merged plot' is something we were taught never to do... but we did it in this instance. (We were greedy.) Fortunately, in our case, we rolled out of the turn in trail - and not in front - of the two speeding enemy MiG-21's. Apparently, they had been just above the 2,000 foot overcast cloud layer continuing northbound, while we were just below it. Out of our hard yet sweeping, 600 knots and 6.5G+ low-level turn, we continued chasing those fast flying and escaping MiG-21J's, almost all the way to Hànôi.

'Although my RO, (call-sign, 'TA') had one of them locked-up on our fire control radar, the MiG remained slightly out of range for our AIM-7 Sparrow missiles, so we had to hold our fire. I had pushed the throttles all the way to a 'two-blocked' full afterburner position and we were screaming along supersonic at a very low level. But because of our configuration-drag that day and their newer 'J' models, the MiGs surprisingly increased slightly their range from us. (Normally, we should have been equal to them or a little faster.)

'Meanwhile, in the long, high speed and low-level chase, we began to become the target of substantial - and obviously alerted - enemy ground fire. Many tracers were flying by, we had SAM warnings on our RHAW gear (Radar Homing and Warning - Related) and we were rapidly running low on fuel for having our afterburners so long engaged. Finally and wisely, we broke off the attack. Going 'feet wet' (over water) and very low on fuel, we desperately sought a 'tanker' to in-flight refuel us, while the two MiG-21Js continued on and landed safely at Kép airfield, to fight another day.'

'Sometime early in my second combat cruise, I regained a little 'religion'. Having now seen a lot of enemy fire directed specifically at us/me as the intended target and now on a near daily basis with the fire getting ever closer, I incorporated a new pre-launch checklist item - the quickie prayer. Well before the hand-salute that signalled the catapult officer to launch us off the aircraft carrier, into the air and into history or oblivion, I made a quickie sign of the cross and whispered my short pre-launch prayer. My quickie prayer was: 'Lord, please allow me/we not to screw up; to live through that day's mission; and (perhaps stretching things) if at all possible, for me to live long enough to enjoy my much anticipated and scheduled leave, then three months hence.'

'I did indeed live three more months, although I doubt it had anything to do with my selfish prayer. Nevertheless, even in a combat zone, we were allowed to have 10% of our crews on leave at any given time. Refreshed and rejuvenated from a spell of leave, I was eager and ready to resume my duties on 'Yankee Station'. While our sister squadron, 'Brand-X', aka VF-161 had shot down a number of MiGs in a short period of time, no one in our squadron had. In fact, no one in our squadron had even encountered any MiGs yet, much less engage any, or shoot any down. I was determined to change that!

'During a short visit to 'Red Crown' (the USS *Truxton* at the time), I was surprised to learn that the VPAF pilots were receiving nearly real-time translations of our fighters' tactical transmissions. Upon learning this, I devised a plan that we executed on our next flight over the North.

'While on CAP (Combat Air Patrol) station well west of Hon Gai we made up some deceptive transmissions, complaining about how our radar and missiles weren't working and we were getting low on fuel, but we would remain on station and just 'fake it'.

'Sure enough, the MiGs took the bait. Shortly after our UHF transmissions, two 'Blue Bandits' launched from Kép. They were coming straight for us. Excitedly, we then called for a 'cross-turn' and 'buster' (180 degree tactical turn and afterburner) to engage them. But our aggressive transmissions must have been immediately relayed to them, as they quickly reversed course back to Kép. We were too far away to catch them. But it was a nice try.

'One day the Skipper let me brief and lead our two-plane mission. It was a 'road-recce' where we were free to look for any enemy targets of opportunity. With my RO and I as lead, flying low-level over the countryside for some time, we encountered no enemy fire. We also had not found any targets of opportunity, until much to our surprise we came upon a steel-span bridge. Now unless they were heavily defended, there should not have been any bridges still standing in this part of North Việtnam, especially one like this - a large one, seemingly sitting out alone in the countryside.

'We popped up and because it was a windy day, we each dropped only two of our six Mk.82 500lb bombs on the bridge for effect. Both missing the bridge, we would adjust for the wind on our next drop of our remaining bombs. With no enemy fire apparent or expected, we set up a lazy, racetrack pattern for our next roll-in attack. Focused on the bridge, what we failed to realize was that it was near one of the most heavily defended cities - Vĩnh. Fixated on 'our' bridge, we never saw the city. Now having unknowingly alerted every enemy gunner in town with our first drop, we were now flying directly over them, obliviously.57mm AAA

'When I once again reached the same roll-in point for my second bombing run on the bridge, every anti-aircraft gun in Vĩnh must have by then been tracking us - and they all suddenly at once, opened fire! Immediately, our F-4 was totally engulfed in a thick cloud of AAA smoke! While I had seen a lot of AAA fire in the past, it thankfully was always in the form of tracers and puffs of smoke at least some distance from my cockpit. This time, however, we seemed to be engulfed in and part of the explosions. We were IFR in AAA flak! That we were not blown out of the sky and didn't take a hit is a true miracle… . and one I cannot explain to this day. Fortunately, we managed to abort our Vĩnh bridge attack to find a less well-defended target and live to fight another day.

'Well into our second combat cruise and now having over a hundred and fifty combat missions, we had a certain level of expectations. We expected successful results from our strike missions (in the form of secondary explosions, or post-strike reconnaissance bomb-damage-assessment - BDA photos). But we also had come to expect certain levels of enemy resistance, in the form of SAM's (Surface to Air Missiles) and AAA, if not any MiGs. When our results or enemy resistance were lacking, I felt disappointed and somehow, inexplicably cheated.

'I had unwittingly become addicted to the repetitive adrenalin rush of combat! (Something I have later learned is not that uncommon for those living under hostile fire, over time.) Thus one day when my expectations of enemy opposition were not met, to compensate, I did something very stupid:

'A squadron mate had informed me of an NVA anti-aircraft gunnery training site located between two karst ridges we called 'Happy Valley'. For kicks, he had flown over the school as a target. But he flew at an altitude he knew was safely above their 23mm and 37mm AAA range.

'One day, having some extra fuel following a CAP mission, we flew over to the NVA Gunnery School. Circling the school at 15,000 as targets and just out of their range, we enjoyed the fireworks of their AAA (Anti-Aircraft Artillery) shells exploding 2,000 feet below us, at their maximum altitude. My wingman that day thought the many puffs looked like a large flock of white and grey 'doves'. Satisfied, we then returned to the ship.

'Two weeks later, we again had some extra gas and returned to the gunnery school. What we did not know was the North Viêtnamese, obviously anticipating our return, had moved in some heavy AAA - 85mm guns - capable of shooting us down at very high altitudes. As we set up our circle over the school as before, a large orange and black explosion occurred just off the right side of our aircraft. As we lit afterburners, turned and quickly vacated the area, the sky was full of big, orange and black explosions - the signature of 85mm - all around us and at our altitude. Needless to say, we never did that again!

'We had been flying combat missions over North Viêtnam since early May. Now, by August 1972 we had fallen into an almost 'comfortable' routine. Yes, our air-wing had lost a few aircraft and pilots, but except for the loss of one of our F-4s off the ships catapult (crew safely recovered), both of our F-4B squadrons had remained mostly unscathed. Unfortunately, that would abruptly change.

'On 25 August an F-4B [153020 crewed by Lieutenant Commander Michael William Doyle and Lieutenant John Clyde Ensch] from our sister squadron, VF-161 was shot down over North Viêtnam. Its crew were two of the most respected and well-liked men in the F-4 Community. 'Jack' would survive, albeit wounded and immediately incarcerated as a PoW. (A few years later Jack and I would be reunited into the same squadron - VF-1 - and in fact, we became for a time, stateroom-mates aboard the USS *Enterprise*.... As most would agree, Jack was one of the finest - and funniest - guys I have ever known.) But my former instructor and friend, 'Mike' sadly did not survive. Whatever feeling of invincibility that was growing in the two F-4 squadrons was suddenly shattered. Then two days later, it was obliterated!

'Still shaken by the loss of our sister squadron's crew, it was then our squadron's unfortunate turn. On 27 August our own 'Ted' and 'Dave' [Lieutenant Theodore W. Triebel and Lieutenant (jg) David A. Everett] were shot down by a SAM and subsequently captured. Once again, it was the loss of two of the most respected and well-liked squadron mates. It was a most bitter blow. Although Dave was far more seriously wounded than Ted and very fortunate to survive given his serious wounds, thankfully both Dave and Ted would eventually be repatriated. Moreover, their loss shook some of us out of our relative complacency, while flying in harm's way. If it could happen to 'them' it could happen to any of us. No longer feeling somewhat invulnerable because of our F-4's speed and manoeuvrability, we wisely began to take a few more precautions, lest we tempt the same fate. Letter to Mom

'Although I always sought MiG-CAP missions, perhaps the most enjoyable missions for me were Photo Escort. Our reconnaissance aircraft were RF-8s - a very impressive aircraft for its time, but unarmed except for cameras. Since they went in by themselves to take 'before' and 'after' photographs of bombed targets, they were always an expected and a single, isolated, main target for the enemy. For this reason, they always received a lot of enemy fire. Indeed, a couple of our RF-8 friends from their small detachment were shot down - one captured, one recovered. We in our F-4s could not protect them from enemy ground fire, other than calling out that fire to them. Our mission was to protect them from enemy MiGs while they prosecuted their dangerous 'photo-recon' mission. To a man, these guys were fearless and always fun and always an honour to escort. We fighter pilots believed in the axiom, 'speed is life' - that a fast moving target is much more difficult to hit than a slow one. And to our exquisite delight, no one flew faster over the 'North' than these photo-recon guys.

'They would come in at extremely high speed, following an Alpha Strike. While sustaining heavy enemy fire, they had to stop 'jinking' to avoid that fire (as escort, we thankfully could continue jinking) and line up straight for their very dangerous photo run. Our guys would nearly always get incredible low-level pictures, far beyond anything expected. Then they had to return to the ship - the F-8 being notoriously most difficult to land on a carrier. As escort, we had to follow these exceptional guys on some of the most dangerous missions of the war. To this day, I still remain in contact with a few of them; they all hold my deepest respect. Although fighter squadrons are notoriously cliquish groups, all our guys respected and embraced our air-wing's fearless RF-8 photo-recon drivers from VFP-63.

'The sky over North Việtnam was not the only place of danger. Indeed the flight deck of any aircraft carrier is some of the most dangerous real estate in the world.

'On 24 October 1972 during combat night operations in the Gulf of Tonkin, a VA-115 A-6 Intruder aircraft [returning with two 'hung' 500lb bombs] lost its right wheel landing aboard the USS *Midway*. The remaining main stub snagged a wire, careening the A-6 into the 'pack' of recently recovered crews, aircraft and flight deck personnel on the ship's bow. Immediate crash crew effort prevented a major conflagration. Nevertheless, five were killed and 23 injured; many critically. [As the right landing gear stub continued in a howling screech to drag up the flight deck, it caused the trajectory of the aircraft to slowly arc to the right, out of the landing area and into the pack of aircraft at the front of the flight deck. ['Immediately in our path' recalled the pilot, Bruce Kallsen, 'was the F-4 just landed by our Air Wing Commander (CAG) [Commander C. E. Meyers], with CAG climbing out of the cockpit. Undeterred, I continued at full throttle, with the aim of shoving the F-4 off the flight deck, following it and ejecting. Again physics intervened and the result was the dismembering of the left wing and tail of my aircraft and a forward displacement of the F-4, breaking CAG's leg rather severely.] Rapid helo MedEvacs to Đà Nẵng saved many lives.

'Of my nearly two years combat flying in SEA (Southeast Asia), the most spectacular and memorable sight occurred on 20 December, the third and worst night of the of the historic 'Linebacker II' Christmas raids, designed to end the war. Although we (F-4s) never flew 'planned' night MiGCAP 'feet dry' overland, some of us were now tasked for this major strike to do so. My RO 'TA' and I set up our CAP station in the vicinity of Hàiphòng and hopefully on the outer ranges of their SAM sites. Fortunately, we took no serious enemy fire that night due to our range, but especially because of the North Viêtnamese concentration on the higher value B-52s targets, rather than us in an F-4. Also, there were no MiGs in our immediate vicinity, so we could somewhat 'relax' and just watch in total amazement.

'We knew the Air Force had taken some serious losses on the first two nights of raids. We hoped that on this night, their tactics and fortunes would change. Looking up, high above our F-4, we could see the B-52s still flying in their familiar, cells-of-three formations, same altitude, streaming observable contrails with each cell directly in trail of another. 'Hadn't these guys ever flown in hostile territory before,' we wondered? Apparently, they hoped their advanced electronic countermeasures (ECM) would protect them. Unfortunately that night, it would not. [We had a six-second rule: If you flew in the same direction and the same altitude for longer than 6 seconds, you were dead. We therefore always 'jinked' (abruptly and aggressively changing heading and altitude, dipping, diving, climbing and turning ... like a white wing dove during hunting season) so the enemy could never draw a good bead on us.]

'That night, not only were the B-52s flying straight and level at a most lethal SAM altitude, but they were in trail. [Enemy gunners usually didn't pull enough lead and their fire often went behind their intended target. Therefore, the last place you want to be obviously is directly behind and 'in trail' of an enemy targeted aircraft ahead.] But what was really incredible to us, they all had their lights on! We immediately knew it would not be a good night for them. And it was not.

'My RO and I had seen a lot of SAMs and flak fired at us and our wingmen in the many months prior. But that night, it seemed the North launched more SAM's and AAA than we had seen in all the many months before, combined! To the west, the darkness was lit up with literally sheets of AAA. It reminded me of the slanting sheets of rain coming from a Midwest thunderstorm. The barrage AAA was so thick, it had to hit some of the B-52s flying through it, we thought, regardless of their very effective ECM (Electronic Counter Measures).

'As spectacular was the sight of the intense Triple-A fire, the many SAMs were totally mesmerizing. Launched repeatedly in pairs, over and over, from a distance they looked like multiple Roman candles fired on the 4th of July. Every few seconds, another pair would be launched from various SAM sites. It was an astonishing sight! Usually, the bright orange glow of the distant SAMs in the night sky continued until their rocket motor burned out and they abruptly disappeared into darkness. Unfortunately, that was not always the case. We watched a few whose glow never went out.B-52 loss over Hànôi Their orange glow rose to altitude, stopped, became much more brilliant, then the glow much more slowly returned brightly back to earth, sometimes splitting. We realized we were witnessing some shoot-downs, both of B-52s and a Navy

A-7. Overall Air Force losses included fifteen B-52s, two F-4s, two F-111s and one HH-53 search and rescue helicopter. Navy losses included two A-7s, two A-6s, one RA-5 and one F-4. Seventeen of these losses were attributed to SA-2 missiles, three to daytime MiG attacks, three to antiaircraft artillery and three to unknown causes.'

'Thankfully, the *Midway* left 'Yankee Station' after we returned that night, to spend Christmas in Singapore and enjoy a Bob Hope show. But the 'Christmas Raids' continued without us. It had been a long and extended line period… we had some losses and we were all long overdue for a break.

'Nevertheless, I will carry forever the vivid memory of that December night's spectacular fireworks display - one that a lifetime of 4th of July's could never approach. (And one I still vividly recall in a flashback - unfortunately - whenever I see spectacular, but now thankfully benign fireworks even today, decades later.)

'Juxtaposed with that spectacular, visual, pyrotechnic memory is also the agonizing and sickening feeling of watching helplessly, some of our courageous brethren dying before our eyes in the glowing night sky over the 'North' on that fateful evening. [In addition to the massive barrage of AAA, a total of 220 SAMs were fired and six B-52s along with a Navy A-6 were shot down on that night!]

'I ended that cruise with 197 combat missions. I was bugging our scheduling officer for extra flights so I could get an even 200 combat missions before the war ended when, fortunately, common sense took hold. 200 missions' patch I decided to accept my normal rotation for combat missions, regardless of whatever my total final number at war's end would be. This was just as well, considering the tragic fate of former 'Blue Angel' lead and highly respected officer, Commander Harley Hubert Hall [CO of VF-143] who was shot down on the official last day of the war [27 January 1973] and listed as missing in action. Much closer to home and more personal was the loss of the two great A-6 guys that lived in the stateroom next to us on the *Midway*, Lieutenants' Alan Clark and Mike McCormick.[1]

'One of my very best memories of the Viêtnam War was to be present at Clark AFB, PI on February 12, 1973. There I was to witness the first flights from Hànôi of our newly released PoWs.

'While the *Midway* was in port in Subic Bay, I had come the 50+ miles or so, to Clark AFB to umpire a teachers versus nurses softball game as a favour for a friend. (Tough duty, not!) However, the unexpected and tremendous 'event' of the day obviously cancelled the softball game. Everyone went to the flight line to witness history. My friend and I both knew a number of returning, former PoWs, (Including two friends from my own squadron, one from our sister squadron, one photo-recon pilot and others; all shot down, wounded and captured on this same cruise, as noted earlier above.) and we were very disappointed we could not personally meet any of them. They were tightly sequestered for debriefing and allowed no 'outside' contact.

'It would be many weeks later - back stateside - before we could personally say, 'welcome back and thank you for your sacrifice.' But to be there, on that historic day at Clark, watching them step off the C-141s to freedom, is one of my fondest memories. [And I couldn't also help but think: There but for the Grace of God could I also have been.]

'None of us who were there would ever be the same. Quite a number of our crews had been shot down or involved in accidents but were safely recovered. Sadly, we did leave some behind: eleven died, seven listed as Missing in Action (MIA) and six PoWs. Our PoWs returned; the others did not. But they remain in my thoughts, prayers and memories.

> *At Fiddler's Green, where seamen true*
> *When here they've done their duty*
> *The bowl of grog shall still renew*
> *And pledge to love and beauty.'*

'For having the most days on line in combat in the history of the Viêtnam War, we were awarded the somewhat rare, Presidential Unit Citation for a Navy carrier and its air-wing. It was nice gesture, but it hardly compensated.

'Finally, after being gone for eleven months, we flew back to NAS Miramar on 2 March 1973. Much had changed. Thankfully for most of us, we could move on to the rest of our gratefully extended lives.'

Endnotes Chapter 6

1   Lieutenant Michael Timothy McCormick and Lieutenant (jg) Robert Alan Clark of VA-115 were shot down and killed in their A-6A on 9 January 1973.

Chapter 7

'Linebacker'

MiG killing was not our objective. The objective was to protect the strike force. Any MiG kills obtained were considered as a bonus. A shoot down of a strike aircraft was considered ... a mission failure, regardless of the number of MiGs killed.

Major General Alton D. Slay, Deputy Chief of Staff, Operations, Seventh Air Force, December 1971-August 1972.

By March 1972 the North Viêtnamese fighter inventory included 93 MiG-21s, 33 MiG-19s and 120 MiG-15s and -17s - although probably no more than 190 of these aircraft were combat ready. American commanders noted that MiG aircraft airborne below 20° North latitude increased from a daily average of five flights in late 1971 to an average of ten per day early in 1972. Notwithstanding the stand-down in North Viêtnam, B-52 strikes continued and USAF fighters flew combat air patrols and escort flights. MiGs began increasingly to penetrate Laos to try to check the B-52 strikes, but USAF F-4s were on hand to greet them. So for a brief period during the inactivity over North Viêtnam, the F-4s engaged MiGs in air-to-air combat over Laos. The end of 'Rolling Thunder' in early 1968 had resulted in the almost total absence of air-to-air combat for almost four years. After 23 February 1968 North Viêtnamese MiGs did not shoot down another USAF fixed wing aircraft until 18 December 1971. This occurred during a top cover mission by Phantoms of the 432nd TRW for a helicopter extracting a Special Forces team from behind enemy lines in north-eastern Laos when VPAF MiGs claimed two F-4Ds in combat and a third Udorn Phantom, which ran out of fuel and crashed after failing to reach a tanker following an engagement with a MiG. Two crews were taken prisoner and the other was picked up by rescue helicopters. The USAF had to wait even longer for a resumption of victories with the destruction of a MiG finally coming on 21 February 1972. More significantly, it was the first at night, over northeast Laos, about ninety miles southwest of Hànôi. Major Robert Alfred Lodge, 31 of Columbus, Ohio was aircraft commander and 1st Lieutenant Roger Clinton Locher, 26, was his weapon systems officer in an F-4D ('Falcon 02') in the 'Triple Nickel' Squadron flying MiGCAP.

'Red Crown' called out bandits at our 060° position and proceeded to vector us on an intercept,' recalled Major Lodge. 'I descended to minimum en route altitude and my WSO detected and locked on a target at the position 'Red Crown' was calling 'Bandit'. The target was level at zero azimuth and closing, with the combined velocity of both aircraft in excess of 900 knots. I fired three AIM-7Es, the first at approximately eleven nautical miles, the second at eight nautical miles and the third at six nautical miles. The first missile appeared to guide and track level and detonated in a small explosion. The second missile guided in a similar manner and detonated with another small explosion followed immediately by a large explosion in the same area. This secondary explosion was of a different nature than the two missile detonations and appeared like a large POL [petroleum, oil and lubricants] explosion with a fireball. The third missile started guiding in a corkscrew manner and then straightened out. No detonation was observed for the third missile. We had no more AIM-7s left and broke off and egressed at low altitude. Two other MiG-21s then attempted to pursue us. We were low, over 500 knots computed airspeed and the MiGs broke off after about a 30-nautical mile chase and continued to drop back. Another F-4 was flying radar trail during the entire flight and was about 5,000 feet higher than us on the final attack.'

On the night of 1 March, the 'Triple Nickel' added another MiG-21 to its expanding list of aerial victories. The red-haired, 43-year old Lieutenant Colonel Joseph W. Kittinger Jr. of Orlando, Florida flying MiGCAP in 'Falcon 54' with 1st Lieutenant Leigh A. Hodgdon of Kingsport, Pennsylvania in the rear seat, emerged victors in an air battle in northern Laos. Kittinger, who had been one of the original 'Farm Gate' B-26 pilots, was serving on his third tour of duty in Southeast Asia, which began in May 1971. He had joined the Air Force in 1949 and eventually became a test pilot. He is best known for his part in Project 'Manhigh' which was designed to test the pressure suit and other equipment that was going to be used in the US space programme. On 2 June 1957, he piloted an experimental balloon which ascended to 96,000 feet. On 16 August 1960 he made another record-breaking balloon ascent, this time to 102,800 feet at which point he climbed out of the balloon in his bulky pressure suit and literally jumped into space. His free fall lasted over four minutes during which he attained Mach 1 with a maximum speed of 614 mph. The parachute he was testing had been designed for astronauts in the event of an emergency in the earth's atmosphere.

Before taking off for their MiGCAP, Kittinger's flight had been briefed to anticipate enemy diversionary flights which sought to lure unsuspecting F-4s into a hazardous environment. American fighter pilots were well aware that the North Viêtnamese monitored all radio conversations between US air defence agencies and airborne fighters and used such information to their advantage. About 2000 hours Kittinger's flight took up a MiGCAP position in north-eastern Laos. 'Disco' soon advised the flight that MiGs were airborne in the area and vectored the Phantoms to make contact. Kittinger set off in pursuit but it appeared that he was not really overtaking the target, so the outboard tanks were dropped. 'At approximately six miles the 'in-range' light illuminated, followed by an increase in the ASE circle. Trigger was squeezed and crew felt a thump as the missile was ejected; however, the missile motor did not ignite. The trigger was squeezed again and held for approximately three seconds; again the missile did not fire. Trigger was squeezed again and missile #3 fired. The missile made a small correction to the left then back to the right and guided straight away. Approximately five to six seconds after launch, detonation was observed. Almost simultaneously, two enemy missiles were seen coming from the vicinity of the detonation. Evasive action prevented more thorough observations of detonation. The flight maintained 9,000 feet, airspeed 500 knots and egressed the area.'

Using the call sign, 'Old Nick two-zero-one', F-4B BuNo 153019 was flown by all the VF-111 'Sundowners' pilots and Radar Intercept Officers at one time or another on the USS *Coral Sea*, but on 6 March it was flown by Lieutenant Gary L.

'Greyhound' Weigand and Lieutenant (jg) William 'Farkle' Freckleton. When they launched off the deck of the *Coral Sea* steaming in the tepid waters and hot humid air of the Gulf of Tonkin that afternoon and headed toward North Viêtnam they had no idea the mission would ultimately end with their engagement and shoot down of a MiG-17. Weigand and Freckleton had flown many missions together over South and North Vietnam and Laos and on 6 March, they were flying wing to Lieutenant Jim 'Yosemite' Stillinger, a former F-8 Crusader pilot and a recent 'Top Gun' graduate and Lieutenant (jg) Rick Olin on a MiGCAP mission fifty miles north of Quảng Lăng airfield where an A-5 Vigilante recon mission was taking place. Between the two aircraft, there was just one pulse radar (this was Rick Olin's radar and it was limited to the search mode which negated any Sparrow employment). There were no Sparrows aboard 'Old Nick 201'; there was only a Sidewinder capability which (for that older model- AIM-9D) meant any shoot down would have to be from the rear quarter.

The two F-4s from the *Coral Sea* had just arrived on station when they were advised by 'Red Crown' that there were 'Red bandits' to the south of them. The controller kept them informed of the MiG's position by constantly giving range and bearing calls: 'Red bandit bearing 230 degrees at fifteen miles, 240 degrees at 10, 250 at 8, 270 at 6, 295 at 4 miles.' Neither crew in the F-4s had obtained a visual contact with the enemy aircraft. Then, as they were in a descending starboard turn, a final bearing and range call of 330 degrees and two nautical miles was given. Senior Chief Radarman, Larry Nowell The 'Red Crown' controller aboard the cruiser USS *Chicago* (who would subsequently be involved in no less than thirteen successful MiG-killing sorties) was now desperate and radioed for them to 'look left and look low'. The lead F-4 manned by Stillinger and Olin took the flight into a left bank and immediately saw what they were being vectored on - a single green MiG-17 at a 1,000 feet AGL aggressively pulling his nose up into them. The Phantom crews' combat training and responsibilities were now going to be put to the real test. Freckleton, who, without radar, immediately loosened his straps and began a twisting and turning in his cockpit visually looking for the MiGs that had been called out near Quảng Lăng. Weigand, a fighter pilot in every sense, followed Stillinger's instructions to go to a high cover position. As Stillinger and Olin engaged the MiG they descended too low altitude losing radio contact with 'Red Crown'.

As they rolled into the MiG and Jim Stillinger began executing a series of scissors manoeuvres in an attempt to get to the MiG's six o'clock. At one point, he fired a Sidewinder which the MiG-17 pilot must have seen because he skilfully and effectively evaded it. The MiG pilot was proving to be extremely aggressive and agile in handling his aircraft and Stillinger called Weigand to cover him as he put his nose down and proceeded to extend away from the MiG. Determined to chase the F-4 down, the MiG-17 pilot lit his afterburner and proceeded to go after Stillinger and Olin to blast them out of the sky.

As the extension was taking place, a sandwich situation soon developed when Weigand and Freckleton came back down from cover position and engaged from the rear quarter. With Weigand at the controls, they easily got into a 6 o'clock position with either the MiG-17 pilot not seeing them or, ignoring them due to his concentration with closing on the F-4 in front of him. With a good Sidewinder tone indicating the missile was locked on a heat source, Freckleton was shouting for a missile launch as Weigand pressed his trigger switch to release the AIM-9D Sidewinder from the port side of NL-201. The missile tracked true to the heat source of the afterburning MiG and went right up its tailpipe. The subsequent explosion took the enemy aircraft's tail off and it immediately began a fatal descent to the ground only a few hundred feet below. With debris from the explosion flying past their aircraft, Weigand executed a hard turn to starboard to avoid it as the MiG crashed to the ground in a huge fireball. There was no parachute seen to indicate that the enemy pilot had ejected and it was readily assumed that he met his demise instantly. But there was no time to contemplate the fate of the enemy pilot; Stillinger, Olin, Weigand and Freckleton were still in deep jeopardy.

The 'Red Crown' controller, who had been out of radio contact with the two Phantoms during their low-level battle, eventually was able to contact the flight and warn that six MiG-21s were closing at a high rate of closure in an attempt to get into Atoll firing position. The two Phantoms successfully outran the MiG-21s and exited North Viêtnam in afterburner. They were refuelled from an airborne tanker off the USS *Constellation* and were able to make it back to the *Coral Sea*. Both aircraft executed victory roles and brought the F-4s back to the flight deck with 'OK-3' wires. Many crew members rushed out to the flight deck to greet the four aviators. Much of the victory that day belonged not just to the aircrews involved, but all those aboard the *Coral Sea*.[1]

A new aspect was added to the air war in South-east Asia on 30 March when the North Viêtnamese formally invaded the south. They quickly moved through the demilitarized zone into Quảng Trì Province. In response to the NVN offensive, American air resources were ordered to active interdiction of MiGs in North Viêtnam. That same day there was one aerial victory. While at Udorn, Captain Frederick 'Fredo' S. Olmsted, Jr. of San Diego, California served as a Laredo Fast FAC and when the air war heated up once again he was selected as one of the special cadre of MiGCAP flight leaders. 'Our mission was to dash ahead of the strike fighters that were bombing Hànôi so as to keep the MiGs from engaging our bomb-laden fighter brethren. On 30th March 'Fredo' and his backseater, Captain Gerald R. Volloy, weapon systems officer, of Cincinnati, Ohio were pulling F-4D alert duty at Udorn late in the day when they were scrambled in 'Papa 01' to take up an orbit near the Laotian border. Olmsted recalled: 'Our covert intelligence sources had uncovered a plan by the NVAF whereby three MiG-21s would trap a 'slow mover' AC-130 gunship north of the DMZ [Demilitarised Zone]. Consequently, I was put on full scramble alert along with two other highly experienced F-4 pilots. Within an hour of the intelligence guesstimated time of scramble, we took off with orders for a max afterburner climb and a full military power dash to the North Viêtnamese/Laotian border.'

'The US Navy ['Red Crown'] took us under its radar control and vectored us to the vicinity of the three blue bandits - the MiG-21s. At fifteen nautical miles, Volloy established radar contact. Volloy recalled: 'A full system lock-on was acquired at twelve nautical miles and all missile-firing parameters were satisfactory.' But as Olmsted said, 'Whenever my backseater would lock-on, the 'bandit' would turn towards the water; the Navy would then lock-on with its shipboard missiles and the MiG would turn back to my onrushing Phantom. The

MiG finally turned head-on to me at a closure speed of greater than 1,000 knots. I fired a Sparrow radar-guided missile. The first missile didn't guide well, so I fired again. Both of us in the F-4 saw the missile guide and in a second or two saw a tremendous fireball as the Sparrow impacted the MiG head-on that lasted for a few seconds and then trailed what seemed to be fiery sparks estimated to be 150-200 feet in length behind it, paralleling our flight path. The Navy then confirmed that the 'bandit' had suddenly disappeared from its radar scopes.'

As the North Viêtnamese offensive continued, it became apparent to American forces that the enemy had to be hit at his supply points. On 15 April the air tasking order for the next day called for twenty Phantoms to fly MiG patrol in the Hànôi area for bombing flights taking off from other F-4 and F-105 bases. These would be the first American raids into the Hànôi-Hảiphòng area since President Johnson's partial bombing halt had been announced on 31 March 1968. The gloves were coming off.

On 16 April strike forces were sent to bomb fuel depots, warehouses and truck parks in the vicinity of Hảiphòng and on the outskirts of Hànôi. At Udorn five flights of four Phantoms each in the 432nd Tactical Reconnaissance Wing had the primary responsibility for providing MIGCAP missions for the strike forces going deep into North Vietnam. Four of the flights were assigned patrol areas in the Hànôi area, covering the main strike of the day. 'Basco' flight led by Captain Fred Olmsted and his WSO, Captain Stuart W. Maas of Williamsburg, Ohio with Captain Steve Cuthbert on his wing was assigned MIGCAP duties for a secondary strike of Phantoms from Korat. Captain Greg 'Baby Beef' Crane with his backseater, Captain Jerald L. Lachman was 'Basco 04'. Major Edward Daniel Cherry was the pilot of 'Basco 03', From January to August 1967 Cherry, of Marietta, Georgia flew 100 missions over North Vietnam in the F-105. 'In 1971the US Air Force offered a checkout in the F-4 to F-105 drivers who had completed a 100-mission combat tour and were willing to volunteer for a second tour. I dearly loved the 'Thud', but with its numbers dwindling due to combat losses, its future was bleak.' Dan Cherry's weapon systems officer on the 16th of April mission was Captain Jeffrey S. Feinstein of East Troy, Wisconsin. Born in Chicago, Illinois on 29 January 1945, Feinstein enlisted in the Air Force in 1963 to attend the United States Military Academy Preparatory School. He subsequently entered the USAF Academy in 1964 and graduated in 1968. Assigned to the 80th Fighter Squadron, he was detached to the 13th Tactical Fighter Squadron, part of the 432nd Tactical Reconnaissance Wing at Udorn. His nickname/tactical call sign was 'Fang'. Having originally been designated as an Air Force navigator, he was given a vision waiver after Viêtnam (Feinstein wore glasses to correct mild nearsightedness to 20/20), sent to Undergraduate Pilot Training and re-designated as an Air Force pilot in the fighter community.

'Basco' flight would rendezvous with the Korat F-4s over North Central Laos and then proceed to the target with them to provide cover for strike forces ingressing and egressing the target area as well as providing the first line of defence for SAR forces orbiting close to the border with northern Laos. Since this was a secondary strike and the major effort included many aircraft 'Basco' flight, each with 600-gallon centreline tanks, two 370-gallon wing tanks, two Sidewinder missiles and three Sparrow Missiles, were not scheduled for tanker support.

'After take-off at 0830 and join-up we proceeded north into Laos continues Cherry. 'We reached the rendezvous point over the Laotian city of Ban Ban and began to orbit while we waited for the strike flight from Korat to arrive. As the minutes dragged on and the strike flight failed to show, we began to think about our secondary patrol area. Finally with our fuel at a critical point, insofar as our briefed primary mission was concerned, we decided to proceed with the secondary mission, which was to patrol for MiG targets of opportunity in an area about fifty miles southwest of Hànôi. About the time we made the decision to go to our secondary mission, the centreline tanks ran dry. Since there were some pretty stringent G and airspeed limitations on jettisoning the centreline tank, it was common practice to punch them off when they ran dry, if combat was anticipated. We climbed, slowed down and punched off all four tanks in unison. Then we put the noses down and, heading straight for Hànôi, picked up speed for our dash into North Viêtnam.'

As anticipated, the enemy resisted ferociously, firing thousands of rounds of anti-aircraft artillery and about 200 surface-to-air missiles and American strike aircraft were met and engaged by MiG-21s. 'As soon as we crossed the border into North Viêtnam' continues Cherry 'we started picking up surface to air missile (SAM) and triple A strobes on our radar warning gear. They were locking on to us and we were all keeping an eye out for SAM firings, as well as searching on the radar and visually for MiGs. Since the Navy had the primary responsibility for the coastal areas, we didn't want to infringe upon their territory, so midway into North Viêtnam we turned due south to an area we called the 'fish's mouth,' which is where Route 7 comes out into Laos, all the time searching on the radar for bogies. When we reached Route 7 we turned 180 degrees and headed back north, almost directly towards Yên Bái just west of Hànôi. As we approached Hòa Bình, two things happened, almost simultaneously. Captain Stu Maas, in the back seat of Olmsted's airplane, picked up a bogie on his radar at twenty miles. About the same time, our airborne controller called and directed us to proceed to an orbit point down by the DMZ. Since we had a contact and an engagement seemed imminent, we disregarded their instructions and turned to put the bogies on our nose. Stu maintained his radar contact and called them out as we closed to fifteen...ten...and at five miles we picked them up visually. We saw two silver MiG 21s about 5,000 feet higher than we were and on a reciprocal heading. Olmsted called for a hard right turn after jettisoning the tanks. We cranked it around, trying to keep the two MiGs in sight. I was on the outside of the turn leading the second element, so I fell behind as we turned. About halfway through the turn, my wingman called a third MiG. It was a camouflaged MiG 21 and he was at 12 o'clock level to me and climbing into position behind Olmsted's element. The North Viêtnamese had apparently been setting a trap, using the two silver MiGs for bait. The camouflaged MiG had been at low level and as we started our turn he had climbed, hoping to roll in behind us as we chased the silver MiGs.

'I rolled out of my turn and headed directly for him. He evidently saw us and turned hard left away from me and into a cloud. There were scattered to broken build-ups about 3,000 feet high all around us. Outside of the clouds, the visibility was unlimited. The tops of the clouds were about 15,000 feet and we were skimming them at 450 knots when the MiG disappeared. I thought: 'Well, I'll never see him again!' Then I figured I might as well go in after him. I might get lucky and spot him as we came out the other side. So we bored into the cloud. After what seemed like hours in the clouds searching for him on radar, I got nervous and pulled up. You're always worried about SAMs anyway and if you can't see them coming you can't do anything about avoiding them. When we popped out of the top of the clouds we looked all around and didn't see anything.

'In the meantime, Olmsted and his wingman were still in hot pursuit of the other two MiGs, so I thought I had better go after him and offer as much support as possible. I made a hard right turn, in the direction I had last seen Olmsted heading. As we rolled out of the turn, my hawk-eyed wingman, Greg Crane, spotted our MiG again! He was about 2 o'clock and 5,000 feet higher than we were in a climbing turn. I went to max afterburner and pulled around to go after him. While I was doing this we could hear radio transmissions from Olmsted. He was locked on to the other MiGs and was about to shoot one of them down.'

Olmsted said later: 'As we closed head-on and came into firing range, I hesitated to fire my Sparrow missiles fearing that the bogeys might be friendlies drifting into our area. I just didn't trust the new, top-secret electronic gear that was installed in the airplane which allowed us to shoot BVR, or beyond visual range. I disregarded Stu's insistent intercom calls to me to 'shoot 'em 'Fredo', shoot 'em; they are MiG-21s.' I saw the two aircraft pass immediately overhead and they were indeed shiny MiG-21s! I immediately alerted my #3 of my visual sighting and made a high-g turn up and to the right to engage the MiGs. As we were rolling out behind the lead MiGs, the third MiG entered the fight from behind. As I pulled OY 463 in behind the two lead MiGs, the MiG leader performed a split-s directly in front of my nose and was gone from the fight, leaving his wingman to fend for himself. I tracked this MiG through a number of high-speed, high-g vertical vector rolls until I got into good Sparrow firing position. I fired a missile at the MiG while we were both in a hard left turn. The missile impacted the aircraft and blew about half of his wing off, but the pilot didn't eject and the aircraft kept on turning hard. So I fired two more Sparrows at him and the second of these two shots scored a direct hit. The missile went through the top of the MiG's canopy and the shiny enemy fighter exploded into two, huge fireballs.

'Doing his usual superb job as an element leader, Dan Cherry had picked up that third MiG-21 up and engaged him in a high-speed fight that I could hear taking place'.

Cherry continues: 'As I pulled the nose of the Phantom up I had a beautiful set-up for a Sidewinder shot. The sun was more or less behind us and there was nothing out in front except the MiG. I pulled the nose out in front of him a little bit as I selected HEAT and pulled the trigger. Nothing happened. I squeezed again; still nothing. Recheck the armament switches... all OK... squeeze again... nothing... squeeze again... still nothing. Despair. The perfect shot and my airplane is broken. But in the meantime, I had maintained position behind the MiG as he went up and over the top and started down in a diving spiral trying his best to get away. My wingman was out about a thousand feet in perfect fighting wing formation and I know he can't understand why I haven't shot. I can't either! We can't get a radar lock on the MiG so when Greg calls; 'I'm taking the lead, passing on the right' I acknowledge; 'Roger, you have the lead.' I rolled around him into fighting wing formation as Greg lined up the MiG in his sights and fired his missiles. His first missile malfunctioned and fell away like a bomb. His next one went into a corkscrew spiral and missed the MiG. Remember that they still didn't have a lock-on and consequently were not firing within optimum parameters for the missile. His last missile was tracking perfectly and headed right for the MiG. However, at the critical point just prior to impact, the MiG driver broke hard and the Sparrow went right by his tail without detonating. When the MiG made his hard break he dissipated all of his energy which made it easier for us to maintain the advantage. I figured that there was way no way he was going to get away from us now. The only thing that could prevent a kill was the fact that we had nothing left to shoot at him. All we had left were my two Sparrows. My Sidewinders had apparently been knocked off, or something, when the wing tanks were jettisoned. We really never figured out what happened to them.

'I made up my mind that I would stay at that MiG's 6 o'clock no matter what. Even if my Sparrows wouldn't fire, I would chase him until I hit 'bingo' fuel....then turn for home. I called Greg that I was taking the lead back. No answer. We were both in max afterburner so I couldn't overtake him easily. His radio had gone down at that exact moment and he didn't know that I wanted the lead back. He was thinking the same as I was. Chase the MiG until 'bingo' fuel. Greg was too far out in front of me for me to risk shooting a missile. I could hit him by mistake. So I continued trying to pass and take the lead, calling him all the time to break out of the way so I could shoot. Luckily, my airplane was a little faster than his and I began to gain on him, all the time tracking the MiG in my gunsight. While this was going on I called Jeff in the back seat and told him 'I've got the sight right on the MiG - lock him up!' He did and the analogue indicator popped out on the edge of the gun sight indicating a good radar lock-on. It seemed like it took forever for me to pull up line abreast on Greg. When I finally did regain lead of the element I clamped down on the trigger again...never expecting the missile to come off. But suddenly, whoosh; that big AIM 7 smoked out in front of us!

'We were in a right descending turn, accelerating through 500 knots and closing on the MiG as the missile came off. The missile did a big barrel roll and at first, I thought it would miss him. It appeared to be going too far out in front of him but it was just pulling lead. The missile and the MiG came together about 4,000 feet out in front of me. The explosion blew the right wing off the MiG and it immediately went into a hard spiral trailing fire and smoke. The MiG pilot ejected and his chute opened right in front of me. I turned hard left to make sure I didn't fly through the chute and that Jeff could see the guy in his chute and the MiG going down in flames. We were really excited. There was a lot of hollering on the radio. The whole thing had a dreamlike quality to it. There we were, smoking by this guy just as his parachute opened. We must have been close to supersonic with the afterburners cooking and I know we weren't more than thirty feet away from him when we passed. Even at that, I got a good look at him. He had on a black flying suit and his parachute was mostly white, with one red panel in it. I thought; 'This is just like in the movies!'

'We could still hear Olmsted's element' continues Cherry 'and, though they were fairly close to us, we couldn't see them because of the cloud cover. Within a minute of my victory, he locked onto the wingman of the silver MiG element. The leader had rolled inverted, headed for the ground and run away, but the wingman didn't seem to know quite what to do. Fred knocked his right stabilator off with his first missile. The MiG went into a gentle right turn and Fred pulled up high, came back down on him and fired a second AIM-7. His second missile hit the MiG dead centre, exploding it in a huge fireball, leaving nothing but fluttering debris. Then came Olmsted's call, 'Scratch another MiG-21,' confirming his kill on one of the silver MiGs.'

'Baby Beef' Crane and Jerald Lachman in 'Basco 04' confirmed 'Basco 03's missile impact and explosion and he and Cherry joined up and headed home.

By this time they were low on fuel and Cherry had but one thought at that point.... 'Let's get out of here before more MiGs show up!

'We dived for the deck and levelled off right on the treetops, heading for Udorn. I wanted to find a tanker so I could get enough extra gas to show off a bit when we got back to Udorn, but there were too many guys egressing North Vietnam that really needed the gas, so we just pressed on for home. We made it back with less than 1,000lbs of fuel. 'Basco' flight had flown the entire mission with only the fuel we had taken off with, shot down two MiGs and we had done it with no help from radar controllers. That was fairly unusual and the length of the engagement (four minutes) was pretty rare also.'

A third MiG-21 was destroyed by the 432nd Wing in a separate engagement. Captain James C. Null of Oklahoma City and his WSO, Captain Michael D. Vahue of Battle Creek, Michigan in the 523rd TFS flying F-4D 'Papa 03', had been scrambled from Udorn and vectored into northern Laos to investigate a possible hostile track. The target was declared hostile shortly after the flight reached the orbit and Null was authorized to initiate the attack. He reported: 'The flight jettisoned all external tanks. 'Papa 04' acquired a radar lock-on when the target was nineteen miles out. He was given the lead and attempted to fire, but all AIM-7s malfunctioned. A flight of two MiG-21s passed overhead and we started a hard right turn. A vector of 275° for twelve miles was received and visual and radar contact was made at that point. We closed on the target, confirmed it was a flight of two MiG-21s and manoeuvred to their 12 o'clock position. Radar lock-on was acquired and when in range three AIM-7s were fired, the second of which proximity fused on the left side of the wingman's tail section, tearing it from the fuselage. We then passed overhead and observed the MiG to be on fire in the aft section of the fuselage and out of control at approximately 2,000 feet altitude. No chutes were seen. We then egressed and heard from a controlling agency that a single hostile aircraft was orbiting in the vicinity of the engagement.'

The Udorn Officers Club was the hot spot that night. Cherry and Fienstein's adversary, Lieutenant Nguyễn Hồng My, had been trained to fly the MiG-21 in the Soviet Union and was presented his pilot wings by Hồ Chi Minh. Hồng broke both arms and injured his back when he ejected but recovered to fly two more years and is credited with downing one American aircraft. Retired Brigadier General Dan Cherry, who flew 185 combat missions, fifty of them over North Viêtnam during the 'Linebacker' campaign and Nguyễn Hồng My, met again 36 years later in North Viêtnam and became friends.[2]

The month of May 1972 was significant in the Viêtnamese war. On the 8th, President Richard M. Nixon announced the resumption of bombing of North

Việtnam and the mining of entrances to its ports. The mines were set to activate on the 11th. The Presidential announcement was in effect the 'execute' order for Operation 'Linebacker' given renewed and generally unrestricted air strikes against military targets in North Việtnam. Throughout April and the first week of May, additional US Navy attack carriers joined the line in the Gulf of Tonkin, large numbers of B-52 heavy bombers were deployed to points from which they could reach Southeast Asia and more tactical fighter aircraft were placed in Thailand to supplement air power there. The stage had been set for implementation of the new policy.

During an air strike in the Hànôi area on 8 May two MiGs fell to USAF F-4D aircrews. Two different MiGCAP flights from the 432nd TRW supported this strike and each encountered MiGs in the target area. Major Barton P. Crews of Fort Lauderdale, Florida and his WSO, Captain Keith W. Jones, Jr. of Flen Ellyn, Illinois flying 'Galore 03', destroyed a MiG-19 - the first enemy aircraft of this type destroyed by an Air Force crew. Major Crews describes his skirmish: 'A flight of four F-4Ds was fragged to provide MiGCAP for strike flights hitting the Hànôi area. I was scheduled as number three. After the flight arrived at the pre-planned orbit point the flight proceeded north of Yên Bái airfield and then made a 180° right turn heading south. After crossing the Red River, the lead aircraft called, 'Bogies, 12 o'clock.' I immediately acquired them visually and identified them as four MiG-19s. I called over the radio, 'They're not friendly.' The lead aircraft commander confirmed that and directed the engagement. I set up my attack on the northernmost element of MiG-19s and started a closure on what appeared to be the number two man. My WSO stated that he couldn't get a lock-on so I pulled the pipper up to the MiG and fired one AIM-7. I estimated the range was below 3,000 feet. I did not see the missile impact as I directed my attention to the lead MiG. Captain Jones stated he saw a yellowish chute go by. As I was trying to get my pipper on the lead MiG he did a hard break and ruined my tracking solution. My number four aircraft said over the radio, 'That's a kill.' Shortly after that my number four WSO, Lieutenant Holland, called 'Bandits at 6 o'clock.'

'I then broke off my engagement and went into the clouds and lost the MiGs. Later, on the ground, 1st Lieutenant William S. Magill and 1st Lieutenant Michael T. Holland, the aircraft commander and weapon systems officer on my wing, confirmed seeing a chute and observing the MiG do a slow roll to inverted position and start down.

'The other MiGCAP flight was trailing the strike force over Hòa Bình and heard the radio chatter as Crews' flight engaged its MiGs. 'Red Crown' requested assistance for a flight of F-4 strike aircraft, which was also engaging MiGs near Yên Bái. Before they could reach the battle area, the flight disengaged, but 'Red Crown' advised that another group of bandits were approaching from the east. Major Robert A. Lodge, flight leader, ('Oyster 01') with Captain Roger C. Locher of Sabetha, Kansas as his WSO, turned his flight eastward and crossed the Red River. Locher soon acquired two targets on his radar and the flight turned to engage them. As Lodge closed on a MiG, he saw another at 1 o'clock. 'I continued to close on our radar target while watching the second, closer one. At about one mile I saw that the other aircraft was a silver MiG-21. We broke radar contact with the leading MiG and locked on to the wingman. We were about Mach 1.4, with the MiG about as fast as us in afterburner. I was low on the MiG and I do not believe he was aware he was under attack. He was in a right turn, initially and then reversed to the left. I fired two AIM-7 missiles in ripple fire at a distance of 4,500 feet, using a pure pursuit attack at about 20° angle-off. Both missiles guided directly to the target. The first hit the MiG's right wing, which was breaking up when the second missile hit the centre of the fuselage. I saw no bailout. I last saw the MiG disintegrating and out of control.

'The lead MiG broke up hard and I lost visual contact with him. My wingman then engaged the MiG unsuccessfully. We disengaged at 'Bingo' fuel and egressed the area. Passing the initial area outbound while descending, I almost hit a parachute to the left of my aircraft at an estimated 300 feet away. There was a yellow canopy and a body in the chute but I did not notice if the pilot was alive. Egress was then uneventful with a normal recovery.'

Operation 'Linebacker' commenced on 9 May and American forces did well in air-to-air engagements. During May and June, the ratio of kills was better than one to one in favour of the American forces. The 432nd Tactical Reconnaissance Wing at Udorn scored the majority of kills. The addition of this role to its mission made it the only composite- strike-interdiction, counter-air and reconnaissance wing in the conflict and, more notable, its role made possible the majority of MiG kills. The wing was the primary counter-air unit in Southeast Asia during 1972. The 432nd Wing's counter-air mission was diversified, including ingress MiGCAP, egress CAP and barrier CAP (different types of combat air patrol). The entire USAF effort, however, was directed toward strikes against enemy military targets. Combat air patrols were employed toward this end and not to destroy MiGs. Counter-MiG tactics, when employed, generally used the fluid-four formation for all daytime MiGCAP and escort missions, while at night the MiGCAP aircraft flew separate two-plane elements, with the second element in manoeuvering radar trail formation. Ingress CAPs were primarily flown for protection of chaff and chaff escort flights from MiG attack. This required two or three flights of four F-4s each, which preceded the chaff mission aircraft into a target area and remained until the mission aircraft left the hostile zone. MiGCAP flights often arrived at the target scene before strike aircraft and remained until the latter departed.

All egress CAP F-4s were freshly refuelled aircraft and able to take over the protection of strike aircraft from the MiGCAP F-4s since the latter would be low on fuel upon egressing. Combat air patrol missions, composed of a flight of four aircraft, were responsible for the protection of all types of allied air forces: fighter-bombers, heavy bombers, reconnaissance aircraft, gunships, electronic communications aircraft and search and rescue aircraft. Egress CAP also was responsible for covering the post-strike reconnaissance flight. Finally, barrier CAP provided a buffer zone between threat areas and specialized friendly aircraft, including refuelling tankers, SAR forces and EC-121 and EB-66 electronic communications and surveillance aircraft. The barrier CAP flight was usually made up of flights of two F-4s. All strike formations were escorted by at least one and sometimes two, flights of F-4s. These aircraft were not limited to the immediate vicinity of the strike force, but were allowed to turn into approaching MiGs - provided advance warning was available. The most troublesome MiG tactic was the low approach and zoom attack. Although the MiGs relied almost without exception on hit-and-run tactics - single passes at high speeds - the F-4s, nevertheless, enjoyed a high success rate because of crew aggressiveness.

USAF pilots scored more victories on MiGCAP flights than on any other type of mission. While on MiGCAP, aircrews flying F-4Ds of the 'Triple-Nickel' Squadron scored the next five USAF victories of the air war to make it six straight for the squadron. Three of these victories came on 10 May and all of the MiG killers were of the same flight. Major Robert A. Lodge the flight leader - call sign 'Oyster 1' - with Captain Roger C. Locher as his weapon systems officer, in 65-0784, was involved in the initial engagement. Fifty miles south of Yên Bái, Captain Locher held two separate hostile contacts on the nose at forty miles. Lodge then positioned his flight into modified fluid-four formation and set up for the impending engagement. The MiGs continued down the centre of the scope and he accelerated to 1.4 Mach. Twenty nautical miles from the radar contact he began a 5° wing-level climb and armed his missiles. At thirteen nautical miles, the 'in-range' light came on. Lodge waited until the ASE circle began to contract and fired one AIM-7 at a range of eight nautical miles at the leading MiG element. The missile came off the aircraft and began climbing at a 15-20° angle, tracking straight away. When the missile motor burned out, the missile detonated. Lodge immediately fired the second AIM-7 at six nautical miles. It began climbing at a 20° angle, tracking straight away and then contrailed for about 5-8 seconds before the missile detonated, followed immediately by a huge reddish-orange fireball. Lodge continued his climb. Five seconds' later a MiG-21 with the left wing missing, trailing fire with pieces falling off passed 1,000 feet to the left side of the Phantom. The aircraft was out of control, the pilot having already ejected. The flight then engaged the remainder of the flight of bandits.

The second MiG-21 shot down by Lodge's flight came minutes after Lodge's wingman, 1st Lieutenant John D. Markle, 25, of Hutchinson, Kansas and his WSO, Captain Stephen D. Eaves of Honolulu, Hawaii scored the aerial victory. Markle, a veteran of 78 combat missions; twenty of them in Viêtnam, reported: 'Lodge initiated the attack. We engaged a MiG-21 that was a threat to the flight. The MiG was engaged with a full system radar lock-on. Two AIM-7 missiles were launched by us. I observed the second missile to climb slightly and turn right approximately 15°. Soon after missile launch, I visually identified a MiG-21 passing from my left to my right. The AIM-7 continued on a collision course with the MiG-21. Upon impact, the missile detonated and a large yellow fireball resulted. The right wing of the MiG departed the aircraft and the airframe immediately began to descend out of control. The kill was witnessed by 1st Lieutenant Tommy L. Feezel and his WSO, Captain Lawrence H. Pettit in 'Oyster 4'.'

The flight's third aerial victory followed immediately. Captain Richard S. 'Steve' Ritchie, of Reidsville, North Carolina and Captain Charles B. DeBellevue of Lafayette, Louisiana, weapon systems officer of in 'Oyster 03' secured the first of five MiG kills which would bring the coveted distinction of 'Ace' and would subsequently make DeBellevue the ranking ace of the Viêtnam conflict. Ritchie accounts for his and DeBellevue's initial aerial victory: 'Upon reaching our patrol area west of Phú Thọ and south of Yên Bái, 'Red Crown' advised us of bandits approaching from the northeast. Shortly thereafter, both Lodge and I obtained a radar contact. The bandits were declared hostile and our flight engaged the flight of four MiG-21s. Lodge fired two missiles at the attacking MiGs from a front-quarter aspect, utilizing a full system radar lock-on. A detonation and fireball were seen as one of the missiles impacted the number two MiG. Meanwhile, Markle achieved a radar lock-on on the number three MiG-21 and fired two AIM-7 missiles. Another yellow fireball was observed and the number three MiG began to disintegrate.

'We switched the attack to the number four MiG, which was now a threat to Lodge and Markle, while Lodge pursued the number one MiG. As we converted to the rear, I achieved a radar lock-on and fired two AIM-7s at a range of approximately 6,000 feet. The first missile guided to the target and appeared to pass just under the MiG-21. The second missile guided perfectly and impacted the target, causing another yellow fireball. As we flew past the falling debris, my weapon systems officer observed a dirty yellow parachute and what is believed to be the MiG-21 pilot.'

Lodge and Locher meanwhile, almost got their fourth MiG-21 of the war, but fell victim to a MiG tactic dubbed 'Kuban tactics' after those of the Soviet WWII ace Alexander Pokryshkin, in which a ground-controlled flight of four Shenyang J-6s were launched after the MiG-21s so that they could be steered behind the American fighters manoeuvering to attack the MiG-21s. Nguyễn Mạnh Tùng of No. 2 Flight came up from below in his J-6 and hit Lodge and Locher's F-4D Phantom with his three 30mm cannon as Lodge and Locher were lining up a second shot on another MiG-21 near Yên Bái. The Phantom immediately went out of control, flopping from side to side. Then fire started coming in the back of the cockpit. As the aircraft yawed the slipstream pushed the flames up over Locher's canopy and he could not see out any more. The aircraft slowed down and went into a flat spin. Locher noted that the right engine's RPM was at zero and the left was decreasing towards idle. It looked to him that the right engine had exploded. Lodge and his WSO discussed their options. They saw that the hydraulic pressure was low and falling. When Lodge tried the autopilot, it did not respond. Passing through 8,000 feet Locher told Lodge that it was getting too hot and he'd better get out. Lodge looked over his right shoulder at Locher and said, 'Well, why don't you eject then?'

Their F-4D was observed to be on fire during descent and impacted the ground in a ball of fire. No chutes were seen or beepers heard from either crewman. About three weeks previously Lodge had told fellow squadron members, as he had done several times before, that he would not allow himself to be captured because of his extensive knowledge of classified and sensitive information.

Ten days' later, on 20 June, John Markle and his backseater, Captain Jim Williams, were forced to eject thirty miles west of Hànôi after two MiGs attacked their Phantom and one other piloted by Steve Ritchie. One of the enemy jets attacked from the right and the other from the left. Ritchie turned into one with Markle on his wing; the other element broke left. The MiG turned faster and got into the 7 o'clock position, where the enemy pilot fired an Atoll missile. Ritchie turned so hard that the missile missed but as Markle turned even harder his aircraft departed and spun out. Incredibly, Markle and Williams were rescued that afternoon. Markle admitted that he simply lost control of the Phantom 'using too much back stick and aileron.'

On 1 June an F-4 on a mission reported a beeper and voice contact with a shot down crew member within seven miles of Yên Bái airfield. It was Roger Locher, who had survived the shoot down of his Phantom on 10 May and had come down in 'a kind of deep-dished valley.' Evading capture he had walked about twelve miles from where he had parachuted and had kept himself alive on fruit, nuts, berries and water from banana trees for 23 days and nights. The many streams had provided him a plentiful supply of fresh water. Search and Rescue (SAR) forces were immediately diverted to the area and established radio contact with the WSO Captain Locher. Minutes later helicopters arrived in the area. The A-1s defending the rescue were receiving heavy anti-aircraft fire. They had not been able to pinpoint Captain Locher's location and the helicopters, equipped with electronic location finders (ELFs), attempted to pinpoint his position. At this point a MiG-21 made a high-speed, low-altitude pass at the helicopters, followed by another pass within minutes. The helicopters were low on fuel and it was decided to suspend rescue for the day. It had been three weeks since 'Oyster 1' was shot down and it seemed unlikely that anyone could evade capture against such heavy odds. Despite the possibility of an ambush, the SAR operation resumed the second day. Operations began with a diversionary strike against Yên Bái airfield. Other F-4s were used to hit anti-aircraft guns in the area. General Vogt authorised a rescue package totalling 119 bombers, F-4 escorts, EB-66s, F-105G 'Weasels' and KC-135 tankers. As the helicopters entered the rescue area, they picked up strong radio signals from Locher. The A-1 escorts were receiving heavy AAA fire and called in more F-4 strikes against the guns. The SAR helicopters, to avoid SAMs and MiGs, flew at an altitude of about fifty feet (all within 3-7 miles of the enemy airfield). As they approached Locher's position, they began taking heavy ground fire from the many villages in the area. The ELF equipment proved to be particularly valuable, as its signals directed the helicopters right to Locher. A jungle penetrator was lowered and Locher brought on board under heavy ground fire. It was not until Locher was actually onboard that SAR forces knew for certain that the rescue had not been a trap.

The 23 days Captain Locher spent behind enemy lines was a record for shot down airmen during the war. His rescue was the deepest inside North Viêtnam during the entire War.[3]

The rescue of 1st Lieutenant Woodrow J. Bergeron of the 558th TFS, 12th TFW in December 1969 is another example of the lengths that the US Forces were prepared to go to too rescue shot down airmen. On 5 December Captain Benjamin Franklin Danielson and 'Woody' Bergeron ('Boxer 22') were one of two F-4C crews sent on a raid on a choke point on the Hô Chi Minh Trail near the village of Ban Phanôp in southern Laos. Bergeron recalled: 'We had just dropped our ordnance and were pulling the nose up when the aircraft suddenly pitched up, then down. I immediately started initiating ejection and due to seat reaction time, I heard both Ben and our flight lead, Major Joe Young say: 'Bail Out'.'

'Boxer 22' had been hit by a 37mm shell at 6,000 feet. Danielson turned to the east but the crew ejected a few miles from the target when they lost control. When he ejected at 1,000 feet, the wind blast ripped off Bergeron's helmet causing a gash and fractured his nose bridge. The parachute canopy fully deployed but during initial descent, one riser or shoulder strap came unbuckled. On the way down, his first thought was how lucky he was to get a hold of that other riser. Both men landed less than 200 yards apart on either side of the Ngo River in a valley. Voice contact was made with them and the rescue forces were called in on what became one of the biggest rescue efforts of the war. Unfortunately, Danielson was caught and killed on 6 December. Bergeron heard shooting and then a scream, after which he could no longer contact his pilot.

Surrounded by the enemy for 51 hours, Bergeron eluded capture after sixteen-failed rescue attempts, until successfully retrieved by an HH-3 helicopter. The 'Boxer 22' SAR effort the largest on record: 336 sorties were flown during the rescue; five A-l Skyraiders received heavy damage and five of ten HH-3 helicopters ravaged by ground fire were later scrapped.

Although the 'Bat 21' rescue in April 1972 received more publicity, Locher's rescue and that of 'Woody' Bergeron are among the most outstanding episodes of the war in SE Asia.

Endnotes Chapter 7

1   NL-201 is now on a pedestal just inside the front gate at NAS Key West, Florida.
2   Edward Daniel 'Dan' Cherry is the author of *My Enemy, My Friend, a story of reconciliation from the Vietnam War.*
3   On 30 September 1977 the Vietnamese 'discovered' the remains of Robert A. Lodge and returned them to US control.

Chapter 8

The MiG Killers

'Buick, Bandits 240/30, Bullseye.'
'Copy 240 at 30.'
'What in the hell are they doing down there?'
'...I've got some friendlies and some MiGs. The MiGs are behind the friendlies right now.
'Buick shows MiGs 10 miles behind friendlies. Stand by for position.'
'This is Red Crown. Bandits at 253/37, Bullseye.'
'Copy that.'
'Bandits on the nose.'
'It looks like two of them at least.'
'Buick flight, fuel check.'
'90 left.'
'This is Red Crown. Bandits 252/51, Bullseye.'
'Buick 4, this is 3. You read me? We've bogies off to the left at 1 o'clock, way out.'
'Tally.'
'This is Red Crown. Bandits 251/57, Bullseye.'
'Roger, I've got 'em.
'I can't believe we're getting a SAM shot at us.'
'Me either.'
'Bandits. We're running in.'
'He's at 1 o'clock right now.'
'... Three miles - 3 ½ miles, 2 o'clock.
'You got min overtake. OK, you are out of range.'
'They are 12 o'clock straight ahead.'
'You're in range. You're in range. Fire.'
'He's coming way high.'
'Splash! I got him! Splash!'
'Good show Steve.'

Radio transmissions between Captain Richard S. 'Steve' Ritchie and his WSO, Captain Charles DeBellevue on 28 August 1972 when they scored their fifth kill. 'Buick 3' was element lead responsible for protecting Buick 1'; Captain Ritchie's aircraft. 'Red Crown' was the Call-sign for the Navy ship in the Gulf who observed and controlled the air war. 'Bullseye' was a reference point in North Việtnam known to aircrews and ground agencies. 'Bullseye' located the MiGs without the MiG pilot knowing that the US transmissions referred to him.

Richard Stephen 'Steve' Ritchie was born on 25 June 1942 in Reidsville, North Carolina the son of an American Tobacco Company executive. He was a star quarterback for Reidsville High School, despite breaking his leg twice, graduating in 1960. In 1964, he graduated with a Bachelor of Science degree in Engineering Science from the United States Air Force Academy, where, as a 'walk-on', he became the starting halfback for the Falcons varsity football team in 1962 and 1963. Ritchie was described by his peers as being a jock and by General Robin Olds, who admired him greatly, as being 'brilliant' but thinking himself 'God's gift' (cocky and egotistical). According to one of the intelligence officers of the 555th 'Triple Nickel' Squadron, Ritchie was often lacking in self-discipline, with a personal trademark of using too much 'Old Spice' cologne. (Ritchie's retort was that the pilots' locker room was too odoriferous.) Professionally, Ritchie was a gifted and dedicated flyer who constantly maintained his skills by flying every two or three days. With consistently high performance evaluations, high scores in undergraduate pilot training and replacement training courses and achieving a thorough understanding of the weapons systems he used, he earned opportunities to place himself in the forefront of USAF fighter pilots, where he became known for his 'intelligent aggression'.

He was a star quarterback in high school. At the US Air Force Academy, he continued playing football, as starting halfback for the Falcons in 1962 and 1963. Graduating from the Academy in 1964, Ritchie was commissioned a Second Lieutenant in the US Air Force. In August 1964 he entered pilot training at Laredo AFB, Texas and finished first in his class. After a stint at Flight Test Operations at Eglin AFB, Florida, where he flew the F-104 Starfighter, he began flying the Phantom at Homestead Air Force Base, Florida in preparation for his first tour in Southeast Asia. Assigned to the 480th Tactical Fighter Squadron at Đà Nẵng Air Base, South Việtnam in 1968, Ritchie flew the first 'Fast FAC' mission in the F-4 forward air controller program and was instrumental in the spread and success of the programme. He completed 195 combat missions.

Returning from Southeast Asia in 1969, he reported to the Air Force Fighter Weapons School at Nellis Air Force Base, Nevada, where at 26 years of age, he became one of the youngest instructors in the history of the school. He taught air-to-air tactics from 1970 to 1972 to the best USAF pilots, including Major Robert Lodge, who later became his flight leader in Thailand. Ritchie volunteered for a second combat tour in January 1972 and was assigned to the 432nd Tactical Reconnaissance Wing at Udorn, flying an F-4D with the famed 555th 'Tactical Fighter Squadron. An advantage that the 'Triple Nickel' pilots had over other US aircrews was that eight of their F-4D Phantoms had the top secret APX-80 electronic set installed. Known by its code-name 'Combat Tree' it could read the IFF signals of the transponders built into the MiGs so that North Việtnamese GCI radar could discriminate its aircraft from that of the Americans. Displayed on a scope in the WSO's cockpit, 'Combat Tree' gave the Phantoms the ability to identify and locate MiGs when they were still beyond visual range.

In 1972 the period 10 May to 15 October produced all five American aces (three USAF and two USN) of the Việtnam War. There was intense rivalry between the two services, not least in the 'ace' stakes. On 10 May when 'Steve' Ritchie claimed his first MiG victory, the NVNAF lost eleven aircraft. Navy fighters destroyed eight MiGs, six by F-4J Phantoms of VF-96 'Fighting Falcons' on USS *Constellation*. Lieutenant Randall Cunningham, better known as 'Randy' or 'Duke' and Lieutenant (jg) William Patrick 'Irish' Driscoll, his RIO became the first American aircrew to qualify as aces solely as a result of action in Việtnam when they shot down their third, fourth and fifth MiGs before their F-4J ('ShowTime 100') was hit by a SAM and went down off the coast. Randall Harold Cunningham was born in Los Angeles to Randall and Lela Cunningham on 8 December 1941. His father was a truck driver for Union Oil at the time. Around 1945, the family moved to Fresno, California, where Cunningham's father purchased a gas station. In 1953 they moved to rural Shelbina, Missouri, where his parents purchased and managed the Cunningham Variety Store, a five-and-dime. After earning his bachelor's degree in 1964 and his Masters in education in 1965 from the University of Missouri, Cunningham began his career as an educator and a coach at Hinsdale (Ill.) High School. As a swimming coach, 'Duke' trained two athletes to Olympic gold and silver medals. In 1967 he earned a commission and pilot wings in the Navy. His first Việtnam cruise was on VF-96 aboard the USS *America* 10 April to 21 December 1970 and then he completed the Navy's 'Top Gun' Fighter Weapons School.

Cunningham returned to combat with VF-96 in 1971 and teamed up with Driscoll a 'Top Gun' graduate like himself. Driscoll who was born on 5 March 1947 in Boston attended Stonehill College in North Easton, Massachusetts, where he earned a Bachelor's degree in Economics. In college, he was Captain of the baseball team and sports editor of the school newspaper and yearbook and a member of the Dean's list. After graduation, he furthered his education by driving a Budweiser truck for eight months in the Boston area. He became interested in Naval Aviation when he first learned that the Navy did things besides drive ships around in the water and he was told that only the elite and most highly competent of people were able to consistently land on a carrier deck, particularly at night and come back and do it the next night. The expertise involved there was of the highest calibre. He joined the Navy in April 1969, was commissioned an Ensign on 15 August 1969 and earned his Wings of Gold on 10 May 1970.

On 1 October 1971 VF-96 'Fighting Falcons' sailed from NAS North Island, San Diego to the Western Pacific. 'There were numerous people in the area protesting the departure of the *Constellation* into the war zone,' recalled Driscoll. 'Jane Fonda and Joan Baez were in town and they had been conducting rallies with their emphasis on 'Keep the 'Connie' home. I believed in exactly what I was doing and it had no effect on my beliefs.' The carrier reached the Philippines, at which time it was loaded up with combat ordnance loads and prepared for detachment to the Gulf of Tonkin to commence operations on 'Yankee Station'.

Cunningham and Driscoll had made their first two kills on separate missions in 1972. Their first, on 19 January was the first Navy air combat victory in almost two years; the 112th MiG brought down in the war and the tenth to fall to a Navy fighter. A Navy RA-5C was performing a reconnaissance mission over North Việtnam, with a flight of Navy F-4Js assigned to perform air-defence suppression. The Phantoms dodged a number of SAMs and then ran into MiG-21s. Cunningham saw two MiG-21s moving fast below him and dived on them. Driscoll got a Sparrow lock, but Cunningham decided to close in and use a

Sidewinder. He fired; the NVNAF pilot broke right and shook off the missile. Cunningham's 'Top Gun' training told him not to get into a turning contest with a MiG, so he went down low and fast to get out of that game and seek a better opportunity. He got it; though the second MiG-21 flew out the fight, the first came out of his turn, the pilot failing to see the Phantom below him. The MiG banked left and Cunningham popped up, firing a Sidewinder on a nice clear target outlined against the sky. The missile scored a direct hit on the MiG, blowing off its tail.

On 6 May a MiG-17 was destroyed by an AIM-9 fired by Lieutenant Commander Jerry B. Houston - aka 'Devil' - and Lieutenant Kevin T. Moore of VF-51 'Screaming Eagles' flying an F-4B from the *Coral Sea*. Two MiG-21s were shot down by a pair of VF-114 crews from the *Kitty Hawk* when they engaged four MiG-21 fighters. Low on fuel in a 90-second fight, Lieutenant Commander (later Admiral) Kenneth W. Pettigrew - aka 'Viper' - and his backseater, Lieutenant (jg) Michael J. McCabe shot down one MiG. The leader, Lieutenant Robert G. Hughes with his RIO Lieutenant (jg) Adolph J. Cruz got another and both F-4s disengaged without an enemy shot fired. One of the difficult decisions required of Pettigrew in his service as a landing signal officer (LSO) in 1972 was when a pilot with a wing on fire wanted to land the plane. As an LSO, Pettigrew helped guide in the planes for landing on the carrier. If he thought the plane was going to land poorly, the LSO had to 'wave off' or get rid of the plane in order to save the ship. The pilot was flying too fast and could not extend the flaps on the plane to help it slow down for a safe landing on the carrier. 'There are times in your life when big decisions arise with little time to react to them,' Pettigrew said. The plane had to crash into the sea and the pilot managed to parachute to safety.

Cunningham and Driscoll scored their second kill on 8 May when they were flying escort for Navy A-6 Intruders mining Hảiphòng harbour. When a MiG-17 leapt out of the clouds, firing at Lieutenant Brian Grant, Cunningham's wingman, Grant broke away and the MiG fired a heat seeking 'Atoll' missile. As Cunningham and Grant twisted and banked and shook the missile, two more MiGs zoomed past, briefly out of the action. Cunningham turned on the first MiG and took a long-range shot at him with a Sidewinder. It turned hard to elude the missile but put himself in front of 'Duke's Phantom. As the other two MiGs returned and began firing, Cunningham stayed focused on his target. He fired a Sidewinder, which locked in and destroyed the MiG. Then two MiGs were right on them. Cunningham sharply turned to escape, damaging his aircraft in the process, only to look up and see the MiG-17 just above. There was no out-turning a MiG-17, but he could out-run it. He ducked into a cloud and fired up his afterburner to give the MiG the slip.

Late in the morning of Wednesday 10 May, the first strike on that day was launched by the *Constellation, Coral Sea* and *Kitty Hawk* consisting of about ninety aircraft. *Constellation*, being the farthest south on the 'Yankee Station', started launching around 07:30, *Coral Sea* followed twenty minutes later and ten minutes later *Kitty Hawk*. Almost half an hour elapsed between the first launch of aircraft from *Constellation* before the last plane joined the strike formation: in total, six A-6 Intruders, twelve A-7 Corsairs, thirteen F-4 Phantoms and one RA-5C Vigilante reconnaissance aircraft started. Around 08:00 *Constellation*'s strike package set a course for Haiphòng, heading up the Gulf of Tonkin. The formations from two other carriers swung into line behind at ten-minute intervals. The North Viêtnamese were well prepared and certainly knew the planes were coming. Not only that the assembly of USN formations and the flight toward Håiphòng took place in full view of early warning radars along the coast, but also Soviet intelligence ship *Kursograf* cruised in the vicinity.

Seven F-4J Phantoms, each carrying 2,000lb of Rockeye cluster bombs for flak suppression duties was launched from the *Constellation*. Their job was to nullify the flak guns while the A-6 Intruders, helped by A-7s armed with anti-radar Shrike missiles to take out the SAM sites, bombed the rail yards. Flak suppression was abandoned, however, when, before the target was reached, an estimated 22 MiGs intercepted the force. The F-4s dropped their bomb loads on a target of opportunity and climbed in hot pursuit before the enemy fighters could get among the A-6s and A-7s.

Ten miles west of Haiphòng, Lieutenant Austin Hawkins led a pair of Phantoms of VF-92 'Silver Kings' from *Constellation* on patrol at 14,000 feet. They did several radar sweeps searching for MiGs, but it seemed that none were coming up to fight. It would appear that the NVAF was indeed surprised by the morning strike of USN and only around 08:30 was the 921 Fighter Regiment ready to launch four MiG-21s from Kép Air Base, in order to intercept formations which started from *Kitty Hawk* and *Coral Sea*. (The USAF and USN fighters would encounter the much-improved MiG-21MF for the first time in combat. The high speed of this fighter at low levels was a considerable surprise. The MiG-21MF was in service with the 921st Sao Do at the time). Hawkins, who was nearing his tour without a single successful MiG engagement, planned that if there would be any MiGs over Kép airfield, he would fly there and attempt to engage some of them. Such unauthorized probes were strictly forbidden and his backseater Lieutenant Charles Tinker had to promise not to divulge the plan to anyone. Following the MiG-call from 'Red Crown', Hawkins accelerated to 600 knots and headed inland. His wingman, Lieutenant Curtis R. Dosé and his backseater Lieutenant James McDevitt followed. The two Phantoms arrived over Kép without any problems and seemingly unnoticed by those on the ground: the defences remained silent. Dosé was on the left, nearer the runway and on glancing down he noticed two silver MiG-21s on a taxiway, beside the runway. He scanned the sky to make sure none of their comrades was already airborne and - while pondering what to do next - McDevitt called that the MiGs were accelerating down the runway in the opposite direction.

Dosé rolled and went supersonic in the descent, ending just to the right of the runway. He tried to position himself behind the MiGs. Out of the corner of his eye, he glimpsed frenzied activity around MiGs in camouflaged blast pens to his right, as maintenance men scurried for cover or threw themselves flat. The Phantom pilot turned his intention to the front and saw the MiGs lift off the ground. Viêtnamese interceptors were flown by Đặng Ngọc Ngự and Nguyễn Văn Ngãi. They hardly got airborne when their tower warned them of Phantoms behind. Both jettisoned their drop tanks and started a hard left turn, going between hills and down valleys. Dosé acquired the wingman and fired one Sidewinder: 'It looked great until it got up to the MiG and then it flew right through the jet plume and detonated on the other side.' The MiG had been turning too sharply for the missile's proximity fuse to detonate at the right time for a kill. Undaunted, Dosé launched another missile and this hit the tail of the MiG-21, slamming the wreckage into the ground.

Ngự remained alone now. However, he continued his turn in low level, deceiving any try of two Phantom pilots to fire at him. Meanwhile, two other MiG-21s, flown by Lê Thành Đạo and Vu Duc Hop, started and tried to catch Hawkins and Dosé, but Hawkins noticed them while turning into a barrel-roll behind the first MiG and ordered a fast break to the right. During the turn, both Phantom-crews noticed that they were in more danger than they had thought: the sky around them was dark with AAA bursts and one SAM was launched against them, but it passed by. The Phantoms went supersonic and sped toward the coast. However, having survived five actual or attempted Sidewinder attacks, Đặng Ngọc Ngự - initially pursued by Hawkins and Dosé - now turned his MiG-21MF around and gave them a pursuit. Hawkins commented: 'At that time we had strong intelligence that the MiG-21 could not do more than Mach 1.05 below 5,000 feet. We were doing Mach 1.15 in combat spread, feeling cocksure as we headed towards the coast.' Dosé continued: 'Then a MiG-21 came up behind, overtaking fast. He made it look effortless. When I saw the MiG it was about three-quarters of a mile behind Hawkins. I called for an in-place turn.'

When Phantoms began turning Ngự fired a missile from the range of 1200 metres at Hawkins. However, Hawkins was in a high-G horizontal turn and the Atoll, which initially guided, flew straight ahead. After attacking, Ngự turned hard to right and flew back to his base, claiming one Phantom as shot down.

After taking fuel from the waiting EKA-3B tanker, Dosé and Hawkins reached *Constellation* as last of the whole strike package. To the delight of those on deck, Dosé performed a victory roll, then made a wide orbit and landed. While the deck crew of the 'Connie' and pilots of VF-92 and VF-96 cheered, Commander Lowell Franklin 'Gus' Eggert, 43, born Milwaukee, Wisconsin, Commanding Air Wing 8, was not delighted. Hawkins actually disobeyed an order, left the strike package without escort and went 'trolling' for MiGs. During his later mission of that day, both Phantom pilots were punished by being 'tied' as an 'Iron Hand' A-7 escort. Their commander told them not to come back at all if they didn't come back together with 'their' Corsairs. They almost did not come back at all. The late afternoon sun sat low in the sky to the west and its rays were diffused by a bank of haze. Suddenly, Dosé saw two SAMs, 'busting out of the haze in our 9 o'clock, doing about Mach 3.' He rolled the Phantom on its back and pulled into a dive trying to outmanoeuvre the missiles, but they corrected to a new collision course. Dosé rolled out and pulled into a maximum G climb, while missiles readjusted their trajectories and continued after the fighter. Now, the SA-2s were too close for any further evasive manoeuvring and closing fast: 'One missile came past the nose; the other went over my canopy. It looked like a killer shot. Those missiles had 280lb warheads, they had us cold. They were so close I could see the control surfaces moving. I gritted my teeth and waited for the explosion. I was looking at 'em, tensed up, ready to die. And they just continued on past, they didn't get off!'

Lieutenant Matthew J. 'Matt' Connelly III, 28, the flight leader of a section of VF-96 Phantoms and his RIO, Lieutenant Thomas J. 'Tom' Blonski, 29, in

'Showtime 106' was also airborne from the *Constellation*. Connelly and Blonski had been flying together for two years and were both on their second combat cruise. Both men were graduates of the US Navy's Fighter Weapons School. A pilot like Connelly could fling the Phantom around the sky like a hotrod and a RIO like Blonski could turn the magnificent AWG-10 radar system into a secret weapon to give 'Showtime 106's crew better situational awareness than their enemies. While 'Showtime 106' flew combat air patrol (CAP) to protect warplanes withdrawing from a target near Hànôi, Blonski maintained visual contact with a formation of approximately sixteen enemy fighter aircraft and warned the retiring strike force of the oncoming threat. The North Viêtnamese had scrambled several dozen MiG-17 and MiG-21 fighters.

Connelly and Blonski found themselves in the middle of a fight while attempting to protect a withdrawing strike force of F-4s, A-6 Intruders and A-7Es. What Connelly noticed, early on, was that no surface-to-air missiles were coming up at them. That meant MiGs. The North Viêtnamese had positioned MiGs on airborne alert - by coincidence - over the target for the day, a Hànôi outskirt known as Hải Dương. Connelly led their wingman, Lieutenant Aaron Campbell, into what was evolving into a complex, high-speed dogfight - a 'fur-ball,' naval aviators called it. Connelly looked down to see a withdrawing A-7 Corsair with two MiG-17s pressing in on its vulnerable six o'clock position. Campbell rolled in on the two MiGs. At just that instant, Blonski's radar screen went blank. He fired off an AIM-9 Sidewinder, which did not need radar guidance. One of the two MiG-17s pulled up, avoided the Sidewinder by a considerable distance and narrowly avoided colliding with Connelly and Campbell.

Amid this confusion, the wingmen became separated and 'Showtime 106' was alone near the centre of the 'fur-ball'. The Navy wrote that Connelly 'engaged the numerically superior aircraft, pressing home hard-fought attacks.' Connelly found himself behind a different MiG-17, which was piloted by Nguyễn Văn Thơ. Had Văn Thơ held his turn he would have escaped, but he suddenly rolled out - probably because he was out of ammunition. The MiG levelled off and Connelly fired an AIM-9 infrared missile for the second time. The Sidewinder departed its rail under the Phantom's wing, leapt ahead in a blur of white exhaust, flew straight and true stabilized by its tandem set of cruciform fins and almost at minimum range travelled just a short distance to go straight up the MiG's tailpipe. At exactly the instant the MiG-17 erupted into red-orange flames, Nguyễn Văn Thơ was hurled up and out like a cork from a wine bottle and landed safely under his parachute. Connelly did not know whether he ejected or was simply blown out of his MiG by the force of the Sidewinder's annular blast fragmentation warhead detonating. No one saw a parachute.

Connelly engaged yet another MiG-17 in what he later termed a carbon copy of the previous engagement. He latched onto the MiG's six o'clock position and watched his adversary repeat his previous foe's manoeuvre - rolling into wings-level position. For the third time, Connelly fired a Sidewinder. It appeared at first to fly wide but it detonated in a black puff just close enough to blow the MiG's tail off. The MiG rolled to the left and the pilot ejected. Connelly and Blonski watched the pilot bail out. With two confirmed aerial victories, Connelly and Blonski tore into yet another MiG-17 until the fuel gauge warned them that they were at 'Bingo' fuel - time to return to *Constellation's* pitching angled deck. Ex-'Blue Angels' pilot Lieutenant Steven C. Shoemaker and his WSO, Lieutenant (jg) Keith V. Crenshaw of VF-96. Shoemaker made three high-speed charges through the target area and came on one MiG-17 to the southwest of the 'fur-ball'. The MiG pilots never saw the Phantom and flew straight, when Shoemaker fired one Sidewinder. After that, the American had to pull up, as he was getting too close to the ground. He lost sight of both the missile and the MiG. He gained some altitude and then rolled over and on the ground was obviously a fighter burning, giving off thick black greasy smoke.

Just after the last of the strike aircraft left the target 37-year old Commander Harry Lee Blackburn's F-4J (155797) on VF-92 was hit in the tail by 85mm AAA. The engines failed, followed by the electrical power system and a fierce fire started to burn away the rear fuselage. Blackburn, of Highland Springs, Virginia was the Squadron's executive officer. His 26-year old RIO, Lieutenant Anthony Rudloff, born in Brooklyn, New York, who was on his third tour of the war and his 295th combat mission. Both were seen to eject and to land only about 100 yards apart. Rudloff was temporarily blinded during the incident and was taken to the Hànôi 'Hilton' but he had no further direct contact with his pilot.[1]

The Phantom flown by Lieutenant 'Rod' Dilworth, Blackburn's wingman was hit by an 85mm shell which damaged his engines and began streaming fuel. He had to shut one engine down. A section of MiG-21s flown by Lê Thành Đạo and Vu Duc Hop on their return to Kép flew between him and an A-7 about 2,000 feet above, heading towards Hải Dương. They could not have seen them because they did not engage. After crossing the coast, Dilworth decided to rid his plane of its missiles and fired the four Sidewinders in turn but the Sparrows were mounted under the fuselage and had to be jettisoned because there was a danger of them igniting the leaking fuel. The first Sparrow bumped aft down the fuselage, waggled and fell away. Then the second waggled a bit and then started sliding across the underside of his wing, cleared it, went nose up and missed the intake of the A-7 by a few feet! The A-7 pilot followed Dilworth back to *Constellation*, where he was able to land safely.

Commander 'Gus' Eggert the Navy commander of the mission that day was now calling all Phantoms and Corsairs to disengage: 'Showtimes' and 'Pouncers', disengage and get out of there if you can!' F-4J 155800 of VF-96 crewed by Lieutenant Randy Cunningham and Lieutenant (jg) Willie Driscoll - Call sign 'Showtime 110' - was in the flak suppression flight for a strike group attacking Hải Dương thirty miles east of Hànôi on the railway line to Hảiphòng and where there were a railway yard, a POL storage site and a bridge. They had just released their six 'Rockeye' cluster bombs on some warehouses when they loitered to cover the A-7 fighter-bombers still engaged. Responding to a call for help, Cunningham took his F-4J into a group of MiG-17s, two of which promptly jumped them. Between 11:00 and 14:15, the *Constellation's* Air Wing, composed of F-4s, A-6s and A-7s was intercepted by a high number of MiG-17s and a well-known series of dogfights developed, in which the F-4Js of VF-96 downed six enemy fighters. South from Hải Dương, Cunningham noticed a MiG in front of him. His and Driscoll's engagement became one of the most celebrated aerial dogfights in the war. They were attacked from 7 o'clock by two MiG-17s - one of them flown by

Nguyễn Hang - and caught Cunningham off guard, but he reversed port and both MiGs slashed beside him. Cunningham fired one AIM-9 and it smashed into the MiG flown by Nguyễn Hang, which exploded in a ball of fire. Seconds later another MiG pulled behind Cunningham, which turned around, trying to invite his wingman, Lieutenant Brian Grant, 'Showtime 110's wingman, to shoot down the Viêtnamese. Grant, who had fired a Sidewinder at the MiG previously attacked by Steve Shoemaker, only to see it detonate well behind the target, was then warned of another MiG behind him and accelerated away. Cunningham followed and both Phantoms disengaged. Grant, called 'break' and the MiGs overshot. The MiG dived away to make a fundamental error of opening the range and presenting his tail. Cunningham made the most of the opportunity. He curved after the MiG, placed the gunsight pipper over it and squeezed the trigger. The Sidewinder detonated beside the tail of the MiG, which burst into flames and simply flew into the ground. Eight MiG-17s were then seen in an anti-clockwise orbit around the target area at 10-15,000 feet and four more dived in column from the Northeast.

Just south of Hải Dương Randy Cunningham and Brian Grant zoom climbed to 12,000 feet and then turned around to attack again. Looking below, Cunningham saw a scene straight out of 'The Patrol.' One flaming MiG was plunging down, eight more circled defensively, while three Phantoms went after the MiGs within the wheel. These were at an extreme disadvantage, due to their low energy state. Diving back, Cunningham almost collided with 'Showtime 112', the F-4J of Commander Dwight Timm, 39, the VF-96 XO and his RIO Lieutenant Jim Fox; neither of whom knew that they had in their blind spot a MiG-17 300 feet behind and another 3,000 feet behind him which already fired at the Phantom and 3,500 feet behind was a MiG-21 in tracking. Cunningham lined up on the MiG-17 nearest to Timm, which kept his port turn and prepared to launch when, out of nowhere, two J-6s appeared and opened fire at Cunningham. 'Showtime 100' easily evaded their fire and then realigned on the MiG-17 close behind Timm, calling the Commander to break starboard to clear the Phantom's hotter J-79 engines from the Sidewinder's heat seeker, thus permitting a clear lock on the bandit. But Timm thought the warning was about the other two, distant MiGs and failed to heed 'Duke's first call. After more manoeuvering, Cunningham re-engaged the MiG-17 still threatening his XO. He called again for him to break, adding, 'If you don't break NOW you are going to die.' The XO finally accelerated and rapidly broke hard right and clear of the nearest MiG. The 'Fresco' could not follow 'Showtime 112's high-speed turn, leaving Cunningham clear to fire. Calling 'Fox Two,' Cunningham squeezed off his second Sidewinder while the MiG still inside the minimum firing range. But the high speed of the MiG worked against it, as the AIM-9 had time to arm and track to its target. It homed into the tail pipe of the MiG-17 and smashed into its rear, knocking the tail off. The MiG wallowed drunkenly and its pilot ejected.

Pulling out of his dive, Cunningham could see to his left that there were yet more MiG-17s and he had begun turning into them when a warning call made him hesitate: 'Showtime heading about one-eight-zero. Heads up! You got a MiG behind you!' The caller was Matt Connelly, also heading for the coast after his successful encounter with the MiGs, fighters, who emphasized the point by launching a Sparrow missile without guidance in the general direction of the MiG.

Initially, Cunningham thought Connelly's Sparrow was coming right at him but the Sparrow went past his tail and past the MiG and served its purpose by making the enemy fighter break away from him.

As Cunningham approached the coast at 10,000 feet, he spotted another MiG-17 heading straight for them and needing just one more kill for ace status, he decided to try and shoot it down. Cunningham tacked onto the MiG and a vicious, twisting dogfight ensued, Cunningham, realising that this was no ordinary MiG pilot. Neither opponent could gain the initiative and finally, the enemy pilot broke off, probably low on fuel and headed for home. The Phantom crew gained their first advantage. Now above and behind the MiG, they seized the opportunity to fire their remaining Sidewinder at the retreating MiG. With the distracting heat of the ground, Cunningham was not sure that a Sidewinder would home in on the MiG, but he called 'Fox Two' and squeezed one off. The missile came off the rail and flew right at the MiG. He saw little flashes off the MiG and thought he had missed but there was an abrupt burst of flame and black smoke erupted from the MiG. It kept slanting down, smashing into the ground at about 45 degrees angle with a resulting explosion and fireball. Seconds later, Cunningham and Driscoll, finding themselves alone in a sky full of bandits, disengaged and headed for the *Constellation*.

Meanwhile, Lieutenants Kenneth L. Cannon and Roy A. Morris Jr. of VF-51 from the *Coral Sea* and Lieutenant Commander 'Chuck' Schroeder piloting another 'Screaming Eagles' Phantom were warned by 'Red Crown' that MiGs were in the vicinity. The two Phantoms closed and found a single MiG-17. Schroeder attacked as first, but was outmanoeuvred and had to accelerate away, while Cannon dived from above, fired a Sidewinder and shot the MiG down. That was the last air-to-air engagement of the day.

Cunningham and Driscoll attempted to exit the target area but they were jumped by a fourth MiG-17 and the F-4J crew attempted to engage but broke off when another F-4J crew called four more MiG-17s at 'Showtime 100's 6 o'clock position. Cunningham broke away and accelerated toward the Gulf of Tonkin. Cunningham had always said a SAM would never hit him but at 16,000 feet the F-4J was hit by an SA-2 fired from the vicinity of Nam Định. Cunningham spotted the SAM just before impact and Driscoll observed an orange cloud after the burst. The Phantom's hydraulic systems progressively failed and both crew were forced to eject about five nautical miles from the mouth of the Red River. Cunningham and Driscoll were rescued by a helicopter from the *Okinawa* and returned uninjured to the *Constellation* to a hero's welcome and to share their victories with their colleagues. [2]

Matt Connelly and 'Tom' Blonski meanwhile, were on afterburner, crossing the coast and heading for the *Constellation*, shortly before Cunningham and Driscoll completed their fight for the day and were being plucked from the Gulf of Tonkin. Phantom crews returned to the carrier deck in time to watch Cunningham and Driscoll very wet, returning to *Constellation* via CH-46 Sea Knight helicopter. The naval total for the day was eight MiGs destroyed, two Phantoms lost, with one of the two crews rescued. Commander 'Gus' Eggert joined Connelly, Blonski, Cunningham and Driscoll in receiving the Navy Cross - the second-highest American award for valour.[3]

The following day (11 May) a MiG-21 shot down by the 'Triple-Nickel' squadron was not officially credited to Captain Stephen E. Nichols of Durham, North Carolina and 1st Lieutenant James R. 'Taco' Bell his 25-year old weapon systems officer of Springfield, Ohio, until 15 July 1974. It was known that the 432nd TRW and the 388th TFW were involved in an intensive engagement on 11 May and that an F-4D aircrew had made the kill. Nichols and Bell were flying 'Gopher 02' in a group of four F-4Ds, providing MiGCAP support for a 'Linebacker' mission against bridge and airfield targets near Hànôi, when the flight encountered MiG-21s, apparently operating under GCI control. A MiG-21 had just shot down an 'Iron Hand' F-105. A MiG also destroyed the F-4D (66-0230) of the flight leader, Lieutenant Colonel Joseph Kittinger who had flown a staggering total of 485 missions. He and his backseater, 1st Lieutenant William J. Reich, who had flown 125 missions, ejected and they became prisoners of war. Kittinger, who had only seven days left before he was due to return home became known as the 'Red Baron' or Grandpa' in the PoW camps.[4] Nichols and Bell knocked down one of the MiGs with an AIM-7E missile, but they had to make a hurried exit because of fuel shortage and therefore did not see the Sparrow hit the MiG. Post-kill analysis, however, confirmed that the MiG-21 was destroyed by a Sparrow and Nichols' was the only US aircraft that shot a Sparrow during the engagement.

On 12 May two lieutenant colonels destroyed the first MiG-19 for the 'Triple Nickel.' Lieutenant Colonel Wayne T. Frye of Maysville, Kentucky, the squadron CO and his weapon systems officer, Lieutenant Colonel James P. Cooney of Newburgh, New York, who headed the 432nd TRW's operations tactics division, were flying MiGCAP northwest of Yên Bái airfield in 'Harlow 02' in a flight of four F-4Ds. Major Sidney B. Hudson, the flight leader observed four MiG-19s taking off with a left turn out. He proceeded to attack the lead MiG-19 and in the ensuing fight his wingman had the second, third and fourth MiG-19s flushed out in front of him. Hudson fired inside range with his missiles and saw none impact. As he reversed and egressed the area, he observed a large yellow fireball in the area of the missile detonations of aircraft.

Colonel Frye's own account provides more details of the skirmish: 'The engagement occurred at low level (500-1,000 feet) approximately two miles southwest of Yên Bái airfield. Three AIM-7s were fired at the fourth MiG-19 in a flight of four in trail at an approximate range of 2,000 feet. After firing these missiles, I momentarily diverted my attention inside the cockpit to check switchology for my two remaining missiles. When I looked back out, a cloud of debris located where the target had previously been, passed under my aircraft almost immediately. Rate of closure at the time of firing was 250 knots.' Frye later noted that he and Cooney had 'probably set a world's record for the total age of an aircrew in an F-4 Phantom for a MiG kill.' He was 41 years old and his WSO was 44. Frye also speculated that they were 'probably the first two lieutenant colonels in the same airplane to get a MiG.' He was correct on both counts.

On 18 May four Navy Lieutenants from VF-161'Chargers' in Carrier Air Group 5 prepared to fly a MiGCAP in support of the strike on the Hảiphòng road and rail bridge from the USS *Midway*, one of the American carriers on the line in the Gulf of Tonkin launching air strikes against North Viêtnam. Lieutenant (jg) Patrick 'Pat' Arwood, 26 of Lynchburg, Virginia and RIO 'Taco' Bell, had reason to feel a little apprehensive as they clambered aboard their F-4J Phantom. Arwood was on his first cruise and it would be his first time across the beach (into North Vietnam). 'It was in support of a pretty big operation. I was nervous before I took off.' Less so probably was 27-year old Lieutenant (jg) Henry Adams 'Black Bart' Bartholomay, born in Chicago and raised in Winnetka, Illinois and his RIO, Oran R. Brown, 29, of Flagstaff, Arizona who crewed BuNo153068. 'Bart', was on his second tour of duty with VF-161 having received his Wings of Gold in 1969 at Naval Air Station Kingsville, Texas after completing fast jet and advanced training in the Grumman F-9F Cougar. Following his first tour of duty to Viêtnam he had been given the role of Weapons Training Officer and in February 1972 had completed advanced fighter weapons and air combat manoeuvering training at the US Navy Fighter Weapons School at NAS Miramar where he achieved the status of 'Top Gun'. He re-joined VF-161 and sailed out for his second deployment in April 1972.

Having refuelled offshore, the pair headed up the Red River and over Hảiphòng to arrive on station in their patrol area. Bartholomay glanced to his right to check on Arwood and saw two sun flashes against a ridgeline at about eight miles range. Closing on the targets at 650 knots, Bartholomay identified them as MiG-19s and called 'shooter' with Arwood providing protective cover. The dogfight between 300 and 500 feet above ground level, with Bartholomay deciding to push the MiGs into a left turn away from their home airfield at Kép. Pulling 3 to 4G at 550 knots, they entered a sustained high energy turn; but, each time 'Bart' tried to get a lock on them, the MiGs would out-rate the bigger, heavier Phantoms, forcing Bartholomay to back off. Arwood was the first to get a shot. The lead MiG was drawing within range of Bartholomay's Phantom getting ready to launch a heat-seeking missile but when he levelled out to fire, he was a good target for Arwood's AIM-9 Sidewinder. This shot missed and exploded behind the MiG. For the next few minutes, the Phantoms were in the 6 o'clock position straight behind the MIGs. As the leading MiG pulled up and to the right, Arwood was able to maintain a position of advantage and fired another missile. Following a bright flash in the tailpipe, the MiG veered out of control with the pilot choosing to eject.

Meanwhile, Bartholomay had positioned himself at the belly of the second MiG as it twisted through 6 and 7G turns in attempts to shake him off. Accelerating to 550 knots, he pulled up and hard left into the MiG. After briefly losing visual on his quarry, Oran Brown regained visual, with the MiG at the Phantom's 9 o'clock and moving towards their six. 'Bart' executed a brilliant nose-up, rolling manoeuvre and made the MiG overshoot, which then countered with its own roll. By this point in the engagement, both jets were down to around 250 knots airspeed; the MiG seemed to be making a run for it as it pitched down. Bartholomay, by coincidence, was lowering his nose to gain airspeed and in unison, both aircraft accelerated to around 400 knots. As they were gaining on the MiG, Bartholomay realized that the enemy pilot had lost sight of them as it was climbing. Around ten seconds after Arwood's missile hit the lead aircraft, 'Bart' pulled up behind his MiG and fired a Sidewinder. In his own words: 'I pulled back at very low altitude into the MiG but couldn't hear an AIM-9 tone. I knew we were desperately low on fuel, so I made a decision to try one more time. This time I still couldn't hear an AIM-9 tone but went ahead and fired. It looked like they guy had gone into afterburner and it apparently hit him in the tail because he spewed fuel or something. Then he pitched nose-up and went into a flat spiral. I broke off to rejoin Pat and I didn't see any chute.'

The two F-4s regrouped and headed back out to sea to refuel and recover to the carrier. Amazingly the engagement had taken place within six to nine miles of an enemy airfield and they had encountered no AAA or SAM launches. More significantly, this engagement would leave the two F-4 Phantom crews as the only Naval aviators to shoot down MiG-19s in the entire Viêtnam War.

The two pilots described the 'classic two-on-two dogfight' near Hảiphòng in an interview aboard the *Midway*,[5] Bartholomay crediting much of his success in the encounter to the training he had received at 'Top Gun'. The two pilots said the MiG pilots were good. 'We happened to come up against two good pilots who knew their planes fairly well,' Bartholomay said. 'They were afraid of us, but they fought well. I respect them highly. Everything they did, we countered. It was a question of who would make the first mistake. They made some mistakes, some pretty gross ones, but recovered from those in time. But then they both made mistakes at the same time. Once we got engaged, our training paid off. We knew just what to do and how to do it. It was a classic two-on-two dogfight and it turned out just as advertised.'

Pat Arwood told how he cured his nervousness on his first mission North Viêtnam by bagging the MiG-19 that was about to draw a bead on his wingman. When the tail of Arwood's MiG exploded he thought, 'that's really neat. It was more a matter-of-fact thing because that's the way you expect it to turn out. I had a sense of relief when my missile hit because he was after 'Bart'. I have no qualms about going back now' Arwood added. 'I've seen that you don't instantly die when somebody starts shooting at you. You just use your training.'

On 23 May a flight of F-4Es flew to the vicinity of Kép airfield as a chaff flight escort. Once the chaff aircraft had completed their activity, the F-4s switched to MiGCAP. Two South Dakotans Lieutenant Colonel Lyle L. Beckers of Gregory and Captain John F. Huwe of Dell Rapids flying 'Balter 01' engaged and destroyed a MiG with an AIM-7 missile during an engagement with eight MiGs. After the chaff flight departed the area, the F-4s passed a few miles north of Kép airfield and spotted four MiG-21s preparing to take off and two MiG-17s airborne, at 8 o'clock low. 'Balter 03' crewed by Captain James M. Beatty of East Clare, Pennsylvania and 1st Lieutenant James M. Sumner of Manchester, Missouri, feinted toward the MiG-17s and they turned tail. Meanwhile, Beckers spotted two MiG-19s south of the field and went after them. 'The MiGs were down around 3,000-4,000 feet, silver in colour and very easy to see. They were in an easy left turn heading east and I was about seven miles away heading south. I probably had 500 knots and was still accelerating. As I came straight down into them, the clouds hindered my attack, but I also don't think they saw me. The MiGs went behind one of the clouds and we lost sight momentarily. When I picked them up again I was about 2,000 feet away with approximately 75° angle-off, which was too much to fire anything. I continued my yo-yo, came around to the outside and then back down at them trying to work for an AIM-7 shot. I pulled in deep at 6 o'clock and descended to 1,500-2,000 feet to get a good look-up angle for the radar. I placed the pipper on the trailing MiG at two nautical miles, 10° angle-off, 550 knots, 2g and used auto-acquisition to get a full-system radar lock-on. They pulled into a climbing left turn, again trying to get away. I paused for settling time and then fired two AIM-7s in ripple. The first missile guided to a direct hit with the second missile guiding within twenty feet but failing to detonate. From the time that I spotted the MiGs heading east, turned south, made my first pass, overshot, rolled back and got a kill, the total elapsed time was about 45 seconds.'

As the MiG went out of control, Beckers saw five other MiG-19s in a 'Wagon Wheel' over the airfield. He made several passes at them but was unable to down another. Meanwhile, Beatty and Sumner set up cover for their flight leader and observed Beckers' MiG kill. Soon thereafter, while Beckers was trying to get another MiG, Beatty spotted two MiG-21s on their tail. Beatty immediately started after these North Viêtnamese and was soon in a position to use his 20mm cannon. 'I had enough time to let the gunsight settle and when the pipper got about one airplane length in front of him, I fired. The tracers helped me a great deal. I thought I had missed him until I closed to inside a thousand feet, where I could see my 20mm was right on. I estimate that I put 50-100 rounds in him and his plane began to come apart and roll to the left.'

On 31 May Phantoms destroyed two more MiG-21s in two separate engagements about fifteen minutes apart. Both F-4 flights came from the 432nd TRW. The MiG-21s were intercepted in pairs while the two Phantom flights were flying MiGCAP in conjunction with strikes. While one flight continued to provide cover for strike flights attacking targets near Kép airfield, the other engaged the first set of MiGs. The second-flight Phantoms quickly decided to enter the fray and turned left to join up. During the turn, 'Gopher 03' the element leader crewed by Captain Bruce G. Leonard, Jr., of Greensboro, North Carolina and Captain Jeffrey S. Feinstein, his weapon systems officer, observed a MiG-21 at 10 o'clock heading toward his flight. When Leonard initiated intercept, Leonard relates: 'We started a level left turn and observed the MiG-21 pass between the elements. The MiG turned away and disengaged. When clear of the MiG, our flight turned southwest toward our assigned orbit point.'

Leonard's flight leader obtained a radar contact at 25 nautical miles. He acquired a visual contact on two MiG-21s, turned left to engage and fired two AIM-7s, front-quartering head-on and missed. Feinstein got a radar contact on two aircraft at six nautical miles and attempted to lock on but the radar malfunctioned.

'Feinstein then saw one of the two MiGs that he had on radar come head-on, shooting two air-to-air missiles at our element. We were on the left of the leader and in a left turn. A MiG-21 came from right to left in front of us at about 4,000 feet range. The angle-off was 90° and I fired one AIM-9 at the MiG with no results. The MiG then went out of view.

'The flight turned another 90° and aircraft 3 and 4 were positioned over 1 and 2. We did not observe the leader fire two AIM-7s at another MiG-21. A MiG-21 then came in front of us and was at 12 o'clock, 3,000 feet in range, turning left. We performed a hard left turn through 40° of heading when the MiG-21 rolled out and started to descend. Our aircraft was then at the MiG's 6 o'clock, about 1 nautical mile. We obtained a high tone from the AIM-9 and fired at the MiG-21. The flight leader called a right turn to 090° and Captain Feinstein called out that there were two MiG-21s at 9 o'clock, 1 nautical mile, turning with us. To maintain flight integrity and cover the flight leader, we had to turn away from the present engagement and could not press the attack further. Because we turned immediately away from the attack, we could not see the missile impact. During the time of the engagement, the flight had continuous SAM radar and missile launch indications. Our wingman observed the flight taking 85mm antiaircraft fire at the time we were firing.'

Meanwhile, the other flight of Phantoms was engaging MiG-21s and Captains Steve Ritchie and Lawrence H. Pettit destroyed one. Ritchie was the flight leader of a flight of four F-4s ('Icebag 01') assigned to MiGCAP northeast of Thái Nguyên. 'Shortly after crossing the coast northeast of Haiphòng, heading generally northwest, 'Red Crown advised us of blue bandits forty nautical miles west-southwest of our position, at a heading of 080°. 'Red Crown' continued to give excellent information on the position of the bandits. With the bandits at 7 to 8 o'clock, fourteen miles range, I began a descending left turn. Shortly thereafter I spotted a flight of two MiG-21s at 10 o'clock high. I continued the left turn and manoeuvred to a 7 o'clock position on the number two MiG. The lead MiG broke up and away. Captain Larry Pettit achieved a full-system lock-on and I fired four AIM-7 missiles. The first missile corkscrewed off and to the right. The next two missiles detonated early. The fourth missile guided perfectly and impacted the MiG in the forward fuselage area. The fuselage from the wings forward broke off and the remainder of the MiG entered a flat left spin until impacting the ground.'

These aerial victories earned for both Ritchie and Feinstein their second kills.

'Linebacker' grew in intensity and enemy resistance remained high. Scores of American fighter-bombers ranged from Hànôi southward to the coastal city of Vĩnh on 2 June, threatening North Việtnam's supply and transportation system. More than 250 aircraft of all services were involved in these strikes, damaging or destroying bridges, trucks, surface craft, supply warehouses and storage areas. During these heavy attacks, a MiG-19 was shot down by an F-4E escorting strike aircraft about 40 miles northeast of Hànôi. The Phantom flight from the 58th TFS, 432nd TRW, encountered two MiG-19s, one of which the flight leader, Major Philip W. Handley of Wellington, Texas and his WSO, 1st Lieutenant John J. Smallwood of Atlanta, Georgia in 'Brenda 01', destroyed with 20mm gunfire. 'After approximately fifteen minutes on station,' said Handley, 'aircraft 3 and 4 became separated from the first element during a particularly violent SAM break. At the same time, they hit 'Bingo' fuel and began egress. Shortly thereafter, while my wingman and I were egressing, we were attacked from 6 o'clock low by a flight of two MiG-19s. After a brief engagement, I shot down the number two MiG-19 with 20mm cannon fire at a slant range of about 300 feet. The MiG-19 was observed to roll slowly off on his right wing and begin to trail smoke from his left wing root. His nose continued to drop and he crashed almost vertically into a green meadow eight seconds after I fired a 300-round burst. The kill was witnessed by Captain Stanley C. Green, aircraft commander and Captain Douglas W. Eden, weapon systems officer in 'Brenda 02.'

'Linebacker' continued unabated except for the period between 14 and 18 June, when the bombing of Hànôi was suspended for the duration of a visit to that city by the President of the USSR. Then in late June and continuing into the next month

Above: F-4E of the 388th TFW taxiing out at Korat RTAFB during the war in South East Asia.

Right: Captain (later Colonel) Joe Lee Burns of the '35th Black Panthers' Tactical Fighter Squadron, 3rd TFW at Korat who with his RIO, 1st Lieutenant 'Mike' Nelson, was shot down in F-4D 66-0265 on 20 July 1972 by AAA near Cẩm Phả, North Việtnam and rescued by a US Navy SH-3 from the *Kitty Hawk* off Haiphòng.

Top: The leaders of 'Oyster' Flight, Major Robert Alfred Lodge, 31, of Columbus, Ohio and WSO 1st Lieutenant Roger Clinton Locher in the 555th TFS 'Triple Nickel' Squadron, 432nd TRW at Udorn scored their first victory on Monday 21 February 1972 ('Falcon 62'); their second on Monday 8 May 1972 ('Oyster 01') and 3rd on Wednesday 10 May 1972 at 9:43 am (as 'Oyster 01') in F-4D 65-0784 after which their Wingman Lieutenant John Markel and Captain Steve Eaves in F-4D 66-8734 warned them of an enemy on their tail but Lodge did not break and was shot down at 9:44 am by 30mm cannon shells. 'Bob' Lodge's remains were recovered on 30 September 1977 and identified on 25 October.

Above: Major Roger Locher, 26, of Sabetha, Kansas, ejected safely. The 23 days that he spent behind enemy lines was a record for shot down airmen during the war. His rescue was the deepest inside North Viêtnam during the entire war.

Left: Major Paul L. Gilmore and 1st Lieutenant William T. Smith of the 480th TFS, 35th TFW beside their F-4C which displays their MiG-21 kill (on 26 April 1966) marking on the splitter plate.

Left: Captain John A. Madden Jr. of Jackson, Mississippi. Flying his first combat mission on 5 October 1965 Madden flew three combat tours in Việtnam, scoring an impressive record of three MiG kills and one damaged. On 28 August 1972 he was part of the same mission when Steve Ritchie made 'ace' status. That same year Madden led over fifty combat flights and he never lost a wingman. Flights under his leadership accounted for five enemy aircraft destroyed and one damaged. He left Việtnam in 1975 and retired from the USAF in 1984.

Below: F-4C Phantoms of the 433rd TFS, 8th TFW at Ubon RTAB tanking from Boeing KC-135A-BN 58-0040. Nearest aircraft is F-4C 63-7684 which on 5 April 1968 was with the 391st TFS, 12th TFW at Cam Ranh Bay when it had difficulty refuelling from a tanker and struck the aerial refueling boom of the KC-135 during an interdiction mission and crashed near Đà Nẵng AB, South Việtnam. Captain G. L. Butler and Major J. G. Kondracki ejected.

Left: 1st Lieutenant Lance Peter Sijan MoH of the 480th TFS, 366th TFW.

Below: On 11 May 1972 a MiG destroyed the F-4D (66-0230) flown by Lieutenant Colonel Joseph Kittinger who had flown a staggering total of 485 missions. He and his backseater, 1st Lieutenant William J. Reich, who had flown 125 missions, ejected and they became prisoners of war. Kittinger had only seven days left before he was due to return home and became known as the 'Red Baron' or Grandpa' in the PoW camps. Both men were released from Hànôi on 28 March 1973. Kittinger finally retired from the Air Force in 1978.

Above: On 6 May 1972 two MiG-21s were shot down by a pair of VF-114 crews from the *Kitty Hawk* when they engaged four MIG-21 fighters. Low on fuel in a 90-second fight, Lieutenant Commander (later Admiral) Kenneth W. Pettigrew - aka 'Viper' - (far right) and his backseater, Lieutenant (jg) Michael J. McCabe (3rd from left) shot down one MiG. The leader, Lieutenant Robert G. Hughes (far left) with his RIO Lieutenant (jg) Adolph J. Cruz (2nd from left) got another and both F-4s disengaged without an enemy shot fired.

Right: The first and only USAF ace in the Viêtnam war Captain Richard Stephen Ritchie in front of F-4D 66-7463 on 28 August 1972. His back seater was WSO Charles DeBellevue. Ritchie's first MiG victory was on 10 May 1972 in F-4D 66-7463 with DeBellevue as back seater; his second was on 31 May with back seater Captain Larry 'Doc' Pettit in F-4D 65-0801 and on 8 July he confirmed two more MiG 21's in F-4E 67-0362 with his usual back seater Captain DeBellevue.

F-4N NE-101 of VF-154 'Black Knights' preparing to launch from the USS *Coral Sea* (CV-43) part of Carrier Air Wing Fourteen (CVW-14)on 1 May 1981.

Above: On 17 June 1965 two VF-21 'Freelancers' F-4Bs from the USS *Midway* (CVA-41) scored the first MiG kills of the war when they attacked four MiG-17s south of Hànôi and brought down two with AIM-7 Sparrow missiles. L-R: Commander Louis C. Page; Lieutenant John C. Smith; Lieutenant Jack E. D. Batson, Page's Radar Intercept Officer; and Lieutenant Commander Robert B. Doremus, Smith's RIO.

Below: On 10 May 1972 Lieutenant Randy 'Duke' Cunningham, pilot of a VF-96 'Fighting Falcons' F-4J Phantom and Lieutenant (jg) William P. 'Irish' Driscoll his RIO operating from the USS *Constellation* became the first American aircrew to qualify as aces solely as a result of action in Việtnam when they downed their third, fourth and fifth MiGs.

Top left: Major Lee T. 'The Bear' Lasseter of VMFA-333 'Shamrocks' on the USS *America* who on 11 September 1972 with his RIO Captain 'L'il' John D. Cummings (both were 'Top Gun' graduates) scored the only all-Marine Corps MiG kill of the war. Below, left: Lieutenant Commander Jerry B. Houston - aka 'Devil' - who with his backseater, Lieutenant Kevin T. Moore - both of VF-51 'Screaming Eagles' - destroyed a MiG-17 with an AIM-9 on 6 May 1972 flying an F-4B from the *Coral Sea*. Top, right: Commander John R. Cheshire USN.

Below, right: Lieutenant (jg) Ralph E.Gaither, who, with his back-seater, Lieutenant (jg) Rodney A. Knutson were one of the two VF-84 'Jolly Rogers' crews (and Lieutenant Roderick Mayer and Lt (jg) David Wheat, RIO of VF-41 'Black Aces') from the *Independence* that were shot down on 17 October 1965 in Long Song Province, northeast of Thai Nguyen and within a few miles of each other. Gaither and Knutson were captured by the North Viêtnamese, spent almost eight years as prisoners and were released on 12 February 1973 in Operation 'Homecoming'. Knutson had been injured and was not fully recovered at the time of his release. Lt (jg) Wheat later was confirmed to be a prisoner and was released in 1973. On 31 October 1977 a Presumptive Finding of Death was issued for Roderick Mayer.

Above: L-R: Lieutenant Oran R. Brown, RIO for Lieutenant (jg) Henry A. 'Black Bart' Bartholomay and Lieutenant (jg) Patrick 'Pat' Arwood and his RIO 1st Lieutenant James R. 'Taco'Bell from VF-161'Chargers' aboard the USS *Midway* celebrate their two MiG 19 victories on 18 May 1972.

On 10 July 1968 Lieutenant Roy Cash, Jr. and Lieutenant Joseph E. Kain, Jr. of VF-33 'Tarsiers' who destroyed a MiG-21 with an AIM-9 about twenty miles northwest of Vĩnh for the USS *America's* first kill of the war proudly point to their MiG victory symbol on the splitter plate of their F-4J.

Right: Captain (later Colonel) Andrew 'Scotty' Dudley Jr. of VMFA-333 'Shamrocks' on the USS *America*.

Centre: Lieutenant (jg) Gareth L. Anderson, 25, of Falmouth, Massachusetts, of VF-114 'Aardvarks' on the USS *Kitty Hawk* and his pilot, Lieutenant H. Dennis 'Denny' Wisely, destroyed a MiG on 24 April 1967. On 19 May Gary Anderson and his pilot, Lieutenant (jg) Joseph C. Plumb, were brought down by a SAM and both men were marched into captivity at the Hànôi 'Hilton'. After spending 2,117 days in captivity, Lieutenant Commander Anderson was released on 4 March 1973. Briefly hospitalized to recover from his injuries he then entered flight training at NAS Pensacola, Florida in October 1973 and was designated a Naval Aviator in May 1975, joining the F-14 Tomcat Replacement Air Group, VF-124, at NAS Miramar, California, but was killed during a training flight on 21 June 1976.

Below: On 20 February 1967 during an attack on a railway siding at Thiên Lin Đông F-4B BuNo150413 flown by Major Russell C. Goodman USAF (pictured) and Ensign Gary L. Thornton of VF-96 on the *Enterprise*, was shot down either by AAA or a SAM. Thornton ejected but Goodman was killed. At the time of his loss, Goodman was assigned to the Thunderbirds USAF Air Demonstration Squadron and was flying with the US Navy on an exchange programme.

Ex-'Blue Angels' pilot Lieutenant Steven Collier Shoemaker, 30, of Iowa Falls and his WSO, Lieutenant (jg) Keith Virgil Crenshaw of VF-96 'Fighting Falcons' on the USS *Constellation* after their MiG 17 kill on 10 May 1972 in F-4J 157295 (which has eight MiG victory symbols on the splitter plate; one for each kill the unit scored). Five more VPAF MiG-17s were downed by two other VF-96 crews that same day; three by 'Randy' Cunningham and his back-seater, 'Willy' Driscoll and two by Lieutenant Michael J. Connelly and Lieutenant Thomas J. Blonski.

Captain Everett T. 'Razz' Raspberry (right) completed 130 combat missions with 100 as flight leader and mission commander in North Việtnam. He returned to the USAF Fighter Weapons School as an F-100/F-4 project pilot and programme manager, He returned to SE Asia and flew an additional 55 combat missions. He retired from the USAF in 1977 with over 5,000 hours of fighter time. .

Above: FG.1 (F-4K) XV574 of 43 Squadron from RAF Leuchars shadowing a Soviet Tu-95 'Bear' over the North Sea. 43 Squadron flew its last Phantom mission on 1 July 1989. It converted to the Tornado F.Mk 3 shortly thereafter. The UK was the only country outside the United States to operate the Phantom at sea.

Left: Lt John Newlin, Operations Officer of VF-74 'Bedevilers' on the *Forrestal* in 1966. (John Newlin)

Below: In a photo he calls 'The Sandwich' John Newlin and his backseater Nick Estabrook flew uncomfortably close between a Soviet Tu-95 'Bear-B' and a Douglas A-3 tanker on 11 April 1966 in a memorable Cold War encounter 150 miles west of Gibraltar.

Above: RAF F-4K-30-MC Phantom XT858 getting airborne. In RAF service the F.G.1 operated in the air defence interceptor role and the F.G.R.2 in the ground attack and tactical reconnaissance role. Forty-eight Phantom F.G.1s were delivered (28 to the Royal Navy). The remaining 118 Phantoms delivered to Britain were F.G.R.2s, which were deployed from July 1970. Delivery of 168 Phantoms to the UK was completed on 29 October 1969.

Below: An 892 Squadron Phantom FG.1 with the unit's 'Omega' insignia on its fin, launches from HMS *Ark Royal* with a load of ten 1,000lb bombs. The last Phantom launch from *Ark Royal* took place on 27 November 1978.

Above: Israeli Air Force Kurnas (Heavy Hammer) 2000, which entered service in the IAF on 9 April 1989, was different from the original F-4E Phantom mostly in its avionics. The RF-4E was called Orev (Raven) in IAF service.

Left: Next to the United States, Israel was the largest user of the Phantom. About 240 F-4Es and RF-4Es were delivered to Israel between 1969 and 1976 under US aid programmes and served with the Tsvah Haganah le Israel/Heyl Ha'Avir (Israeli Air Force).

Below: F-4E 250 of the Israeli Air Force. By the end of the 20th Century there were still 112 F-4s serving with the IDF, in three Squadrons.

F-4E 674 of the Israeli Air Force during an air-to-air refuelled sortie.

the ratio of kills was reversed in favour of North Việtnam's MiGs.

The problem of losses to enemy air defences was serious. Even though SAM defences were extensive and well disciplined, their effectiveness was seriously degraded by friendly chaff, support jamming, ECM pods on US aircraft and special SAM suppression missions. MiGs, on the other hand, became increasingly effective, instead of becoming less of a threat as anticipated. The North Việtnamese constantly refined MiG tactics, employed excellent GCI radars and further improved their warning and identification system of American forces. (In June thirteen Phantoms were lost. During July seventeen USAF Phantoms and a US Navy F-4J were lost - seven to MiGs and six to SAMs and small arms fire). Nevertheless, USAF fighter aircrews succeeded in destroying seven MiG-21s between 21 June and 29 July.

The first of this series of kills took place on 21 June when a flight of four F-4Es of the 469th TFS at Korat escorted two flights of chaff-dispensing aircraft over Route Package 6 in North Việtnam. One of the MiG-21s attacked the chaff force and the other pursued 'Iceman 01' the lead Phantom, flown by Colonel Mele Vojvodich, Jr. and Major Robert M. Maltbie. 'I saw three different MiGs and got off a shot at one of them. I didn't see the missile impact because I was distracted by a MiG-21 on my right,' Vojvodich commented.

'Iceman 03' crewed by Lieutenant Colonel Von R. Christiansen of Seattle, Washington and Major Kaye M. Harden of Jacksonville, Florida, probably saved Vojvodich from destruction. Christiansen recalled: 'As the MiGs came abreast of the chaff force, they executed a hard nose low turn to the left, quickly positioning at 6 o'clock and the lead MiG-21 commenced an attack. While following his leader through the turn, the number two MiG appeared to sight Vojvodich and his wingman below him. He then pulled high momentarily to gain a favourable position and initiated an attack on the two F-4s. Possibly because our element was positioned high on the left in fluid-four formation, it appeared that the number two MiG did not see me and my wingman. We called Vojvodich and his wingman to break left. The MiG's rate of closure was such that he continued neatly straight ahead after firing two 'Atoll' missiles at 'Iceman 02', who managed to evade both of them with his hard turn to the left. By going to maximum power and performing an acceleration manoeuvre, we were able to stabilize our position at 5 to 6,000 feet behind the number two MiG in a slight descending turn. He was in afterburner power.

'After acquiring a full system radar lock-on, we attempted to fire two AIM-7 missiles, but neither missile launched. We then switched to heat and picked up a strong IR [infrared] tone from our second AIM-9 missile when the number two MiG was positioned in the gunsight reticule. Three AIM-9 missiles were ripple-fired at the MiG, who was in a level, gentle bank to the left. The first missile appeared to guide normally but detonated about fifty feet right of the MiG's tail. Major Harden observed the second missile guide directly into the MiG's tail, causing the aircraft to explode and burn fiercely from the canopy aft. The pilot ejected immediately and was observed to have a yellow parachute. I did not observe the second AIM-9 impact on the MiG because I immediately transferred my attention to the number one MiG, which was pulling off high after attacking an F-4 of another flight.

'We initiated a maximum power pull-up toward the number one MiG and thereafter manoeuvred with him at very high speed until achieving a position at his 6 o'clock. The MiG executed numerous evasive manoeuvres while descending from 20,000 feet to 1,000 feet as we closed for a gun attack. Radar lock-on was obtained and although tracking was by no means perfect, firing was initiated from about 3,000 feet with a short burst. Thereafter, we fired several short bursts while slowly closing range and attempting to refine the tracking solution. Suspecting a gunsight lead prediction problem, we began to aim slightly in front of the MiG and observed strikes on the left wing just as the gun fired out. The engagement was terminated due to 'Bingo' fuel state.' The kill marked the first confirmed victory by a 388th TFW aircraft since 23 August 1967.

At sea, two of *Saratoga's* F-4Js of VF-31 'Tomcatters' attacked three MiG-21s over North Viêtnam. The Phantom crewed by Commander Samuel C. Flynn Jr. and Lieutenant William H. John out-manoeuvred four SAMs and shot down one of the MiG-21s with a Sidewinder. (On 10 August *Saratoga* scored another air-to-air victory when an F-4J flown by Lieutenant Commander Robert E. Tucker Jr. and Lieutenant (jg) Stanley B. Edens from VF-103 'Jolly Rogers' destroyed a MiG-21 with a Sparrow missile during a night interception. This was the first and only night MiG kill by the Navy during the entire war).

On 23 May while leading a section of F-4s on a CAP north of Hànôi near the enemy airfield at Kép, Lieutenant Commander Ronald E. 'Mugs' McKeown, a native of Ysleta, Texas who was on his fourth combat deployment to Viêtnam and Lieutenant (later Commander) John C. 'Inchworm' or 'Jack' Ensch of VF-161 the 'Chargers' on the Midway attacked two MiG-17s with AIM-9 Sidewinders in their F-4B 'Rock River 100'. 'Jack' Ensch and his usual RIO, Lieutenant Commander Michael 'Ratso' Doyle, 29, had already flown a dozen combat missions together and 'Jack' considered 'old double nuts' a lucky aircraft. 'Jack' Clyde Ensch, born in 1937 in Springfield, Illinois had originally planned to be a high school teacher after doing a hitch in the Navy. At Illinois State University he had been a wrestler. In what has been described as one of the longest and most exciting dogfights of the war, fighting often at tree-top height, McKeown and 'Jack' Ensch actually tumbled their F-4B end-over-end during the engagement. What is more remarkable is that Ensch could not detect the low flying MiGs that they had been warned about by the 'Red Crown' controller on the USS *Biddle* and their wingman, Lieutenant Mike Rabb and Lieutenant (jg) Ken Crandell had a radar failure. McKeown lost a pursuing MiG-17 and found another ahead of him. He turned into the enemy jet's blind spot and destroyed it with an AIM-9G. Rabb, meanwhile, had another MiG-17 on his tail that had fired at him and missed and he 'dragged' it out for McKeown to blast it off his wingman's tail with his second Sidewinder.

For this action, McKeown and Ensch were awarded the Navy Cross. Following this action Lieutenant Commander McKeown received orders to become the first Commanding Officer of 'Top Gun', the Navy Fighter Weapons School. Born in the city of New Orleans, 'Ratso's close-cropped sideburns framed a 5 o'clock shadow so pronounced that it was clearly evident by noon, giving him persistent unshaven look. This had, no doubt been responsible for one of his several 'call signs' or nicknames (others were 'Paw' and 'Dou Dou' Doyle) that aviators pick up in the course of their flying careers. Recalling the perpetually unshaven character portrayed by Dustin Hoffman in Midnight Cowboy, 'Ratso' seemed a perfect moniker. His old roommate from his days in San Diego had been 'Jaybee' Souder when they shared their Mission Beach bachelor pad.

Thirteen days after 'Mugs' McKeown departed *Midway*, on 25 August 1972, 'Jack' Ensch and 'Ratso' Doyle flew together again. In 'Jack' Ensch's own words: 'Soon after going 'feet dry' we were taken under attack by what seemed like every SAM and AAA site in North Viêtnam. Our electronic detection and warning gear was lit up and our headsets were alive with such a cacophony of warning alarms. The MiGCAP mission quickly took a back seat to the immediate problem at hand; avoiding the myriad of SAMs being fired at us. We manoeuvred hard, keeping up the speed, expending chaff and turning this way and that to avoid the missiles. I counted at least five that we successfully defeated when the world caved in on me: there was a dazzling light and tremendous concussion over the cockpit as a SAM we didn't see detonated. I looked down to see shards of canopy Plexiglass strewn about the cockpit and my left hand laying in my lap, covered in blood. 'Oh my God, no!' I screamed. Embodied in those words was the thought that 'this can't be happening to me.' I guess that after 285 combat missions over four cruises, I thought I was immune. Others might get shot down, not me! How very wrong I was.

'I screamed into the intercom at 'Ratso'. 'Are you OK? Can we make it back to the water?' But there was no reply. I looked forward to seeing him slumped forward over the controls as we hurled toward the ground at 3 to 4,000 feet and almost 500 knots. Realizing that we were in a dire situation, I reached between my legs with my good hand and pulled the ejection handle to get us out of the plane. (The command ejection system allowed either crew member to eject both cockpits). I felt the initial surge as the seat started up the rail and the tremendous blast of air as I hit the wind stream and then I was hanging in my chute surrounded by a peaceful silence.

'Looking around, I saw the plane crash and 'Ratso's deployed chute some distance from me. Then I looked up to check my chute, looked down to assess my landing area (rice paddies) and reached for my survival radio to get out a broadcast of my position and condition. It was then that I realized my hands were not doing what my brain was telling them to do. I looked down to discover that the high-speed ejection had caused my limbs to flail violently in the wind. In addition to a badly mangled left hand, both elbows were dislocated, the forearms pushed half way up the inside of each upper arm. I was helpless!'

It was extraordinarily quiet except for the annoying sound of unseen 'insects' buzzing by his ears, until, of course, he realized that they were not insects at all but bullets being fired at him from various groups of armed peasants and Viêtnamese militia. Eight days following the shoot down, on the first Saturday evening in September, North Viêtnamese guards deposited 'Jack' Ensch in the small bamboo hut in the middle of the courtyard at Camp Unity. Of 'Ratso' there was no sign, not now, not ever.[6] During 'Jack' Ensch's long incarceration 'Mugs' McKeown steadfastly refused to accept the Navy Cross, stating that he and 'Jack' had won them together and would wear them the first time together. After repatriation 'Mugs' was also able to work the Navy personnel system and have 'Jack' Ensch assigned to 'Top Gun' as an instructor where they would, once again, fly together.

On Sunday 11 June Lieutenant (later Rear Admiral) Winston W. 'Mad Dog' Copeland and Lieutenant Donald R. Bouchoux of VF-51 on the USS *Coral Sea* and another F-4B flown by Commander Foster S. 'Tooter' Teague and Lieutenant Ralph M. Howell were assigned to be a MiGCAP 'blocker' between Văn Hóa and the aircraft carrier over 100 miles out to sea. Neither F-4B had a serviceable radar and 'Mad Dog' Copeland's Phantom had no radio either; a common occurrence during the perils of the Viêtnam conflict but four MiG-17s that loomed above them in no time at all were acquired visually from the CAP's 3,000 feet altitude at as distance of three miles. Copeland and Don Bouchoux went behind the lead MiG, fired and took the wings off the enemy aircraft with a AIM-9 Sidewinder. There was a huge fireball to avoid. The two MIGs on the left took off in seeming retreat.

'Tooter' Teague, born 21 November 1934 in Bossier City, Louisiana and Ralph Howell managed to launch a Sidewinder against another MiG. The AIM-9 exploded close enough to damage the enemy jet but in the ensuing battle Teague lost track of it and a victory could not be confirmed. Teague and Howell launched a second Sidewinder against another MiG but it had been launched too close to arm and failed to detonate. According to Copeland one never deserts their wingman, so they went back to check on him. Together, the jets headed out to sea, towards the carrier and out of North Viêtnam. On the way home Copeland's fire light came on, but they hadn't noticed being hit. Regardless, one always has to respect a fire light. 'Planes on fire tend to blow up,' said. Copeland 'and that can ruin your day.' The radio came back on. 'Tooter' Teague came over, saw that they were on fire and quickly retreated to a safe distance. Copeland shut down the burning engine, yet it was still ablaze. He and Don Bouchoux thought of ejecting, but decided against it, since the dangers in the water included sharks and sea snakes as well as being easy targets for enemy fire. Despite all the problems and with MiG-21s vectored onto them they made it back to the *Coral Sea*. But the carrier refused to let them land. Tradition states that for each kill a pilot does one roll before they land. 'Tooter' Teague's F-4B did two, one for his own and one for them, since they were in a dangerously damaged aircraft. The carrier suggested that both pilots eject to which Copeland responded, 'Jeez, we could have ejected yesterday. We want to land this thing!' They went fifteen or twenty miles out to sea and waited until the flames subsided. After the landing they looked under the Phantom. The aircraft had been hit by ground fire before the dogfight had even begun. The fuel line had been severed and it had welded the F-port Sparrow to the fuselage. Aircraft 149457 never took flight again. It was so badly damaged that it was eventually struck off and set aside to be used for spare parts. According to Copeland, 'Tales get retold and stories get embellished. But, I assure you, I put my pants on just like you do; one leg at a time.'[7]

On 27 June Captain Dick Francis in the 432nd TRW at Udorn was shot down by a SAM over Hànôi. Following completion of training as a Weapons Systems Officer in the F-4, Francis had been assigned to the 523rd TFS at Clark AB, Philippines. However, as a result of North Vietnam's invasion of South Viêtnam in March 1972, his squadron had been deployed to the 432nd TRW to participate in the Operation 'Linebacker' airstrikes over North Viêtnam. 'Having arrived in theatre only about two weeks earlier, I had flown a couple of lower risk missions into Route Pack 1 (the part of North Viêtnam just north of the DMZ) and a few missions into Laos and South Viêtnam. However, I kept worrying about how I would hold up once I had to go 'downtown' to Hànôi, at that time the most heavily defended city in the history of aerial warfare. Somewhat nervous about the situation, I wondered if I would survive this temporary duty assignment (TDY) of unknown duration. Normally aircrew members stationed in Southeast Asia either flew 100 missions over North Viêtnam or served a combat tour of one year, whichever occurred first. Then one morning my flight was scheduled to fly north so we attended the Wing briefing in the Deputy Commander for Operations (DCO) complex. When the briefing officer pulled the curtain back, the map showed the order of battle for a raid on the Hànôi rail yards. As the briefing progressed a feeling of dread and anxiety began to creep over me. Upon completion of the briefing, I ducked into the men's room on my way back to the squadron. Taking temporary refuge in a toilet stall just to calm my nerves, I noticed some graffiti on the door that provided some comic relief that helped reduce some of my anxiety. It said, 'I've got 364 days left on my tour and it seems like I just got here yesterday.'

After he was shot down by a SAM over Hànôi, Francis was captured, spent 274 days in the Hànôi 'Hilton' and 'Zoo' prisons and was repatriated on 28 March 1973. Dick's front seater that day, Lieutenant Colonel Farrell Sullivan, 37, of Caddo Mills, Texas, the 523rd Tactical Fighter Squadron commander, was killed in action by the SAM.

Three MiG-21s became the prey of US Air Force aircrews on 8 July during two separate engagements involving two different squadrons. A flight of four F-4s from the 4th TFS gave that squadron its first MiG victory of the war. The flight was, on that morning, providing escort to a chaff flight in the Hànôi area and had just escorted the aircraft from the threat area. Returning for a sweep the flight again departed when 'Red Crown' warned that bandits were attacking. Captains Richard F. Hardy of Chicago, Illinois and Paul T. Lewinski of Schenectady, New York in 'Brenda 03' then engaged and destroyed a MiG-21: 'The flight turned into the MiG threat and the turned outbound again. While egressing, 'Brenda 02' called a break to our element; a MiG-21 was attacking. We broke and the flight leader and his wingman attacked the first MiG. When 'Brenda 03' and '04' reversed, a second MiG-21 had just overshot and we fired an AIM-9 which did not guide due to his entry into a cloud. We attempted to fire three more AIM-9s which did not come off the rails. We locked-on in boresight and fired two AIM-7s. The first AIM-7 guided to a direct hit and the second guided into the wreckage. The MiG's right wing was blown off and the fuselage tumbled end over end. No chute was observed.'

The two other MiG-21s destroyed on the same day were shot down by Captain Steve Ritchie and Charles DeBellevue flying the lead F-4E ('Paula 01') in a flight of four on MiGCAP in support of a 'Linebacker' strike, flying at medium to low altitude west of Phú Thọ and south of Yên Bái Cà. Ritchie recalled: 'Disco' and 'Red Crown' advised our flight bandits southeast of our position at 35-40 nautical miles. The flight headed towards the threat in patrol formation and crossed Black River on a southerly course. 'Red Crown' and 'Disco' shortly thereafter advised that the bandits and our flight had merged. The flight then turned to the north, met two MiG-21s at 10 o'clock, made a slight left turn and passed the MiGs head-on. I unloaded and executed a hard left turn as the MiGs turned right. I manoeuvred to a 5 o'clock position on the number two MiG, obtained an auto-acquisition boresight radar lock-on and fired two AIM-7 missiles. The first missile impacted the number two MiG, causing a large yellow fireball as the MiG broke into parts. It continued to disintegrate until impacting the ground. I then unloaded again for energy and turned hard right in pursuit of the lead MiG-21, who was now in a rear-quarter threatening position on 'Paula 04'. I manoeuvred into a similar position on the lead MiG as was achieved on his wingman previously. Another radar auto-acquisition lock-on was obtained and one AIM-7 missile fired. The missile impacted the MiG, resulting in a large yellow fireball. This MiG also broke into parts and began to disintegrate. The front of the aircraft was observed impacting the ground in a large fireball.'

The flight remained in tactical support formation throughout the flight and egressed as a flight of four. For Ritchie, these two aerial victories increased his score to four. DeBellevue now had three MiG kills, all earned while flying with Ritchie.

On 11 July Captain George E. Nolly turned off his Big Ben alarm clock at 0230, the usual wake-up time for a 'Linebacker' mission. 'When the scheduling board simply indicated 'Special', we knew it would be a 0400 mass briefing at Wing Headquarters for a bombing mission over North Viêtnam. We wouldn't know our target until the mission briefing. The schedule was normally posted at the end of each day's flying and the previous day I had seen my name listed for the number four position in 'Jazz' Flight for today's Special. My Weapon Systems Officer would be Bill Woodworth.

'F-4 pilots quickly become creatures of habit mixed with ritual and I walked the short distance to the Ubon Officer's Club to have my standard breakfast: cheese omelette, toast with butter and coffee. I had successfully flown thirty-one Counters - missions over North Vietnam - and I wasn't about to change anything without a pretty compelling reason. A few weeks earlier, the Thai waitress had misunderstood me when I had ordered and brought me a plain omelette. I politely ate it and the mission on that day was the closest I had come - up until then - to getting shot down.

'After breakfast, I walked to the 8th Tactical Fighter Wing Headquarters building and performed my usual routine of stopping by the Intel desk and checking the Shoot-down Board. The Shoot-down Board was a large Plexiglas-covered board that listed the most recent friendly aircraft losses, written in grease pencil. We could tell, at a glance, if any aircraft had been shot down the previous night, the call sign, aircraft type and survivor status. There were no friendly aircraft losses over North Vietnam to enemy action in the previous day. That was not surprising. The Special for the previous day had been cancelled when the strike leader, my Squadron Commander, Lieutenant Colonel Brad Sharp, crashed on takeoff when his left tyre exploded at 160 knots. He aborted, taking the departure end barrier and his aircraft caught fire when pieces of the shredded tyre pierced his left wing fuel tank. Brad's emergency egress was delayed when he got hung up by his leg restraint lines. As he sat in his seat, seeing the canopy melting around him, his WSO, Mike Pomphrey, ran back to the burning aircraft and pulled him out, saving his life. As Mike dragged him to a drainage ditch 100 yards away to hunker down, the ejection seats, missiles and, eventually, bombs cooked off. Ubon's only runway was out of commission and the entire 'Linebacker' mission, for all bases, was cancelled. Overnight, the runway at Ubon was repaired and our mission was on for this day. [8]

'The mission briefing was in a large auditorium. The Wing Commander led the Mission Briefing, followed by an Intel Briefing and Weather Briefing. Slides were projected onto the screen to show the targets on a map of North Vietnam, then reconnaissance photos of the individual targets for the strike flights. 'Jazz' Flight's target was POL (Petroleum, Oil, Lubricants) storage near Kép airfield, north of Hànôi. During the briefing, we all received our mission line-up cards, showing our Estimated Times En route (ETE), fuel computations, strike frequencies and flight de-confliction information.

'A mass strike over Route Package Six, the area of North Vietnam covering Hanoi, Haiphong and points north, required a massive orchestration effort. The run-in directions, Time Over Target (TOT) and egress plan for each of the sixteen four-ship strike flights, plus all of the same information for support flights, such as MiGCAP, were designated to exacting specifications.

'After the mass briefing, we assembled in our respective squadrons for our individual flight briefings. When I walked into the 25th Tactical Fighter Squadron, my first order of business was to check the Flight Crew Information File Book. The FCIF was a book that had last-minute changes to procedures and other instructions for aircrews. After reading the latest entries in the book, each crewmember would initial his FCIF card and turn the card over in the vertical card file so that the green side of the card was facing out, instead of the red side. That way, the Ops Officer could instantly see if all the crews were flying with the most current information.

'The briefing for Jazz Flight lasted about 45 minutes. Our flight lead briefed engine start and check-in times, flight join-up, frequencies, tactics and our munitions load. Today we would each carry two 2,000lb Mk.84L laser-guided bombs. After the briefing, we waited our turns for the most important part of the pre-flight.

'The building that housed our squadron had not been designed for a mass launch of 32 crewmembers all needing to use the latrine at the same time. It was a three-holer and everyone always badly needed to use the facility before a mission up north. It was a major bottle-neck to our individual plans.

'After that essential stop, we went by the Life Support section to leave our personal items, such as wedding rings, wallets and anything else we wouldn't need for the flight, in our lockers. The only thing I would carry in my pocket was my ID card and my Geneva Convention Card. And, of course, I had my dog tags around my neck. Then we would pick up our G-suits, helmets, survival vests and parachute harnesses and board the 'bread truck' for transportation to the flight line, with a quick stop at the armoury to retrieve our .38 calibre Smith & Wesson revolvers. Our Thai driver always had a cooler stocked with plastic flasks of cold water and we would grab several and put them in leg pockets of our G-suits. I also grabbed several piddle packs.

'The F-4 did not have a relief tube, so we carried piddle packs. The piddle pack was a small plastic bag with a two inch by six inch sponge inside and a spout at one end. When you used this portable urinal, the entire assembly would expand to about the size of a football. This flight was scheduled to be a bit longer than the standard mission, so I grabbed three piddle packs.

'There were two ways to get to Pack Six from Ubon: right turns and left turns. With right turns, the missions are about 45 minutes shorter. Head north over Laos; refuel on 'Green Anchor', make a right turn at 'Thud Ridge' and proceed to the target. Left turns takes us to the east coast of Viêtnam and proceed north 'feet wet' and then make a left turns toward Vĩnh to strike our targets. Today we would make left turns.

'We launched off at dawn and headed into the rising sun. Our route of flight took us east across Laos to Đà Nẵng, then north to the Gulf of Tonkin, then northwest to our target in the area of Kép. Our refuelling would be along 'Purple Anchor' as we headed north for pre-strike and south for post-strike.

'One of my rituals during every refuelling, in between hook-ups, was to break out one of the water flasks, finish off an entire pack of Tums and fill one of the piddle packs. Using the piddle pack in the seat of the Phantom was easier said than done. It required a bit of manoeuvering. I handed the jet over to Bill, my WSO, as I loosened my lap belt, loosened the leg straps on my parachute harness and unzipped my flight suit from the bottom. Then I did my best to fill the piddle pack without any spillage. Our route was already taking us feet wet and I wasn't looking forward to becoming feet wet in any other respect.

'Bill flew smoothly and I finished my business with no problem and took control of the airplane again for our refuelling top-offs. We conducted our aerial ballet in total radio silence as our four airplanes cycled on and off the refuelling boom, flying at almost 400 knots, as we approached the refuelling drop-off point.

'When we finished refuelling, we switched to strike frequency and headed north-northwest to the target area. Typical for a 'Linebacker' mission, strike frequency was pretty busy. There were 'Bandit' calls from 'Disco', the Airborne Early Warning bird, an EC-121 orbiting over the Gulf of Tonkin. And SAM breaks. And, of course, the ever-present triple-A that produced fields of instant-blooming dandelions at our altitude. We pressed on. In the entire history of the Air Force and the Army Air Corps before it, no strike aircraft has ever aborted its mission due to enemy reaction and we were not about to set a precedent.

'Weather in the target area was severe clear and Flight Lead identified the target with no problem. We closed in to 'fingertip' formation, with three feet of separation between wingtips. 'Jazz' Flight, arm 'em up.'

'We made a left orbit to make our run-in on the designated attack heading. Then a left roll-in with 135 degrees of bank. My element lead, 'Jazz Three', was on Lead's right wing and I was on the far right position in the formation. Our roll-in and roll-out was in close fingertip position, which put me at negative G-loading during the roll-out.

'During negative-G formation flying, the flight controls work differently. I was on the right wing and a little too close to Element Lead, so I needed to put the stick to the left to increase spacing. Totally unnatural. At the same time, I was hanging against my lap belt, which I had forgotten to tighten when I had finished my piddle-pack filling procedure. My head hit the canopy, as dust and other detritus from the cockpit floated up into my eyes. But I maintained my position.

'We rolled out on the correct run-in heading and reached our delivery parameters right on profile. Five hundred knots at 20,000 feet. Lead called our release. 'Jazz' Flight, ready, ready, pickle!'

'We all pushed our Bomb Release 'pickle' buttons on our stick grips at the same time and eight 2,000lb bombs guided together to the target that was being illuminated by the laser designator in the Lead's 'Pave Knife' pod, guidance performed by his WSO. Immediately after release, we performed the normal 4-G pullout. And I was instantly in excruciating pain. I screamed out in pain on our 'hot mike' interphone. 'Are you okay?' Bill called. 'I think I've been shot in the balls!' I screamed.

'Then I realized what had happened. I had carelessly neglected to tighten my lap belt and parachute harness leg straps after relieving myself during the refuelling. My body had shifted and my testicles had gotten trapped between the harness and my body. With a 4-G pull, my 150lb body was exerting 600lbs of pressure on the family jewels.

'As soon as I knew what the problem was, I unloaded the aircraft to zero Gs, to try to readjust myself. But I was still headed downhill and Mother Hanoi was rushing up to me at 500 knots. And I was getting further out of position in my formation. So I gritted my teeth and pulled. When we got onto the post-strike tanker, I adjusted myself, but the damage had been done. I was in agony all the way back to Ubon.

'As soon as I landed I went to see the Flight Surgeon and told him what had happened. He told me to drop my shorts and show him my injury. 'Wow! I'd heard you guys had big ones, but these are even larger than I expected.' I looked down and saw that my testicles were swollen to the size of large oranges. The Flight Surgeon put me on total bed-rest orders, telling me I could only get out of bed to use the bathroom until the swelling subsided. While I was flat on my back, waiting for the pain to subside, I couldn't get that stupid old joke out of my head, the one where the kid goes into a malt shop and asks for a sundae with nuts and the clerk asks, 'Do you want your nuts crushed?' And the kid has a wise-crack answer. All of a sudden, it didn't seem so funny.

'After about five days I was feeling much better. The Flight Surgeon had offered to submit my injury for a Purple Heart, but I declined. For starters, my injury was not due to enemy action, it was due to my carelessness. And I wasn't too keen on standing in front of the entire squadron at my next assignment while the Admin Officer read the citation to accompany the award of the Purple Heart. 'On that day, Captain Nolly managed to crush…' No thanks!

'A few months later, the Flight Surgeon showed up at our squadron. 'You're famous and made me a famous author,' he beamed, as he held up the current issue of *Aerospace Medicine* magazine. In the article, he recounted how a 27-year-old pilot had experienced a strangulation injury to his testes that came very close to requiring amputation. Castration! 'There was no use in telling you and making you worry when there was nothing we could do for you other than bed rest and wait to see if you healed,' he commented.' [9]

On 18 July another MiG-21 was destroyed. This one fell victim to Lieutenant Colonel Carl G. 'Griff' Baily of Denver, Colorado and his WSO, Captain Jeffrey S. Feinstein, of the 13th TFS, 432nd TRW in 'Snug 01'. This F-4D team was one of four MiGCAP aircraft protecting strike flights hitting targets near Phúc Yên airfield. Colonel Baily later said of the air battle: 'At 0224Z, as our flight was ingressing west of Hànôi, 'Snug 04' called out, 'Bandits,' and broke hard right. This caused the elements to be separated, but I elected to continue inbound as the other flight was requesting our assistance. They were low on fuel and were being pursued by MiGs.

'At 0227Z, Captain Feinstein got a radar contact and vectored me and our wingman toward it. At a range of three miles I got a visual contact with a single-silver MiG.' The WSO locked on the MiG and Colonel Baily fired four AIM-7 missiles as the MiG dived, attempting to separate. They missed their mark, but he quickly followed with an AIM-9, which did not miss. It blew off the MiG's right wing and caused the enemy aircraft to snap-roll to the right. During the second snap it hit the ground and disintegrated.

Baily and Feinstein repeated their performance on 29 July with another MiG-21. They were flying lead in a four-ship MiGCAP formation which was sent into North Việtnam during the early morning hours to protect forces attacking targets on the Northeast Railway near Kép airfield. Feinstein describes his fourth aerial victory: 'Red Crown' gave the code words for 'MiG activity.' A minute-and-half later I picked up radar contacts in the vicinity of Phúc Yên airfield. 'Red Crown' began vectoring our flight toward the southwest on two bandits and I had radar contacts at that position. I obtained a radar lock-on and the flight began a hard left turn, attempting to close within firing range. Baily was able to close to five miles but could not get in range due to the bandit's high rate of speed. We lost the radar lock-on at six miles. After completing the turn, we reacquired another contact which was probably the same bandit. We closed in on an attack as 'Red Crown' continued to call the bandit's position. Colonel Baily began firing AIM-7 missiles. The first missile did not ignite. The second and third missiles ripple-fired at 2½-miles range, guided down and to the left, bursting into a large fireball.'

'The MiGs were coming at us at a very high rate of speed,' Baily later described the aerial victory to newsmen. 'They managed to get by us before we engaged them. We turned as hard as we could, started toward them and got them right in front of us, coming head-on. Jeff [Feinstein] locked-on the MiG and I fired two missiles. They both guided right in and splashed him good. The credit all goes to Jeff. When you get them head-on, the guy with the radar does all the work. I just sat up front and squeezed the trigger.'

The same morning Lieutenant Colonel Gene E. Taft of Ventura, California and his WSO, Captain Stanley M. Imaye of Honolulu, Hawaii in the 4th TFS, 366th TFW, flying F-4E 'Pistol 01' were escorting a chaff force deep into North Việtnam when SAMs and MiG-21s threatened the strike force. The two chaff flights withdrew from the strike area while the two F-4 escort flights engaged the MiGs. One got in firing position behind two of the F-4s and Taft and Imaye manoeuvred their aircraft behind the MiG before he could fire. Taft recalled: 'As the MiG approached 11 o'clock, the acquisition switch was activated with no lock noted. The 'GIB' went out of 'boresight to radar in an attempt to lock on. The MiG was called level at that instant. The switch was returned boresight and auto-acquisition attempted with successful lock-on. The range bar indicated MiG at approximately 4 o'clock position, 9,000, feet. Four seconds were counted and the trigger squeezed once. One AIM-7 left the aircraft and tracked smoothly to the MiG. Missile detonation was observed and simultaneously the MiG's wing appeared to separate, fire was observed out of the wing and the MiG rolled uncontrollably. No chute was observed. No impact was observed. After detonation occurred, our flight rolled off in a fairly tight descending turn. After approximately 150° of turn, an F-4 was observed, out of control, on fire, in an inverted flat spin on the inside of our aircraft. Approximately five seconds later two good chutes were noted and the aircraft impacted on a mountainside.[10] Our flight began an orbit of the area, but 'Pistol 04' was 'Bingo' fuel and the flight egressed with no other encounters or sightings.'

Late in July the US put a more sophisticated MiG warning system into operation and the kill ratio again turned in favour of the Americans. For the remainder of 'Linebacker' operations, US pilots destroyed four MiGs for every Phantom or Thunderchief lost.

The next aerial victory, on a weather reconnaissance mission in North Việtnam on 12 August, was unique in that the USAF F-4E was piloted by a Marine; Captain Lawrence G. Richard of Lansdale, Pennsylvania and his WSO, Lieutenant Commander Michael J. Ettel of St. Paul, Minnesota was a naval aviator. Both were exchange officers attached for duty with the 58th TFS, 432nd TRW. They were flying 'Dodge 01' the lead F-4E in a flight of four aircraft. Captain Richard reported: 'As I crossed the Red River, I was informed by 'Red Crown' that bandits were airborne, out of 'Bullseye' heading 180°. I was 35 nautical miles northwest of them, proceeding on my fragged route. The bandits then turned to a heading of 360° and commenced an attack. With the bandits at my 6 o'clock at thirty nautical miles, I turned the flight to a heading of 180° and accelerated the flight. 'Red Crown' continued giving bandit information and I visually acquired two aircraft at my 9:30 about four nautical miles, starting a turn to my 6 o'clock. I did a slice turn to the left, sending my supporting element high. I acquired a boresight lock-on on the lead aircraft, which was a silver MiG-21. I closed to 1½- nautical miles with 30° angle-off and fired one AIM-7, which appeared to guide, but missed as the MiG-21 broke hard into the AIM-7 and met me head-on. I unloaded and went after his wingman who was in about a 2- to 3g turn. I acquired a boresight lock-on to this MiG-21, which was light green camouflage in colour, closed to one nautical mile and fired another AIM-7 which impacted just forward of the vertical fin. The aircraft pitched up and some pieces of the aircraft broke away. I turned the flight and egressed the area. The kill was witnessed by Lieutenant Colonel Lee Williams and Major Thomas Leach, his weapon systems officer on 'Dodge 03'.

The 8th Tactical Fighter Wing again temporarily entered the MiG-killer business on 15 August. 'Date 04' a chaff-dispensing F-4E in the 336th TFS, crewed by Captains' Fred W. Sheffler of Akron, Ohio and Mark A. Massen of Downey, California engaged a MiG-21 while their flight was supporting routine 'Linebacker' strikes in Route Package 6. The MiG-21 apparently hesitated, believing that the chaff aircraft carried no air-to-air missiles. Sheffler recalled: 'Our mission was to provide support for two strike flights targeted with laser-guided bombs against a thermal power plant and a rail bridge along the Northwest railway at Việt Trì and Phú Thọ respectively. We were the right outside aircraft in a formation of two flights of four. One minute prior to our first target our escort, the other flight, called a single bandit coming down from high 6 o'clock and attacking us on the right. Our flight began a hard turn to the right in an attempt to negate the enemy's attack. Escort told us that there were now two MiGs in the attack. We continued our turn, trying to visually pick up the MiGs. A camouflaged MiG-21 overshot on my right, no further than one or two thousand feet away. Massen called for me to auto-acquire. [11] I placed my pipper on the MiG and toggled the proper switch on my throttles. We achieved an immediate radar lock-on. I continued our turn to the right, striving to pick up the second MiG. Unable to achieve firing parameters, 'Date 03' gave me the lead and at the same time Massen cleared me to fire. I made a quick check to see if the MiG-21 was still at my 12 o'clock and then squeezed off an AIM-7 missile. By now the MiG-21 was about four to five thousand feet in front of me. For the next ten seconds, until missile impact, I divided my attention between monitoring the AIM-7's flight and checking our 4 to 6 o'clock for his partner. The missile made two minor corrections in flight; one just prior to impact on the left side just forward of the tail section. He did not appear to take any evasive action up until the last second when he hardened up his turn to the left. After impact and explosion, the MiG-21 entered a 45° dive, trailing smoke and flames from his aft section. I estimate his altitude when hit at between 9,000 and 10,000 feet MSL. The second MiG-21 came by on our right in a hard left turn and went between our two flights head-on. We continued our turn and egressed the area at low altitude. Because of the ensuing engagement with the second MiG-21, I was unable to observe a chute or impact of the MiG-21 with the ground. However, the back-seater of an aircraft of the follow-on strike flight observed a large fire on the side of a hill near the area of the engagement during ingress and it was still burning during his egress fifteen minutes later.'

Four days later, on 19 August, another MiG-21 was destroyed when Captain Sammy C. White of Hot Springs, Arkansas, flying his final 'Linebacker' mission and his WSO, 1st Lieutenant Frank J. Bettine of Hartshorn, Oklahoma in 'Pistol 03' in a flight of four chaff-dispensing F-4Es fired an AIM-7 which tracked on the MiG and detonated. The MiG began to smoke and burn, followed by the ejection of the aircraft's pilot. Having reached minimum fuel, White egressed the area.

After seven years of air-to-air combat in Southeast Asia, the US Air Force finally produced its first ace of the war when Steve Ritchie had his fifth MiG victory confirmed for 28 August 1972. Ritchie (along with his backseater, Charles DeBellevue and Jeff Feinstein, another weapons systems officer) joined Navy Commander 'Randy' Cunningham (along with 'Willie' Driscoll, his RIO) as the only two pilots among the five American aces during the Việtnam War. (It will be recalled that in 1971 General John Dale Ryan, Chief of Staff of the US Air Force changed the rules governing a victory so that a pilot and his backseater each received full credit for a victory). There was a competition being waged between Ritchie and Feinstein and the latter had tallied his fourth MiG victory on 29 July. Ritchie's fourth had been scored on 8 July. The question was whether Ritchie, a pilot, or Feinstein, a WSO, would become the Air Force's first ace in Southeast Asia. Each had had a potential fifth claim disallowed. Feinstein, flying with Major John L. Mesenbourg, had claimed an aerial victory in an engagement on 9 June, but approval was denied by the Seventh Air Force's Enemy Aircraft Claims

Evaluation Board because of a lack of sufficient evidence. Ritchie's claim of a MiG-21 on 13 June was also rejected because of insufficient evidence. The 28 August skirmish resolved the issue. Ritchie flew the lead aircraft ('Buick 01') of a MiGCAP flight, with Captain Charles B. DeBellevue as his WSO, during a 'Linebacker' strike mission. 'We acquired a radar lock-on on a MiG-21 that was head-on to us,' Ritchie said. 'We converted to the stern and fired two AIM-7 missiles during the conversion. These missiles were out of parameters and were fired in an attempt to get the MiG to start a turn. As we rolled out behind the MiG, we fired the two remaining AIM-7s. The third missile missed, but the fourth impacted the MiG, which was seen to explode and start tumbling toward the earth. The kill was witnessed by Captain John A. Madden Jr., of Jackson, Mississippi, aircraft commander in 'Buick 03'. 'It was an entirely different situation,' Ritchie noted to newsmen. The MiG flew at 'a much higher altitude than any of my other MiG kills and at a much greater range. I don't think the MiG pilot ever really saw us. All he saw were those missiles coming at him and that's what helped us finally get him.'

The new ace complimented the ground crews who kept the F-4s combat-ready: 'There's no way we could have done it without them,' he said. 'In fact, I got my first and fifth MiG in the same plane. Crew Chief Sergeant Reggie Taylor was the first one up the ladder when the plane landed and you just couldn't believe how happy he was. I think he was more excited than I.'

DeBellevue, whose total victories rose to four with this day's kill, commented on teamwork: 'The most important thing is for the crew to work well together,' he said. 'They have to know each other. I know what Steve is thinking on a mission and can almost accomplish whatever he wants before he asks. I was telling him everything he had to know when he wanted it and did not waste time giving him useless data.'

One of two F-4E crews of the 34th TFS, 388th TFW flying a hunter-killer mission with two F-105G two-seat 'Wild Weasels' made the next MiG kill on a SAM suppression in the vicinity of Phúc Yên airfield on 2 September. A MiG-19 made a hard right turn and fired an Atoll air-to-air missile at the F-105 flown by Major Thomas J. Coady and Major Harold E. Kurz, narrowly missing the Thunderchief's left wing by approximately twenty feet. The MiG pilot then pressed a cannon attack against the lead F-105 crewed by Major Edward Y. Cleveland and Captain Michael B. O'Brien. A hard right turn also saved them. As the MiG broke off, it passed over 'Eagle 03' flown by Major Jon I. Lucas of Steubenville, Ohio and 1st Lieutenant Douglas G. Malloy of Dayton, Ohio. 'He came in from our 4 o'clock position,' said Major Lucas 'and I started a left turn to manoeuvre into firing position. The MiG then started a left-descending turn at which time Malloy went to boresight and confirmed the switch settings. I hit the auto-acquisition switch with the MiG-19 framed in the reticule. Malloy confirmed a good lock-on. I counted four seconds and squeezed the trigger. The left aft missile light went out, indicating expenditure of an AIM-7. I started to select 'Master Arm and Guns' to follow up with a gun attack. A SAM tracked our aircraft and a turn was initiated into the SAM to negate its track. We then turned back towards the MiG and observed a pastel orange parachute with a man hanging in the harness. Missile impact was not observed due to the turn into the SAM, but Cleveland and his wingman called the MiG-19 burning and spiralling towards the ground and also observed the parachute.'

During 'Linebacker' strikes on 9 September, a flight of four F-4Ds on MiGCAP west of Hànôi shot down three MiGs. Two were MiG-19s shot down by flight leader ('Olds 01') Captain John Madden and his WSO, Captain Charles B. DeBellevue. For Madden, the victories constituted his first and second MiG kills. Flying his first combat mission on 5 October 1965, Madden flew three combat tours in Vietnam, notching up three kills and one damaged. For DeBellevue the victories on 9 September were numbers five and six, moving him up as the leading MiG destroyer of the war. Before their MiG victories, however, Captain Calvin Bryan Tibbett, 25, of Waynesville, Missouri and 1st Lieutenant William 'Buddy' Stone Hargrove, 24, of Harlingen, Texas in 'Olds 03' destroyed a MiG-21.

The flight was alerted to the presence of MiGs fifty miles away. 'We knew the MiGs would be returning soon to land at Phúc Yên airfield,' Captain Madden later reported. 'We just kind of sat back and waited for them.' When DeBellevue acquired the MiGs on radar, the flight manoeuvred to attack. Madden made the first move: 'We got a visual on a MiG about five miles out on final approach with his gear and flaps down. Getting a lock on him, I fired my missiles but they missed. We were coming in from the side-rear and slipped up next to that MiG no more than 500 feet apart. He got a visual on us, snatched up his flaps and hit afterburners, accelerating out. It became obvious that I wasn't going to get another shot at the MiG. That's when Captain Tibbett closed in on the MiG.'

Tibbett had been watching the engagement carefully and saw that the two AIM-7 missiles fired by Madden did not guide. He recalled: 'Madden then cleared us to fire since we were in a good position for an AIM-9 attack. We fired two AIM-9 missiles which appeared not to guide, closed to gun range and fired the 20mm cannon. The MiG-21 sustained numerous hits along the fuselage and left wing. The pilot ejected and the aircraft started a gentle roll and nose down attitude toward the ground. The altitude was approximately 1,000 feet.

'As the flight made a turn to withdraw, two MiG-19s swarmed in for an attack. DeBellevue describes the next two engagements: 'We acquired the MiGs on radar and positioned as we picked them up visually. We used a slicing low-speed yo-yo to position behind the MiG-19s and started turning hard with them. We fired one AIM-9 missile, which detonated 25 feet from one of the MiG-19s. We then switched the attack to the other MiG-19 and one turn later we fired an AIM-9 at him. The missile impacted the tail of the MiG. It continued normally for the next few seconds and then began a slow roll and spin downward, impacting the ground with a large fireball. Our altitude was approximately 1,500 feet at the moment of the MiG's impact.'

Madden and DeBellevue returned to their base, thinking they had destroyed only the second MiG-19. Only later did investigation reveal that they were the only aircrew to shoot at a MiG-19 which crashed and burned on the runway at Phúc Yên that day. Captains William J. Daleky and Terry M. Murphy, in number 4 position, were hit by anti aircraft fire in the fuel tank and they lost their fuel shortly thereafter as the flight left the battle area and headed back for Udorn. They were soon rescued from northern Laos, over which they were forced to bail out. When they were returned to their base that same afternoon, crews had a fly-by to celebrate their return and the MiG shoot downs. Their report of the MiG-19 engagements, along with photo analysis and debriefing interviews of other flight aircrews helped confirm the destruction of the first as well as the second MiG engaged by Madden and DeBellevue. Even without the extra kill, Captain DeBellevue was the Air Force's second ace of the war. As events would later demonstrate, he emerged as the leading MiG-killer of the conflict, for no one later matched his score. When asked how he felt about becoming an ace, the navigator commented: 'I feel pretty good about it. It's the high point of my career. There's no other job that you have to put out as much for. It's frustrating and yet when you do shoot down a MiG, it's so rewarding.'

'So far, no Marine Corps aircrew had shot down a MiG during the entire Viêtnam War' recalls J. M. Shotwell, Captain John 'Bud' Linder's radar intercept officer (RIO) in VMFA-333 'Trip Trey' on the USS *America* (the only Marine Corps Phantom squadron that deployed on board a carrier for duty in the war). Throughout the war, Marine F-4 units were relegated to close air support for troops on the ground. 'Naping' (dropping napalm), strafing and low-level dive-bombing were vital to the grunts but gutter work for the proud Phantom, arguably the Free World's finest fighter jet at the time. The Phantom was little more than two huge jet engines strapped together with a couple of stubby wings and radar in the nose. Add two average-size guys strapped to the ejection seats and an F-4 will tip the scales at about twenty tons. To propel a chunk of metal that heavy to twice the speed of sound or send it spiralling into the stratosphere takes two giant 'huffers' - the J-79-GE-10 jet engines, each capable of producing up to 17,900lbs of thrust. They're incredibly powerful, but in a supersonic engagement, those power plants could go through a tank of fuel in minutes. I'd heard tales of fighter crews who had downed MiGs only to flame out over the Hànôi 'Hilton'. Hardly an even trade.

'Our good fortune extended back through our previous cruise, which also had been accident-free. Because USS *America* was based in Norfolk, she was normally deployed to the Mediterranean. Exactly one year before this mission, we had been anchored in Souda Bay, off the barren, rocky western coast of Crete, on call in case Middle East tensions escalated to a degree requiring US military intervention. At that time our biggest concern centred on whether military operations might interfere with a much anticipated port call in Athens, where many of us planned to meet our wives. The war in Viêtnam, half a planet away, seemed to be winding down and very remote.

'For the Marines of VMFA-333 - known as 'the Shamrock Squadron' for the three cloverleaf patterns on the tails of its aircraft - fate took a hairpin turn on 30 March 1972, though we didn't know it at the time. Our squadron, based at the Marine Corps air station at Beaufort, South Carolina was getting ready for a second Mediterranean cruise on *America* when the North Viêtnamese launched a massive invasion of South Viêtnam that became known as the 'Eastertide Offensive'. Three heavily reinforced NVA divisions trooped across the DMZ to attack the fire support bases along the border and more NVA divisions attacked farther south at Kontum and Ăn Lộc. It was Hànôi's test of America's 'Viêtnamization' programme, President Richard M. Nixon's plan to gradually turn over the conflict to the South Viêtnamese. By 1972 there were fewer than 100,000 American troops in the war, which had reached a force of about a half million in 1969. There had been a corresponding reduction in US air support. After Hànôi's March 30 incursion, President Nixon ordered the Pentagon to beef up the sea and air attack forces in Southeast Asia for an all-out airborne retaliation against the North. USS *Constellation* had orders to head for home, which meant that only two carriers would be left on 'Yankee Station'. The decision to divert *America* from the Mediterranean to the western Pacific was highly classified prior to our deployment. Some Marines in our squadron showed up the night before departure with surfboards in tow, visions of Majorca and the Riviera swimming in their heads. Word had leaked out to the anti-war community, though. When the tugboat team dislodged *America* from Norfolk's Pier 12 on 5 June 1972, thirty demonstrators in canoes and small sailboats had stretched in formation across her bow in a frail attempt to prevent the ship from leaving on schedule. Coast Guard ships had swiftly swept them out of the way.

'The last Marine squadron had pulled out of the country several months before we arrived at 'Yankee Station'. The only other Marine squadrons still in the fight were based at a desolate, dusty airfield at Nam Phong, Thailand, known to Marines as the 'Rose Garden' - something the Marine Corps didn't promise to prospective enlistees in a popular recruiting poster of the time.

'Since VMFA-333 was the first Marine F-4 squadron to fly combat missions from an aircraft carrier, we were assigned the same missions as the Navy Phantoms: air to air, trolling for MiGs. We did some bombing over the South, but we were there mainly to protect the fleet and bombers. Most of the time, enemy aircraft stayed away, perhaps out of respect for the Phantom's lethality.'

On 10 September an 'Iron Hand' flight of A-7 Corsairs from the USS *America* attacked SAM sites during a 'Linebacker' raid in the Hànôi area supported by a MiGCAP flight of four F-4Js from VMFA-333. They were led by Major Lee T. 'The Bear' Lasseter the 38-year old Squadron Executive Officer and his RIO, Captain 'L'il' John D. Cummings (both 'Top Gun' graduates) in 'Red One'. 'Bud' Linder and J. M. Shotwell were 'Red Two'. Shotwell recalled: 'On this particular mission we were assigned as the MiGCAP. In a Navy 'Alpha' strike - a coordinated attack involving all seven or eight squadrons aboard a single carrier - the MiGCAP F-4s were sent in ahead of the bombers to stations surrounding the assigned target. We were there to ward off any enemy planes that might try to thwart the strike by hassling the slower attack aircraft. The MiG-21 presented the greatest threat to the strike force. The fastest and most sophisticated aircraft in North Viêtnam's air force, the MiG-21 could pack up to four radar-guided air-to-air missiles and a twin-barrelled 23mm gun.'

The first warning 'Red' flight had of MiGs in the locality came from 'Red Crown' as Shotwell recalls:

'Red One', this is 'Red Crown'. Got a bandit at your six o'clock, two-two-nine at nine miles.'

'Roger. Red Flight, let's go port.'

'Bud slammed our F-4J into a tight left turn. I strained to find the MiGs before they spotted us. That was unlikely; the MiG-21, given the incongruous NATO code name 'Fishbed,' was not much larger than half the size of our Phantoms, was almost as fast - capable of Mach 2 - and much more manoeuvrable. 'Red Crown', the radar controller aboard USS *England*, a positive identification radar advisory zone (PIRAZ) ship in the Tonkin Gulf, monitored the MiGs for us that day.

'I was less worried about the MiGs than I was about their buddies on the ground. We were just over the suburbs of Hànôi (code-named 'Bull's-eye'). An engagement with MiGs would place us directly over the greatest concentration of North Viêtnamese Army (NVA) anti-aircraft artillery (AAA) and surface-to-air missile (SAM) batteries. In a dogfight, we might be too busy trying to bag a MiG to dodge all the flak from below.

'Red One' from 'Red Crown', bandits attacking. I repeat; bandits are attacking.'

'By the time we'd steadied our turn, my electronic countermeasures gear was lit up and buzzing like a pinball machine. That meant enemy fire control radar had painted our aircraft. 'Red Flight' from 'Crown'. SAM launch, vicinity 'Bullseye.'

'A loud warble and a flashing red light told me that a SAM missile had indeed selected our aircraft as its target.

'Red Two's got a singer high,' I said. I twisted my head as far as I could in the cramped rear cockpit and saw neither MiGs nor missiles.

'Where were The MiGs?

'Airburst!' said Bud over the intercom. A SAM detonated off our starboard wing. It could have been yards away or a mile. We felt no impact. The puffs of prickly flak we'd dodged since we took our station southwest of Hanoi were getting thicker. And closer. And where were the MiGs?

'Bogey dope, 'Red Crown',' demanded L'il John from 'Red One'.

'Red One', 'Red Crown'. Bandits now at your two-two-eight at seven.'

'L'il John, like myself, was a radar intercept officer (RIO). The F-4J was akin to a multimillion-dollar pistol. Unlike the Air Force's F-4E Phantom, which had an internal 20mm cannon, the F-4J had a maximum of eight big bullets - four Sparrows and four Sidewinders - to expend on targets that could move at supersonic speed through three dimensions and shoot back. Close coordination between the tandem cockpits of the Phantoms was essential. A RIO's job in a dogfight included operating radar to detect and track enemy aircraft and helping his pilot, in the forward cockpit, to manoeuvre the fighter into a position where he can fire one of the Phantom's missiles. In an air engagement, a good RIO was worth his weight in fine Scotch. An incompetent RIO was just so much dead weight. L'il John was worth about 120lbs of Chivas Regal. He was only 5 foot 4, but at age 39 the former enlisted Marine had the build and stamina of a high-school halfback. He'd already flown more than 500 combat missions in Viêtnam. In contrast to his diminutive RIO, 'Bear' was 6 foot 3 and 220lbs of solid muscle - plus another 50lbs of assorted other tissues that I suspected were nerve endings camouflaged as fat cells. He had a bull's head planted directly on expansive shoulders, no neck to speak of and a non-regulation handlebar moustache, from under which a big stogey protruded when he wasn't in the cockpit.

'Red One' from 'Red Crown'. Bandits attacking again.' I tried to find them on my radar, but it was useless in the glare of the afternoon sunlight. Normally I carried a rubber scope boot to shield the screen from the direct light, but I'd left the thing aboard the aircraft carrier when I'd detoured through the head on my way to the pre-flight briefing. Some guy was probably sitting there right then, wondering what that black rubber thing was hanging on the tissue roller. It was one of many things that would go awry on this mission.

'Another occurred after 'the Bear' called for tank jettison. Bud pulled a couple of g's as he punched off our centreline external fuel tank to cut down on aerodynamic drag during the engagement. When he pushed the nose back over, everything that wasn't strapped down flew toward the top of my canopy. I'd left my flight bag open and its contents - maps, frequency cards, checklists, cookie crumbs - floated like big snowflakes throughout the cockpit until a resumption of gravity brought them down, mostly to the floor and out of reach.

'L'il John, far more focused than I, picked up the MiGs on his radar. 'Gotta target high, gang. Let's go after 'em....

'Ten left....Steady up....He's at nine miles. We're losing overtake. Gotta get some speed now.'

'The 'Bear' lit his plane's afterburners, which gave the engines rocket like thrust and a flaming exhaust. A split second later I felt the acceleration as 'Bud' fired our afterburners. We were well into the supersonic envelope, hurtling through the air at more than twelve miles a minute.

'L'il' John lost sight of the MiGs when his AWG-10 radar died. The AWG-10 was not the most reliable system in the best of circumstances. The shock of locking onto an actual enemy target probably blew its transistors. But 'Red Crown' monitored the intercept on his radar.

'This is 'Red Crown'. Bandits on your one-niner-niner at eight.'

'Roger, roger,' answered L'il John.

'Bandits at two-oh-five at eight. Bandits headed southwest. Bandits now your two-oh-four at eight.'

'It was a tail chase, I realized. These guys weren't going to fight us. They were baiting us. We were over Hanoi headed inland. The farther in we went, the greater our chances of getting blown out of the sky or simply falling out of it because of fuel depletion.

'My electronic countermeasures gear loudly signalled the imminent arrival of a SAM. 'Red Two, singer high!' I shouted. I saw the missile at my 7 o'clock. Long and narrow - a flying telephone pole with a warhead. Bud jerked our warplane directly toward it. It was like charging at a striking cobra, but it worked. The little radar in the missile's nose broke its lock when our relative velocity abruptly increased. The SAM went stupid, careened wildly for an instant, then exploded, a bright white flash amid tangerine smoke and black shrapnel shards. Our aircraft buffeted and dipped its nose and I reached for my ejection handle. But then we levelled off.

'Once again I said a brief, silent prayer of thanks that Bud was my pilot. Prior to carrier cruises, pilots and RIOs were paired to fly their missions as a team. In most cases, the partnership was based on friendship or chemistry. I regarded Bud as my best friend, but my deeper motivation for asking him to be my pilot was his extraordinary flying prowess. He'd earned his private pilot's license as a youngster and looked at his tour in the Marines as an opportunity to hone his aviation skills and build up flight time to enhance his chances for acceptance by a major airline. A devout Christian, he had no lust for combat. While many of the pilots saw our deployment as a path to glory, Bud just loved to fly.

'How's it lookin', Bud?' I asked.

'Not sure. Gauges look good. Stick response okay....

'Red Lead', 'Red Two'. Can you check me over real quick? We got some vibration off that SAM.'

'But where was 'Red One'? While we were concentrating on evading the missile, we'd lost sight of our lead. For a queasy moment, we were up there all alone.

'You got us in sight, 'Red One?' I asked. After a very long second, I heard, 'Uh - rog. Check your two o'clock high.'

'We saw him, a speck among lots of puffs of AAA bursts. It was hard to tell how much flak had been aimed at us. The smoke - grey, white or black depending on the size and type of munitions - usually lingered in the sky for a while after the rounds detonated.

'Red One' moved in to inspect us. 'Looks good, Bud. Don't see any holes or leaks....'Crown', 'Red One'. Where's our bogey?'

'Bandits headed north at nineteen miles. Break engage. You've got another bandit. Bandits now your three-oh-six at nine, heading south-southwest.'

'Roger, pulling starboard,' came L'il John's voice.

'Red One', 'Crown'. Aircraft down from your strike. Call is 'Silver One'.'

'Silver One'? Was that an A-7 Corsair II or an A-6 Intruder? I couldn't remember from the pre-flight briefing. The pilot could have been someone I'd had Post Toasties with that morning.

'Roger, you have his position?'

'Negative....Your bandits are now three-one-eight at twelve. Looks like they're headed north.'

'They were sucking us in again.

'We're five-point-oh,' Bud transmitted, indicating we were down to only 5,000lbs of JP-5 jet fuel. At first, I thought that maybe we'd taken a hit after all and were losing gas. Then I realized what had happened. Since I didn't have a fuel gauge in my cockpit, I hadn't caught the mistake and it was as much my fault as Bud's. I'd failed to remind him to transfer the fuel out of the external tank early in the flight. He normally did it automatically and I'd become complacent. As a result, the centreline we'd jettisoned earlier - the one that had probably landed in somebody's chicken coop - was full of precious gas.

'I tried to do some quick mental math to determine whether we had enough fuel to get to the coast. Our rescue odds were much better if we ejected over water. If we parachuted over land, our best chance of survival would be immediate capture by the NVA. As PoWs, we'd be political capital and they might just let us live. Less desirable was a confrontation with local denizens. A North Viêtnamese farmer wasn't likely to be very hospitable, especially if American bombs had just creamed his water buffalo. Or his daughter.

'While all this went through my head, we were getting farther from the MiGs and closer to the buffer zone around the Chinese Communist border. An F-4 can normally outrun a MiG-21 in straight and narrow flight, but we were constantly having to reel our airplanes around to evade all the junk.

'Red Crown', 'Red One'. We're going to have to break it off and get some fuel. Has the strike group egressed?'

'Affirmative. Going feet wet now.'

'Roger. 'Red Flight's coming starboard to one-three-zero. 'Red Two', what's your state?'

'We're four-point-two.' That was about twenty minutes worth at the rate we were burning. That might get us to the coast, but making it back to the ship was out of the question. We'd have to rendezvous with an airborne tanker as soon as we got out of enemy range. We descended to 1,500 feet. At lower altitudes, enemy radar would have trouble tracking us because of ground return interference. We were still drawing a few flak bursts and an occasional SAM warble, but they were having to fire optically and not getting too close.

'Red Two' from 'Bear', what's your state?'

'Red Two's two-point-niner.'

'Red Crown' from 'Red One'. We'd like a tanker to meet us as close to the coast as God'll allow.'

'Stand by. I'll see if I can find one. 'Raygun 521', 'Red Crown'. 'Raygun 521', 'Red Crown', over.'

'We were down to 2,500lbs of fuel and I could see only dry land around us. The terrain below must have been strategically irrelevant since it looked virtually unscathed by war. There were a few little round ponds - water-filled bomb craters - but nothing like the destruction around the Demilitarized Zone, Hànôi or Thành Hóa. It was dark green and lush below, beautiful in another context. Patches of thick vegetation divided the little farms and villages. I even saw something that looked like a church - a little brown building with a steeple and a cross. A good omen? I wondered. Our squadron had been lucky so far. No losses due to accident or combat action after nearly two months on station.

'Red One', 'Red Crown'. Bandit on your one-three-seven at seventeen and he's very low.' I wondered where he'd come from.

'Get on the scope,' said Bud over the intercom, unaware that I didn't have a scope boot. With L'il John's radar out, I was the only hope for locking the enemy on the scope for a head-on launch of a Sparrow radar-guided missile. I hunched over the radar with my nose about a half inch from the screen to try to shield it from the glare. The bandit was low, but so were we. I levelled my antenna. At first, I saw nothing but green snow. I reduced my gain control and made out a little blip above the ground clutter. I locked onto it and an attack presentation popped up on the screen. The overtake looked good. It was him.

'Red Crown', 'Red Two's got radar contact,' I announced. 'Dead ahead. Eleven miles'. We were closing at 1,200 knots, in range for a Sparrow shot within seconds. 'Red Crown', 'Red Two'. Copy me?' Where was 'Crown'? They had to clear us to fire. We were in optimum range and the bandits weren't turning this time.

'Red Crown', 'Red Crown'. How do you read? Over!'

'Red Flight' from 'Crown'. Disregard! Disregard! Break it off! It's friendly. I repeat. Bogey is friendly.' Seconds later two Air Force 'Wild Weasels' zipped by to our port. I imagined the pilots giving us congenial little waves, blissfully unaware we'd nearly vaporized them.

'Red Two, what's your state?' asked L'il John.

'One-point-five.'

'Red Crown', anything from 'Raygun' tanker?'

'Nothin yet. We're still tryin'.'

'Better hurry. Gonna be suckin' fumes in a minute.'

'The 'Bear' hadn't said anything to us over the air about blowing a full centreline fuel tank. He knew what had happened but was far too professional to ream us over the air. He'd wait until we got back. And even then he wouldn't yell. He never needed to raise his voice. When 'the Bear' was displeased, he had a glare that could turn a young officer's blood to cherry slush.

'The Bear' passed us the lead as we crossed the coast. 'Red Crown' had reached 'Raygun' tanker and switched him over to our frequency.

'Raygun 521', this is 'Red Crown'. You have two fox fours just going feet wet. Need gas pretty bad.'

'Roger. I can give 'em four thousand apiece,' came the response from the tanker.

'Raygun 52' from 'Red Crown'. Vector two-seven-zero. 'Red Flight', your Texaco now your zero-nine-three at twenty, in a port turn.'

'The tanker was one of the ship's KA-6Ds that we fighter jocks liked to call 'pregnant guppies' - very ungainly looking but highly sophisticated all-weather bombers that could be fitted with four big external refuelling tanks. As we pulled in behind it, the tanker was already trailing its drogue. We had 700lbs of gas left. Suckin' fumes. Bud extended our in-flight refuelling probe, which jumped out - plock - from beside my canopy. As we approached 'Raygun', I steered Bud to the drogue. On the first attempt to hook up with the tanker, the probe, an appendage about 4 feet long, pressed against the top of the basket. The fuel line buckled and then oscillated and the drogue rap-rap-rapped across our canopies.

'After the hose stopped swaying, we began another approach. We were at just under 500lbs of fuel. 'Okay, Bud, a little to the right this time. Steady... steady...looks good....Got it!'

'We took our gas, headed back to the carrier and trapped (landed) uneventfully. When we pieced together the flight during the debriefing, I learned that at one point the MiGs we had tracked were nearly between us and the strike force, which had been about twenty miles southeast. The MiGs turned west, away from the strike force, when L'il John locked them in on his scope, possibly lighting up their electronic countermeasures gear and chasing them off, eventually to the north. Had they turned east, they might have tangled with the strike force, disrupting the ground attack and possibly exterminating some of the friendlies. Maybe our flight had accomplished something after all. As years separate me from the mission, that's what I choose to believe.'

The next day, 11 September, VMFA-333 provided a CAP flight of two F-4Js for a major strike on the Cô Giàng SAM assembly depot when Major 'The Bear' Lasseter and Captain 'L'il' Cummings in 'Shamrock 201 / 'Red One' (BuNo155526) were accompanied by their wing position aircraft flown by Captain Andrew 'Scotty' Dudley Jr. and 1st Lieutenant James 'Diamond Jim' Brady in 'Red Two'. They were on the second flight of the day and both F-4Js were armed with Sparrow AIM-7E2 and four AIM-9D missiles. The 'Red' Flight met an airborne KA-6 tanker to top off for the mission and was still refuelling when the strike force aircraft they were assigned to cover arrived and began their attacks. 'Red Two' had not completed refuelling but Lasseter felt that his wingman had enough fuel to complete the mission and ordered 'Scotty' Dudley to disconnect from the tanker and join him to their assigned CAP station. Prior to their arriving at their CAP location, Chief Radarman 'Dutch' Schulz on the USS *England*, the tactical air commander and ground control intercept officer, reported locations of two MiGs at 20,000 feet over Phúc Yên airfield. Lasseter's flight closed on the MiGs and at seven miles they recognised two MiG-21s low at 1,000 feet. Dudley called, 'Tally Ho' 'Tally Ho! Twelve o'clock. Keep going straight.' Lasseter fired two Sparrows but the MiG turned inside the missile and climbed. The second MiG reversed course and flew out of the area to the north. Lasseter and the remaining MiG engaged at subsonic manoeuvres below 1,000 feet directly over Phúc Yên. L'il' Cummings reported SAM and AAA warnings were going off. Lasseter fired two more Sparrows and two Sidewinders during the chase but the MiG stayed close to the ground and evaded the missiles. 'Scotty' Dudley, now dangerously low on fuel, was ready to disengage from the chase. Suddenly, the MiG reversed his turn and Lasseter, who had a clear shot, fired a Sidewinder and the MiG-21 exploded in a fireball. Cummings shouted, 'Okay, splash one MiG-21!'

Both Phantoms rejoined and headed back to the *America* but a third MiG made a pass on 'Red Two'. Lasseter and 'Scotty' Dudley each fired their remaining Sidewinder and the MiG beat a hasty retreat. Dudley was now critically low on fuel and both F-4s slowed to 14,000 feet in an effort to reach the safety of the sea. They flew directly over Hảiphòng on their way to the Gulf and a waiting tanker to cut short their departure route. As AAA warnings could be heard inside their cockpits the air began to fill with SAMs and flak bursts. Despite the evasive action, 'Shamrock 201' was hit by an SA-2 at 15,000 feet which damaged the wing. 'Red One' was hit by a SAM and began burning. 'Red Two' was unable to meet up with a tanker and stayed with Lasseter and Cummings as the latter's engine flamed out. Eventually, hydraulic failure led to loss of control and they ejected over the Gulf of Tonkin and into the sea about 35 miles southeast of Haiphòng, where they were rescued by an SH-3 helicopter of HC-7 operating from the USS *England* and recovered aboard the *Biddle*. 'Scotty' Dudley's aircraft had also been hit, by flak in the wing and fuselage, as he flew over Hảiphòng on the way out to sea, causing a massive fuel leak. The engines flamed out from lack of fuel when the aircraft was about 45 miles south of Hảiphòng and the crew ejected. They were rescued by the SAR destroyer USS *Biddle*. All four men were returned to the *America* with barely a scratch to celebrate 'The Bear' and Cummings' victory was the only all-Marine Corps MiG kill of the war.

On the 12th when the primary target was the Là Đánh storage caves 35 miles north of Hànôi, 'Finch', a flight of four F-4Es in the 388th TFW protected 'Date' flight, one of two chaff flights on the raid. 'Finch' ingressed near Hon Gai on the east coast near Haiphòng. The chaffers were about three miles ahead in line-abreast formation. Immediately, 'Red Crown' began issuing warnings of bandits in the area and anticipated an attack on the chaff force. Two MiG-21s disregarded the escorts or failed to see them and closed in on one of the 'Date' flights from 4 to 6 o'clock in a pincher-type geometry attack as the chaffers approached the target area. 'Finch 01', the lead F-4E crewed by Lieutenant Colonel Lyle L. Beckers the squadron commander of the 35th Tactical Fighter Squadron - the Black Panthers - and 1st Lieutenant Thomas M. Griffin of New Orleans, Louisiana, observed one of the MiGs in a high speed right turn aligning itself to the rear of the chaff flight from which point he could launch a missile. Beckers obtained an auto-acquisition lock-on and attempted to fire two AIM-7 missiles but they failed to launch as the MiG closed on the left hand chaff flight tasked to dispense a chaff corridor from the initial point to the target in order to provide radar shielding for a follow on strike force. Just then the MiG-21 fired an Atoll missile at the breaking chaffers and broke straight down. The missile narrowly missed 'Date 04' and impacted in the aft section of 'Date 03' flown by Captain Rudolph W. Zuberbuhler, who continued his mission and constructed the valuable chaff corridor. Zuberbuhler, born in 1940 in Lowman, Idaho, was on his 368th mission of the war, of which 146 were over North Viêtnam. His WSO was Captain Frederick Charles McMurray, 27, of Coeur d'Alene Idaho.

Captain Zuberbuhler nursed the crippled F-4E toward the Gulf of Tonkin hoping to get 'feet wet' before ejecting, but as they neared 'Phantom Ridge' north of Håiphòng both crew had to abandon their aircraft after it became uncontrollable. Zuberbuhler and McMurray, who received a compression fracture during ejection, were taken prisoner. During one of McMurray's initial interrogations, the weather was quite hot and the interrogators brought in an electric fan and placed it so it would blow on them, not him. 'Due to the faulty wiring of the outlet, it was only working intermittently. This was bothering the interrogators so they decided to stop in the middle of the interrogation and try to fix it. While one of them was working on it he got a bad electrical shock that knocked him on his rear. Although I wasn't in a jovial mood at the time I almost broke out laughing when I saw him get shocked.'

Beckers stabbed his throttles into afterburner and reset switches to fire a Sidewinder and went in pursuit of the MiG which dived toward the ground in a split-S manoeuvre typical of a hit and run tactic. Beckers and his wingman followed the MiG down through the manoeuvre and 'Finch 01' fired an AIM-9 Sidewinder, which failed to guide. As the flight bottomed out and pulled up in a steep climb, Beckers fired a second Sidewinder, which impacted the MiG's left wing without appearing to detonate. But then smoke and flames were observed coming from the left wing. Beckers then selected guns and proceeded to fire 520 rounds of HEI (High Explosive Incendiary) tracer from about 1,000 feet. As he opened fire Beckers noticed his tracers passing behind the MiG and he eased the pipper ahead of the enemy jet until he could see projectile impacts and additional fire on the fuselage of the MiG-21, which fell off on a wing and was last observed on fire in a steep descent.

Meanwhile, Major Gary L. Retterbush of Lebanon, Indiana with 1st Lieutenant Daniel L. Autrey of Hialeah, Florida in the back seat in 'Finch 03' attacked another MiG-21. Retterbush recalled: 'The MiG's came from high and behind my flight and dived down through us firing their missiles as they came. It was a rather chaotic time! During the manoeuvering that followed, our flight broke apart and we ended up as two elements of two F-4s. I manoeuvred to the six o'clock position behind a MiG-21 and Dan Autrey got a good radar lock on the MiG. Conditions were excellent; almost text book. I fired two AIM-7 Sparrow radar guided missiles but the first failed to guide and the second did not detonate. They simply went ballistic and did nothing except alert the MiG pilot to his impending peril. I had a lot of overtake and continued to close on the MiG. I changed my armament switches from the AIM-7 to the AIM-9 Sidewinder heat-seeking infrared missile. As soon as I was within AIM-9 range (approximately 9,000 feet), I got a good audio tone for the AIM-9s. I fired three Sidewinders at the MiG, but they either did not guide or their proximity fuses did not work. The first Sidewinder narrowly missed but caused the MiG to execute a Split 'S'. The MiG pilot eased his turn as he pulled out, allowing me to fire two more AIM-9s. Both missed by a matter of feet but failed to detonate. One went just under the MiG; the other over the canopy. The last missile went close by the cockpit and got the MiG pilot's attention! He broke hard and I followed and continued to close on him. I fired a couple of short bursts with 20mm cannon, firing approximately 350 rounds. The 20mm with tracer was observed impacting the fuselage, wing and canopy and the MiG started burning immediately. I was now closing way too fast. I did a high speed yo-yo. The manoeuvre once again put me in position to fire another burst from my gun. These bullets hit in and around the cockpit and in a few seconds the MiG went into an uncontrolled climb with its nose 65 degrees up, slowed to 150 knots, apparently stalled and pitched downward in a wingover attitude. I saw the pilot slumped forward in the cockpit. I watched the burning MiG until it hit the ground and exploded in a cloud of smoke and fire.' As the F-4Es left the battle area, they observed a smoke trail and a large fireball.

Later in the day, another F-4 flight in the 388th TFW escorted a strike flight in a raid on the Tuân Quán rail bridge when two MiG-21s attacked. The first MiG appeared in an 8 o'clock position and lined up on the strike flight. The lead aircraft fired one AIM-7 missile ballistically to distract the MiG and then turned in pursuit as the MiG broke away. This 'shot across the bow' detonated about 1,000 feet in front of the Phantom. In hot pursuit, the flight leader then fired another AIM-7, followed by three AIM-9 missiles. They all missed. The second AIM-7 detonated 500 feet from the target and the nearest AIM-9 detonated about 200 feet from the MiG. Captain Michael J. Mahaffey of Patterson, California with 1st Lieutenant George I. Shields of Georgetown, Connecticut in the rear seat in 'Robin 02' had better luck with its ordnance during the engagement when a second MiG-21 dropped between the two F-4s.

'It went right across in front of us,' Mahaffey said 'and it looked a lot bigger than I thought a MiG was supposed to look. We rolled right, tracked and fired one AIM-9 which guided and impacted the MiG in the tail section, blowing off parts of the aircraft. The MiG went into a spin from 16,000 feet and more pieces fell off the aircraft. It was last seen below 8,000 feet, about twenty nautical miles southwest of Yên Bái airfield.'

Another MiG-21 was destroyed during 'Linebacker' operations on 16 September. The victors again were Captain Calvin Bryan Tibbett and his WSO, 1st Lieutenant Bill 'Buddy' Hargrove, Texas who were flying 'Chevy 03' in a flight of four F-4Es of the 'Triple Nickel' on escort for US strike forces. It was their second aerial victory within a week. Tibbett recalled: 'A MiG-21 was spotted going southeast down the Red River. A low-level chase started and Captain John A. Madden and Captain Michael A. Hilliard fired two radar and four heat-seeking missiles, none of which detonated or appeared to guide. The flight leader cleared us to fire and we fired four heat missiles, the last of which guided and detonated near the aft portion of the fuselage. The MiG started a turn and then pitched down.

The MiG pilot ejected just before the aircraft struck the ground.' [12]

Air Force fighter crews scored no additional aerial victories until the first week of October, although 'Linebacker' operations continued uninterrupted. On the ground, five MiGs were destroyed and nine others damaged on 1 October at Phúc Yên, Yên Bái, Vĩnh and Quảng Làng airfields. On 5 October when MiGs from Kép airfield opposed a strike force an escort flight of F-4Es in the 388th TFW engaged the enemy in a heated battle. A MiG-21 was shot down by Captain Richard E. Coe of East Orange, New Jersey and 1st Lieutenant Omri K. Webb III of Leesville, South Carolina in 'Robin 01'. Coe reported: 'We received vectors from 'Disco' for two MiGs off 'Bullseye' on ingress to initial point. They seemed to be heading in our direction. 'Disco' gave continuous vectors until the flight we were escorting called MiGs at 8 o'clock high. The formation began a hard left turn. After two turns I observed two MiG-21s in route formation at 10 o'clock high, at about three miles. We began a lazy one-g descending turn to get to 6 o'clock. The auto-acquisition switch was activated with the MiGs still in the pipper. I then fired one AIM-7. Someone called: 'One of you has a MiG at 6 o'clock, tracking.'

'We rolled up to check 6 o'clock. I then checked 12 o'clock where I saw a smoke trail entering a black smoke cloud and a large white column exiting the other side. We then broke hard right and on roll-out observed the white column leading down to two large dirt clouds rising from the ground.'

The following day two F-4E aircrews of a hunter-killer team destroyed a MiG-19. 'Buick 01' was manned by Major Gordon L. Clouser of Norman, Oklahoma and 1st Lieutenant Cecil H. Brunson of Eddyville, Kentucky and 'Eagle 04' by Captain Charles D. Barton of Greenville, South Carolina and 1st Lieutenant George D. Watson of Trenton, Missouri. The manner in which this MiG was destroyed was unusual. 'Disco' warned the flight of approaching MiGs when in the vicinity of Thái Nguyên. The F-105 flight leader and his wingman moved out of the area as pre-briefed while Clouser and Barton turned to make contact with the enemy. Clouser then saw a MiG-21 sliding into a 7 o'clock position; Barton observed a MiG-19 attempting to achieve a 6 o'clock position on the element. Clouser called a hard left break to provide self-protection for the Phantoms and to divert the MiGs from the F-105s. Because of the ordnance on board, the manoeuvrability of the F-4s was limited and therefore they jettisoned the ordnance and fuel tanks. The MiGs were dangerously close to a firing position and the two backseaters, Branson and Watson, warned their pilots of the danger. To disrupt enemy tracking, Barton went into a vertical dive in afterburner with a weaving pattern. Meanwhile, Clouser was able to manoeuvre out of the MiG's range without resorting to a dive. The MiG-19 pilot followed Barton's aircraft, its guns blazing and Clouser rolled in behind the MiG to create a sandwich. The MiG-21, in turn, sandwiched Clouser. Barton continued the dive and bottomed out at 300 feet above a valley floor between two mountain peaks. The MiG-19 pilot was apparently so engrossed with the chase that he failed to notice the vertical dive angle until it was too late. His aircraft impacted with the ground. Both F-4Es recovered and the MiG-21 hastily withdrew from the battle. Each F-4E crew member was subsequently credited with one-half of a MiG kill.

The next MiG fell on 8 October. Major Gary L. Retterbush, this time in 'Lark 01' with Captain Robert H. Jasperson of Minneapolis, Minnesota crewed the lead aircraft in a very small strike package of F-4Es dispatched by the 388th TFW. Retterbush recalled: 'My backseater had a problem getting his canopy to lock just prior to takeoff. Bob cycled his canopy several times. He finally pulled it down on the rails and got it to lock. Bob told me later that he knew this would be his last Southeast Asia flight and he didn't want to abort on the ground. Thanks, Bob!

'After we refuelled from the KC-135 tankers on the ingress route, one of my F-4s in my flight had a mechanical problem. I sent that airplane and a wingman home. Under the rules of engagement at that time, I should have aborted the mission since I only had two fighters in my flight, but I chose to continue the mission.

'As we approached the border of North Viêtnam, 'Disco' (the USAF airborne EC-121 warning aircraft orbiting in Laos) warned us that a MiG was scrambling and that we were probably its target. As we continued inbound, 'Disco' gave us frequent warnings of the MiG's progress and location. It was indeed coming our way. The engagement was almost like a GCI (ground controlled intercept) in reverse. 'Disco' announced the MiG was at our 10:30 high. Sure enough, Bob Jasperson pointed out a silver glint in the sun as the MiG turned down on us. I called a 'hijack' and had the fighters jettison their external fuel tanks and light afterburners as we turned into the MiG. A few seconds later I had the F-4 bomber flight break as the MiG came closer to the bombers. The MiG dived down trying to attack the breaking bombers. I was on his tail but at a very high angle off. Angle off is the angle between the attacking airplane and the target if you extended a line straight back from the target's tail and then measured the angle between the attacker and the extended line. The book said that the AIM-9 Sidewinder would not guide to the target if the angle off at the time of firing was greater than 45 degrees. I fired two AIM-9 heat seeking missiles at the diving MiG. I did not expect either of them to guide because the angle off was far beyond the limits. Both missiles went ballistic as I anticipated. I then tried to jettison the rest of my missiles including the three AIM-7 Sparrow radar guided missiles. I was yelling for Bob to give me a caged gun sight because the reticule was completely off of the windscreen due to the high angle off and the high Gs we were pulling. Bob got the gun sight locked. I very quickly did a little Kentucky windage estimate, pulled the pipper way out in front of the MiG and high and fired a short burst from my 20mm Gatling gun. To my pleasant surprise, the bullets hit the MiG in the fuselage near the left wing and it immediately burst into flames. The pilot did not hesitate and ejected immediately. Then came an even bigger surprise; he had a beautiful pastel pink parachute! I circled him one time and then regrouped the flight for our trip home. The entire engagement was visible from the Yên Bái airfield tower if anyone was in it at that time. The engagement lasted only a minute or two from start to finish. When I landed, I checked the gun and found that I had fired only 96 rounds, including the exciter burst that was probably about the half bullets fired.

'I was extremely pleased that I had a gun camera for this mission (not all birds had them) and it had checked out good going in. When I removed the film pack it looked like it had functioned correctly. I gave the film to the gun camera guys and told them to really take care in developing it. About an hour later they came to me with the results and a great film, but all of it was flying straight and level after the refuelling. I tested the gun after leaving the tanker and the camera apparently continued to run after the test firing. All of the film was used long before the dogfight began. So, unfortunately, I did not have the great MiG kill camera film that I had hoped for!

On 12 October another manoeuvering action resulted in a third aerial victory for Captain John A. Madden, Jr. and a second MiG kill for his WSO, Captain Lawrence H. Pettit. They were flying 'Vega 01' on MiGCAP in support of 'Linebacker' operations. 'We ingressed North Việtnam over Cẩm Phả on a westerly heading,' reported Madden. 'Two bandits were airborne from Phúc Yên and heading northeast. We vectored now on a more northerly heading to position ourselves between the MiGs and strike forces. 'Red Crown' stated that the MiGs were in a port turn and we then engaged a silver MiG-21 head-on. As the MiG passed abeam, we sliced around in a right turn to get behind and beneath him. Coming out of the right sliding turn, we sighted the MiG-21 in a port turn. We passed within 1,000 feet behind him as we slid to the outside of his turn. We turned back to the left to get behind the MiG. He pulled up, rolled over and Split-S'd into the clouds. We were 20,000 feet and the cloud layer was solid undercast between 16,000 feet and 18,000 feet. We rolled over and dived after the MiG through the cloud deck. We picked him up underneath and pressed after him. He was last observed at 9,000 feet, entering a 7/8's cloud deck with an unknown base. We broke off our attack just at the top of these clouds and egressed.' The MiG crashed. Because the aggressive attack and hot pursuit caused the MiG to execute and prolong a manoeuvre from which he could not recover, Captains' Madden and Pettit submitted a claim for the MiG's destruction. Captain George Norwood and 1st Lieutenant David F. Bland served as Madden's wingman during these manoeuvres but did not submit a claim for a portion of the MiG-21's destruction. On the 20th credit was given for the aerial victory to Madden and Pettit. In 1972 Madden led over fifty combat flights and he never lost a wingman. Flights under his leadership accounted for five enemy aircraft downed and one damaged.

The third and final USAF ace of the war in Southeast Asia obtained his fifth aerial victory on 13 October. More significantly, Captain Jeffrey S. Feinstein was the second WSO ace. Flying as back-seater for his squadron commander, Lieutenant Colonel Curtis D. Westphal of Bonduel, Wisconsin during a MiGCAP near Kép airfield, Feinstein later recalled, 'We received a call that bandits were in the area and heading our way. There were two of them and I got a visual on them when they were about two miles off.' Colonel Westphal describes the engagement:

'We received initial word that two bandits were airborne from the vicinity of Hànôi, heading north. Our flight, under 'Red Crown' control, turned to engage the MiGs. Shortly thereafter Captain Feinstein obtained radar contact at seventeen nautical miles. 'Red Crown' confirmed the contact as being the bandits and our flight closed on a front quarter attack. Due to the presence of friendlies in the area, we decided not to fire at that point. After closing to one mile, Feinstein obtained a visual contact on one of the two MiG-21s. We turned left to engage. We fired three AIM-7 missiles. All eight members of the flight observed the second AIM-7 hit the MiG-21 in the aft section, at which time it burst into flames. We saw the MiG pilot eject at approximately five seconds after missile impact. The entire flight then observed the MiG-21 going down in flames until it disappeared through the undercast.'

Air combat on 15 October led to the destruction of three additional MiG-21s by Air Force fighter crews. The first kill was credited to Major Robert L. Holtz of Milwaukee, Wisconsin and his WSO, 1st Lieutenant William C. Diehl of Tampa, Florida in 'Parrot 03'. The flight had been dispatched by the 388th Wing to escort three flights of F-4 strike aircraft to the vicinity of Việt Trì. Holtz recalled: 'We were vectored by 'Red Crown' to two MiGs in my 12 o'clock position. These bandits were picked up visually at about two miles and a hard left turn was made to engage as they passed overhead and away at a rapid rate. Seeing that these two were no longer a threat, we started to return to escort duties when my wingman saw and engaged another MiG-21 with myself flying fighting wing. This MiG headed for the clouds and disappeared. The strike flights were too far ahead of us to catch, so I called for an orbit in the vicinity of Việt Trì to cover the strike flights on egress. While in this orbit my wingman and I re-engaged one more time each, with negative results, until we got separated by numerous F-4s going through our flight after another MiG. While in a right hand turn to rejoin my wingman I circled a cloud and noted a white parachute about 3,000 to 4,000 feet AGL. 13. I told Lieutenant Diehl to mark the time and position in case it was one of our pilots.

'I then noted a silver MiG-21 orbiting the descending parachute about the same altitude (3,000 to 4,000 feet). The MiG was not manoeuvering but instead was in a lazy right bank and about 3,000 feet ahead. I fired an AIM-9 which came off the rail, did a slow roll and then went straight up the MiG's tail and exploded, blowing pieces of tail section and almost one complete elevator off the aircraft. The MiG rolled violently to the right and started towards the ground, nose down and on fire. I disengaged and egressed the area.'

Northwest of 'Bullseye' one of the MiGCAP flights, which the 432nd TRW was providing for strike aircraft targeting a fuel storage area in the Thái Nguyên area, was vectored south while under 'Red Crown' control against a pair of MiG-21s. A radar contact was established at sixteen nautical miles, followed by a visual contact shortly thereafter. Lieutenant Colonel Carl Funk and Major James Malaney the flight lead in 'Buick 01' attempted to attack the MiG, but the radar in their 'Combat Tree' F-4D broke lock twice in succession and Funk cleared 'Buick 03' in to fire. 'Buick 03' was crewed by Captain (later Brigadier General) Gary M. Rubus of Banning, California and his WSO Captain James L. Hendrickson of Columbus, Ohio. Hendrickson recalls: 'The F-4 radar, whatever the variant, wasn't supposed to be able to track a 'look down, shoot down' target. We were the only ones in the flight able to track the target. We were lucky to have a radar that was better 'tweaked' than the others and it would happily track a target below us in ground clutter.

'The gun attack took place in a near-vertical dive, in afterburner at about Mach 0.95 just as the MiG neared the bottom of his dive. Rubus fired at 1,100 feet and again at 800 feet, seeing cannon shell explosions on the silver jet with its thin green camouflage.'

Rubus recalls: 'I fired an AIM-7 at a range of four nautical miles which detonated prematurely in front of my aircraft. A second AIM-7 was fired at a range of 4,500 feet which did not guide. I closed to cannon range and fired a burst from approximately 1,100 feet, followed by a second burst from approximately 800 feet.

Both bursts impacted the MiG-21 and the pilot ejected. The MiG-21 was trailing grey smoke, rolled left and impacted the ground about two nautical miles beyond the point where the pilot ejected.'

Rubus attributed his kill to overall teamwork in the engagement. After he shot down the MiG-21, 'Red Crown' advised the flight that four more MiGs were airborne and coming their way, but Funk's flight had reached 'Bingo' fuel level and so they beat a rapid retreat.

'Red Crown' informed 'Chevy', the third MiGCAP flight, that 'Buick' flight was engaged with MiGs and for them to remain with the strike flight and then called 'new bandits airborne from Phúc Yên'. This flight was led by Major Ivy J. McCoy of Baton Rouge, Louisiana with his WSO, Major Frederick W. Brown, of Grand View, Washington in 66-7463, Steve Ritchie's Phantom, which was available because having got his fifth MiG he could go home. After that, the other squadrons got the MiGCAP lead in turn. 'Chevy 01'was equipped with 'Combat Tree' which McCoy's WSO thought was 'the berries' but McCoy was not impressed by it.

McCoy recalled: 'We were vectored towards them. 'Red Crown' estimated their altitude at 12,000. We continued the vectors until we merged. Having no visual contact, we made a 180° left turn and continued towards bandits. I saw contrails at 1 o'clock. 'Red Crown' informed me that they were probably my bandits. My wingman called 'Bandits visual at 2 o'clock'. I turned and visually acquired a MiG-21 in a right descending turn. I spiralled down with the MiG-21, calling for Major Brown to lock on. Then I fired three AIM-7s during an elapsed time of 23 seconds. The first two missiles I did not observe. The third fell away to the left. I never had much confidence in the AIM-7! I was frustrated because Fred still didn't have a lock-on and I couldn't see any missile out in front. The MiG was continuing down in a right 20° bank turn. I then selected 'heat' and fired three AIM-9s. I visually acquired the third missile at 200-300 feet aft of the MiG-21 and saw it fly up the tailpipe. Colonel Robert E. Wayne my wingman verified that the entire aft section of the MiG-21 was one large fireball. Captain Glenn A. Profitt saw the MiG pilot eject and also observed chute deployment. Our flight then egressed as a flight of four.'

Meanwhile, the strike flights were unable to reach their primary target and hit the alternate target: Yên Bái airfield. At least one MiG was destroyed and two were damaged on the ground during this attack.

Operation 'Linebacker' came to an end on 22 October 1972 and many of the fighter squadrons which had been temporarily deployed to Southeast Asia were returned to their home bases or sent elsewhere in the Far East. 'Linebacker's demise was premature, however, for it soon became apparent that the North Viêtnamese had no intention of stopping wholesale infiltration into South Viêtnam so long as American aircraft remained south of the 20th parallel. President Richard M. Nixon, who on 7 November had won a massive presidential election victory, was determined to end the long drawn out war in Viêtnam, even if it meant using B-52s to bomb Hànôi to destruction. On 18 December he gave the order to attack the enemy in his home territory once again, this time with a concentrated force unprecedented in the Viêtnam conflict. The new operation - actually a resumption of the previous campaign - was coded 'Linebacker II'. Primary targets consisted of rail complexes, storage facilities and supply areas, power plants, radio broadcasting stations, air bases and SAM sites in the area around Hànôi and Haiphòng. The mission of protecting the B-52s was generally assigned to F-4 MiGCAP flights which accompanied every bomber wave over North Viêtnam. Beginning with 18 December, except for a stand-down on Christmas Day when no missions were flown, targets were attacked day and night. That first night F-4 'chaffers' and an F-4 chaff escort were included in the force of 39 support aircraft.

On 21/22 December Lieutenant Colonel James E. Brunson of Eddyville, Kentucky and Major Ralph S. Pickett of Beulaville, North Carolina in 'Buick 01' were leading the ingress MiGCAP that was escorting strike aircraft in Route Package 6. Brunson recalled: 'After pre-strike refuelling, the ingress MiGCAP proceeded north toward Phú Thọ Hòa en route to the assigned CAP area near Kép airfield. 'Red Crown' was controlling the flight as two bandits started climbing out through 26,000 feet to the northwest of Hànôi. The MiGs turned south toward us and other friendlies. 'Red Crown' vectored us for a head-on intercept and called the MiGs at sixteen miles from us when we got a radar lock-on. 'Red Crown' cleared us to fire if a visual identification was made, as friendly aircraft were still in the area. Our flight jettisoned the centreline fuel tanks and accelerated. The MiG was about 10,000 feet higher than the flight and as I started my pull-up to centre the radar steering dot, I saw a silver MiG-21 above. I put the MiG in my gunsight pipper and fired four AIM-7 missiles in rapid succession with full radar lock-on, maintaining a steep climb toward the MiG. Pickett saw one of the AIM-7s detonate in the tail section of the MiG-21, causing the tail section and large pieces to separate. The MiG went into an uncontrollable spin. No bail-out was observed. The flight was still in good formation and I turned to engage the second MiG in the flight but this MiG escaped and the flight returned to base due to fuel.'

Captain Gary L. Sholders of Lebanon, Oregon and his WSO, 1st Lieutenant Eldon D. Binkley of Winston-Salem, North Carolina, who were 'Bucket 01', the lead aircraft scored a victory without even hitting the MiG. Sholders recalled: 'Intelligence sources confirmed (on 24 December) that an enemy aircraft went down in the early morning hours of 22 December. Ours was the only flight in the area that engaged an enemy aircraft for any length of time on 21/22 December; in addition, the only flight that pursued an enemy aircraft after he had apparently attempted a landing at Yên Bái airfield. We claimed one enemy aircraft destroyed due to continued pursuit which resulted in fuel starvation for the enemy aircraft.'

B-52 losses mounted alarmingly and on the 22nd the support package included not only F-4 'chaffers' and an F-4 chaff escort as before but also an F-4 MiGCAP, an F-4 B-52 escort and an F-4 hunter/killer flight. On the 23rd the same elements were included in the support package of seventy aircraft. It was same again on Christmas Eve and on 26 and 27 December when Air Force and Navy F-4s comprised the MiGCAP. On the morning of 27 December when F-4s began raiding SAM sites around Hànôi, two MiG-21s acting as 'bait' climbed to high altitude, hoping to draw the Phantoms away from the bombers. Meanwhile, another MiG took off and flew at a low altitude along Highway 1 heading towards Phúc lý. This ploy worked as nearly all of the 24 escorting F-4Es [of the 432nd TRW] dived for the two MiGs at the higher altitude, leaving the twelve fighter-bombers to fend for themselves. One of the Phantoms was hit. A yellow ball of flame was seen and then a black trail of smoke seemed to burst out of it before it went straight into the ground, crashing in Hòa Bình province. The two-crew safely ejected and were saved. Later that afternoon, a second Phantom was shot down; the two-crew ejecting safely after their aircraft was hit in the right wing, sending it spinning into a hill. [14]

On the night of 27/28 December F-4E's 'Vega One' and 'Two' from the 432nd TFW in one of the MiGCAP flights were attacked by MiGs in the vicinity of 'Thud Ridge'. 'Vega Two' was piloted by 25-year old Captain John Wesley Anderson, of Portland Oregon. His WSO was 1st Lieutenant Brian H. Ward of Huntington Beach, California who recalled: 'Vega One' was engaged by a MiG-21 and we were flying on his wing. We were at three to five hundred feet and flying about 600 mph when we were hit by an 'Atoll' air-to-air missile. The plane went out of control and we ejected about thirty miles west of Hànôi. I estimate that my chute opened about fifty feet above the ground. I landed in a ditch next to a village and was captured immediately [as was Anderson, both of whose arms were broken during ejection]. The plane crashed a couple of hundred yards away. During the ejection I received a separated right elbow, fractured right and left shoulder, compression fracture of the lower back, a broken rib and some cartilage damage to the right knee. The trip to Hànôi was probably the worst part. My pilot and I had to ride in the back of a jeep. They made us sit on the rim of the spare tyre instead of on the seats. The trip lasted one night and morning over some unbelievably rough roads and at the wild pace of a Bangkok cab. When we arrived at Hànôi we were kept at the Hànôi 'Hilton.' Three weeks later we were moved to the 'Zoo.'

'Vega Two' was the last USAF aircraft shot down by a MiG and also the only US aircraft lost in air-to-air-combat at night during the war. [15]

On the 28th when 99 Support aircraft accompanied the Route packages to Hànôi once again, F-4 chaffers and F-4 chaff escort, Air Force and Navy MiGCAP F-4s and Air Force B-52 escort and F-4 hunter/killers were included. 'Red Crown' called the position of a 'bandit' heading west of Hànôi said Major Harry L. McKee of Austin, Texas in the 'Triple Nickel' Squadron, who with his WSO, Captain John E. Dubler of Omaha, Nebraska was on MiGCAP duty in 'List 01'. 'Captain Dubler made radar contact with the bandit at ninety nautical miles range at approximately 2150 hours. We were in trail with the MiG and had radar contact 30° left at eleven nautical miles. We were cleared to close by 'Red Crown' and a full system lock-on was made at ten nautical miles. My wingman [Captain Kimzey W. Rhine] called 'locked on' shortly thereafter. Both aircraft fired on my verbal command with the radar dot centred. I fired two AIM-7 missiles. Rhine fired one AIM-7 at the same time. We all observed a large fireball approximately four nautical miles distant at 12 o'clock. It appeared that all three AIM-7s guided. Further, it appeared that the first missile impacted the MiG, followed immediately by the impact of the missile fired by Rhine. At missile firing our airspeed was Mach 1.05, altitude 30,500 feet and heading 010°. Moments later I observed a fireball on the ground in the vicinity of the shoot down. We continued to operate as a flight of two in a MiGCAP capacity until 2235 hours, whereupon we egressed.'

At sea on 28 December Lieutenant (jg)'s Scott H. Davis, 26, and Geoffrey Hugh Ulrich of VF-412 on the *Enterprise* in an F-4J destroyed a MiG-21with an AIM-9 Sidewinder. Wildly manoeuvering between altitudes of 50-7,000 feet, Davis and Ulrich made their kill about five miles to the south of the outskirts of Hànôi. The

24th MiG shot down by Navy and Marine Corps pilots that year; it was also the first and only one for *Enterprise* during her Viêtnam tours.

During 18-29 December all-out, intensive aerial bombardment of industry, communications, ports, supply depots and airfields in the Hànôi and Hàiphòng areas were among the most effective of the war. Pilots who flew the missions (on the last day five forces of F-4s were among the 102 support aircraft committed) claimed that 'the North Viêtnamese had nothing left to shoot at us as we flew over. It was like flying over New York City.'

In the Hànôi 'Hilton' and the dozen other prisons scattered in and around Hànôi with nicknames like 'Alcatraz', 'Briarpatch', 'Dirty Bird' and the 'Zoo' there was no doubt in the minds of the American prisoners that now the raids were hitting the Hàiphòng-Hànôi area it could only hasten their release and not before a moment too soon. Michael Thomas Burns' weight had dropped from about 178-180lbs when he and Major Crumpler were shot down on 5 July 1968, to 155-165lbs. 'Basically, food was soup twice a day. From October until March it was boiled greens and little pieces of pork fat with the hair sticking up. From March through the summer up until late October 1972 it was boiled pumpkin with pork fat. A half or a third loaf of bread had boll weevils - we called them little black bugs - that guys just ate because they said they were dead. It was probably protein anyway.' [16]

When John 'Spike' Nasmyth was shot down and captured on 4 September 1966 he was subjected to constant torture and near starvation during his first three years in captivity. The guards would find any reason to humiliate him and try to break his spirit. Refusing to acknowledge that Nasmyth was a prisoner of war, they referred to him as a war criminal and, as far as they were concerned, the Geneva Convention did not apply to war criminals. After several months of solitary confinement, he was allowed to mix with the other 'American air pirates,' as they were called by their captors. He received no medical treatment for his wounds. Bandages which some civilians had given him were taken off so his wound could fester. The tortures, which he and 95% of the other prisoners underwent, were in the forms of solitary confinement, leg irons and bindings with nylon straps which stretched the tendons and numbed the limbs. These tortures were not only severe, they were long; many spent months and months in leg irons and years in solitary confinement. Time was the prisoners' biggest enemy and only Nasmyth's positive outlook got him through dark times where others would have given up.

Some men, like Lieutenant (jg) Porter Halyburton, who had been shot down on 17 October 1965, had been incarcerated in the Hànôi 'Hilton' for longer and for two years his wife Marty had not known whether he was alive or dead. But once on the ground after safely ejecting from his Phantom, peasants surrounded him and hours later Halyburton was blindfolded and riding in a jeep to Hànôi. In January 1967, the military called Marty. Just checking up on how you're doing, she was told. Oddly, they asked if she had remarried. Days later, she answered a knock at the door. Six government men flashed their IDs. 'Oh my God!' she gasped. 'Porter's alive, isn't he?'

One of Halyburton's favourite Christmases was in 1968, when he and eight other PoWs exchanged imaginary gifts. 'We did anything to keep us going.' Back home, Marty did the same. By then the government had informed her they had evidence that Porter had not died, but instructed her not to divulge that secret. 'This was a bigger shock than when I found out he'd been killed,' she said. 'Here I had thought that he had been saved from capture and torture and now I was learning that probably that was his fate. On the one hand, I was really happy he was still alive. On the other, my worst fears had been realized.'

For a man who had relished the freedom of roaming the woods outside Davidson, North Carolina the beatings, the constant interrogations, the leg irons, the watery soup and moldy bread, the isolation and the bricked-up windows were almost too much to bear. Soon Major Fred Cherry, an F-105 pilot, was dumped in his cell, badly injured. Halyburton fed Cherry, washed him, cleaned his wounds and nursed him back. 'Up until Fred came in, I was concerned about my own situation. I was depressed and feeling pretty sorry for myself. Helping Fred gave me something meaningful in life to do.' Halyburton kept his wits by exercising his body daily. He exercised his mind by imagining life on the outside, imagining what the day was like for his wife and daughter Dabney. After the Hànôi bombing began in July 1966, the torture began. Halyburton had his hands bound behind his back 'like pretzels.' When he refused to talk, restraints were tightened and his arms raised until they nearly popped out of his shoulder sockets.

While at the Zoo 1st Lieutenant Brian Ward was in the 'Pigsty Squadron'. 'Our area was called the 'Pigsty' because when it rained the small courtyard outside our building turned into a mud-hole. While we were locked up we passed the time by playing cards and holding a German class. One individual in our group was a qualified German instructor. When they let us out each day we were required to make coal balls and sweep the courtyard. They have a very poor grade of coal in North Viêtnam; it is real soft. Coal balls are made by wetting the coal and then forming them into balls, which in turn were allowed to dry and harden. These were used as fuel to cook the food and boil water. After making coal balls, we were sometimes allowed to play volleyball and mingle with prisoners in other sections of the camp. While we were mingling or playing volleyball we were watched very closely by the guards. Due to our location in the camp we were the C-141 watch. Every time a scheduled release was made, we manned the lookout for the C-141s going into Giá Lâm. When we spotted one coming in or heard the big turbines whining we would alert the rest of the camp. It was a great feeling to see those big silver birds floating in and knowing that some fellow PoWs were going home. Then on 28 March it was our turn to board the C-141s. That had to be one of the most beautiful sights I have ever seen.'

Unrestricted use of air warfare had finally forced the North's hand. When the Communists indicated their desire for a peace settlement on 30 December, the bombing above the 20th Parallel was halted. Nasmyth recalled how the men endured a very violent two weeks that ended as quickly as they had begun. 'After we bombed Hànôi, the Viêtnamese decided they'd had enough, so they signed the Paris Peace Accords on 3 January 1973.'

One of the stipulations of the accord was that it had to be read to all the prisoners, so they were marched outside the Hànôi 'Hilton', where someone read the whole thing to them - in Viêtnamese. 'None of us understood two words of it and it took them about an hour to read,' Nasmyth recalled, adding that an interpreter eventually read it in English.

'Approximately 300 men were released.' says John 'Spike' Nasmyth. 'For most this was the first chance they'd had to see each other. Inside the prison, they had never been allowed to all be together. My big worry the whole time was that I'd wake up from a dream. Even the day I was released, I kept poking myself, saying 'don't wake up man'. When I was on that C-141 Starlifter and flew out of there, I was still thinking it was a dream. But it wasn't.'

When Colonel Fred V. Cherry was released after more than seven years as a prisoner of war, he came home to find that his wife, who had deserted him, had been paid a total of $121,998 by the Air Force - his salary, his subsistence allowance, his flight pay and his savings.

Porter Halyburton's only regret was: 'In the end, we didn't accomplish what we set out to accomplish. We didn't ensure the freedom of the South Vietnamese people.'

Despite the Peace Accords, for the first half of January 1973 bombing missions and the fighting continued south of the 20th Parallel and American pilots were permitted to cross the parallel in pursuit of North Viêtnamese aircraft attacking B-52s and other US aircraft. At 0230 hours on 8 January 1973, this resulted in the destruction of the 137th and last USAF victory of the Viêtnam War. Captain Paul D. Howman of Wooster, Ohio and his WSO, 1st Lieutenant Lawrence W. Kullman of Hartley, Delaware in 'Crafty One' of the the 4th TFS, 432nd TRW were leading a flight of two fighters on a MiGCAP in Route Package 3, eighty miles southwest of Hànôi when they received a warning from 'Red Crown' steaming in the Gulf of Tonkin, providing radar coverage for the fighters. 'Crafty One' ingressed North Viêtnam through the 'Gorilla's Head' and established their CAP about seventy miles southwest of Hànôi. Howman recalled: 'About five minutes after arriving on station, we were advised by 'Red Crown' that a MiG-21 was airborne out of Phúc Yên and was heading southwest toward the inbound strike force. They vectored us northwest and told us he had levelled at 13,000 feet. Passing through [a heading of] north, we picked him up on radar at about sixty miles. We were able to follow him most of the way in as the range decreased. At about thirty miles, I called 'Crafty Two' and we jettisoned our centreline tanks. We descended to 12,000 feet at 400 knots, still taking vectors and obtained a visual contact with the MiG's afterburner plume at ten nautical miles and a full system radar lock-on at six nautical miles. I called him out to the backseater and put the pipper on him. At six miles Lieutenant Kullman got a good full-system radar lock-on. The range was about four miles and overtake 900+ knots when I squeezed the trigger. The missile came off, did a little roll to the left and tracked toward the 'burner plume.' It detonated fifty feet short of his tail. I squeezed another one off at two miles range. This one just pulled some lead and then went straight for the MiG. It hit him in the fuselage and the airplane exploded and broke into three big flaming pieces.' [17] After determining there were no more MiGs in the area 'Crafty' returned to orbit for their remaining CAP period. They returned to base without further incident.[18]

Medford, Oregon's Lieutenant James A. Wise did not know that when he and his pilot Lieutenant Victor T. Kovaleski and Lieutenant (jg) Patrick 'Pat' Arwood and Ensign Lynn Oates in another F-4B of VF-161 launched from the deck of the USS *Midway* on 12 January that he would help make history. Over the air control radio Wise heard the unthinkable: a MiG-17 was over the Gulf of Tonkin while a

Viêt Công delegation sat at the peace table in Paris. 'I couldn't believe it,' said Wise, who served two stints in Viêtnam: March to November 1971 and April 1972 to March 1973. 'There were only two other times when the North Vietnamese sent fighters over the Gulf of Tonkin because they knew the sophistication of our aircraft.' Little did they know they would accomplish the 197th and final MiG victory of the war. 'It's a testament to our superior training that we were able to do what we did because MiGs turned so fast and if they didn't want to fight, they'd go and you'd never see them.' Wise remembered flying through overcast skies, the hot humidity heavy on his face. 'We caught up with the MiG,' Wise said. 'It saw us and rolled behind us. Then, it turned right and got in front of us. We hit it with a Sidewinder, which hit the left tail. The second missile hit the tailpipe and the pilot ejected.' Later, Wise found out the MiG had been targeting a C-130 in the Gulf of Tonkin.[19] Because of the actions of Wise and the other pilots, the Air Force crew escaped attack by the MiG. The pilot was found dead in the Gulf of Tonkin. 'You have an empty feeling,' Wise said. 'You know you did what you had to do, but you know you shot somebody down.'

Two days later while escorting a 'Blue Tree' photographic reconnaissance mission near Thành Hóa Kovaleski and his RIO, Ensign Dennis Plautz was shot down by 85mm anti-aircraft artillery approximately ten miles south of their objective. The aircraft began leaking fuel and after flying offshore, the crew ejected. (It was the 4,181st US aircraft lost in the war). Both men were rescued by helicopter.[20]

All air operations were due to end at midnight when a cease-fire that had already been announced, made 27 January 1973 the last day of combat operations. That Friday morning, Ernie Christensen met Commander Harley Hubert Hall, 36, of Vancouver, Washington, the exec of the VF-143 'Pukin' Dogs' briefly on the flight deck of the USS *Enterprise*. They reflected on what would be the final combat mission of the Viêtnam War. Hall, a 1955 Evergreen High graduate and a 1957 Clark College grad, who had commanded the 'Blue Angels' flight team for two years and Christensen, who wound up as commander of the USS *Ranger* before retiring as a rear admiral, had never tested their skills against MiG jets. Christensen reminded his friend that Hall's only kill was a 'Buffalo Hunter,' an unmanned US reconnaissance aircraft. 'We never got our MiGs, did we?' Christensen said in their brief conversation. 'Harley Hall said, 'No, we never did.'

'I said it's hard to believe that this is it,' Christensen told Hall. 'He looked at me and he was really mellow. He said, 'Yeah, we're done after today.' He was really quiet.'

That was the last time Christensen saw Harley Hall alive. He took off in F-4J 155768 with Lieutenant Commander Phillip Allen Kientzler in the back seat and was shot down by AAA near Quảng Trị. They were pulling up on their third pass during the bombing a cluster of trucks on a road about eight miles north of the city when the Phantom, codenamed 'Taproom 113', was hit and caught fire. Both men ejected at 4,000 feet after the flying control system failed, leading to loss of control. They were seen to land 100 feet apart near a village on an island in the Dam Cho Chữa and Cửa Viêt Rivers. 'Al' Kientzler, a veteran of over 500 combat missions, was hit by heavy ground fire while in his chute and was wounded in one leg. He was fortunate to survive. Earlier that morning he had seen the two man crew of an Air Force OV-10A FAC destroyed by a shoulder-launched SA-7 fired from a force of about thirty Viêt Công and both men were shot and killed as they parachuted down. Commander Hall was seen to be moving about and to discard his parachute but later, in prison, when Kientzler asked his guards about his pilot he was told he had been killed.[21]

'It was a killing field that day,' said Christensen. 'On the previous day I was working that same area and we caught two boats going across a river. We killed twelve to fourteen of them and they probably were really pissed with US air.'

A Presidential order halted all bombing of North Viêtnam and on 29 January the Viêtnam cease-fire went into effect. More F-4 Phantoms were lost than any other type in service with any nation in the war in South-East Asia; a total of 445 Phantoms and 321 aircrew with another 135 men taken prisoner. The USN lost 71 F-4s (five to enemy aircraft, thirteen to surface-to-air missiles and 53 to AAA and small arms fire) in combat and 54 in operational accidents. The Marines lost 72 F-4s in combat (only one to a MiG, 65 to AAA and small arms fire and six in mortar or sapper attacks on their bases) and 23 in operational accidents.

The USAF, USN and USMC could at least draw some solace from the fact that the final intensive campaign had persuaded Hànôi to seek an end to the war and conclude a peace treaty. USAF F-4 crews were credited with 107.5 MiG victories. Navy F-4 crews were credited with the destruction of 57 MiGs June 1965-January 1973.

Although all US ground forces were withdrawn from South Viêtnam, air raids into neighbouring Cambodia and Laos continued until August 1973. Both countries then fell to the Communists and the North turned its attentions to the final take-over of South Viêtnam. Inevitably, the South, now without US military support, collapsed under the full might of the Communists' spring offensive. On 12 April 1975 the American Embassy in Sàigòn was evacuated and 287 staff flown to carriers offshore. F-4s and F-14 Tomcats provided air cover during the final evacuation of South Viêtnam. On 29 April 900 Americans were airlifted by the Navy to five carriers. Next day Sàigòn was in Communist hands and the South was under the control of North Viêtnam. [22]

Endnotes Chapter 8

1   Rudloff was released on 28 March 1973 and later became an F-14 Tomcat instructor pilot. Commander Blackburn is presumed to have been killed either during or soon after capture. His remains were returned to the USA on 10 April 1986. Hobson.

2   The incident is described in detail in Cunningham's book *Fox Two*.

3   Adapted from an article that first appeared in *Air Power at Sea: A Century of US Naval Aviation*.

4   Both men were released from Hanoi on 28 March 1973. Kittinger finally retired from the Air Force in 1978.

5   *Lt. Bags MIG19 On 1st Mission, Cures Nervousness* by Donald Bremner, *Pacific Stars and Stripes* 27 May 1972.

6   In February 1980 the Department of the Navy changed Lieutenant Commander 'Ratso' Doyle's status to 'Presumed Killed in Action'. His remains were returned in July 1985.

7 149457 has been on display at the Hinsdale American Legion Post since November 2002.

8 Lieutenant Colonel Sharp had been shot down during a Wolf FAC mission in southern Laos on 3 December 1969 in an F-4D. He and his backseater escaped and were eventually recovered by a USAF SAR helicopter.

9 George Nolly is a retired Air Force pilot and retired from United Airlines as a B777 Captain and is the author of the *Hamfist* novel series, available at Amazon in Kindle and printed formats.

10 A raid on Kép ran into trouble when it was engaged by several MiGs. F-4E 66-0367 of the 4 TFS, 366 TFW at Takhli from the chaff-escort flight was hit by an 'Atoll' missile fired by a MiG-21 at about 10,000 feet 15 miles northeast of Kép. Captain James D. Kula and Captain Melvin K. Matsui ejected a few moments later when it was realised that their burning aircraft was no longer responding to the controls. Kula and Matsui were soon captured. They were released on 29 March 1973. Horner.

11 Refers to detecting, identifying and locating the target (MiG) in enough detail so that the pilot can fire the missile. Unable to track the MiG visually, the pilot wants this acquisition to be automatically picked up on radar.

12 Captain Tibbett and William Stone 'Buddy' Hargrove were killed on 21 November 1972 when their Phantom crashed following a control failure during a training sortie over Thailand. 'Buddy' was engaged to be married when he returned home from South East Asia.

13 Above Ground Level

14 *MiGs Over North Vietnam: The Vietnam People's Air Force in Combat, 1965-75* by Roger Boniface (Stackpole Books). The first F-4E was reportedly hit by an AAM from a MiG-21during a MiGCAP mission in search of a F-111 crew Southwest of Hànôi. The second was shot down by a MiG-21 30 miles west of Hànôi.

15 Hobson.

16 Adapted from the transcript of an interview with Michael Thomas Burns by R. Stuart.

17 Their victim was Hoàng Cường, who failed to eject and was killed. *MiGs Over North Vietnam: The Vietnam People's Air Force in Combat, 1965-75* by Roger Boniface (Stackpole Books).

18 See *The Tale of Two Bridges; and The Battle for the Skies Over North Vietnam* by Major A. J. C. Lavalle USAF, editor, Office of Air Force History, Washington DC. Howman and Kullman's Phantom (F-4D-29-MC 65-0796) served another seventeen years before being retired. Today, it is on display at William E. Dyess Elementary School, Abilene, Texas.

19 Senior Lieutenant Lưu-Kim-Ngọc, 28, was listed as KIA on that date. *MiGs Over North Vietnam: The Vietnam People's Air Force in Combat, 1965-75* by Roger Boniface (Stackpole Books).

20 Their Phantom - 153068 - had shot down a MiG-19 on 18 May 1972 when flown by Lieutenant Henry A. 'Black Bart' Bartholomay and Lieutenant Oran R. Brown.

21 Kientzler was the last Navy aviator to be taken prisoner. The last Navy Phantom aviators killed were Lieutenant Allyn Duensing and Lieutenant (jg) Roy Elbert Haviland when their F-4J was one of two from VF-21 on the *Ranger* that collided in mid-air during a BARCAP mission on 30 January. The other crew survived. On 26 May 1973 F-4D 65-0645 of the 31st TFW, one of two Phantoms flying an armed reconnaissance mission along Route 13, was shot down over Cambodia during an attack on a bridge near Kratié. Both crew survived although the pilot's ejection seat failed and he had to manually jettison the canopy, which then allowed the seat to fire.
F-4E 67-0374 of the 4th TFW attached to the 8th TFW was the last US aircraft lost to enemy action when it was shot down by ground fire on a strike mission in Cambodia on 16 June. Captain Samuel Blackmar Cornelius, 30, and 27-year old Captain John Jackie 'JJ' Smallwood call sign 'Wolf' were killed. Sam Cornelius was on his third tour having flown over 360 combat missions.

22 At war end Phantoms remained the only fighter aircraft in service with the Fleet Marine Force until the arrival of the first F/A-18 Hornets in January 1983. The last F-4Ss were finally phased out early in 1989, the last being VMFA-134 at MCAS El Toro, California, which received F/A-l8As in spring 1989. In the Marine Air Reserve F-4Bs were first delivered in December 1973 to VMFA-321 at NAF Washington. F-14As progressively replaced F-4Bs and F-4Js in most deployable squadrons except the six squadrons assigned to the older and smaller CVAs' USS *Midway, Franklin D. Roosevelt* and *Coral Sea*, which were eventually re-equipped with F-4N/S Phantoms. On 24 March 1986 VF-151 and VF-161, the last active duty carrier-based squadrons, were launched from Midway for the last time. The last Phantoms in reserve service were replaced by F/A-18s in 1990-91.

Chapter 9

Keeping the Bear at Bay

Fundamental to any nation's air defence requirements is the need to monitor all air traffic so that any irregular aircraft movements can be highlighted. So far as Britain's defence needs are concerned, this monitoring is achieved by the air and ground based radar systems of the UK and NATO, closely co-ordinated with Civil Air Traffic authorities and interlinked by comprehensive data analysis and communications systems. If an aircraft is picked up by the air defence sensors and cannot be identified by routine means it must then be visually identified to establish its bona fides - a task fulfilled by the RAF by scrambling a Quick Reaction Alert (Interceptor) or QRA(I) aircraft to intercept the unknown aircraft. Once or twice in a year, such a scramble may result from a fault in the air traffic notification system, but most of the unknown tracks appear over the South Norwegian Seas, north of the Faeroes and are intercepted by a Phantom or Lightning fighter, supported by airborne refuelling often many miles out to sea. These unknown tracks, accounting for as many as six scrambles a week in 1981, invariably turn out to be Russian military aircraft going about their lawful business over international waters. Nevertheless, NATO air defences must be continuously vigilant to ensure that any intrusion into national airspace is deterred. This article presents an account of a typical QRA(I) sortie and is written by a pilot on 43 Squadron, which flew Phantom FG.Mk.1s from RAF Leuchars.

RAF *Yearbook* 1982. During peacetime, unannounced and uninvited Soviet reconnaissance aircraft frequently pass through and operate within the UK ADR. Aircraft of 11 Group are charged with identifying and shadowing these aircraft within the UK ADR. Within minutes of an 'intruder' being detected, one or two fighters can be winging their way towards the visitor - not in anger, but as what may be termed the 11 Group UK ADR escort service. The fighters will observe the behaviour of the Russians, collect visual and photographic reminders of their visit - for later evaluation by intelligence officers - and ensure that they eventually leave the ADR. This role is carried out unceasingly by the QRA or Quick Reaction Alert Force, 24 hours a day, 365 days a year, in fair weather or foul for an average of 200 incursions annually.

'Mission 40', Vector 340, climb to flight level 350, to CAP 'Lima Echo Charlie', call Buchan on fighter stud 44, Scramble! Scramble! Scramble!'

The still night air is rent apart by the whine of two Rolls-Royce Spey jet engines starting up as the pilot, navigator and ground crew work feverishly to get the Phantom fighter ready for take-off inside the 5-minute time limit. '40 scramble taxi?'

'40 clear taxi for runway 09, QFE 1008.'

'The Phantom taxies from its lair at the end of the runway, the pilot calls '40 take off?' and is cleared by the airfield controller one mile away in his glass-topped air traffic control tower. The pilot swings the aircraft onto the runway and, with all pre-flight checks complete, pushes the twin throttles 'through the gate' and up to the maximum reheat position. Any lingering idea that this is just a quiet agricultural stretch of the East Scottish coast is now shattered by the enormous roar of the Phantom at full combat power as it thrusts itself down the mile and a half of concrete on two thirty-foot streams of yellow flame.

'As soon as the aircraft is safely airborne the pilot banks hard round onto the vector given during the scramble message and continues climbing to 35,000 feet. Meanwhile, the navigator is quickly bringing the radar into operation to search the sky ahead.

'Buchan, this is Mission 40 heading 340, climbing to flight level 350, radar and weapons serviceable.'

'So, barely four minutes after receiving the order to scramble, a Royal Air Force Phantom of 43(F) Squadron is beginning its long and lonely transit 500 miles north to the area known as the Iceland-Faroes Gap to intercept another unidentified intruder.

'The Quick Reaction Alert (Interceptor) Force, in service abbreviation QRA(I), keeps four fully-armed fighter aircraft at the highest peacetime readiness state, for 24 hours a day, 365 days a year. RAF Leuchars in Fife holds Northern QRA(I) with at least two Phantoms all the year round. In the south, QRA(I) is held alternately by RAF Binbrook (Lightnings), RAF Coningsby (Phantoms), both in Lincolnshire and RAF Wattisham (Phantoms) in Suffolk. These three southern bases share the task of providing at least two fighters all the year round.

'To support these fighters, Victor K.2 air-to-air tankers are always available at a high readiness state, in order to keep the Phantoms or Lightnings airborne as long as required - sometimes up to seven or eight hours. These Victors are based at RAF Marham in Norfolk and will soon be supplemented by the VC-10s modified from their civilian roles to serve as tankers, which will greatly extend the endurance of the United Kingdom's fighter force.

'In the north of Scotland, near Elgin, RAF Lossiemouth is the home of the RAF's Airborne Early Warning (AEW) force of Shackleton AEW Mk.2s. These Shackletons are capable of travelling great distances and providing radar cover over large areas which are beyond the range of land-based radar sites and can control the fighters to intercept targets as an airborne radar-equipped operations centre. The Shackletons will be replaced in the coming years by AEW Nimrods, which will give a multi-fold increase in the UK's air defence capability.

'Of course, Phantoms or Lightnings would never be scrambled if targets were not detected in time, so a chain of long-range radar sites exists from Iceland to Norway and down through Europe. On a typical QRA sortie, approaching aircraft will have been tracked for many miles before they are finally detected by UK mainland radar sites.

'The role of QRA(I) is to protect the integrity of the piece of airspace allocated to the UK by NATO. As a result, any unidentified or potentially hostile track in what is known as the United Kingdom Air Defence Region (UKADR) is intercepted by an RAF fighter, which will then escort the aircraft, known in Air Force jargon as 'trade', until it either leaves the UKADR or is no longer considered a threat.

'To keep all these RAF resources permanently ready for action is no easy task, but it is considered to be essential to prove to any potential aggressor that the country intends to defend itself and be seen to be capable of doing so - yet another form of deterrence.

'Mission 40' to Tanker 56, request join.'

'Our Phantom has now been joined on its transit north by a Victor tanker scrambled from RAF Marham. '40 clear join.'

The Phantom pilot eases his 25 tons of aeroplane behind the huge Victor, from which dangles a 50 feet fuel hose. To make contact with this hose is like hitting 'double tops' in darts every throw - only the board is bobbing up and down! Lights on the Victor illuminate to show that contact can be made and with tiny control movements the pilot nudges up and into the refuelling basket on the end of the hose. With only an eerie glow from the luminous cat's eye beads on the basket's rim, the navigator has talked the pilot in and now both can relax a little as the vital fuel exchange proceeds, between aircraft 15 feet apart, 35,000 feet up and travelling at 500 mph.

Once the refuelling is complete, the fighter gently drops back clear of its own airborne petrol station and then continues north to its pre-briefed combat air patrol (CAP) position. As many as six air-to-air refuels can be required on a long-range QRA sortie, making this one of the most demanding of all flying skills.

RAF Leuchars sits on the northern shore of the Eden estuary in Fife. On the other bank a mile away the visiting golfers to St Andrews can hear Phantoms on routine training missions, but most will be unaware of the role of the grey hangar-like building at the end of the runway. This is the 'Q-shed', which houses RAF Leuchars primary peacetime task - two menacing looking Phantoms fully fuelled and armed and waiting only for the word to go.

The Phantom is getting old now but is still better equipped to do the job of defending the UK from air attack than any other fighter, apart perhaps from the US Navy's F-14 Tomcat and, soon, our own Tornado Air Defence Variant. The Phantom's major advantages over other types are its pulse doppler radar associated with four Sparrow or Skyflash radar guided air-to-air missiles, giving a look down, shoot down capability; four heat-seeking Sidewinder missiles; a highly accurate gun pod and, most important of all, a two-man crew which spreads the work load and ensures greater mission success and survivability - very important when, as now, we are outnumbered.

The Q-shed is big enough for only two Phantoms and their paraphernalia to keep them 'gassed and oiled' at permanent readiness. The eight missiles on each aircraft are armed and the safety locks removed, only the Pilot's Master Arm switch and a trigger press being required for a missile launch. Next to the shed, in a connected bungalow-type building, are the two crews and seven engineers waiting for the scramble order. Each crew of pilot and navigator shares a bedroom and the two crews share a small lounge with a TV and magazines. They all remain in the shed in their flying kit, minus life jacket and helmet, for a 24-hour period of duty, a third crew being nominated as a reserve but waiting at home for a phone call that can have them rapidly airborne if needed. The six airmen ground crew and their Senior Non-Commissioned Officer are in the same building but have a separate lounge and two bedrooms where they spend a seven-day duty period;

air and ground crews share the same simple kitchen.

The flying kit the aircrews wear is hot, bulky, uncomfortable and very expensive, but all necessary to protect their lives in a rapid decompression at 40,000 feet or in the event of an ejection into the icy waters of the North Atlantic.

The two resident squadrons at Leuchars, 43(F) 'The Fighting Cocks' and 111 Squadron, split the year into two-three week segments and alternate QRA duties over the whole year. Each squadron will hold either Christmas or New Year QRA but swop round the following year. Both squadrons, like all the other QRA(I) squadrons, have a distinguished history dating back to World War One and there is much friendly rivalry in the messes.

'Shackleton 66 this is Mission 40 on CAP in Mike Lima Echo Charlie, flight level 350, looking 040°.'

'40 this is 66, your trade bears from you 050° at 150 miles.'

'40 Roger.'

One hour after take-off our Phantom has transited under a canopy of stars to a position 500 miles north of Leuchars, half-way between Iceland and the Faeroes. From the dark and cramped confines of the Shackleton AEW, a radar operator gives the fighter crew the information they need to find the intruding Soviets.

'40 your trade is now 050° at 120 miles, tracking 230°, height unknown.'

In the Phantom, the navigator is searching the sky ahead with the electronic beam of the radar hoping to catch an early 'pick-up' in order to give himself enough time to direct the pilot into a perfectly controlled intercept. A late radar pick up often means a rushed intercept which puts more strain on the crew.

'Mission 40, your trade has turned west and bears 040° at 100 miles.' This means that the intruders have altered course and now the Phantom navigator has to work out a different intercept pattern.

'Roger Shackleton 56, 40 is now vectoring 020° for intercept.' The navigator has made his counter move and hopes that if the trade maintains its course he will pick up the tell-tale 'blips' on his radar scope in a few minutes. Still, he searches the huge area of sky ahead of the Phantom, from sea level to 60,000 feet. The crew together maintain an 'air picture' in their heads of what is going on around them: where the 'trade' is now; where the Shackleton and tanker are; what range it is to base, the nearest diversions and what their weather is like; how long before the fuel gets too low and they have to air-refuel again and a multitude of other considerations.

'40 in contact two targets bearing 035°.'

'Roger 40, you are clear to investigate. Check your weapon switches are safe.'

Interpreting the information displayed to him on the radar scope, the navigator tells the pilot his own assessment of the intruders' heading, height and speed and then gives directions to fly that will bring the fighter up behind the target aircraft for an identification.

'They're in five mile trail, which one do you want to go for first?' the navigator asks the pilot.

'We'll take a look at the leader first and then throw an orbit behind the trailer. We'll shadow them both from the rear man until told otherwise,' the pilot's reply is immediate whilst still concentrating on flying as accurately as possible the navigator's requested datums for the intercept and staring vainly out into the night blackness hoping for that glimpse of a flashing navigation light which would be the first visual sign of the unwelcome intruders.

'We're getting close now and I still can't see any lights, we'll have to go for a VID (visual identification profile).' The navigator controls the intercept carefully to roll out two miles behind the lead aircraft and then the pilot and navigator together use the radar to control the VID which, as they close below a mile, requires very precise flying to the exact knot of speed and foot of height. A mistake now would mean a break off and set up again - five minutes and precious fuel wasted.

Through the reflected red glow of his instrument lights on the canopy, the pilot makes out an area of even darker blackness in the night sky just ahead and above the Phantom. At the same time, a gentle rumbling starts and noise can be heard from outside the fighter, both caused by resonance from the blades of eight huge thrashing the cold night air and driving the mighty bomber forward.

'It's a 'Bear'!'

The intruders that QRA(I) are most regularly called on to intercept are the Tu-95 'Bears' and Tu-16 'Badgers' of the Soviet Long Range Air Force and Soviet Naval Air Force. Occasionally other types such as M-4 'Bisons' and Il-18 'Coots' come down far enough south to be intercepted by QRA fighters.

The Soviet aircraft are practising their war roles of maritime surveillance, anti-shipping, anti-submarine warfare and simulated strike attack against the mainland UK. QRA intercepts provide valuable information on Soviet aircraft and equipment and any changes to the tactics they may employ in a future conflict.

The number of Soviet aircraft in a group requiring intercept varies from singletons to quite large groups at one time. If large numbers of 'trade' penetrate the UKADR several QRA fighters with AEW Shackletons and Victor tankers in support can be involved all at once. Squadrons holding QRA, therefore, have to be able to generate extra armed aircraft if required. The Soviets are no respecters of Western culture and the UKADR has been known to be full of 'trade' with many fighters airborne even on Christmas and Easter holidays.

'Shackleton 66 this is 40, we are in company with the lead aircraft which is identified as a Bear Delta.'

The pilot now has to hold the Phantom as steady as possible just underneath the Bear while the navigator looks through the magic green eye of the hand held image intensifier to discern any unusual features of this particular aircraft. This is a maritime surveillance aircraft and its number is recorded to be passed on for intelligence analysis. If the intercept had taken place during daylight the navigator would have taken photographs of the Bear which again would have been forwarded to the intelligence services after landing.

'40 is departing the lead aircraft and going to identify the rear.'

After flying an orbit the Phantom rolls out two miles behind the rear aircraft of the Soviet pair and the same procedure for an identification is followed - again it's a 'Bear Delta' maritime surveillance bomber.

'40, this is Shackleton 66; you are to RTB (return to base).'

The Phantom now leaves the 'Bears' as they exit the UKADR and the crew decides whether any fuel is required from the Victor to get them safely home with enough to divert to another airfield if they cannot land back at Leuchars because of poor weather.

'Leuchars tower, Mission 40 'finals' gear down to land.'

'40 clear land, wind 080° eight knots.'

As the dawn is beginning to break the Phantom screams in over the airfield fence and touches down on the runway with a flurry of grey smoke from the tyres. The pilot taxies back to the Q-shed as alarm clocks all over the country are beginning to wake others to a new day's work. As the weary crew unstrap from their rigid ejection seats after several trussed hours and climb down the aircraft ladders the engineers begin busily preparing the Phantom to be ready to go again to meet the next intruder.

After writing their reports, handing in any film used and checking their Phantom after turn-round, the pilot and navigator wait for the 0830 hours crew changeover. As others are normally on their way to work, Mission 40 is on its way home to bed after a normal 'day at the office' on the Quick Reaction Alert (Interceptor) Force.

In the Mediterranean in March 1966 Lieutenant John Newlin USN, who flew the McDonnell F-3H Demon and the F-4B Phantom and also accrued flight time in the F-8D Crusader and the F-14 Tomcat, flew 'eye to eye with the Bear' while operations officer of VF-74 'Bedevillers' aboard the carrier *Forrestal*.

'After a long deployment in the Mediterranean Sea, the *Forrestal* set a course for its home port, in Norfolk, Virginia. As soon as we'd cleared the Strait of Gibraltar, the ship went on 'Bear Watch.'

'Bear' is NATO's designation for the Soviet Tupolev Tu-95, a large strategic bomber, sometimes armed with missiles but primarily used for electronic surveillance. Powered by four Kuznetsov NK-12 engines driving contra-rotating propellers, the Bear is an unusually loud airplane: The tips of the blades on those propellers rotate at supersonic speed, creating an unholy racket. The 'Bear' went into service in 1956 and the design remains in use by the Russian Air Force even today. 'Bear Watch' was a mission requiring two VF-74 F-4 Phantoms, two VMF-451 Marine F-8 Crusaders, a VFP-62 F-8 photo aircraft and a VAH-11 A-3 tanker. All were manned during the daylight hours on the flight deck. The Phantoms and the Crusaders were hooked into the ship's catapults, ready to launch within five minutes of the order. Our flight crews manned the 'Alert Five' birds on the catapults for an hour at a time. Each evening, it was my job to write and post the schedule for the next day's 'Alert Five' crews.

'One evening I was in the squadron ready room making out the next day's schedule when the officer in charge of the *Forrestal's* highly classified Supplemental Radio section dropped in. We were both bachelor lieutenants; we'd become buddies exploring the bars and cafes of La Rambla in Barcelona, Spain. He told me two Soviet 'Bears' were expected in the vicinity of the *Forrestal* around noon the next day. They would take off from Murmansk, Russia, just before dawn and would refuel over the Faroe Islands before continuing south to overfly the *Forrestal*. Unable to resist the chance to spot a 'Bear' with my own eyes, I scheduled myself and radar intercept officer Nick Estabrook, one of the squadron's best F.4 backseaters, for the 12 pm to 1 pm 'Bear Watch'.

'The next day, Nick and I climbed into our F-4B just before noon. The Phantom was armed with two AIM-9 Sidewinder heat-seeking missiles and two AIM-7

Sparrow radar-guided missiles. In the cockpit on the deck, time passed slowly. I began to worry that either the Bears were late or the intelligence on their flight was wrong.

'Then, with just ten minutes remaining on our watch, our commanding officer walked up to our aircraft. As he approached, the air boss called out on the flight deck public address system, 'Rank has its privileges, John!' My CO. looked up at me and asked 'Would you like to be relieved early, John?' Ha! Apparently, he didn't have the nerve to order me out of the cockpit. Something was up.

'I politely refused and I will never forget the sixty seconds or so that followed. The skipper didn't know what to do. He stood there on the flight deck, shifting his weight from foot to foot. When the order 'LAUNCH THE ALERT FIVE' came booming from the PA, Nick and I closed our canopies, I started both engines and we were off. See ya, Skipper!

'The rules of engagement were very strict: We were to intercept the lead 'Bear' as close to 100 miles from the ship as possible. Nick turned on the radar and we made contact with the 'Bears' immediately. The blips on Nick's scope were so large they looked like bananas, he told me. He skillfully guided us through an intercept course that placed us on the starboard side of the lead 'Bear' 98 miles from the Forrestal. Our wingman was positioned on the second Bear, which was in a 1.5-mile trail from its leader. The Marine F-8s remained clear. But one A-3 tanker pilot decided to get a closer look.

'The Tu-95 has a pair of large, Plexiglas blisters located at the rear of the fuselage, under the horizontal stabilizers. As we pulled up alongside the 'Bear', I noticed in the blister a crewman with a large, folding bellows camera on a tripod. He began signalling with his hands - it was evident that he wanted me to position our aircraft for a photo-op. I played along and when our F-4 was in the optimal position, the crewman ducked under the camera hood. He emerged seconds later and gave me a vigorous thumbs-up.

'Ironically, while the 'Bear' crewman was taking our picture, Nick was taking his. The *Forrestal's* intelligence officer had supplied Nick with a state-of-the-art 35mm camera that captured 72 images on a regular 36-frame film cassette. Nick used all 72 frames.

'The lead 'Bear' was a variant known as a 'Bear-B'. The 'Bear' in trail was a 'Bear-D', an electronic surveillance version distinguished by two long pods located on either side of the fuselage, just ahead of the tail section. It was obvious the D's mission was to analyze the radar and communications signals from the *Forrestal* and its airborne aircraft.

'After the photo-op, I pulled up close and adjacent to the 'Bear's outboard engine. Unknown to me, the A-3 tanker pulled up close on our starboard wing. I call the photograph above 'The Sandwich.' Nick was unnerved that our aircraft was tightly sandwiched between two very large and less manoeuvrable ones. It bothered me less because I had to focus on maintaining our position on the 'Bear' and I couldn't see how close that A-3 was. Every time I look at that photo I wonder: If I had lost control and collided with the 'Bear', would that have triggered WWIII?

'The risk of that mishap was actually quite low. I'd had plenty of experience flying close wing on another aircraft. One thing I distinctly recall was the intense vibration of the canopy when I positioned my head directly abeam of the gap between the 'Bear's counter-rotating propellers.

'About twenty miles from the *Forrestal*, the 'Bears' initiated a slow descent from their 33,000-foot cruising altitude. The pair flew over the carrier at 1,500 feet and then began a slow climb to the north. We stayed with the lead 'Bear' until we were again 100 miles from the *Forrestal*. When I signalled to the copilot that we were breaking away, he dropped his oxygen mask and gave us a big Russian grin and a thumbs-up. For about an hour that day, we weren't cold war enemies - just airmen enjoying the shared good fortune of flying some pretty awesome aircraft.'[1]

After the end of the war in the South Atlantic, with Argentina just 350 miles away from the 778 islands of the Falklands, Britain took steps on 17 October 1982 to provide for air defence within the Falkland Islands Protection Zone (FIPZ) by stationing a 29 Squadron detachment of FGR.Mk.2 Phantoms at Mount Pleasant (RAF Stanley). At the time, the air defence variant of the Panavia Tornado was still in development, so that the Phantom was the UK's primary air defence aircraft (supported by two remaining squadrons of Lightnings). To fill the gap in the UK's air defences fifteen ex-US Navy F-4Js in storage in Arizona and the Naval Air Rework Facility at NAS North Island were purchased. After extensive refurbishment they were given the designation F-4S, which was the last variant in service with the US Navy, the only differences being the absence of leading-edge slats and a helmet gun sight.

Air Vice-Marshal Ian MacFadyen CB OBE FRAeS describes his unexpected task, as Officer Commanding 29 Squadron, to provide Phantoms for air defence of the Falkland Islands.

'On 31 March 1982 I stepped into my Phantom FGR2 early in the morning to fly back to my home base, RAF Coningsby, after a month of delightful gunnery practice in sunny Cyprus. When I got home I first heard stories of 'a spot of bother' in the South Atlantic. Although I did not know it then, the next 18 months of my life were to change dramatically.

'Like many others, after the invasion of the Falkland Islands on 1 April, I listened intently to the drama unfolding in the House of Commons in the debate the next morning - a Saturday. There were rapid deployments of ships and some bigger aircraft, but I did not expect much involvement personally as the runway at Port Stanley - at 4,100 feet - was far too short for Phantom operations. It was therefore with some surprise that my Station Commander, Group Captain Wratten (now Air Marshal Sir William Wratten of Gulf fame), told me in his office some two weeks later that if Phantoms were to be involved, it would be my Squadron to go. This was naturally an exciting prospect and we immediately set about planning what should be done by way of operational training, together with the necessary logistic and personnel aspects. The next few months were to be intensive indeed.

'Plans were already in hand to re-take the islands and to enlarge Port Stanley's runway using the US-manufactured AM-2 matting system to enable Phantoms to operate. This was to be a very high priority because of the FGR2's look-down/shoot-down capability which was in 1982 still advanced for its day - and a capability not possessed by the Royal Navy's Sea Harriers; such was the priority for the aircraft's capability that we even considered using the existing runway at Port Stanley as a war measure. However, arrester cables (RHAGs) would clearly be necessary to stop the aircraft from either running off the end of the runway or into the hazardous ditches alongside. Part of our early training, therefore, included arrested landings and flying approaches into the only available 4,000 feet runway - at the British Aerospace airfield at Brough. That runway looked alarmingly short!

'We also set about an intensive period of bringing crews up to a high operational readiness, practising dissimilar air combat training (DACT) with a variety of aircraft including the Mirage, a type in extensive service with the Argentine Air Force. Besides this, we considered options for using the full capabilities of the multi-role Phantom, but opted eventually for air-ground strafe as the only practical additional role to our specialised air defence primary task. For old hands like myself who had only been involved in air-air training previously, the prospect of some 'mud-moving' was exciting.

'Whilst all this was going on, work was set in hand to make improvements to our aircraft. First, the AWG-12 radar got a much needed 'reliability package', but others quickly followed, including the fitment of chaff and flare dispensers. These were very new indeed to the RAF (I recall the first trial fit when the armourer concerned had to don the full fireman's protective clothing!). Next came supplies of the AIM-9L Sidewinder, far more capable than our old AIM-9Gs.

'It was around mid-May, at yet another conference at HQ 11 Group that we learnt of a likely deployment to Ascension Island. This soon became a reality and Squadron markings had to be removed from the aircraft to be deployed. Although the Squadron had some aircraft in the then new grey paint scheme, two more had to be repainted over the weekend before the planned deployment to Ascension Island - quite a task for RAF St. Athan, where the aircraft had to be sent.

'On Monday 24 May 1982 the first two 29 Squadron aircraft made one of the longest non-stop fighter transit flights in the RAF's history on the 4,000-mile flight to Ascension Island. It was to become more of a routine over the next few months. Diversion airfields en route were few and far between and there was no prospect of one at the other end. Ten and a half hours later, the first Phantoms were in the South Atlantic. The detachment immediately set up on Quick Reaction Alert (QRA) in case of an Argentine attack and was under the command of Squadron Leader Roy Trotter (now OC 29 Squadron at Coningsby). The detachment was to remain there, uncertain of its future, for the next five weeks before it returned to the UK once the war was over.

'Events, however, were far from over for the rest of the Squadron, since the next problem was to protect the Falklands in peace from possible further aggression. But first, the runway at Port Stanley had to be prepared for safe peacetime operations. There was nevertheless an urgency about matters, not least because aircraft carriers, with their Sea Harrier and Harrier complements, could only remain in theatre for a limited period. It was, however, not to prove easy to extend the runway and airfield for our use.

'First, the task of clearing the airfield of unexploded ordnance proved formidable and took much longer than anticipated. Secondly, the runway was holed in one place by a 1,000lb bomb dropped on the first Vulcan raid; this was to become a permanent problem due to subsidence of the temporary filling. Thirdly, the runway could only be extended one way - to the West - and this entailed moving a huge tonnage of rock and subsoil in order to make it reasonably level.

Lastly, the planned dispersal area for Phantoms at the end of Runway 27 proved to be such difficult ground that a new site well down the runway had to be found.

'In anticipation of a move early in September, the Squadron once again deployed an element to Ascension Island towards the end of the month; during the month the ground crew and equipment set sail for the Falkland Islands, under the leadership of Warrant Officer Geoff Bland. It was soon evident that plans had been optimistic. The advantage, however, was that it allowed those at Ascension Island to concentrate on some excellent operational flying in perfect conditions. With tanker support, sorties rarely lasted less than four hours and it was not long before six aircraft were clocking up more flying hours than a whole Squadron would normally do in a month.

'The difficulties at RAF Stanley, as it was by now known, kept delaying the deployment further South, not helped by some fierce winter weather. Thus it was not until 1 October that I flew down to RAF Stanley in a Hercules to view the airfield and to meet my people before I was to take the first Phantom south. This proved most valuable because the whole scene had to be seen to be believed. RAF Stanley was totally unlike any airfield I had ever seen. Besides the bleak setting, facilities were crude, but above all the impression was of a tiny airfield; not for us the space we were used to back home. For example, the Harrier dispersal was 10yds from the edge of the runway and my new Phantom dispersal not much more.

'About 5,000 feet of the 6,000 feet of AM-2 matting had been laid at the time of my visit, but the squadron dispersal was anything but complete with no hangars, a few tents and nowhere to park the aircraft. Two weeks later it was to be transformed thanks to the remarkable work both of the Royal Engineers who worked round the clock, backed up by the enthusiasm of the Squadron's advance party who had already been in the South Atlantic for a month. In the interim, it was back to Ascension Island, where the weather, balmy breezes and wonderful flying seemed a far cry from our future location.

'Sunday 17 October 1982 dawned bright and clear on Ascension and the forecast, after a couple of problem days, was good for the Falklands. Six serviceable Phantoms had been prepared for my trip. The aircraft had shown unusually good serviceability in such a benign climate - but today was to be different! Two aircraft went u/s on the pre-flight, the next went u/s on crew acceptance and the fourth, my intended aircraft, had a complete radio failure. With seventeen Victor tankers to support me, all ready to go, these setbacks were becoming increasingly embarrassing, especially with not a little interest from on high.

'Eventually, I climbed into the sixth aircraft and got started with a back-up aircraft ready with me. The story did not stop there because just after take-off the radar in my aircraft failed totally; to complete the saga the inertial navigation system (INAS) motored to 180° South of its own accord at the top of the climb - and we had no TACAN! This might have been a prudent moment to return to Ascension Island, but we had Victors as escort all the way down to the last 1000 miles and my navigator, Squadron Leader Pete Simpson, was a highly experienced Nav Instructor and mental D/R was no problem for him! The sortie subsequently was remarkably uneventful, with nine refuellings.

'After 1½ hour in cloud, having left the last Victor, we heard the first sound on the radio of our welcoming Sea Harriers, who approached to escort us in. It was an unforgettable sight to pop out of cloud in the descent at 18,000 feet into a clear sky with RAF Stanley just below us. Twenty minutes later, after 9¾ hour, we were safely on the ground having made the first arrested landing on the new runway. The welcoming party was huge by Falklands standards with people all around the airfield as far as minefields and the like would allow. One hour later, after a magnificent operational turn-round by the 'boys', Flight Lieutenant Andy Maddox took the aircraft on its first sortie over the islands. During the next three days, further aircraft gradually began arriving and we took over QRA duties from the Royal Navy just four days after we had arrived.

'Flying in the Falklands was certainly difficult. First, there was nowhere else to go, so the weather dominated all we did, as safety was clearly paramount. No more than two Phantoms were allowed to be airborne except in the case of operational need. We nearly always flew with a Hercules tanker airborne to both prolong flight time and to keep us airborne in an emergency; if it was not airborne it was on immediate standby. We invariably intended to land back into one of the five arrester wires straddled across various points of the AM-2 covered runway. Occasionally, if there was a sudden weather deterioration we had to opt for a conventional landing as it took a few minutes to get one aircraft into a cable, clear the runway and then reset it. In such an eventuality, with large ditches, either side of the runway, use of braking had to be done carefully despite the much shorter than normal runway as a burst tyre could have catastrophic consequences. Fortunately, there was usually plenty of wind. It was, however, not always down the runway. I am one of a few who have experienced 50-knot cross wind landings (into the cable I may add) but looking through the side of the cockpit to land was certainly a novel experience.

'Training flying took us out over to the West of the Falkland Islands where we would work with the Royal Navy whose air defence ships were on constant alert. All flying was done with live armament and special rules had to be developed to ensure adequate safety. We found (to our surprise) there was a hole for a safety pin in the trigger which added still further to the safety - and to the need to be fully alert if a real threat emerged. It never did. The Hercules normally operated at medium level but it was not uncommon for AAR operations to be at low level. Refuelling amongst the numerous islands around West Falkland provided views of some superb unspoilt scenery and when the sun shone, bright sandy beaches.

'Besides operating the Phantom we worked with our Harrier colleagues who had recently converted to the air defence role. This, along with affiliation training with the Hercules, provided plenty of training variety. Crews were able to fly about twenty hours per month, roughly at UK levels, but the number of sorties was relatively few because they often lasted over three hours. The adverse weather ensured frequent no flying days, but there was always the constant QRA requirement. Half of the detachment was on some kind of alert and a minimum of four aircraft were on QRA at any one time. This placed great demands on the engineers and those on the station who supported us, but there was little else to do and at least the work prevented boredom.

'The working week was seven days with the occasional rest day (always different). Those on QRA were in comparative comfort, with Portakabins provided; these were the only ones on the site initially apart from the Ops Room. My office was a tent, complete with strip lighting, a purpose built wooden entrance, with corrugated iron door - and cardboard boxes as In/Out trays (the only thing we had fortunately omitted from our deployment pack!).

'Night flying was always testing. I have rarely experienced total darkness and then only really in the South Atlantic where there was not even a light to be seen. One evening Peter Simpson and I were recalled to the circuit via a GCA approach; we were a little disconcerted to see the airfield lights disappear at about twelve miles range and were somewhat alarmed when we went into cloud at 400 feet! Being forced to overshoot because we were still in cloud at 200 feet we were highly relieved to find that half-way down the runway we were back into clear air. This meant we were forced to land in the other direction. We had not been briefed, however, that a 30-knot crosswind had suddenly brewed up, so on my first circuit, I found I could not line up on the runway. It was good to be back on the ground safely a few minutes later. Many of us had similar experiences.

'We had only one incident in the air of note and that was on the day the Secretary of State for Defence, John Nott, visited RAF Stanley. This was a week after our initial deployment. Andy Maddox was sent airborne, in marginal weather, to demonstrate an arrested landing. Having failed to see the runway on his first approach there was already a certain tension when he made the second, but it was with some relief that we saw the Phantom emerging out of the mist. What followed was fairly dramatic. The aircraft arrester hook engaged the wire, but the latter promptly severed under the strain, slicing bits off the tailplane in the process. Fortunately, Maddox managed to stop the aircraft on the runway having wisely decided whatever happened he was going to stay on the ground.

'In the early days, off-duty accommodation was a ship in the middle of Port Stanley harbour. The *Rangatira* [the world's last surviving ship with steam-powered turbo-electric transmission] was a former New Zealand ferry ship which had been hastily converted for operations, complete with a helideck. If you were lucky, you might get a lift from a passing helicopter refuelling in a dispersal immediately next to ours; there were plenty around in those early months. Otherwise, it was a long drive to town, along a road which could only passably be called that, to catch the LSL to the *Rangatira* - one of five ships in the harbour. Such a process could take well over an hour, so helicopter lift procedures had to be developed in case of an alert. I always admired our Harrier cousins because they firmly slept on site - in accommodation that had been honed to perfection over years of field operations!

'During my seven months on those islands, I saw many changes to the airfield and its surrounds. The *Rangatira* was not long used by 29 Squadron (which with a turnover of people became 'Phandet' and later 23 Squadron) before a Swedish Coaster accommodation vessel arrived from the Gulf of Mexico to provide not only much-improved comfort for all but a short land link to the Squadron. The airfield was gradually transformed, roads were constructed and life became more normal.

'I look back on those months leading up to and in the South Atlantic with satisfaction and pride. It was one of the most challenging periods of my life, with certainly the most demanding flying. I got deep fulfilment from not only the work but also from commanding people who were in every way outstanding. The British seem to thrive in adversity, providing ingenuity and good humour just when needed. But that all seems a long time ago now.'

At the time of writing Air Vice Marshal I. D. MacFadyen CB OBE FRAES RAF is Assistant Chief of Defence Staff - Operational Requirements (Air) at the Ministry of Defence.

On 30 March 1983 29 Squadron transferred its Phantoms to 23 Squadron, when it disbanded at Wattisham, reforming the same day at RAF Stanley to replace the Phantom detachment provided by 29 Squadron. On 19 October 1984 74 Squadron reformed at Wattisham on F-4J(UK) Phantoms to fill a gap caused by the need to deploy a UK-based FGR.Mk.2 squadron to the Falklands. (Early in 1991 the F-4J(UK)s were withdrawn and were replaced on 17 January by FGR.Mk.2s released by RAF Leuchars.) On 1 November 1987 29 Squadron became the RAF's first operational Panavia Tornado F.Mk.3 interceptor squadron. With the reduction of the threat in the South Atlantic, on 1 November 1988 23 Squadron was redesignated 1435 Flight, enabling the squadron to return to the UK and reform with Tornado F.Mk.3s at RAF Leeming. 43 Squadron continued operating the FG.Mk.1 Phantom at Leuchars, adding the FGR.Mk.2 version in May 1988 and converting to the Panavia Tornado F.Mk.3 in September 1989. Also at Leuchars, 'Treble One' Squadron began replacing its FG.Mk.1s with the Tornado F.Mk.3 on 31 January 1990. 92 Squadron disbanded on 5 July 1991 and 19 Squadron disbanded at the end of the year. During 1992 56 Squadron, 1435 Flight and the Phantom Training Flight all disbanded, followed on 1 January 1993 by 74 Squadron.

Phantom aircraft were retired and parked at former RAF airfields in East Anglia and beyond, marked with a blue cross to let the satellites of the former Soviet Union verify that the aircraft had been put out to grass.

It was the end of an era.

Endnotes Chapter 9

1   *Air & Space Smithsonian*, January 2015. John Newlin retired from the Navy in 1980.

Chapter 10

The Sword Of David

The F-4 was a large behemoth of an aircraft, fast and strong but not very manoeuvrable. We called the Phantom the Kurnass, or 'Sledgehammer'. When the F-4 arrived in 1969, it was a very hot airplane. It was difficult to reach in our Mirages. The Phantom was a more sophisticated aircraft. It was not easy to fly but it gave you a special feeling when you succeeded. The MiG-21 was a good match for both the Mirage and F-4 in air-to-air combat. Our high rate of success came from our appropriate tactics and training and from the good weapons that the MiGs didn't have, namely the Mirage's two 30mm cannons that ensured destruction if they hit and the Israeli Shafrir and American Sidewinder IR-seeking missiles.
Brigadier General Iftach Spector, who scored twelve aerial victories; eight while flying the Mirage III and four while flying the F-4 Phantom.

Israel had first expressed an interest in acquiring the Phantom in 1965, but the US was not yet willing to sell the fighter to Israel and agreed to provide A-4 Skyhawks instead. But on 1 July 1968 Israel and the US signed the 'Peace Echo' agreement for the supply of fifty F-4Es and six RF-4Es to the Heyl ha'Avir (IAF).[1] To say that they were badly needed would be an understatement. The 1967 Arab-Israeli War, which Israel had emerged victorious, laid the foundation for future discord in the Middle East and massive re-equipment of the Tsvah Haganah le Israel (Israel Defence Force) and the Israeli Air Force followed. In September the Arab states formulated the 'three no's' policy, barring peace, recognition or negotiations with Israel. Egyptian President Gamal Abdel Nasser believed that only military initiative would force Israel's withdrawal from Sinai and hostilities soon resumed along the Suez Canal. By 1969 the Egyptian Army judged itself prepared for larger-scale operations.

On 25 March Israeli crews began training on their new Phantoms. Although the War of Attrition, which Egypt had launched on 8 March, was still going on at the time, the Israeli Air Force sent its best pilots and navigators to the US, headed by the two future F-4 squadron commanders: Avihu Ben-Nun and Shmuel Hetz. On 10 March McDonnell Douglas and Israel Aircraft Industries concluded a licensing and technical assistance agreement. Phantom deliveries began on Friday, 5th September when four F-4Es for Israel landed at Hazor AFB to join the new 201st 'Ha'ahat' ('The One') Squadron, commanded by Shmuel Hetz, a Deputy Commander of an Ouragan squadron during the Six-Day War. Deliveries of the 'Kurnass' (Sledgehammer) as it was called, continued at a rate of four a month, the last aircraft arriving in May 1971. On 23 October 1969, the 69th 'Patishim' ('Hammers') Squadron was reformed at Ramat-David, headed by Avihu Ben-Nun, born in Givat Ada in 1939, who during the Six Day War had destroyed two of the four aircraft he would take down in his career in the IDF.

With the War of Attrition raging along the Suez Canal, the new Phantoms and their crews were only given a short adjustment period before being thrown into the fighting. The first operational Phantom sortie took place on 5 October 1969, a combat air patrol in the southern Sinai led by Shmuel Hetz. On 22 October, only eight weeks after their arrival, the Phantoms flew their first ground attack mission, against an Egyptian SA-2 battery near Abu-Sweir. In November 1969 the IAF initiated operation 'Helem' ('Shock'), in which Phantoms routinely conducted low-level supersonic passes over Cairo in order to demonstrate the IAF's ability to operate unhampered over Egypt. The first such sortie took place on 4 November and these flights continued until January 1970. On 29 January, after a lone Syrian MiG-21 managed to infiltrate Israeli airspace and conduct one such flight over Haifa, Israel responded by sending Phantoms on similar missions over five major Syrian cities.

The War of Attrition was characterized by large-scale shelling along the Suez Canal, extensive aerial warfare and commando raids but the Egyptian Air Force and Air Defence Forces performed badly. Egyptian pilots were rigid, slow to react and unwilling to improvise. On 11 November 1969, the Phantom scored its first kill, an Egyptian MiG-21 downed by Ehud Hankin and Achikar Eyal of 69 Squadron, flying a 201 Squadron aircraft. On 17 November F-4Es attacked a pair of Jordanian radar stations which had provided radar coverage of Israel to the Egyptians and Syrians. Both stations were destroyed for the loss of a single Phantom, once again flown by Ehud Hankin.

According to US intelligence estimates, the War of Attrition cost Egypt 109 aircraft, most in air-to-air combat, while only sixteen Israeli aircraft were lost, most to anti-aircraft artillery or SAMs. The Phantoms spearheaded the IAF's destruction of SAM missile sites, an attempt that lasted right up to the end of the war in August 1970. Large scale attacks took place during late November and on Christmas Day 1969, both resulting in the destruction of the entire Egyptian missile array. These losses were, however, rapidly made good by Soviet assistance and the SAMs soon returned to pose a threat to the IAF.

On 7 January 1970 Israel launched operation 'Priha' ('Bloom') with attacks by Phantoms against camps and military installations in the Nile Valley near Cairo while A-4s attacked artillery and fortifications. The last deep penetration strike by F-4Es took place on 13 April, when the IAF raided SAM sites near Cairo International Airport, bringing the operation's total to 45 such strikes. On 18th and 23rd January and on 8 February the IAF began attacking Egyptian Air Force bases. During this last attack a 69 Squadron F-4E flown by Aviam Sella, born 7 January 1946 in Haifa and Shabtai Ben-Shoa scored the squadron's first kill by downing an Egyptian MiG. As Soviet assistance continued to pour into Egypt, the Egyptians attempted to disrupt these strikes by positioning their SAMs along the IAF's penetration routes. The F-4Es, along with their Dassault Mirage escorts, nonetheless continued their attacks against both the SAM sites and against other Egyptian military targets, such attacks taking place on average once every ten days. On 26 February the F-4Es attacked two SA-2 sites when Egyptian MiGs attempted to intercept them. In the ensuing dogfight, three MiGs were destroyed by the Mirage escort.

MiG-21J interceptors made their appearance in the spring and many battles ensued. In March thirteen MiGs were shot down during the month. On 15 March the first fully operational Soviet SAM site in Egypt was completed, part of three brigades which the Soviet Union sent to Egypt. Israeli Phantoms repeatedly bombed Egyptian positions in Sinai. On 8 April the Israeli Air Force carried out bombing raids against targets identified as Egyptian military installations. A group of military bases about thirty kilometres from the Suez Canal was bombed but in what becomes known as the Bahr el-Baqar incident, Israeli Phantoms attacked a single-floor school in the Egyptian town of Bahr el-Baqar after it was mistaken for a military installation. The school was hit by five bombs and two air-to-ground missiles, killing 46 schoolchildren and injuring over fifty.

On 25 April two Egyptian Air Force Ilyushin Il-28s attacked two Israeli strongholds in the Sinai. Three IAF F-4s were scrambled to intercept the intruders and Shmuel Hetz destroyed one with an AIM-7 Sparrow, the missile's first IAF kill. The second Il-28 was downed by a Mirage. On 16 May an Israeli aircraft was shot down in air combat, probably by a MiG-21. On 30 June Soviet air defences stationed in Egypt shot down two F-4 Phantoms. Two pilots and a navigator were captured, while a second navigator was rescued by helicopter the following night. On 18 May a dozen F-4Es flew a long range strike on Port Said in response to the sinking of an Israeli trawler and the mining of another. After two Egyptian ambushes on 30 May led to the deaths of fifteen Israeli soldiers, the IAF conducted three days of heavy strikes against artillery positions on the western bank of the Suez Canal. Three Egyptian MiGs were destroyed trying to intercept the IAF strike aircraft.

A pair of Phantoms on a mission against a SAM site at Abu-Sweir on 24 June was fired upon by a number of batteries. One of the F-4Es was hit but managed to return safely to base. On 30 June the IAF launched a furious attack on Egyptian defences after it had been discovered that dozens of SAM batteries and hundreds of AAA guns had been advanced the previous night. Two Phantoms were lost on these strikes, both falling prey to Egyptian SAMs. Another Phantom was lost on 5 June when it too was destroyed by a SAM. The IAF broke off its attacks for two weeks in order to rethink its tactics and to come up with new methods to deal with the SAM threat.

On 18 July the IAF resumed its missile suppression strikes, attacking five missile batteries that came within twenty miles of the Canal, this time with new ECM pods supplied by the USA. American experts had suggested a new method of countering the SAMs; high altitude tight formations that would form an electronic barrier against the missiles. This tactic, however, was completely wrong and coupled with the ECM pods' inefficiency proved disastrous to the attacking aircraft as Captain (later Brigadier General) Yoram Agmon, the leader of the 69 Squadron formation recalled: 'In front of me was a formation from the 201st 'Ha'ahat' Squadron, led by Lieutenant Colonel Shmuel Hetz, who was shot down and killed. [His navigator, Menachem Eini was captured].[2] I saw him hit. He was a number of miles in front of me. I saw the missile battery that fired at him. They also fired at us, around fifty to sixty missiles which we evaded safely. I wasn't very worried. I began an attack on the battery that had fired at Hetz. As I approached the battery I saw a missile being launched at me. I told my No. 2 to be prepared, that they were shooting at us from the battery at 10 o'clock. He acknowledged that he saw the battery and the missile. We broke to fly towards the battery, to attack it, as the missile came towards us. Until this time all the missiles that were fired at us were of the SA-2 type, very large and easy to see from a distance; in Viêtnam the Americans called them 'flying telephone poles'. The routine was to break hard when you saw the missile at its normal size; the missile would not be able to follow the turn and would fly on harmlessly. This time they fired a new missile of the SA-3 type, which is smaller and more manoeuvrable. As expected, I saw the missile coming towards me. I saw that when I dived it dived and was drawing a lead to intercept me. I decided to wait until I could see the missile large enough and then I would break to shake it off. But this missile was smaller than the SA-2 of course, and so the break was rather late. It managed to save me from a direct hit but the missile exploded very close to me. The aircraft was entirely sprayed with shrapnel: we found about a thousand holes, some of them right through the cockpit.

'I was able to look out of the Phantom's cockpit through the holes. Some of them were around me and there were tears in my flight suit, but I wasn't really wounded. The aircraft had been hit very hard, however. I said to myself that I would make every effort to avoid being captured. I succeeded in turning the aircraft homewards, on one engine with the other one on fire, at the lowest possible speed and with a number of missiles pursuing us and AAA filling the sky.

'My No. 2 saw the hit but he still had his bombs and decided that he could not jettison his bombs to help me; he continued the attack, bombed the battery and then rejoined me, flying nearby. I didn't have any radio communication with him; I couldn't even speak to my navigator who was sitting behind me. Communicating with signs, I said that we were all right. I had to jettison the armament to make the aircraft lighter. The aircraft jumped as if it had been hit by a missile. The navigator thought that we had been hit again, so I gave him the sign that everything was okay, we were still flying. We managed somehow or other to cross the Canal, flying with all the cockpit lights lit up and one engine on fire. We decided to fly on and land at Refidim, eighty kilometres from the Canal. I don't know how, but we succeeded.

'As we lowered the wheels I saw that we couldn't lower the flaps. I also saw that the aircraft couldn't fly straight at less than 400 kph, about 220 knots. It was plain that the landing would have to be made at this speed. We landed believing that we still had the emergency brakes, the only remaining hydraulic system. But then we found out that this too had been hit. So there was nothing to stop the aircraft on the ground. We touched down at 300-400 kph and the aircraft ran on down the runway at this speed while we sat there, unable to do anything to stop it or keep it on the runway. The mistake we made was not to eject at this stage. This was one of the hardest decisions I've ever made, but after coming all this way to eject now would have been like leaving a friend in trouble.

'We left the runway at a speed of 200 kph and the aircraft ran another kilometre on the ground, passing within a metre or two of ditches, walls, damaged aircraft (MiGs abandoned at Refidim), cannon, AAA, all sorts of things. Finally, the aircraft stopped on a small hill or pile of dirt. The nose wheel broke. We climbed out and saw that we had been even luckier than we thought. When we jettisoned the armament we had forgotten about the missiles under the fuselage. The engine fire had continued to burn and had destroyed the structure around one of the missiles, melting its warhead. It had melted drop by drop as the aircraft ran along the ground.'[3]

West of the Suez Canal on Thursday, 30th July the Egyptian radar site at Sohana in the Gulf of Suez was attacked by 69 and 201 Squadron Phantoms, 110 Squadron Vautours, 113 Squadron Ouragans and 115, 102, and 116 Squadron Skyhawks, encountering no aerial opposition. Once all aircraft had returned to base, Operation 'Rimon ('Pomegranate') 20', which was prompted by the growing Soviet involvement in Egypt, could commence. The aim was to lure MiG-21s flown by Soviet pilots into an ambush using a flight of four Mirage III CJs flying a high-altitude reconnaissance pattern over a known Soviet sector of operations south-west of Suez City as bait. They were positioned above the attacking 'Kurnass' strike aircraft and a second flight of F-4Es of 69 Squadron configured with air-to-air missiles below the attacking F-4Es. Positioned further to the rear were four more Mirage jets. When the Russians failed to respond, the lead section of the Mirage fighters simulating an A-4 'Ahit' ('Eagle') flight profile continued further into Egypt in an attempt to force the Soviets into action. The Soviets finally took the bait and scrambled eight MiG-21s of the 135th Istrebitelnaya Aviatsionnaya Diviziya (IAP, Fighter Air Division) led by Captain Kamencev plus two four ship formations of MiG-21s from Beni-Suef and a large-scale dogfight began. Three Soviet pilots were killed in action. The IAF suffered no losses except a damaged Mirage. A fifth MiG-21 was possibly hit and later crashed en route back to base. Two of the victors were 'Kurnass' crews. Avihu Ben-Nun and his back-seater Shaul Levi destroyed a MiG-21 at incredibly low altitude with an AIM-7. Avihu Ben-Nun recalled: 'Suddenly I and my number 2, along with a lone 117 Squadron Mirage pursued a MiG flying at low level and almost at the speed of sound. As we saw it, the biggest threat was that the 117 pilot would claim our MiG. We launched a Sparrow, though one shouldn't at that altitude and in those conditions, just so that 117 wouldn't get him'. The Mirage pilot was closing into cannon range when the AIM-7 passed him by, struck its target and killing the Soviet pilot.[4] Aviem Sella and Reuven Reshef chased the MiG-21 flown by Captain Georgy Syrkin from 15,000 feet down to 2,000 feet where it was destroyed by an AIM-9D.[5] A fifth Soviet pilot ejected but died in his parachute.

In an interview for the Israeli Press, Aviem Sella said: 'I started looking for a MiG to kill. Finally, found one, its pilot making a right turn, trying to close in on my number one who broke to the right. The MiG left my number one and started chasing me! We stuck together for a while, dropping to about 15,000 feet; at that point, he was only about 150 metres from me. I could see the pilot's helmet clearly. By this time I'd realized the Russian pilot was inexperienced; he didn't know how to handle his aircraft in a combat situation. At 15,000 feet he proved this feat by trying to escape in a steep dive to 7,000 feet. All we had to do was follow him and lock our radar onto him and fire a missile. There was a tremendous explosion but the MiG came out of the cloud of smoke apparently unharmed. That made me mad and I fired a second missile which turned out to be unnecessary. The Russian aircraft had been severely damaged by the first missile. Suddenly it burst into flames and fell apart. By the time the second missile reached it, it wasn't there anymore.'[6] Captain Georgy Syrkin ejected and was rescued. The engagement had lasted a little less than three minutes. As the Soviets could yet scramble more aircraft to the scene, the order for all remaining aircraft to disengage and withdraw was given. While the Mirages headed to Rephidim to refuel prior to their return to their home bases, the 69 Squadron Phantoms made their way directly to Ramat David.

Finally, an American-sponsored ceasefire came into effect on 7 August 1970. Minutes after the cease-fire, Egypt began moving SAM batteries into the zone even though the agreement explicitly forbade new military installations. By October there are approximately one hundred SAM sites in the zone. The end of the War of Attrition did not bring about an end to IAF operations and although the Phantom squadrons spent most of their time in training, some saw combat action. During September 1970 combat air patrols were flown over Syrian armour pushing into Jordan in order to dissuade the Syrian Air Force from intervening. On 18 September 1971, following the destruction of an Israeli Stratocruiser by Egyptian SAMs on 17 September, IAF Phantoms and A-4s attacked SAM batteries along the Suez Canal, enjoying only limited success. 1971 also saw the beginning of Soviet and Arab reconnaissance flights over Israeli territory with the arrival of the MiG-25 'Foxbat'. IAF attempts to intercept these high flyers failed, although Phantoms were routinely launched against them and missiles were fired on a number of occasions. (The MiG-25 overflights only ceased with the arrival of the F-15 in 1976). On 8 January 1972 strikes were conducted against Syrian and Lebanese terrorist camps and on 12 February an Egyptian MiG-21 was shot down attempting to intercept a Phantom reconnaissance flight and the Egyptian Air Force came under orders not to attempt to intercept Israeli fighters. On 9 September 1972, following the massacre of Israeli athletes in the Munich Olympics the F-4s conducted strikes against terrorist positions in Lebanon and Syria. A Syrian SAM battery was destroyed on 9 November, while two Syrian MiG-21s were shot down on 21 November, after another raid on Syrian targets. On 21 February 1973 IAF Phantoms shot down a Libyan Air Airlines Boeing 727 after it infiltrated Israeli airspace and attempted to flee when intercepted by the fighters.

By late September 1973, 127 Phantoms were in service with the IAF. In 1971 24 ex-USAF Phantoms were delivered under 'Peace Echo II' and 'Peace Echo III' and twelve more ex-USAF F-4Es were acquired under 'Peace Patch', while 52 more examples were delivered under 'Peace Echo IV' beginning in 1972. Twenty-four of these were newly built aircraft. These deliveries enabled the formation of 107 'Abirey Hazanav Hakatom' ('Knights of the Orange Tail') Squadron and replacement of the Mirage IIICs in 119th 'Atalef' ('Bat') Squadron. (Under 'Peace Echo V', a further 48 Phantoms were supplied to the IAF, allowing the formation of a fifth Phantom squadron in July 1974 when 105 'Akrav' ('Scorpion') Squadron replaced its ageing Dassault Super Mystère Sa'ars ('Storm') with the newly supplied F-4s). [7]

In a prelude to the Yom-Kippur war, Phantoms and Mirages engaged Syrian MiGs over northern Syria on 13 September 1973 and destroyed twelve of them for the loss of a single Mirage. On Saturday, 6th October the Sinai was once again the scene of conflict between Israel and the coalition of Arab states led by Egypt and Syria, the fifth such occasion. Anticipating that Israel might not be prepared, Egypt and Syria had decided to invade Israel on the holiest day in Judaism. Operation 'Badr' began at 14:00 (Israel time, 15:00 in Egypt) under cover of an artillery barrage and the Egyptian assault force of 32,000 infantry began crossing the Suez Canal in twelve waves at five separate crossing areas to enter the Sinai Peninsula. The IAF conducted air interdiction operations to try to prevent bridges from being erected across the Suez Canal but took losses from Egyptian SAM batteries and the sectional design of the bridges enabled quick repair when hit. Syrian forces meanwhile, crossed ceasefire lines and entered the Golan Heights. F-4s were fully armed to carry out a pre-emptive strike against Egyptian SAM batteries but were prevented from doing so by political reasons, as well as by adverse weather conditions. Prime Minister of Israel Golda Meir had made the controversial decision not to launch a pre-emptive strike for fear of being accused of starting the war but agreed to the mobilization of the entire Air Force and four armoured divisions. The Hey! ha'Avir had 432 aircraft in its inventory, of which Phantoms were the second most numerous aircraft. Israel faced 600 Soviet-supplied aircraft operated by Egypt and 210 by Syria and hundreds of SA-2 'Guideline', -3 'Goa' and -6 'Gainful' SAM missiles, SA-7 'Grail' infrared directed, shoulder launched AA missiles and ZSU-23-4 Shika radar-directed mobile AA guns. The interlocking air defence system was superior even to the belt protecting Hànôi in the Việtnam War. A concentrated air attack by 250 Egyptian aircraft well-coordinated between the Egyptian and Syrian fronts and other services of the Arab armed forces conducted simultaneous strikes against several military targets in Israel. The airfields at Refidim and Bir Tamada were put out of operation.

The first aerial victory of the war came soon after the beginning of Operation 'Badr'. At Ofira Air Base near Sharm el-Sheikh at the southern tip of the Sinai Amir Nachumi and his backseater, Yossi Yavin was one of two F-4 crews in 107 Squadron on quick reaction alert duty. Neither Nachumi, born in Jerusalem in 1945, nor Daniel Shaki, the pilot of the other Phantom were qualified as pair leaders, but when it became clear that war was imminent Nachumi was promoted Lieutenant Colonel on the phone by Squadron Leader Iftach Spector. Sitting in their aircraft when radar detected Egyptian Air Force formations heading for Ofira the two Phantoms were not scrambled yet but Nachumi knew that the day would not end quietly. Despite orders to the contrary, he scrambled the two jets himself. 'The controller was screaming that there were orders not to take off. However, I decided that the orders were 400 kilometres away and they didn't know what was going on. I cranked the engine and told my number two to do the same and to scramble as quickly as possible. Standby was very close to the runway so we cranked the engines, went out and took off. I looked back to see that number two was airborne and that everything was OK and I saw smoke plumes on the runway, like cotton balls. And I didn't understand. I told my navigator, 'Look! What do you make of this?' He said, 'They are bombing the runway, this must be war!'

A total of 28 EAF MiG-17s and their MiG-21 escorts had arrived to attack Ofira and had Nachumi not made the decision to scramble, the Phantoms would not have been able to take off from the damaged runway. He jettisoned his external fuel tanks and the two aircraft separated, each going after his own targets. 'The sirens were sounding when the aircraft left the runway and began to gain height' Nachumi said. 'I looked back to see my No. 2 and there were smoke columns rising from explosions on the runway. 'This is really war', I thought. I pulled up hard, releasing my tanks and made a pass at a MiG-17 just pulling up from his bombing run. The Egyptian dived, but my AIM-9 Sidewinder impacted and he blew up.

Now the sky was full of aircraft; three MiGs tried to get on my tail, bursts from their cannon coming past. I broke hard and one MiG disengaged while I pressed the attack on the other two. They dropped to 150 feet, flying under antennae and electric wires; one MiG broke hard and disappeared into the sea. The remaining MiG was tougher; the pilot pulled high g and I stayed with him. Suddenly my left engine suffered a compressor stall. I began to lose speed and height and was almost on the deck before I got a relight. A MiG came in on my tail, cannon firing; I reversed and came behind him, firing my own cannon. No hits. Then I put my last missile to him and he crashed on the shoreline.' [8]

Egypt acknowledged the loss of five aircraft during the concentrated air attack (eighteen Egyptian aircraft were shot down and these losses prompted the cancellation of the second planned wave). Shaki and his backseater, David Regev, had downed three other aircraft and both Phantoms landed on the damaged runway, avoiding bomb craters and debris.

The second major Egyptian Air Force action on the first day came at dusk with a commando assault involving dozens of Mi-8 helicopters. Seven helicopters, including one deliberately driven into the ground by the jet wash from a Phantom's afterburners, were destroyed by Phantoms of 201 Squadron. 'Bat' Squadron F-4Es which took off from Rephidim shot down an AS-5 Kelt missile and a Sukhoi Su-7.

Amir Nachumi scored his fifth kill on 13 October when 107 Squadron attacked the Syrian air base at Saiqal. A MiG-21 was attempting to down his wingman when Nachumi manoeuvred behind it and fired an AIM-9D from 1300 metres away. He scored two more kills on the following day when the 'Knights of the Orange Tail' was tasked with attacking the Egyptian airfield at Tanta, but Nachumi and wingman Meir Most were intercepted en route by a pair of MiG-21s from El Mansoura. After shooting down a MiG that had gone after Most, Nachumi battled with the other aircraft which eventually crashed into the Mediterranean. By the war's end Nachumi had become the IAF's top Phantom ace, with seven confirmed kills. He and Daniel Shaki and their backseaters received Israel's third highest decoration, the Medal of Distinguished Service for their conduct during the battle. Nachumi would score another seven victories in the F-16 Fighting Falcon in fighting over Lebanon and he participated in Operation 'Opera', the 7 June 1981 raid that destroyed an Iraqi nuclear reactor. On 14 July when a flight of Syrian MiG-21s attempted to intercept Israeli A-4 Skyhawks over Lebanon but were intercepted by their 110 Squadron escorts, Nachumi shot down a single MiG to become the world's first pilot to shoot down an enemy fighter in the F-16.

The scale and effectiveness of the Egyptian strategy of deploying anti-tank weapons coupled with the Israelis' inability to disrupt their use with close air support (due to the SAM shield) greatly contributed to Israeli setbacks early in the war and the IAF was obliged to mount long-range strike missions against enemy ground forces in Egypt and the Suez Canal Zone before tackling the SAMs. The Heyl ha'Avir initially lost forty aircraft to Syrian anti-aircraft batteries, but Israeli pilots soon adopted a different tactic; flying in low over Jordan and diving in over the Golan heights, catching the Syrians in the flank and avoiding many of their batteries. Israeli aircraft dropped conventional bombs and napalm, devastating Syrian armoured columns. However, the Syrian Air Force repeatedly struck Israeli positions during this period. On the second day of the war, the Heyl ha'Avir attempted to take out the Syrian anti-aircraft batteries. Codenamed 'Doogman 5'(model 5B), the attempt was a costly failure. The Israelis destroyed one Syrian missile battery and lost six aircraft.

On 7 October also the IAF carried out Operation 'Tagar', aiming to neutralize Egyptian Air Force bases and its missile defence shield. Seven Egyptian airbases were damaged with the loss of two A-4 Skyhawks and their pilots. Two more planned attacks were called off due to the increasing need for airpower on the Syrian front. The Heyl ha'Avir carried out additional air attacks against Egyptian forces on the east bank of the canal, reportedly inflicting heavy losses. By 8 October Israel had encountered military difficulties on both fronts. In the Sinai, Israeli efforts to break through Egyptian lines with armour had been thwarted and while Israel had contained and begun to turn back the Syrian advance, Syrian forces were still overlooking the Jordan River and their air defence systems were inflicting a high toll on Israeli aircraft. Israeli jets had by now carried out hundreds of sorties against Egyptian targets, but the Egyptian SAM shield had taken a toll and losses had mounted to three aircraft for every 200 sorties, an unsustainable rate. The Heyl ha'Avir lost 33 of its 140 F-4Es, mainly to SAMs. Israel admitted to total losses of 115 aircraft (US estimates were nearer 200) sixty of them in the first week of the Yom Kippur War. To evade the SA-2 the F-4E pilots found that they had to enter the zone of the SA-6 and there the only effective counter action was to dive inside and below the missile before it had time to gain high altitude and speed. Then they ran headlong into the range of the SA-7 and SA-9 and the massed array of ZSU-23-4s. Israel was supplied with AGM-54A 'Shrike' anti-radiation missiles but these were largely unsuccessful against the continuous wave-guidance SA-6, which the Phantoms had great difficulty in outmanoeuvring once they had been launched. Eventually, the IAF gained the upper hand on the Sinai Front by making massed attacks using squadrons of attacking aircraft rather than in groups of four and ground targets were bombed accurately by American-supplied 'smart' bombs and the F-4Es were fitted with decoy flares to counter the heat-seeking SAMs.

On 9 October Syrian FROG-7 surface-to-surface missiles struck the IAF base of Ramat David, killing a pilot and injuring several soldiers. Additional missiles struck civilian settlements. In retaliation, seven Israeli F-4Es struck the Syrian General Staff Headquarters in Damascus. The jets attacked from Lebanese airspace to avoid the heavily defended regions around the Golan Heights, attacking a Lebanese radar station along the way. The upper floors of the Syrian GHQ and the Air Force Command were badly damaged. A Soviet cultural centre, a television station and other nearby structures were also mistakenly hit. One Israeli Phantom was shot down. The strike prompted the Syrians to transfer air defence units from the Golan Heights to the home front, allowing the Heyl ha'Avir greater freedom of action. The Syrian Air Force attacked Israeli columns, but its operations were highly limited due to Israeli air superiority and it suffered heavy losses in dogfights with Israeli jets.

It became clear by 9 October that no quick reversal in Israel's favour would occur and that IDF losses were unexpectedly high. During the night of 8/9 October, an alarmed Moshe Dayan told Golda Meir that 'this is the end of the third temple.' He was warning of Israel's impending total defeat, but 'Temple' was also the code word for nuclear weapons. In a cabinet meeting Dayan warned that Israel was approaching a point of 'last resort' That night Meir authorized the assembly of thirteen 20-kiloton-of-TNT (84 TJ) tactical atomic weapons for 'Jericho' missiles at Sdot Micha Airbase and F-4s at Tel Nof Airbase for use against Syrian and Egyptian targets if absolutely necessary to prevent total defeat. The United States learned of the nuclear alert on the morning of 9 October and President Nixon ordered the commencement of Operation 'Nickel Grass' and Israel began receiving supplies via US Air Force cargo planes on 14 October, although some equipment had arrived on aircraft from Israel's national airline El Al before this date. By now, the IDF had advanced deep into Syria and was mounting a largely successful invasion of the Egyptian mainland from the Sinai, but had taken severe material losses. 'Nickel Grass' ensured that Israeli losses were made good with the urgent delivery of 36 F-4Es from USAFE and TAC units.[9] By the end of 'Nickel Grass', the United States had shipped 22,395 tons of matériel to Israel. By the beginning of December, Israel had received between 34 to 40 F-4 fighter-bombers alone.

Attacks on SAM sites punched a hole in the Egyptian anti-aircraft screen and enabled the Heyl ha'Avir to more aggressively strike Egyptian ground targets. The combination of a weakened Egyptian SAM umbrella and a greater concentration of Israeli fighter-bombers meant that the Heyl ha'Avir was capable of greatly increasing sorties against Egyptian military targets, including convoys, armour and airfields. The Egyptian bridges across the canal were damaged in Israeli air and artillery attacks. Israeli jets began attacking Egyptian SAM sites and radars, prompting the withdrawal of much of the Egyptians' air defence equipment. This, in turn, gave the Heyl ha'Avir greater freedom to operate in Egyptian airspace. Israeli jets also attacked and destroyed underground communication cables at Banha in the Nile Delta, forcing the Egyptians to transmit selective messages by radio, which could be intercepted. The Egyptian Air Force attempted to interdict IAF sorties and attack Israeli ground forces, but suffered heavy losses in dogfights and from Israeli air defences, while inflicting light aircraft losses on the Israelis. The heaviest air battles took place over the northern Nile Delta, where the Israelis repeatedly attempted to destroy Egyptian airbases.

An article called *The Hardest Mission of My Life*, which appeared in the *Israeli Air Force Journal* in October 1981, describes the intensity of combat during Yom Kippur:

'It all began on 11 October when the squadron participated in an attack on Binhaha airfield in the Delta. The aircraft were caught on their way home by MiGs, attacking from their 6 o'clock. There began a vicious air battle. A few MiGs were shot down, as well as two of our Phantoms. Yonatan Ophir and Aaron Cohen, the crew of one of the aircraft, managed to eject safely but were murdered on the ground, apparently by villagers. This battle made a deep impression on the squadron.

'On the morning of 14 October, a formation of Phantoms went to Mansura. It was clear that this was going to be difficult, perhaps very difficult. Mansura was in the heart of the Delta, defended by SA-2 and SA-3 missile batteries. MiGs were also expected in the target area and the prospects of surprise were weak.

'The first part of the approach was over the sea. As we flew we scanned the sky constantly in an effort to see signs of MiGs or missiles. At first, all was quiet, but a little before we crossed the coastline the controller called: 'Heads up. There are MiGs over your target.' 'I receive,' answered the leader. To the formation, he said: 'Continuing as usual.' OK, now there were missiles and MiGs. The tension in each of the aircraft rose. The journey across the Delta was a long one. We flew at very low altitude, so low that from time to time you had to manoeuvre to pass over the electric cables which stretch all over the Delta. We would have to remember those cables on the way home. As we approached the target the controller reported on the MiGs in the area. No longer any question: surprise was not on our side. We would have to perform the attack as quickly as possible: if you waste too much time at altitude the missiles zero in on you; if they aren't able to lock on, the MiGs go for you instead. And we didn't have enough fuel to become involved.

'We arrived and broke over Mansura. We looked around. Still, we couldn't spot the enemy aircraft, though we could see the MiGs' drop-tanks spinning towards the ground. We heard the MiGs above us: they could see the Phantoms and were beginning to get organised to go after the formation. A hard decision: whether to turn tail to the MiGs and dive for the target? During the aiming stage, you fly a long time without any manoeuvres and it is very easy for an enemy fighter to set up on you. Only three days before two of our aircraft were shot down when they were caught from behind by MiGs. Or to jettison the armament and try to escape? But then what was the purpose of this long and dangerous flight if in the end, we did not attack the target?

'My No. 2 and I decided to attack, hoping that the MiGs would not be able to launch until after bomb-release. We rolled in and bombed the runway. Another second and large smoke columns rose from exactly where we wanted them. Stage A completed, now for Stage B, safe return to base. We performed a hard break. There still wasn't any sign of MiGs, but we knew where they were - behind us. And then No. 4 reported that he was burning. One of the pilots said afterwards that his first thought upon hearing this was: 'What do you want me to do? Bring a fire extinguisher?'

'We turned towards No. 4. The Phantom didn't appear to be burning, but now there were two MiGs closing the range behind him. 'No. 4 break hard left. They're on you.' No. 4 broke left and I broke to get on to the threatening MiGs and dropped the remaining armament to lighten the aircraft. I still wasn't thinking in terms of a dogfight, but only to rescue my wingman who was in trouble. The MiGs gave up, turned towards us and then broke away. No. 4 headed home, still thinking that he was burning. His navigator was a very young man. He had had very few flights in the Phantom when the war started. During the attack, he had heard the radio warnings of MiGs firing. Then, looking outside, he saw the condensation coming from the wings because of the high speed. He thought that this was smoke and reported it to the pilot!

'The MiG break didn't seem right to me. It appeared as if they had received a warning from someone. There were MiGs still in the area and sure enough in another moment, Baram, my navigator warned: 'Break, they're on us.' I broke and looked behind: two MiGs; range 600-700 metres. Suddenly two smoke trails appeared, coming towards us from the MiGs. Air-to-air missiles! I moved the stick a little more. The missiles missed and the MiGs passed in front. At this point, I had to decide whether to fight this pair or go home. Then Baram warned me again to break. Another pair of MiGs was on us. I didn't know if this was the first pair or if I was fighting six. I had performed two hard breaks and my speed was low. I began to worry. Another break and my speed would fall even more.

'I didn't have enough fuel for a dogfight. 'No. 3 stuck with MiGs.' I reported. I hoped that someone would come to rescue me. We were at low altitude and I could see the MiGs beginning to set up. I manoeuvred sharply. 'They still behind?' I asked Baram. 'Affirmative,' he replied.

'You sure?' I asked him.

'Yes,' he said 'and now they are firing.'

'Two things were especially difficult in this battle. The first was that I was alone over Mansura, stuck with four or six MiGs, and nobody was coming to help me. Nobody. The rest of my formation had already managed to leave the area. When you're alone you sink or swim. The second thing was that the lessons of Binhaha were still clearly in my mind. This was definitely the time to leave. I had good speed stabilised in a turn, but nothing else was right. So I decided to try something else. Then Baram warned: 'Break, they're firing.' I pulled the nose up sharply and looked behind to see what was happening. The MiGs raised their noses after me. If they reached us we were finished. We were now completely vertical, losing speed. The MiGs were behind, but they weren't overtaking and they gave up. I raised my head: above were two MiGs waiting for me to fall off so that they could set up on us. I had to fall off because my speed was gone. This is what we call jumping from the trap into the snare.

'I pushed the nose down into a vertical dive. Nobody can fire in such a situation, nose-down. As the altitude fell I reached the point at which if I didn't pull up now I would never pull up. I waited for a second and pulled on the stick with all my strength. We came out of the dive at tree-top height. The MiGs were still behind, range 1,000 metres. They were beginning to set up. Should I head home in military power? My brain was working at top speed. My fuel load was now less than the minimum required to return home safely. If I went to military power close to the ground they would find it easy to aim and hit us. But how far away were the electric cables? I would have to manoeuvre over them and this would enable the MiGs to get us. There was no choice: I had to turn and pass in front of them. I turned hard. The two MiGs were still behind and Baram warned me from time to time to break when they launched missiles or fired their cannon. Then I reverted to the manoeuvre I had performed before. I suddenly raised the nose 90°, as sharply as possible. Would they reach us this time? Fortunately, they didn't and I saw them diving away in front of us.

'We were now very low on fuel. During the last manoeuvre, I had decided that I would continue to evade until I had half my present fuel load. If I hadn't disengaged by then I would head north and try at least to eject over the sea. But I now had doubts whether I would make it home on even the existing fuel.

'We continued to climb vertically. The MiGs behind had fallen away and I could see no-one in a threatening position. I lowered the nose vertically once more and then pulled up and levelled out over the trees. I couldn't see anyone behind, and so I decided to go home, flying as low as possible. Baram watched our tail all the time. It is not easy for a pilot to admit this, but if Baram hadn't been with me I wouldn't have been able to leave Mansura safely. He simply gave me the best help that I could have asked for.

'We were now approaching the electric cables. I manoeuvred for a moment and descended back to low level. Our fuel was dwindling fast, so I cancelled afterburner and speed fell a little. The engines were now in military power, and our biggest problem was fuel. We crossed the shoreline with the fuel gauges reading minimum approaching zero. It was still impossible to go directly home because of Port Said and its missile batteries. And, sure enough, as we passed directly north of Port Said they launched a few missiles at us, but they fell into the sea.

'Where to go from here? Even Refidim was rather far. Just north of Port Said, and we had only 1,000lb of fuel left. There was only one other place, Baluza. It had one short narrow runway and was inside the missile threat area. I called: 'No. 3 landing at Baluza. Prepare the runway for landing.' I silently hoped that we would find Baluza before the fuel ran out. But then No. 4 suddenly came on the air: 'I am also going to land at Baluza.'

'Baluza can accept only one aircraft at a time, however, and I had only 700lb of fuel and couldn't go anywhere else. It was Baluza or eject. I reported this to No. 4. 'OK,' he said to me, 'I don't have much fuel either. The first to reach Baluza can land.' I told him firmly that he would go to Refidim. He managed to land there. I wouldn't have.

'I called the Baluza control tower. Someone answered faintly: 'We hear you, where are you coming from?' It was clear that he was not used to dealing with aircraft, and I could only just hear him. Baram and I searched for the runway and started on finals. There were people and vehicles near the runway. Then the tower called: 'Go around, it's impossible to land.' I was not sure if I had enough fuel to go around but felt I had no choice. I added power for five seconds and went around. 'What's the problem?' I asked him, thinking to myself that at any moment we would have to eject. 'It's impossible to land safely,' said the man in the tower, 'there's a direct crosswind!'

'This was just too much for me: 'Idiot!' I said, 'because of this you make me go around? You only have to tell me whether the runway is clear to land.' The runway is clear,' he said to me, 'but the crosswind ...' My fuel load was now less than 300lb and from time to time the gauge would hit zero. I started on finals again, expecting the engines to cut out at any time. Another five seconds, four, three - we were down and rolling along the runway. It was like a narrow road. As we turned off the runway the engines cut. We had done it! We left our cockpits and embraced.'

A ceasefire came into effect on 22 October but it broke down and fighting was renewed.[10] On 23 October ten Phantoms and four Neshers ('Vultures'; Israeli version of the Dassault Mirage 5) engaged twenty Syrian MiG-21s near Damascus and shot down nine of them, four falling prey to the Phantoms. The IDF also destroyed the Syrian missile defence system. The Heyl ha'Avir utilized its air superiority to attack strategic targets throughout Syria, including important power plants, petrol supplies, bridges and main roads. The strikes damaged the Syrian war effort, disrupted Soviet efforts to airlift military equipment into Syria and disrupted normal life inside the country.

In the eighteen days of the Yom Kippur conflict that became known as the

'Phantom's War', the four 'Kurnass' squadrons bore the brunt of IAF operations, flying virtually any mission assigned to them. Nearly 100% of IAF strategic strikes were conducted by the F-4s, which flew as many as six sorties per plane every day while carrying out SEAD, anti-runway, interdiction and strike missions, as well as close air support, interception, reconnaissance and combat air patrol missions. Responsible for 30% of all IAF aerial kills, 27 Phantoms were lost by the war's end, the majority of them to enemy air defences. In total the Heyl ha'Avir lost 102 aircraft. Between 341 and 514 Arab aircraft were shot down; 334 of these in air-to-air combat for the loss of only five Israeli aircraft.

The last aerial engagement on the Egyptian front, which took place on 6 October, saw Israeli F-4s engage North Korean-piloted MiG-21s deployed to Bir Arida to protect Egypt's south. Two F-4 'Kurnass' ('Sledgehammer') pairs from 69 and 119 Squadrons were scrambled from Ramat David Air Base for a patrol over the Gulf of Suez sector. The F-4Es of the two squadrons were teamed together and the 69 pair (crewed by Shadmi and Gur on board the first aircraft and Shpitzer and Ofer on the other) led the mission. It was only after a long patrol, when the jets were already low on fuel, that the F-4Es were vectored towards Egypt's west-northwest: even if they were flying at the high altitude, between 20,000 and 25,000 feet, Gur spotted the pair on his radar, at lower altitude, in a position where achieving a radar lock would be extremely difficult. With the help of a GCI (Ground Control Intercept) station, the Israeli Phantoms tracked the enemy formation. Although at suitable distance for an AIM-7 shot, the two F-4s could not engage the enemy planes because bad weather prevented them from identifying the 'bandits.' However, seconds later, the Israeli pilots saw the two MiG-21s and immediately engaged them: one of the MiGs disappeared, while the other 'Fishbed' was forced into a 1-v-2 combat.

Alone against the two 'Kurnass' (supported by two more F-4Es from 119 Squadron which were flying overhead), the MiG pilot could not escape missile-lock: first, Shadmi and Gur launched an AIM-9D; a second later, they launched another Sidewinder which was followed by a third AIM-9D launched by Shpitzer and Ofer from the other Kurnass. All the missiles exploded very close to the MiG, but the 'Fishbed' continued flying. With little fuel remaining for more dog-fighting, the Israeli Phantoms were forced to skip the engagement and return to base. As they turned eastbound, Gur looked at the MiG and noticed the 'Fishbed' was leaving a white smoke trail. Suddenly, after the F-4s had crossed the coastline, Gur saw the trail of a SAM and then an explosion at around 20,000 feet quite close to the MiG-21: Egyptians had shot down one of their aircraft. Only after the end of the war, the pilots became aware that the MiG-21 belonged to North Korea.[11] Though most heavy fighting ended on 28 October, the fighting never stopped until 18 January 1974.

In the spring of 1981 Israeli reconnaissance photography revealed a sinister new development. Syria had begun to move SAM batteries into the neutral territory of Lebanon. During the course of the following year, Syria built up an overlapping network of SAMs, which included Soviet SA-2, SA-3 and mobile SA-6 missiles in the Beka'a Valley and along the Zabadani mountain range above it. The density of SAM site locations was unmatched anywhere in the world - including the Soviet Union itself! 'Operation Peace for Galilee' began on Sunday 6 June 1982 when the

Israel Defence Forces invaded southern Lebanon after repeated attacks and counter-attacks between the Palestine Liberation Organization (PLO) operating in southern Lebanon and the IDF that had caused civilian casualties on both sides of the border. The most spectacular achievement of the war was the destruction of the Syrian surface-to-air missile (SAM) sites in the Beka'a Valley by F-4Es armed with anti-radiation missiles and bombs. During the course of combat operations, the Heyl ha'Avir conducted successful ground attack missions against Syrian and PLO targets, with Israeli attack helicopters inflicting heavy losses on Syrian armour. Israeli jets shot down between 82 and 86 Syrian aircraft in aerial combat without loss. A single Israeli A-4 Skyhawk and two helicopters were shot down by anti-aircraft fire and SAM missiles. This was the largest aerial combat battle of the jet age with over 150 fighters from both sides engaged.

Operation 'Mole Cricket 19' which was mounted to destroy the SAM batteries in the Beka'a Valley began on Wednesday, 9th June. Brigadier General Avi Barber, who was captured and taken hostage by the Syrians during the Yom Kippur War in Operation 'Model 5', commanded 201 Squadron. About half of the Phantom crews were trained for the operation and the other half was instructed to blow up the SAM bases using traditional methods if the first team failed. That Wednesday, Barber supervised the preparations of the aircraft very carefully. The operation was scheduled to begin at noon. At 1000 hours he assembled all the squadron members in the operations room. The first to speak was navigator Captain Doron Dovrat, who was familiar not only with the location of the SAM batteries but with all of Lebanon's terrain. Each Phantom carried two electro-optical bombs (precision guided missiles), which weighed one ton each. According to the principle of redundancy, the navigators were supposed to drop four bombs on each battery. Each bomb cost $1 million. The navigators were supposed to drop the bomb in the exact centre of each battery. Dovrat reiterated the plan, especially the details that were particularly important for the navigators to know, even though they had been practicing for this mission for years.

Next, it was Barber's turn to speak to the group. When he finished his speech, he threw down the stick he'd been using to point to targets on the map and said dramatically, 'Each one of you has a great responsibility on his shoulders to make this mission a success. You've all learned how to fly and have been given all the necessary tools. Now make it happen!'

The start of the operation was delayed to 1300 hours and then again to 1400. At 1345, maintaining radio silence, the fighter jets took off, one after another. 'We followed the prepared route over the sea until the Lebanon coast came into view,' Barber recalled: 'When we were 32 kilometres from the SAM 6 battery, we identified our target. I moved a little closer to ensure that the bomb would reach the target and then I released the bomb. At first, the bomb flew on autopilot, but then Dovrat took over the controls and steered it toward the target. Suddenly, the control centre announced to us 'Alfa,' which meant that the bomb had hit its target. I realized that something historic had just taken place. I had hit and destroyed the target on my first try.'

It had taken only 110 minutes for the IAF to methodically destroy fifteen of nineteen SAM batteries in the Beka'a Valley. (This was the first time that a Soviet-built SAM missile battery was destroyed without the use of ground troops). At that point, it was decided to halt the operation and not to try to destroy the remaining four SAM batteries, so as not to endanger the lives of the pilots. The next day, two more batteries were destroyed and on the last day of the mission, the last remaining batteries were destroyed. During the three day operation, no fewer than 97 Syrian jets had been destroyed, without even one Israeli aircraft being hit. The Syrian air defence was effectively nonexistent from then on.

On Friday, 11th June two F-4Bs were on a routine reconnaissance in Lebanese skies. In the west the artillery still thundered and thick smog covered Beirut, a reminder of the massive shelling of the previous night. In the east, there was nothing new. Here and there smoke columns rose in the area of Lake Karoun. The Phantom pilots did not expect any surprises. One of them was Lieutenant Colonel Ben Ami Peri, a veteran who already had four kills to his name, the first of these in 1969. From his experiences in the past, Ami Peri knew not to raise his hopes too much, though he was keenly aware that this was perhaps the last chance for the Phantom to shoot down something in this war. 'There wasn't anything for us to be ashamed of. On the contrary, the Phantoms distinguished themselves in the attack missions during the beginning of the war. But we wanted meat and this patrol was the sort of thing that was thrown to us.'

'The tension which is characteristic of the take-off faded away as the Phantoms flew on tranquilly, accepting the directions of the controller. But then the tranquillity evaporated as the controller suddenly turned them east towards unidentified aircraft. We dropped our tanks, went to afterburner and proceeded east at full power. My excitement grew from the beginning of the 'warm-up' and continued to rise as speed increased. As we headed towards the unknown, eyes scanning the horizon for prey, our thoughts were concentrated on the mission, everything else forgotten. All my attention was directed at spotting the target.'

But then came disappointment as the Phantom crews failed to spot the targets. The Phantoms had turned for home when the controller called them again, directing them to a target in the west, at low altitude.

'We went to afterburners again' continues Ben Ami Peri' 'and flew west until we saw them, two brown dots over Lake Karoun, heading towards us. Later we found that these were two MiG-21s that had tried to intercept our helicopters. But D's formation wasn't the only one turned towards the MiGs: two F-15s were also racing in to intercept. It was Phantoms against Eagles. 'The 'F' beat me to a firing position on one of the MiGs, launched first and missed. I launched immediately after him and missed also. The MiG was now very close to me, but it was the F-15 that launched last and the MiG exploded into debris and smoke in front of me. More disappointment.

'The second MiG had disappeared, apparently heading west at low altitude. The controller turned us towards him. We turned hard and the F-15s, because of their superior performance, left us behind. There was nothing for us to do but search for the MiG on the radarscope. We couldn't see anything and I was worried that our last chance was slipping away. I told the navigator that I was giving up on the radar and trying to acquire him visually. It was now or never.

'After some seconds I saw him: a dot over Jebel Bruk, heading towards us. We weren't sure if this was a MiG until it launched a missile at the F-15s, who saw it and broke. The missile passed them and hit the ground. Now the MiG was coming directly towards me. Was he aware of me? But all his thoughts were on the Fs and he passed in front of me, heading south to north, trying to evade the Fs and not thinking about anything else except his success in fooling the two Eagles.

'I broke hard right and after a short period, I was sitting on his tail. From here on everything was simple. I pursued him until he was centred in my sights, and then I launched. I waited long seconds as the missile headed off on its way to the target and I tried to guide it by willpower. I waited for the MiG to break and the missile to fly on harmlessly. But this didn't happen: the missile entered his engine and blew the MiG to pieces.

''End of story. On the way home I reported that I had had a kill and was coming in for a buzz (victory roll) over the base. They had not yet heard about the kill. We quickly organised a celebration.'[12]

Stripped of its surface-to-air defence, Syria continued to flood the Beka'a Valley with fighters over the next few days. By now Israel had F-15s and F-16s and Kfir C-2 air superiority fighters, which roamed the area without fear of SAMs and raised the total number of aerial victories to about ninety. Incredibly, not a single Israeli fighter was lost during the hazardous attack against the SAMs or in the ensuing dogfights. The IAF once again proved that it was master of the skies.

By the end of the 1980s 110 F-4Es still equipped five squadrons of the Heyl ha'Avir. Israel planned to replace the J79 engines with 20,600lb thrust Pratt & Whitney PW1120 engines, fit canard surfaces, install more modern systems and equipment and strengthen the airframes to extend service life, but budgetary considerations forced most improvements to be cancelled. By now most of the Phantoms were high-time aircraft and it would not be very cost effective to modernize them.

Endnotes Chapter 10

1   Israel obtained the loan of two RF-4Cs August 1970-March 1971 pending delivery of the RF-4Es which were increased to twelve with the delivery of a second batch.
2   Eini was later appointed Israeli air attaché in Washington. Hetz was replaced by Ran Ronen (Peker).
3   *Motivation That Rises from the Ground a combat narrative* by Brigadier General 'A', as told to Hanah Zamar, *Israeli Air Force Journal* October 1981.
4   Levi was killed on 7 October during a strike on the Syrian missile defences while flying in a Phantom piloted by Lieutenant Colonel Ehud Hankin.
5   See *Israeli F-4 Phantom Aces* by Shlomo Aloni (Osprey, 2004).
6   Quoted in *The Sword of David: The Israeli Air Force At War* by Donald J. McCarthy Jr. (Pen & Sword, 2013).
7   By 1978 204 F-4Es had been delivered to the Heyl ha'Avir, of which about 65 had been lost in combat and operational accidents. In total the Heyl ha'Avir received 240 F-4Es including 86 Phantoms ordered under FMS contracts and F-4Es transferred from the USAF inventory.
8   See *Israeli Air Force Journal*, June 1980.
9   Many modifications were made to the F-4Es throughout their service life. A non-retractable refuelling probe canted upward and outboard to place the nozzle within easy sight of the pilot was attached to the starboard fuselage and connected to the dorsal fuel receptacle. Provision was also made for carrying indigenous 'Shafrir' and 'Python' air-to-air missiles and 'Gabriel' air-to-surface missiles, Elta EL/M-2021 radar and a forward-looking infrared (FLIR) sensor. The 20mm M-61A1 rotary gun was replaced by two 30mm DEFA cannon.
10 A second ceasefire was imposed cooperatively on 25 October to end the war.
11 Today the 69 Squadron 'Hammers' is based to Hatzerim Air Base and flies the powerful F-15I Ra'am ('Thunder') which replaced the F-4 Kurnass beginning in 1998.
12 See the *Israeli Air Force Journal*, February 1983.

Chapter 11

Phantom Phorever

Dear Mr. F-4 Phantom,

Your days are numbered. In a few short days you will be leaving the Kansas Air National Guard forever to go to the bone yard in Tucson, Arizona - the plane cemetery. I know it's sad for you, but it's sad for me too. Just thinking about this good-bye has made me think back and reflect on all the years we've had together.

In the 15 years that we've shared my husband, I've spent many hours waiting on you to bring him home from some faraway place. I've watched proudly as you and he did a flyby at an air show, river fest, or parade and I've cursed your loud engines as my babies cried from you noise.

You took our family to live in many far way places that we may have never seen if not for you. We lived in Florida, Arizona, North Carolina, West Germany and Kansas. You took my husband to many more than that - England, Spain, Turkey, Italy, Norway, Hawaii, Thailand, Alaska, Korea, Philippines and nearly every state in the union, to name a few.

I first became acquainted with you in 1972 and it was love at first sight. My husband was learning to fly you so he could hurry over to help fight the war in Southeast Asia. What a job you did there! You were on the news nearly every night and a familiar sight in most Americans' living rooms. You were a very welcome sight to many marines and army ground personnel there who were fighting the mud, heat, the enemy, exhaustion, homesickness and fear. They would shout for joy when they saw you coming to their rescue - their black, mud streaked faces turning to all white teeth and smiles. I would have hated to see you dive towards me when you were mad. Your smoking, loud engines made you look so mean and you could be when you wanted to. Your noise and size are greater than any other modern fighter. Sometimes you didn't make it back, but it was rarely your fault. The bullets just came too fast or someone didn't turn you quick enough. Your protected my husband well and my children and I thank you for that.

After the war there were many TDYs (temporary duty) away from home where the two of you would go off together. You and my husband would go away to fly in dogfights with the newer planes, (F-5s, F-15s and F-16s) and he'd still win with you strapped to his seat. You may not have been able to turn as tight or as fast, but the two of you were old friends and worked as a well oiled cog, a part of the team. They had the new paint jobs - you didn't. They had the fancy radar - you didn't. They had the better maneuvering capability - you didn't. But you and he still won!

We had many happy reunions where us (moms, wives, babies, kids) greeted you (Mr. F-4, our husbands and fathers) on the ramp all tears, goose bumps and smiles to see you home safely again.

I will never forget the 36 ship take off of F-4s we had here at McConnell for a change of command. The town's people thought there was a war. One by one you taxied out to take off in sets of two ships at a time. By the time you were all airborne, which seemed an eternity, the sky was black with smoke, F-4s filled the air and I don't think there was a dry eye or an unmoved person to be found in this city.

You know, sometimes I even felt jealous of you or mad at you. Even after a six week T.D.Y. of nothing but flying you, talking about you in the Officers' Club after flying you, being with others who flew you and getting up in the morning to do it all over again, my husband would come home and still talk about you with his hands in the air describing everything in detail that you'd done together. Never mind the beautiful candlelight dinner, how much the kids had changed or the ever faithful dog lapping as his heels. He still had you on his mind. I also felt at times that if it weren't for you I wouldn't have spent a year alone raising a child or fixing broken water pipes alone or getting kids over the chicken pox alone. At times, I think you even knew him better than I did and possibly are the only one who could understand him. There's a mystique and a mythical quality that you and the men who fly you share that cannot be understood by most other people. I also think he was the happiest after he'd been with you. But I didn't mind so much. That is a given. That is the way life is when you are married to one who flies you. You were something to be proud of. You had it all. Besides us wives probably got back at you a bit when we made you look a little silly taxing Santa Claus in from the North Pole for all the kids. You were no war machine on those days; you were the sleigh that brought squeals of delight to young and old alike.

Just think Mr. F-4 of all the places in the world and all the events that you've been to or seen. From our Aircraft Carriers to the walls of our living rooms (or our 'I Love Me' walls) - you are or were there. On our children's T-shirts, clothes, hats, posters- down main street of my own hometown - you are or were there. You were the best of the best, a Thunderbird and the best they'll ever have. You've been the main attraction, the tear in my eyes, the goose bumps on my skin, the vibration in my chest and down to my very soul at funerals, memorials, 4th of July celebrations, River Fests, air shows, parades and yes, you've also portrayed the missing man - the comrades who never came home. I would feel so proud of you, my husband, all the other wonderful hard working folks who kept you so well maintained that you could fly this long and all the men who gave their lives and yours so we could live free. I also felt proud of my country, being an American and the freedom that you have helped to maintain.

But now, it is time to say goodbye. There will be those who will say, 'out with the old, in with the new - progress moves forever onward' and they'll act like they don't care. But you and I know better. There is no man alive who really knew you who could not miss your uniqueness, your size, your style, your noise or something about you. You were a class act!

So the celebration is planned. Fighter pilots and backseaters and their ladies and many others will be here from all around the globe to bid you farewell. There will be songs sung, stories traded (a few stretched), reminiscing will about and hands will be in the air demonstrating the dogfight they won. Wives will again be left out of the conversation because of you, but you know we really won't mind because there have been fighters before you and have been newer fighters since, but none that can compare with you. You are one of those rare legends who stands alone - in a class all your own. Yes, you are old and tired and are going to the bone yard. You deserve the rest. But don't feel sad Mr. F-4 Phantom. A lot of people the world over will be there with you in mind, heart and spirit. You will continue to fly in the hearts, souls and minds of men and women for a long time to come. You are also breaking the hearts; I want you to know, of new and young dreaming-to-be fighter pilots like my sons who will never get to fly you. You will have the good fortune however, of living on in the history books forever.

So I say good-bye faithful old friend. I thank you for a job well done, a country well served and I thank you for keeping my husband safe and happy for all these years. I'll miss you.

Sincerely,

Beverly R. Kavouras

Letter written about 1987 by the wife of Lieutenant Colonel Larry B. Kavouras on the occasion of the phasing out of the last Phantoms from the Kansas ANG.

Spanning the generation gap the next war the US Phantoms were involved in was 'Desert Storm', the Gulf War of 1991. It was also their swan song in battle. Though their numbers were few in a conflict viewed appropriately as the first real 'electronics war' fast aging F-4G 'Wild Weasels' crammed with avionics performed superbly in a hunter-killer partnership with F-16s. Forty-eight F-4G 'Wild Weasels' (unofficial reports indicate the actual number of F-4Gs involved may have been closer to 70) flew more than 2,800 sorties during 'Desert Storm' using call signs taken from popular American beers. Aircraft were drawn from both George AFB, California and Spangdahlem, Germany to form an all-F-4G force based Sheikh Isa, Bahrain. There was an additional mixed F-16C/F-4G unit made up for Spangdahlem assets at Incirlik AB, Turkey. The right-forward Sparrow well was always vacant, but the left-forward one carried an ECM pod. For aircraft from George this was the ALQ-184 ECM pod, while the Spangdahlem aircraft used the deep ALQ-131 pod. Also standard were aft-fuselage-mounted AIM-7F Sparrow medium-range AAMs. Up to four AGM-88 HARMs were carried on the wing pylons. The more normal load was two HARMs on the inboard wing pylons and two outboard fuel tanks. Bahrain was the focal point for receipt and distribution of all AGM-88s. More than 1,000 HARMS were fired during the war, about 400 or substantially more by F-4Gs. During a three-to-four day period AGM-45 Shrikes were substituted for HARMs. This stopped once units in the field were able to convince higher headquarters about HARM capabilities, showing them the missiles were not being wasted. The Incirlik-based 23rd TFS operated mixed F-4G/F-16C formations. The F-16Cs were totally dependent on information from and basically served as an extra set of pylons for, the F-4Gs. They flew three four-ship formations for daytime strikes and two for night. Compositions of these formations varied, but the first two were a mix of the two types of aircraft, while the third was all F-16.

Six F-4Es from Clark AB, Philippines deployed to Incirlik AB, Turkey, during 'Desert Storm'. It is most probable that they were brought in for their PGM (Precision Guided Munitions) capability, which included both the GBU-15 TV/EO glide bomb and the AVQ-26 Pave Tack pod. The centerline-carried Pave Tack pods did not show up until after the war had ended and it is unclear if the F-4Es saw any combat.

The 106th TRS, 117th TRW, Alabama ANG at Birmingham led by Colonel (later Major General) James F. 'Jim' Brown was deployed with its RF-4Cs to Sheikh Isa Bahrain on a voluntary basis August-December 1990 with six aircraft (being attached to the 35th TFW (Provisional) as the only RF-4C unit with LOROP (Long-Range Oblique Photography). Their journey to the war zone may have been the longest nonstop flight made by operational warplanes until that time, requiring sixteen air-to-air refuellings and spanning 8,000 nautical miles in 15½ hours. Using KS-127 66-inch focal length cameras the RF-4Cs flew cross-border reconnaissance missions at distances of up to fifty miles before the start of hostilities. One RF-4C (64-1044) crewed by Major Barry K. Henderson and Lieutenant Colonel Stephen G. Schraam of the 106th Tactical Reconnaissance Squadron was lost in an operational accident on 8 October 1990 during Operation 'Desert Shield'.

Major (later Major General) Stephen L. Vonderheide was one of the fliers from the 192nd TRS, Nevada ANG, who relieved Brown's personnel in November but kept their Phantoms. 'We spent a lot of time anticipating what kinds of targets we might be asked to look at,' said Vonderheide. 'We were very much aware that the Iraqis had formidable air defences.' When the first air strikes against Iraq took place on 17 January 1991 the RF-4Cs were in action from the start. At first, they were limited to tactical reconnaissance missions, flying over Kuwait almost every day in search of Republican Guard units. They flew over Baghdad looking for such targets as rocket fuel plants, chemical weapons plants and command and communications centres. At a combat weight of 51,000lbs with three external fuel tanks, the RF-4C could cover the 540 miles from Shaikh Isa to Kuwait or the 573 miles from Incirlik, Turkey to Baghdad and loiter for two hours taking pictures. But its cameras and sensors were out of date even in 1991 and the RF-4C had no way to relay images. When Lieutenant Colonel Lloyd 'Pappy' Rowland arrived at Incirlik with a second wave of RF-4Cs from the 38th TRS at Zweibrücken, Germany in January 1991 he found himself wishing for 'a multi-function display with real-time capability and some up-to-date instruments in this antique airplane.' Also arriving late in theatre were RF-4Cs from the 12th TRS at Bergstrom Air Force Base, Texas. 'On one of my early missions we flew to Kirkuk,' said Captain (later Colonel) Ken 'Razor' Rizer of the 38th TRS 'the photos showed that the Iraqis had taken their MiGs and distributed them in urban housing areas. We were the first to see and report that. We flew repeated missions to a dam near Mosul. There was a 57mm gunner on that dam. It was almost as though we developed a relationship with him. One day, when the flak was heavier than normal, he was shooting and we climbed above it.'[1]

The RF-4Cs were repeatedly diverted from other photographic missions to search for mobile 'Scud' missile launchers in western Iraq. 'We burned a lot of gas...on the 'Great Scud Hunt' Major Steve Vonderheide of the Nevada Air National Guard said in a 1991 interview with author Robert Dorr. 'Looking back, I guess you'd say our leaders were panicked about the Scuds but never understood how hard it was to find their launchers.'

In support of RF-4C operations, numerous airmen and aircraft were used, among them C-21A Lear Jets, to move finished imagery around the theatre. In the Combined Air Operations Centre (CAOC) in Riyadh, Saudi Arabia known as the 'Black Hole,' coalition air commander Lieutenant General (later General) Charles 'Chuck' Horner scrutinized RF-4C images of Iraq's forces every day and used the information to organize aerial strike 'packages,' or formations. Deployed RF-4Cs maintained a 'mission capable rate' (MCR) of 85 percent on the eve of 'Desert Storm'; the MCR declined to 78 percent during the conflict, still a respectable number for an aging, high-maintenance system. Off to a slow beginning - with six aircraft in theatre only 42 sorties were flown in January - the RF-4C eventually logged about 1,800 sorties as numbers were increased and the war progressed. One airframe flew 172 sorties.[2] None of the RF-4Cs were lost in action, although 64-1056 of the 106th TRS crashed into the Persian Gulf on 30 March 1991 after a bleed air duct failure and a catastrophic engine failure after take-off from Bahrain. Fortunately, Captain John Norman and Captain Jeffrey R. Kregel ejected safely. (By the end of hostilities the Alabama ANG had been relieved by the 192nd TRS, 152nd TRG, Nevada ANG who continued to fly the original RF-4Cs deployed). Attrition replacements were made with RF-4Cs of the Mississippi and Nevada ANGs.

Following the Gulf War the 52nd TFW were assigned to Operation 'Southern Watch' to patrol the no-fly zone over southern Iraq on F-4G defence suppression/destruction missions in conjunction with 'Wild Weasel' F-16C/Ds. The last active-duty RF-4C flight was in 1994. The last RF-4Cs in inventory belonged to the Nevada ANG and were retired on 27 September 1995. At that time the only active-duty USAF unit flying F-4G 'Wild Weasel' sorties was the 561st Fighter Squadron at Nellis AFB, Nevada. Major Tom Pfeiffer, one of the pilots, had flown over 130 F-4G missions over Iraq enforcing the no-fly zone, having scored a SAM site kill during 'Desert Storm'. Of firing a missile at SAM radar he recalled: 'There was a loud rumble that sounded like a bottle rocket going off, then whoosh! It comes off the wing. It's really exciting and after all the training and practice, I felt a real sense of accomplishment.' His father-in-law flew F-15s and before that was a 'Wild Weasel' pilot himself. Describing the no-fly zone missions Pfeiffer said, 'Occasionally [the Iraqi troops] turn on their early warning radar to get a quick view of where we're flying. They've gotten quieter and quieter with each temporary-duty rotation. Sometimes we'll fly 24-hour operations and sometimes we'll have crews up for just a couple of hours or half a day. We try to keep them off balance so they can't predict when or where we'll be. We don't jam the enemy's radar, the only thing we jam are HARM missiles down the enemy's throat!'

With the retirement of the F-4G from the USAF on 26 March 1996, the 561st inactivated and the SEAD mission was assumed by F-16s in different squadrons. Following the retirement of the last two F-4S Phantoms from the Strike Aircraft Test Directorate of the Naval Air Test Centre, the only Phantom remaining in USN service towards the end of the 20th century were F-4Ss at NAS Point Mugu (with VX-4) and QF-4 drones at PMTC Point Mugu and NWC China Lake.

On 24 July 2015 Lieutenant Colonel Todd Houchins, commanding officer of the 53rd Test Support Squadron and one of a dwindling number of qualified F-4 Phantom pilots in the United States Air Force, strapped into the front seat of a QF-4 Phantom, readying himself to depart from Tyndall AFB, Florida for

Holloman AFB, New Mexico. With the canopy still open while taxiing the Phantom out, he briefly waved the Hawaiian 'hang loose' gesture to onlookers before returning to an all-business demeanour. Closing and locking the canopy, Houchins was cleared for takeoff and with a smooth and practiced motion, he pushed the throttles of the Phantom forward, eliciting a mighty roar from the twin General Electric J79 engines as they kicked into afterburner, lifting the big grey jet into the air. Waving his wings in a salute to Tyndall and the folks on the ground, he turned westbound as he climbed, settling in for the ride over.

What made this particular flight unique (and extremely depressing) is that it was the final takeoff of the QF-4 as part of the 82nd Aerial Target Squadron. An ominous sign that the end of the F-4's days with the US military was fast approaching. It would remain at Holloman before being destroyed as an aerial target. With the QF-4s gone, the 82nd ATS has adopted the QF-16 as its next aerial target, which better simulates fourth and fifth generation air-to-air threats that American fighter pilots might possibly face in the next 15-20 years. The QF-16, like the QF-4, can be flown either manned or unmanned. While some of us at TACAIRNET don't like the fact that the last of the American Phantoms will most probably be blown to smithereens by Air Force (or Navy or Marine Corps) pilots during training exercises, I personally feel that there's no better way to go out for a jet that's built to fight.

Phantoms phorever, my friends.[3]

Flying the F-4G is like driving a classic '68 Corvette. It's just fantastic! Sheer, raw power.

What a superb epitaph for one of the world's truly great aircraft.

Endnotes Chapter 11

1   See *Gulf War 20th: RF-4C Phantom II in Desert Storm* by Robert F. Dorr, Defense Media Network, 14 February 2011.

    See *Gulf War 20th: RF-4C Phantom II in Desert Storm* by Robert F. Dorr, Defense Media Network, 14 February 2011.

3   Ian D'Costa, editor-in-chief of the Tactical Air Network.

Acknowledgements

I am indebted to all the contributors for their words and photographs. Thanks also go to my fellow author, friend and colleague, Graham Simons, for getting the book to press ready standard and for his detailed work on the photographs; to Pen & Sword and in particular, Laura Hirst; and Jon Wilkinson, for his unique jacket design once again.

Special thanks to Linda Marks and CONAM, John Newlin and the indispensible Joe Baugher and his serial number listings.

Index